Music Making Community

Music Making Community

Edited by

TONY PERMAN

AND STEFAN FIOL

UNIVERSITY OF
ILLINOIS PRESS
Urbana, Chicago, and Springfield

Publication of this book is supported by a grant from the
Bruno Nettl Endowment for Ethnomusicology.

Library of Congress Cataloging-in-Publication Data
Names: Perman, Tony, 1973- editor. | Fiol, Stefan Patrick,
    editor.
Title: Music making community / edited by Tony
    Perman and Stefan Fiol.
Description: Urbana : University of Illinois Press, 2024. |
    Includes bibliographical references and index.
Identifiers: LCCN 2023049022 (print) | LCCN
    2023049023 (ebook) | ISBN 9780252045806 (cloth) |
ISBN 9780252056680 (ebook)
Subjects: LCSH: Music   Social aspects. | Community
    life. | Social participation.
Classification: LCC ML3916 .M8757 2024 (print) |
    LCC ML3916 (ebook) | DDC 306.4/842—dc23/
    eng/20231018
LC record available at https://lccn.loc.gov/2023049022
LC ebook record available at https://lccn.loc.gov/
    2023049023

for Tom

Contents

Prologue   1
Bruno Nettl

Introduction: Music Making (and Unmaking) Community   7
Stefan Fiol and Tony Perman

PART I: DIFFERENTIATION

1   Re-membering Pontic Sociality: Musical Longing
    as Community Surrogation   37
    Ioannis Tsekouras

2   Choreographic Participation of a Presentational Kind:
    Sound, Movement, and the Politics of Belonging in
    Bulgaria's Armenian Diaspora   61
    Donna A. Buchanan

3   Making a Jewish Neighborhood: In-Group/Out-Group
    Sonic Dynamics and Affective Leverage in an
    Argentine Soccer Stadium   85
    Eduardo Herrera

4   Assembling Indigenous Communities:
    The Making of South Africa's Intellectual Property
    Laws Amendment Act of 2013   103
    Veit Erlmann

PART II: FEEDBACK

5 Teaching Music as Social Life: Performance-Based
   Pedagogy in Ethnomusicology 129
   Joanna Bosse

6 Musical Competition as Community in Highland Bolivia 151
   Thomas Solomon

7 Sustaining Musical Collectivities Through Competition:
   Christmas Bands in Cape Town 173
   Sylvia Bruinders

8 Affective Assembly and Participatory Politics
   at the Palestine Music Expo 190
   David A. McDonald

PART III: MUTUAL INDEBTEDNESS

9 Love and Debt: Performing Difference on the Mbira 209
   Tony Perman

10 Sounds and Social Belonging in Southern Africa:
    Collective Improvisation Versus Pan-African Jazz 232
    Rick Deja

11 Visions of Community and the Perils of Safeguarding
    a Himalayan Festival 248
    Stefan Fiol

Epilogue 271
Stephen Blum

Contributors 281

Index 285

Prologue

Tom Turino: Musician, Scholar, Teacher, Colleague, Friend

BRUNO NETTL

I'm very pleased to have known Tom Turino for four decades as a friend, a colleague, a collaborator, a member of my discipline and of my university department, and even as a great source of musical entertainment. Tom has excelled, has been wonderful, in all of these roles. But today I ask myself, what is it that makes him different from other colleagues and friends, from other collaborators, from many other scholars? I'm happy to have been invited to write a few words of appreciation and would like to provide a rather personal perspective.

Here is what comes first to mind, and what is perhaps most important: Tom is a person of great integrity. He has strong opinions about what is right and what is wrong, in academics and everyday life, and he sticks to them. They may not be everybody's opinions of right and wrong, and sometimes they have amused and even bemused me. But he was never easily pushed around. From his early days at Illinois, he was willing to be the lone dissenter on dissertation committees and a lone voice for an outlier opinion as one of five authors of the textbook he co-wrote with Charles Capwell, Isabel Wong, Philip V. Bohlman, and me (Nettl et al. 1992).

Along similar lines, take Tom's very successful book *Music as Social Life* (2008), which has become widely used as a text. I have always had the feeling that the principal purpose of this book, perhaps never stated precisely, is that music can be—is—a force for changing the directions of a society and its culture, and that we thus have an obligation to use it for positive advancement. And that music is best, morally best, in what Tom calls the "participatory" mode—for people in a society to make music together—rather than as "presentational" for an audience or in its modern electronic formats. I have not necessarily agreed with Tom's analysis, but I have respected and admired his insistence that music should be a force for good. As a teacher, advisor, and collaborator, Tom has, in my experience, always acted ethically, sometimes making decisions that caused others to be displeased, holding to standards that are important to him.

In this way and others, Tom has been consistent. But, perhaps more important and surely more entertaining, his life and career have also been full of interesting inconsistencies. For one thing, Tom is a man who has constantly reinvented himself, in ways personal, academic, geographical, and cultural. Most obviously, in the minds of ethnomusicologists, he has changed specialties. Beginning as a Latin Americanist, he made major contributions to the understanding of music in the culture of Peruvian Aymara villagers, small-town dwellers, and city folk (Turino 1993). But then, somewhat suddenly, one found him in Zimbabwe, dealing with issues of nationalism and cosmopolitanism (2000). Well, that's not so unusual for ethnomusicologists, many of whom have developed a kind of bifurcation of geographic interests. But a few years later he was contemplating several musics of the United States (e.g., in Turino 2008). But Tom also changed his life from an emphasis on scholarship with musical performance a kind of auxiliary career of fun, to an existence in which he sees himself mainly as a performer with some interests in scholarship, and back again. And he repeatedly reinvented his principal musical allegiance, playing guitar and some Carnatic vina, then concentrating on panpipes, and then on the mbiras of Zimbabwe, then to banjo, fiddle, and accordion. He loves all of these instruments and plays them all well, but in my experience, he might say, on one day, "I'm playing a lot of banjo these days," and a month later, "I'm really enjoying my violin," and so on. And concentrating on old-time American music one day, jazz-influenced songs another time, a charango ensemble next, a mbira group, then zydeco, something derived from bluegrass, and contradance music. What has been particularly interesting to me is that Tom seems quickly and easily at home in all of these musics.

Tom's geographic reinventions aren't so much about the world map as they are about the nature of venues, both in his research and in his personal choice of dwellings. A bit of personal recollection: When Tom was appointed to teach at the University of Illinois and was finding it hard to find housing in Champaign-Urbana, I realized that a neighbor of mine, a history professor, was about to take a sabbatical in Europe and was looking for someone to rent his house for a year. I made the introduction, and Tom lived with his family in a very small house on my street for a year. He soon moved to a larger house in a very non-university neighborhood for a few years. Then suddenly one day he told us that he had found a new place. It turned out to be a very large house, in southern plantation style, on a six-acre wooded plot, abandoned—so to speak—by a professor who had lived alone with several dozen cats but passed away without notifying anyone about those cats, who in turn were desperate. The house needed lots of work, including techniques to get rid of the cat odors, and lots of intricate carpentry, at which Tom was an expert, and it became a wonderful home for entertaining and musicking. But after some years Tom decided to retire and moved to Kentucky, first to a small house in town and then to his present abode, a mountaintop cabin. I (who have lived in the same house for fifty-five years) marvel at Tom's adaptability and interest in change. At least five very different abodes in less than thirty years!

Clearly, Tom is a man for whom change and variety are important. But I want to say a few words about areas of scholarship in which he has maintained principles and attitudes throughout his career. They may define his place in the history of our discipline. One of them concerns Peircean semiotics. I don't know when Tom became interested in Peirce, but a couple of years after his arrival at Illinois he made known to me that he would like to teach a course on music and semiotics. I was ignorant of this kind of endeavor but knew some names—Eero Tarasti, Jean-Jacques Nattiez, Steven Feld—and thought he would wish to base a course on the work of their and related scholarship. But no, Tom insisted, he wanted to go back to the origins, as he saw them, in the work of Peirce, to have students read it and use it directly as a guide. Well, Tom taught that course (really a seminar) repeatedly, and others in which Peircean semiotics played the leading role, and he attracted a large number of students to his viewpoint. Until recently, at least, some thirty years later, he was still at it, insisting, in an article titled "On Theory and Models: How to Make Our Ideas Clear" in a book dedicated to me (Levine and Bohlman 2015), that "C. S. Peirce's ideas about different sign types offer a crucial foundation for creating analytical concepts and models" (380). For more than two decades Tom has been a kind of crusader for the efficacy of Peircean concepts and procedures in the analysis of music in culture. He has been, in my view, quite successful, persuading some people but also finding lots of opposition. But this clearly has been one leitmotif of his scholarly career. Indeed, the importance of this body of thought to Tom is clearly stated in a major article of his (2014).

The second one involves his insistence on the importance of first two, then four, "fields" of music making, some (and later all) of which characterize the world's musics and have enabled him to make statements about "music" in a very general, synthetic way: presentational and participatory music, then recorded (high-fidelity and studio) music. Here, too, he has stuck with one version or another of this scheme for a long time, beginning with his work on Zimbabwe (2000, 43–44) and continuing into later works, especially *Music as Social Life* (2008), where it becomes a leading concept for the book's main arguments.

The third characteristic of Tom Turino's work from its beginnings is the emphasis he places on theory and the care he takes to define the types, terminologies, and uses of theory. His tendency to reinvent himself has led him to emphasize different approaches, but the idea that in research, theory should come first, seems to me to have been there always, from my first conversations with him circa 1988 until his 2015 essay dedicated to me. We used to argue, because I countered, "You should have data first, and if it suggests patterns or regularities, then you may bring a theory to explain this." I didn't persuade him, and he brought powerful arguments to support his position. In his 2015 essay he states very clearly his belief that theoretical thinking has been and continues to be central in his discipline, as he points out: "Ethnomusicologists have long used existing theory in a rather ad hoc way, fitting their data into preexisting conceptual boxes picked from here and there. I advocate for a more critical, creative, and holistic way of working with theory" (379). I think this sentence perhaps characterizes Tom's approach to his scholarship throughout his career (so far).

And the fourth characteristic: Scholarly life for Tom as a music researcher requires participation in music. I didn't know this when we first met, but during his time in Austin, as a student, he had organized bands and made recordings that, in unexpected ways, were wildly successful. After he came to Illinois he soon invited students and colleagues to an evening at his house, and when we arrived we were told that we were expected to perform something. A determined nonperformer, I came up with an Arapaho peyote song learned in 1950, but we discovered unexpected talents. Tom, during his residence in Illinois, always had one or several bands with gigs in the local entertainment scene, always directed at least one student ensemble (panpipes, mbiras, country), and when he retired, devoted himself for a long time almost entirely to performing (a lot of it with his son Matt, an expert fiddler). Part of his tendency to self-reinvention is moving from emphasis on playing to emphasis on writing, and back. He sometimes combined these interests with his lifelong emphasis on personal relations. One of my favorite memories concerns his arrangement of a popular Native American "Forty-Nine" song usually called "The One-Eyed Ford," made known nationwide by the famous jazz musician Jim Pepper, which I had made the centerpiece of some of my lectures. Tom arranged it in Zydeco style, playing and singing with accordion and fiddles, making fun of the whole business of cultural fusion and of the self-importance of ethnomusicologists.

In all of these examples of "Turino ness" one senses the concept of community, the fact that communities of humans are what drives music, its existence and its practice, what gives it its unique place among the arts.

To me, principally, Tom has been—is—a scholar who sticks to principles while living a life of variety, a demanding teacher whose enthusiastic and devoted students regularly followed him from class to his office to imbibe further, and

a musician with enormous talent. We at Illinois are still sorry that he decided
to retire at an early age, but we see him frequently on his visits from Kentucky. I
close with a verse I wrote to read at his retirement party that summarizes much
of this prologue, a parody of the American broadside ballad "Sam Bass," about
a man who, as is well known, was "born in Indiana" but ended up in Texas, a
man who also reinvented himself. In other respects, though, the careers of Sam
Bass and Tom Turino have nothing in common at all.

> Tom T was born near the eastern shore, which was his native home.
> At the age of twenty-some, young Tom began to roam,
> And so went down to Texas, an ethno for to be,
> A harder-working student you seldom ever see.
>
> He studied first with old Behague and then with young Steve Feld,
> Impressed the people at UT, at homework he excelled.
> Did fieldwork down in old Peru for music of the Andes,
> And there discovered pisco, which is what they call their brandies.
>
> And then forthwith to Illinois this brand-new doctor went,
> Wrote a book about the Aymara, that time was not misspent.
> He got promoted pretty soon, then off to Africa.
> His book about Zimbabwe sure is no ephemera.
>
> He also came to study a philosopher named Peirce,
> Whose weighty publications sure don't lend themselves to verse.
> An authority on semiotics Tom in time became,
> And icon, index, P-symbol got connected with his name.
>
> He published many articles, and book reviews as well,
> And gave a lot of lectures, and read papers, but to tell
> The truth, he never really liked conventions, it's a fact;
> Instead, for singing, playing, dance he was a maniac.
>
> *Music as Social Life*, that book is quite another story.
> On music presentational or else participatory.
> He taught the mbira, panpipes, banjo, fiddle and charango,
> Played everything from zydeco to samba and fandango.
>
> He loves the music of the folk but doesn't like that term,
> And thinks because I use it still I'm an ancient pachyderm.
> He calls it old-time music, and that's just OK with me;
> I like it both presentational and participatorily.
>
> And Tom has now retired from the U of I, it's true,
> It absolutely makes his colleagues and his students blue.
> But now, instead of hearing him pontificate in classes,
> We'll listen to him musicking while emptying our glasses.

Bibliography

Lindsay Levine, Victoria, and Philip V. Bohlman. 2015. *This Thing Called Music*. Lanham, MD: Rowman and Littlefield.

Nettl, Bruno, et al. 1992. *Excursions in World Music*. Englewood Cliffs, NJ: Prentice Hall. See chapters on Africa and Latin America by Turino.

Turino, Thomas. 1993. *Moving Away from Silence: The Music of the Peruvian Altiplano and the Experience of Urban Migration*. Chicago: University of Chicago Press.

Turino, Thomas. 2000. *Nationalists, Cosmopolitans, and Popular Music in Zimbabwe*. Chicago: University of Chicago Press.

Turino, Thomas. 2008. *Music as Social Life: The Politics of Participation*. Chicago: University of Chicago Press.

Turino, Thomas. 2014. "Peircean Thought as Core Theory for a Phenomenological Ethnomusicology." *Ethnomusicology* 58:185–221.

Turino, Thomas. 2015. "On Theory and Models: How to Make Our Ideas Clear." In Levine and Bohlman, 378–90.

Introduction

Music Making (and Unmaking) Community

STEFAN FIOL AND TONY PERMAN

Music Is Social Life

With an idea so central to his scholarship that it provides the title of his 2008 book, Thomas Turino examines music as social life. With this volume presented in honor of that scholarship and to push past it, we argue that music *is* social life. On the face of it, that is a rather banal statement, at least to ethnomusicologists. For others, it may even seem absurd. Our goal is to advocate for this simple claim and demonstrate its profound utility in musical scholarship and community engagement. Music is social life. Our argument, clarified and qualified by our fellow contributors, is that in the moments when music is being made by and for members of different kinds of human groups, this doing of music (musicking) is a productive act. That which is produced is the social, a concept to which we return below. When musicking is done effectively, the social bonds that it engenders can coalesce into communities that last beyond the time constraints of musicking itself. The ways in which music shapes the relations that comprise the social are variable and unpredictable. Music can generate new relations, solidify or even sever existing ones, and reinforce old divisions. Music can effectively and efficiently augment the similarities and differences that constitute the boundaries of our communities. In essence, the manner in which musical relations relate to social relations determines how that music is valued and made meaningful (see Kockelman 2020). Musicking is relating (Small 1998). Community is not a given and its boundaries are never natural; they are made. One way in which it is made is through the unique, deliberately combined and context-specific sounds identified (at least in English) as music (or countless approximate alternatives such as musique, musiki, mimhanzi, and jaylliphust'a).

The breadth of Turino's scholarship is daunting. Our contributors focus on a few key tools: semiotics, the five fields of music making (Turino 2016), processes of identity formation, and distinctions between cultural cohorts and formations (including the cosmopolitan, diasporic, and immigrant trans-state formations). Underpinning this is a career-long reliance on Peircean phenomenology, which, he argues, should be foundational to ethnomusicological training (2014, 185). Our contributors qualify the distinctions Turino draws between participatory and presentational fields of making music, emphasizing how choices to perform specific musical values impact social life. They examine the relation between cultural cohorts and cultural formations, exposing gray areas between these "neat" categories while demonstrating how music helps cohorts potentially transform habits foundational to the formations from which they emerge. Although Turino critically engages both individuals and groups using the fulcrum of habits, he doesn't explicitly engage with community, per se. Despite this, we argue that his scholarship ultimately elucidates the ways in which music and community are mutually implicated.

This is not a utopian project, but nor is it dystopian. Musicking is a human universal, one that is as foundational to our humanity as language, in part because of the possibilities it offers to human flourishing. It provides hope; it helps imagine human ideals and then helps render those imaginings. Turino asserts that

> as a specially-bounded activity *about* synchrony which includes immediate semiotic feedback (sounds and motion) regarding how the participants are doing, as well as learned, stylized models for being in sync, music and dance performance have a special potential for creating the experience of direct social bonding. (2009, 13, emphasis in original)

This potential underpins Turino's scholarship and the hope for positive social change that it inspires. While critics may question the apparent idealism of such an approach, Turino's consistent acknowledgment that the possible and the actual productively interact—that creativity is the foundation of experience (Collins 2019)—has much to say about shaping an equitable and productive future for ethnomusicology.

We define *community* as the composite relations grounded in similarity and difference among agents who act on their interdependence or mutual indebtedness. Stefano Harney and Fred Moten advocate for this "debt" as a principle of social life (2013, 154). A community cannot exist unless its members distinguish themselves from others. Nor can it operate as such unless its members feel indebted to one another, however asymmetrically. This indebtedness moves beyond the potentially coercive elements of obligation. Debt, if mutual and explicitly acknowledged (159), is more constructive for community-building than obligation, because it implies reciprocity and an understanding of power dynamics. Music is a powerful technology/activity with which to express shared habits but also to distinguish, differentiate, and bond *based on those differences and senses of indebtedness*. When interactive experiences form habits, they can draw people into collectives productively labeled as communities.

Our main theoretical intervention is to phenomenologically highlight how processes of social differentiation impact the feedback dynamics involved in music making and community making as mutually constitutive processes dependent on feelings of mutual indebtedness. To that end, each section of the book emphasizes one of these three core elements: differentiation, feedback, and mutual indebtedness. Each chapter in this volume enters this dialectic from a particular vantage point.

Part I, with chapters by Tsekouras, Buchanan, Herrera, and Erlmann, emphasizes processes of differentiation and the resulting consequences of variable interpretations of sameness and difference. The vagaries of history, as manifest in dislocation, emerging Pontic Greek and Armenian diasporas, and the consequences of institutionalized antisemitism and racism, respectively, in Argentinian soccer stadiums and post-apartheid South African legislation impact how people employ musical and cultural practices to assert their own position in relation to others.

Part II, with chapters by Bosse, Solomon, Bruinders, and McDonald, builds on these dynamics but prioritizes the feedback dynamics between music and community. Each of these authors highlights the potentials of participation (as theorized by Turino) to allow musicians to harness the feedback potential of musical practice to transform the communities that matter to them, whether in North American classrooms, competitive performance settings in Bolivia or South Africa, or on the stages of Palestinian music festivals.

Finally, Part III, with chapters by Perman, Deja, and Fiol, addresses the central role that obligation and debt play in the dynamics of differentiation and the cycles of feedback that define the music/community dialectic. When playing Zimbabwean mbira in American classrooms, drawing on Afro-jazz conventions in the context of collective free improvisation in South Africa, and transforming a Himalayan festival into "universal heritage," competing and unequal visions of community—and contrasting ideals of participation—are in dialogue. Unpacking the social possibilities of independence and interdependence across a range of musical contexts, our contributors reveal under what circumstances communities shape musical lives, and music serves community.

Community Now! Sameness and Difference in Twenty-first Century Music Scholarship

At first glance, our project may seem a little old-school. In many ways ethnomusicology has moved beyond some of the questions we wrestle with here, openly challenging each of the nouns of our title. Sound studies and scholarship concerning the Anthropocene have led the charge away from the potentially ethnocentric valuations behind the imposition of such terms as *music, identity,* and *culture*. Ideas of community are slowly moving beyond the human, encompassing animals, the environment, the spiritual, and the divine (Kohn 2013). Actor-network theory calls into question the very nature of the social across the disciplines (Latour 2007).[1] The premise of musical exceptionalism has been rejected in ways that coincide epistemologically with the recent tilt toward sound studies, acoustemologies, and soundscapes (Bigheno 2008; Feld 2015; Steingo and Sykes 2019). We resist this somewhat, not because sound studies is misguided, or because musicology can account for all the ways in which sound is made meaningful, but because there *are* ways in which music is exceptional. We argue that decades of ethnomusicology have, if nothing else, shown that music is indeed unique in the ways it can communicate and generate feelings among and between participating subjects. This has been a hallmark of Turino's writings since his earliest publications about Aymara music in the Peruvian Andes.

Attitudes about community (whether to accept it uncritically, deconstruct and remake it, or ignore it entirely) are intimately connected to the fields of scholarship from which they emerge. Jim Sykes questions how music is often reductively studied as if it "belonged" to a community of musicians, obfuscating histories of sonic interaction and gifting between different populations, and more important, driving a wedge between them that reinforces simplistic fictions of purity (2018, 5). This reduction equates identity with territory in colonialist, patriarchal, and exclusionary ways (Rivera Cusicanqui 2020, 68).

But communing musically does not simply affirm or construct identity. Music obviously can do this, but it also carries the unique potential to provide people with the capacity to experiment with different modes of social organization, bring people together, reveal modes of relation, and highlight levels of interdependence that reinforce music's impact on the social without merely confirming predetermined collections of identities.[2] As Blum reiterates in the epilogue, putting moral indebtedness at the center of community elevates it beyond an identity framework.

In many ways, this potential exposes the danger of inequality and imbalanced distributions of power. The sociologist and activist Silvia Rivera Cusicanqui's application of *ch'ixi* to social theories of culture and "hybridity" offers hope for a more equitable postcolonial political economy of knowledge regarding human collectivity. In a critique of Nestor Garcia Canclini's hybridity and northern literatures of decoloniality, Rivera Cusicanqui explains ch'ixi as an Aymara juxtaposition of elements that can be confused with "mixing" but is actually a heteronomy that reveals the existence of multiple cultural differences (Rivera Cusicanqui 2020, 66). In ch'ixi, these differences do not extinguish one another but are productively antagonistic and complementary. Ch'ixi puts difference at the center. Without subsuming her theoretical work within other approaches, ch'ixi augments Black feminist theories of intersectionality and Turino's own approach to cultural cohorts and formations rooted in habits to suggest a way beyond what Sykes calls the "identity episteme" (2018). Music's ability to make us feel for one another in real time brings moral indebtedness to these sounded feedback processes of community.

Approaches often glossed as "applied ethnomusicology" can be described as a turn toward advocacy and activism that emerged in response to critiques of positivism, objectivity, and global systems of inequity at the end of the twentieth century. Applied ethnomusicologists build from a commonsense idea of community as the focal point of their advocacy in multiple contexts. The goals of applied scholarship vary widely but are often motivated by a desire to *serve the needs of local communities* as opposed to generating disciplinary knowledge for its own sake. Increasingly, this motivation inspires activist modes of scholarly intervention, in part to reimagine ethnomusicology itself. As Deonte L. Harris argues, "The crises of the moment demand a commitment to action through advocacy and informed activism in order to bring about transformative and long-lasting change within the field of ethnomusicology" (2022, 214). If the "needs of the community" are the point of departure in such studies, they can also be a point of contention. In applied projects we can observe that there is rarely a unified vision for what a community is or what it needs. Applied ethnomusicologists often navigate competing agendas to create a plan for action and advocacy. In order to improve coordinated action, Klisala Harrison underlines the need to identify and mediate multiple "epistemic communities" that are defined by networks of skilled people with claims to knowledge in any given domain (2012, 521).

Contemporary ethnomusicologists, pulled between ideological commitments to sound studies, the Anthropocene, applied study, and advocacy, evidence a wide range of attitudes about community. Yet ethnomusicology is practiced by its own scholarly community, in which the diversity of scholars and subjects is a core value and, in theory if not always in practice, any kind of sounding can be studied by any kind of person. Unfortunately, this ideal obscures a pernicious reality; it is similarly mediated by unresolved histories of racism and colonialism. Danielle Brown asserts that ethnomusicology, "whose predominantly white members by and large research people of color, *is and can be nothing other than a colonialist and imperialist enterprise*" (Brown 2020, n.p., emphasis in original). This charge might lead some to bury their heads in the sand or throw their hands up in frustration, particularly because some ethnomusicologists have long been in engaged in antiracist and anticolonialist politics. Yet ethnomusicologists—in particular, white cisgender males—have an obligation to accept this statement at face value, to acknowledge the ways in which the disciplinary community has been formed on the fault lines of difference and exclusion as much as belonging and inclusion. While encouraging diversity within our circumscribed fields of study, ethnomusicology rests on conformity to white, patriarchal, heteronormative systems of authority, privilege, and prestige. Just as unmarked whiteness predominates in the shadows of racially classified Others, the unmarked privileging of Western art music rests on the classification and segregation of other musics. Ethnomusicology's very existence as a field dedicated to the study of musics of largely nonwhite Others serves as a discursive and institutional space to contain Otherness without challenging the underlying power dynamics of who gets to study whom. Unsettling the boundaries of inclusion and exclusion in ethnomusicology's community might end up dissolving the field or radically reconstituting its modes of engagement and participation.

We believe that fieldwork and ethnography *can* be useful tools for understanding the current worlds in which we live and the histories that shape them, provided that they are grounded in sustained engagement with local community values, an awareness of positionality, and an ethic of anticolonial reciprocity (see Harris 2022; Schultz 2020; Fox 2020; Solis 2012). Ethnographic practice must reflexively confront empire and colonialism (Robinson 2020, 68) while allowing us to find similarities in unfamiliar contexts or differences in our most familiar contexts. When carried out with an honest exploration of one's own "critical listening positionality" (10), ethnography can teach how to listen in ways that help undo lifetimes of listening habits rooted in one's own history of normative socialization. These habits of mind carry the potential to humanize while accommodating difference as a fundamental aspect of our being (Koskoff 2014, 186). By focusing on habits, we hope that researchers can reserve judgments of musicking and community making as either utopian or dystopian, face-to-face or virtual, real or imagined.

As ethnomusicology works toward more decolonial futures, it is vital to understand how its intellectual foundations have ossified into norms that unnecessarily reinforce exclusive ways of thinking and modes of identification. Unfortunately, the scholarly community of ethnomusicologists is not as diverse or inclusive as many of the communities in which we live and do research, and our methods of representing culture are similarly less three-dimensional than the world in which we are embedded. Despite its best intentions, ethnomusicology has long been a community that ensures conformity and sameness within its ranks even as it documents and celebrates difference. Decolonizing music studies involves acts of refusal and disengagement (Robinson et al. 2019) as well as an antiracist commitment to lay bare our disciplinary habits of body and mind. The discourse of ethnomusicology, as a mode of Thirdness (see below) mediating between the signs and objects of musical life, is one of the symbolic contexts that shapes how music is lived and understood. As a community of scholars that has worked to elucidate the music/community relationship for many years, it is critical to address how the social dynamics that ethnomusicologists study can be more equitably reflected in the institutions, practices, and interpersonal dynamics that define us.

This challenge is not unique to ethnomusicology or music studies. It confronts all humanistic disciplines and returns us to the amorphous definition of *community* as relations of sameness and difference that include a sense of mutual indebtedness. How do communities incorporate sameness without using it to police who does and does not belong? How do communities acknowledge difference without threatening that which binds the community together? More concretely, how do we build more diverse, equitable, and inclusive communities in our scholarly work and in our classrooms, universities, and neighborhoods? Inspired by the Southern African philosophies of unhu/ubuntu, how can we learn better to be a person among others (Rukuni 2007)? These are questions that many are asking in the wake of Black Lives Matter, #MeToo, and other ongoing social and environmental justice movements around the world that reinforce the need to acknowledge mutual indebtedness as a necessary condition of community.

In the remainder of this introduction we theorize the relation between music and community with the goal of promoting a more equitable and decolonial vision for ethnomusicology.[3] We first examine the dialectical relation between music and community through the concept of feedback. Then we explore the broader valences of the interaction between music and community as alternately hopeful or discouraging. While scholars may feel inclined toward utopian or dystopian visions of this interaction, we argue for the need to tack between them while holding the value for cultural difference at the center of scholarly practice. Finally, we extend Turino's application of Peircean phenomenology within ethnomusicology by applying the concepts of Firstness, Secondness, and Thirdness to the relations of sameness and difference in sonic and affective practices that underpin community formation.

Community and the Arts as a Feedback System

"Feedback is hard to think" (Tomlinson 2018, 19). This is how the musicologist Gary Tomlinson opened his chapter on feedback as one of the central components of biocultural coevolution in *Culture and the Course of Human Evolution*. Committing to an understanding of feedback's mechanics in any dynamic system (such as social life) reveals the ongoing and essential tension between stability and dynamism, stasis and change, order and chaos, that is essential to our understanding of community itself as a dynamic process rather than a

fixed product. Turino foregrounds this feedback system when he defines ethnomusicology as

> the study of the dialectical interplay of music making and social life within spe-
> cific instances toward the goal of understanding the special potentials of musical
> sound and motion (including dance) as well as understanding the individuals,
> social groups, situations, movements, and exchanges in which music plays a role
> (2014, 185).

Feedback is the consequence of a system's output being "fed back" as input
(Novak 2013, 146). These systems are inherently dynamic, ever-changing, and
constantly transforming (140). This idea has been employed off and on in social
analysis and ethnomusicological scholarship for a long time.[4] Music studies
have been enriched by attention to literal manifestations of feedback through
amplification systems as metaphorical pathways of insight to the communities
who interact with those systems. Kenneth Gourlay argues that humans' search
for meaning leads to the creation of signs that create human beings. We make
music because of who we are; we are who we are because we make music (1982,
412). Extended cycles of feedback between relations of human sociality and elements of musical interaction generate emergent qualities of community that, in
turn, shape the kinds of musicking those communities use to understand and
represent themselves.

But if feedback has quietly been a theoretical tool for generations of ethnomusicologists, it has usually remained an undertheorized and underutilized one.[5]
Tomlinson focuses precisely on the functions and implications of feedback for
the history of humanity and the music that has helped define it for, as he puts
it, a million years (2015). But the classic symbiotic processes of feedback need
to be applied with caution. Music doesn't change community at every instance,
but always carries the potential to transform how people relate to one another,
interact, or reflect on their mutual similarities and differences.

In Tomlinson's exploration of music's origins, the "cultural" is one of three inheritance systems that interact to inform biocultural evolution (2018).[6] Organisms
respond and select traits to shape the environment in which they find themselves
in a process called niche construction (35–58). If we accept, as Turino does, that
musicking is semiosis, then Tomlinson's basic assertion about the role that culture
plays in evolutionary processes becomes vitally important; "all semiosis is niche
construction" (73). People use music as a tool in order to shape their environments.
These environments are then the contexts from which this music making emerges.
Foregrounding this dynamic *process* of never-ending feedback illuminates the
reality that music and community have a great deal to say about how the other is
formed, maintained, and experienced. This assertion is consistent with the Black
feminist thought of Patricia Hill Collins, whose conception of community is built

in part on the same American pragmatist foundation as our own (2019). She argues that human creativity is essential in making sense of human experience, and that experience itself is foundational to understanding the social self (172). Her advocacy for a pragmatic approach to nonreductive identity is a key aspect of intersectionality and is compatible with Turino's approach to identity built on shared habits. The feedback loops between creativity (as in music) and experience (as with sociality) are the foundation of community.

It is crucial to note that feedback is not a kind of chaos that disrupts the stability of social life; it is essential to that stability, organizing chaos via selective differentiation. The immediacy of musical experience, the moments in which flow and communitas emerge, occur in symbolic contexts that can seem rather static. History, religion, race, family, and political economy may seem external and impervious to the subtle dynamics of musical life, but they are all embedded in dynamic feedback systems. Questions remain as to whether the inherent conservatism of many "traditional" musics (e.g., mbira, old-time music, Garhwali d'hol) operates as "negative" feedback tending toward homeostasis or whether emphases on innovation and creativity in other musics (e.g., jazz, mid-century avant-garde) provide "positive" feedback tending toward dynamism. Yet music is just one of countless technologies of transformation employed by people, as organisms, to engineer their ecosystems. Dynamism itself can be restrained by feedback. The feedback model is useful in that it exposes how susceptible rigidity is to transformation and chaos is to order. Affective semiosis depends on such feedback.

Tacking Between Utopia and Dystopia

Community emerged as a term within academic discourse at the end of the nineteenth century and has been used with increasing regularity with each ensuing decade. The term carries a range of associative meanings in academic discourse, even if these are not always made explicit. For Kay Kaufman Shelemay, there is value in the vagueness and polysemy of such a concept (2011). Communities cross boundaries (geographic and otherwise), can operate as a "mode of experience" (Cohen 1985) or reconceived as "musical pathways" (Finnegan 1989), "micromusics" (Slobin 1993), "scenes" (Straw 1991), "affective assemblages" (Deleuze and Guattari 1987), or a "deep comradeship, founded in shared language, political interests, ethos, and blood" (Waterman 1990, 11). Despite the broad range of collectivities encompassed by its many definitions and the stretching of this term to encompass virtual communities or imagined communities at the scale of the nation and beyond (Anderson 1983), the term continues to carry a strong indexical association with intimacy in local social settings (e.g., *Community of Music*, Nettl 1993).

Community endures in humanities and social science discourse in part because it signifies promise and positivity in times of political, economic, and spiritual decay. Raymond Williams noted that *community* always seems to be used favorably (1976, 76). It tends to privilege the face-to-face and to prioritize organic communing rather than institutional formations. The term carries optimism, even idealism, stemming from longstanding indexical associations with such concepts as participation, sharing, equality, fellowship, kinship, obligingness, and "communitas" (Turner 1969, 134). The pedagogue Parker Palmer attributes the vogue of discoursing about community to feelings of disconnection that permeate our society. He describes a therapeutic model of community that relates the health of the person to the health of the broader collectives of which they are part (2007, 202–3). This approach is prevalent in such fields as medical ethnomusicology and "community music therapy" (Jones 2014; Mitchell 2019). A therapeutic model stresses human love and intimacy, perhaps the most cherished forms of sociality.

In many ways, the keystone of Turino's ethnomusicological project is to identify, explain, and then celebrate the ways in which music helps people become the best social versions of themselves. Turino lays his cards on the table by connecting these hypothetical possibilities to the realities of contemporary life. He theorizes five distinct fields of music making that shape habits of interaction and sonic ethics in different ways: participatory performance, presentational performance, high-fidelity recording, studio audio art recording, and telemusical performance (Turino 2016, 300). For Turino, participatory music involves all participants' contributing to an activity "considered integral to the performance" (Turino 2009, 3). There is no distinction between audience and artist, and performance is judged more by the extent to which everyone was compelled to participate than by any autonomous standard of beauty or virtuosity. It is the field to which Turino dedicates the most attention regarding community formation and sustenance. He emphasizes the potential of participatory music to direct habit change toward sustainable living (1), arguing, "As relatively cooperative, egalitarian spaces that are about sociality, bonding, and fun, rather than about hierarchy, competition, financial achievement, or the creation of art objects for listening, participatory performance provides a powerful experiential model of alternative values and ways of being for people in capitalist societies" (14). Musicking both creates experiences of social bonding and models idealized ways of being.

Unfortunately, musical power can also be harnessed for division, rupture, and the dismantling of solidarity. Musical modes of sociality can be exploited to reinforce the kinds of human differences that generate social inequality and violence. For every protest movement emboldened via participatory singing, there is an exclusionary nationalist movement performing propagandistic modes of sonic violence. Both love and hate can be fomented in collective sound, and the processes of interaction and feedback between meaningful musical sounds and the communities to which they connect are similar in both cases.

A corollary to Turino's aspirational project is the scholarly responsibility to expose the dark side of these processes and clarify music's semiotic potential to divide humans from one another as often as it unites them, hence Turino's provocative coupling of the inspirational power of music to affectively augment the possibilities of collective flourishing in the face of brutality among African Americans during the civil rights movement with the cautionary horrors that participatory practices in Germany helped enable during the Third Reich leading up to World War II (2008). David Hesmondhalgh (2013, 19) questions Turino's idealism, arguing that Turino "draws too strong a line between emancipatory and repressive forms of communality. . . . This downplays the complexity and ambivalence surrounding more ordinary modes of musical collectivism." To paraphrase Sherry Ortner, "dark ethnomusicology" would insist that an ethnomusicology of community must account for the negative sides of boundary-making, the failures of utopian musical practice, and the need to address the centrality of social inequality (2016). That which feels like optimism and hope to one person at one moment can be a painful exclusionary experience for another person or at another moment. Understanding this pain as "unmaking" as much as "making" community is an essential step toward achieving an understanding of social justice (Scarry 1985, 279, as cited in Wong 2019, 169). Music contributes to both dynamics as two alternatives of community in process. Community can't be assumed.

Difference and Differentiation

Human difference and differentiation lie at the heart of these aspirational claims and the harmful impact of social distinction, whether tied to class, race, sexuality, or otherwise. As we enter the middle of the twenty-first century, social and political desires to overcome social difference and advance projects of acceptance and inclusivity make these conversations timelier than ever. It is easy to slip into a quest to eradicate human difference and distinction as a way to right the wrongs of historical racism, class struggle, and the persecution of marginalized communities everywhere. Music's role in nationalism and propaganda makes it a complicit practice in centuries-old histories of social inequality.

For Jean-Luc Nancy, being is necessarily being-with-one-another (2000, 13). A sense of self emerges from interactions with non-self, and subjectivity almost always implies a form of intersubjectivity. This is the foundation of both community and identity. From birth, one's sense of self and the world are shaped by relations with others and the growing awareness that self is different from other. Differentiation is the dawn of the ego. One can only acknowledge being together (or being alone) and sharing once the difference between me and you is understood.

Thus difference is not a wrong to be righted any more than music is inherently good or bad. It simply is. Rivera Cusicanqui's advocacy for differences coexisting among equals (2020) reinforces Gary Tomlinson's celebration of differentiation as the key to humanity's flourishing over the millennia (2015). The human capacity to adapt and produce variable cultural practices in evolving environmental conditions enabled the rise of modernity (in the broadest sense). Put another way, the uniquely human capacity to generate cultural difference is essential to human flourishing. It is not something to be erased but, rather, celebrated and nurtured. Perhaps paradoxically, music is uniquely positioned to bring people together in solidarity as the very differences between us are identified and protected.

But experiences of differentiation are dynamic and unpredictable. In each case there are plural conceptions of community, inevitable moments of unpredictability, and a lived interplay between imagination and reality. Any sense of stability in the boundaries of either musical form/style or community can be elusive, revealing instead a process of constant volatility. Like musical styles, communities are typically nested and intersectional, and only loosely bounded by space and time. Because musicking enables interaction between the actual and the possible, it can sometimes be difficult to tell whether a community coheres during a specific performance or whether performance takes shape around a community. A phenomenological analysis of the feedback cycles of music and community allows us to examine how individuals, experiences, and discursive contexts collectively inform the making of community through processes of differentiation and understandings of mutual indebtedness.

The Phenomenology of Community

Firstness, Secondness, and Thirdness are the foundational categories of the phenomenology of Charles S. Peirce and the basis of the complex theory of signs for which he is more widely known. Firstness is possibility; Secondness is actuality; Thirdness is representation.[7] Turino advocates for a phenomenological ethnomusicology rooted in Peircean thought in part because musical experience is so powerful yet elusive. We employ Peirce's categories of being as tools in our examination of community in order to show how community emerges when the complex whole (First) is narrowed down via the distinctions and differences generated by experience (Second) and stabilized in discourse (Third). Each of these elements of being—differentiation, experience, and context—are fundamental influences on the mutually constitutive dynamic processes of musicking and communing.

There is an obvious relation between community and identity, although communities are not coterminous with identity formations. We feel a sense of belonging to communities with which we identify. Whether this is always something felt *for* itself depends on the specific circumstances under investigation, but there is often something intentional about it. In our own exploration of community, we find it instructive to consider the distinctions between self, subjectivity, and identity as manifestations of Firstness, Secondness, and Thirdness as modes of being, in order to provide insight into the nature of community itself. Turino advances a distinction between self and identity that is productive in this regard (2008, 100). Habits provide the foundation on which people align themselves for and against others into communities. Perman extends Turino's original distinction, inserting moment-to-moment experiences of subjectivity in between more holistic senses of self and mediated and partial senses of identity. Both Turino and Perman explicitly link these distinctions to Peirce's fundamental categories. The self is a First and includes one's physical body and all of one's habits; subjectivity, a Second, is the partial selection of habits and capacities engaged in the immediate here and now; identity is a representation, a Third (Perman 2020, 60). If selves are holistic and stable and identities are partial and habitual, subjective experience is in between.

Subjectivity is to intersubjectivity as identity is to community. If intersubjectivity refers to the lived engagement with others in real time as a dimension of subjectivity (Perman 2020, 64), then community is somewhat analogous to "inter-identity," although this comparison has limits. Turino defines *identity* as "a partial and variable selection of habits and attributes that we use to represent ourselves to ourselves and to others, as well as those aspects that are perceived by ourselves and by others as salient" (2008, 102). The making of a community is the real-time bonds and ruptures that form according to how people *feel* similar to or different from others. *Community* refers to collectives based on habits of thinking, feeling, and doing that are made in those intersubjective experiences of life. When discussing the thousands of dancers coming together through taiko in California, Deborah Wong says, "Community is not abstract in this environment. The sight of hundreds upon hundreds of people making the same movements is powerful—even more so, feeling one's own movements amplified through hundreds of other bodies" (Wong 2019, 75). Community emerges from the moments of intersubjectivity (as in musical performance) that put sentient beings in relation to one another.

Firstness and One World

But how to begin? The distinctions and decisions that shape identity or social relations are not predetermined. The anthropologist Jaimie Weiner asks quite simply, "Why not start with 'one world,' wherein peoples, languages and more-or-less well understood 'laws' contingently and praxically exist, and posit as our subject matter the differentiating activity that emerges from it—and results in such categories as 'indigenous' and 'non-indigenous'?" (Weiner 2002, 3, quoted in Strathern 2006, 192). The world comes first; only later do our intersubjective experiences shape identities, communities, cosmologies, and their accompanying languages and laws.[8] If being is always being-with (Nancy 2000), then suddenly the self doesn't really exist in the atomistic ways it is conventionally imagined. My sense of self is me, but it has never been solely or only me, from the moment I heard my mother's voice or saw my father's face. My being has always been "with." Any good therapist will tell you that people who were not "with" anyone in productive or safe ways as children have attachment issues for the rest of their lives. Not being-with another is a kind of social dismemberment.

Thus, community becomes a by-product of differentiation, retreat, and subtraction, emerging from the confrontations of Secondness and the reflections of Thirdness. The "world," in Weiner's suggestion above, is an undifferentiated First. For Nancy, community retreats from or subtracts something, relying on finitude and differentiation (cited in Shelemay 2011, 357). Kofi Agawu suggests that this differentiation toward people and objects asserts a kind of power over them (2003, 119). His point is not that there isn't difference but, rather, that it shouldn't be the way we a priori make sense of the world. Instead, he presumes the reality of sameness before action and representation (126). Theorizing one world as a starting point acknowledges this sameness while accepting the inevitability of differentiation. Communities emerge from the limits and distinctions of Secondness in a retreat from the abstract unity of one world to find one's place in that world.

Secondness, Affect, and Group Flow

Music and dance are temporally and spatially bounded activities that require concentration and engrossment. As such, these activities are well suited to engender experiences of "flow." In a flow state, as theorized by Csikszentmihalyi (1990) and employed by Turino (2008), we become one with the activity we are performing; self-awareness and fear melt away and perceptions of time and space can become distorted. Psychologists have predominantly studied flow experiences at the level of the individual (Rahaim 2019). Csikszentmihalyi listed "direct and immediate feedback" as one of the preconditions for flow, but he was mainly thinking about the information relayed back to an individual actor to focus the mind on the activity at hand. Similarly, he discussed joy as the product of internal positive sensations during an individual flow state (1990).

Yet studies have shown that joy also results from interaction in a field of human relationships and that collective experiences of flow enhance the positive effects that we feel (Walker 2010; Hamilton et al. 2019). Given that flow involves a dissolution of self-consciousness, might it not also bring a heightened sense of "we-ness"? Victor Turner's (1974) concept of communitas, uncoupled from the structuralist paradigms against which he wrote, links the obvious personal ·benefits of flow states to the interpersonal and intersubjective experiences that help shape community. Beyond Turner's narrow applications of communitas to ritual rites of passage (Fiol 2011), it can be helpful to consider communitas as a unique form of intersubjectivity in which social differences temporarily disappear (Perman 2020, 65). Within these moments during the bounded constraints of musical performance, only sameness matters (Turino 2008, 18). Communities are forged in such ways.

How might this happen in phenomenological terms? Over time, in communities all over the world, activities have been essentially engineered to facilitate human flourishing. Music is one of many technologies of transformation employed to shape how individuals relate to one another. It can transform anxiety into hope, possibility into reality, mediums into spirits, placidity into euphoria, and collections of individuals into communities. Like any technology, one must learn how to use it, but when done sincerely and cooperatively, musicking makes communities.

Music is ubiquitous in ritual life, where transformation is often the intended purpose. This is when music's status as a technology of transformation is perhaps most apparent yet difficult to explain. Theorists of social cognition have identified a number of psychosomatic processes that contribute to a sense of "we-ness," whether consciously or not. It is not surprising that many of these processes are central to musical experience. Motor stimulation and entrainment, for instance, involve the subconscious alignment of activity between agents both inside and outside the body (Pacherie 2014, 31). We know from research on mirror neurons that to imagine a musical pattern or phrase stimulates the same neural pathways involved when playing that musical pattern or phrase. Mentally rehearsing patterns—or silently following the kinesthetic and aural cues of a performer—triggers biological effects that are virtually identical to those of performers (Schiavio, Menin, and Matyja 2014). Extending Alfred Schutz's contention that music can forge a sense of community because participants share both subjective and objective senses of time, the music philosopher Kathleen Higgins argues that music's impact on solidarity depends on the use of hearing to detect movement and agency (2018, 4).

Something like a proto-community forms from lived intersubjective experience, preceding any conscious awareness of its distinctiveness. This is a state of Secondness. Drawing on the experiences of members of the Danish String Quartet, Salice, Høffding, and Gallagher (2019) explore the way in which reiterated performances cultivate a collective empathy that is more than simply motor resonance or explicit coordination between performers. There is also an affective, "interkinesthetic awareness" that one's individual sense of agency has been sub-sumed into a group agency—a "we-agency"—in which one's perception-action loops are responsive to, and modulated by, those of the other members. Inter-kinesthetic affectivity involves a deep sense of trust, feel, and responsibility for the sounds and actions of others. In the context of a string quartet this involves "intersubjective proprioception," an implicit knowledge of when the group as a whole will shift its bowing or initiate an acceleration, for instance. This experi-ence of playing and moving together in synchrony also involves interoception, a sense of knowing the body internally, via the vibrational resonance of others' playing. During music- or dance-induced experiences of collective flow or com-munitas, bodies merge, and joint actions and various forms of intersubjective interaction result in what Merleau-Ponty called "intercorporeity" (1968).

The anthropologist Csordas argues that people don't encounter social things, only intersubjective relations (2008, 113). The more that is shared, the more likely the participants of an intersubjective experience will *feel* like they belong to the same community. In his summary of theoretical issues in ethnomusicol-ogy for *Oxford Music Online*, Martin Stokes points out, almost as an aside, that music's impact on social life is precisely in its potential to generate affect during performance (2007, 3). Music can make or break community because of this affective potential. Bonding with others, feeling included or excluded, acting in solidarity: These are all emotional experiences. As a real-time practice that can be liberated from the generality and abstraction of language, music and dance are perhaps the sine qua non of emotional sociality. They are powerful tools for emoting and directing those emotions toward specific but unsaid goals.

Affects integrate the epistemological, the biological, and the ontological as agents evaluate the signs of their experience against the world in which they find themselves. They are ambiguous but intense quests for meaning as lived in real time. The affective dimensions of musical experience help people transform insignificant musical details into the grandest ideals of social life. Community is one such potential ideal. But these connections don't always realize these ideals. As the affective engagement with musical signs triggers emotional responses, senses of self, community, and reality can be transformed for better or worse. Relations between sound and society shape emotional responses that, in turn, change the conditions of those relations in a never-ending feedback cycle.

Thirdness, Discourse, and Differentiation

Feelings of belonging and difference are semiotic and phenomenological. At-tending to difference as Secondness is a way to make sense of the whole, or Firstness. This attention takes place in a context of Thirdness through lan-guage, discourse, and context (Kohn 2013, 38). The feelings of experience and the acknowledgment of sameness and difference are represented in language, made resilient through discourse, and understood in context. Unlike the communities rooted in shared experience, described above, imagined communities (Anderson 1983) are often conceptualized discursively (Thirdness) before they are ever experienced (Secondness). Thus if community requires differentiation, is it also rooted in shared knowledge, which is what makes communication, even community, possible.[9]

Yet there is a tension, one that is reflective of the music/community feedback cycle, between community and knowledge. In learning of and connecting with the other, knowledge is necessary, but one can't begin to really know before seeking a social connection, a being-with-one-another. Stable communities necessitate shared knowledge. Embodied relational knowledge, such as that relied on in music and dance, is the connective tissue between self and other, mind and body, and experience and community. Yet the possibility of valued interpersonal relations also requires a sense of commonality. Each reinforces the other.

The missing ingredients that bind knowledge and community together are mutual investment and indebtedness. Beyond shared knowledge, community depends on habits that are mobilized in social life (Amit 2010, 362). We follow Vered Amit to assert that shared knowledge is not enough to generate community; interdependence is essential (360). The "with" must be nurtured and protected if it is to continue. Sentient beings, whether humans, deities, spirits, or otherwise, constantly interact with others. These moments when habits of interaction are in play during daily life can be understood via intersubjectivity. The intersubjective is the ongoing present of being-with. As we invest in and identify with the habits that develop by means of these interactive experiences through ever-changing feedback loops of social relations and musicking practice, we develop those habits and foreground the relations that we like to be with. This is community.

Turino uses the paired concepts of cultural cohorts and cultural formations to extend his habit-oriented understanding of identity (Thirdness) to groups of people. Partial sets of shared habits characterize cultural cohorts, and more comprehensive sets, cultural formations (2008, 112). We understand these as two nested categories of community. The modes of connection, distinction, bonding, and alienation that emerge in cohorts and formations have different foundations with vastly different consequences: One is experiential, the other discursive. Cultural cohorts are the shallower and more transitory collectives that emerge from shared experience, which music is ideally designed to facilitate. Discursive communities and cultural formations provide the symbolic context in which the chaos of musical sign making takes place. But community is also the product of experience, including past musicked or languaged moments.

The visceral feelings of experiential communing, good or bad, can shape the ways in which the more stable discursive formations unfold over time. There is ongoing feedback between them, hence Turino's (2008, 115) hopeful suggestion that the habits shaped at the local level during midwestern contradances (within a cultural cohort) could eventually change the United States (as a cultural formation). Relying on phenomenological categories of being allows analysis to more specifically reveal how cohorts can shape formations. Over time, the discursive generalizations of Thirdness can render the potentially transformative experiences of Secondness more habitual and more stable.[10]

At the close of *Moving away from Silence*, Turino tells the story of Conima migrants living in Lima returning to their ancestral home to convene with their brethren and musical elders in the group Qhantati Ururi (1993). What they hoped would be a triumphant return and reunion became a bittersweet disappointment. Although the migrants in Lima all identified with the people who remained in Conima, the habits they had acquired in their very different environment in Lima led to different expectations, values, and interpretations of the world around them. They led meetings like the urban dwellers they had become; their Conima counterparts responded with the collectivist silence that cultivated consensus. Urban competitive values that prioritized sonic quality confronted rural preferences for participatory inclusivity accommodating differing degrees of musical competence. In the end, everyone was left unsatisfied. As Turino says,

> Equally important to musical sound among Conimeños in Lima is verbal discourse about social identity and community within which "sounding like Conima" is embedded. Qhantati's music has been abstracted from the "whole way of life" of the ayllus and inserted into new ways of life in the city. In spite of the relatively close similarity in sound between a Qhantati [from rural Conima] and a Centro Social [from urban Lima] sikuri performance, their distinct processes of creation and contrasting musical conceptions lead me to ask whether the two groups are, in fact, even playing the same music. I believe that the residents would answer this question adamantly in the affirmative; the response of older musicians from the ayllus might be a more tentative "Well, yes and no." (1993, 247).

Community here emerged from difference as much as from similarity. Sadly, for urban Conimeños, their efforts to *make* a broader Conimeño community unwittingly helped *unmake* the community they presumed already existed. Diverging habits foreclosed hopes for inclusivity. Like many aspects of life rooted in direct experience, desires and ideals were never easily reified.

For Qhantati members in Conima, music was uniquely suited to overcome these generations of difference because of its affective potential: "For the Qhantati members who wanted to play panpipes on the last day of the Fiesta de San

Miguel, performing was a matter of moving away—as in that morning's meeting—from all the things that could not be said, and of making one's mark on the soundscape" (Turino 1993, 251). Music became the means of overcoming the negative consequences of their interaction with the musicians from Lima. If music helps Conimeños move away from silence, it moves them toward the collective. Community is not silent.

As myriad crises in the early 2020s shape the world in which we write these words, our responsibility as teachers, scholars, and performers to harness these idealized ways of being for the sake of equity and social justice weighs heavily. Kathleen Higgins calls music educators to action regarding the pedagogical mission to employ music education for the sake of engendering solidarity and combating inequality (2018). She relies on Turino's attention to the participatory urge for a musical effort to shape a more peaceful and just world. Scholarship grounded in equity and justice demands theoretical frameworks that untangle the processes of music and community as the foundations of transformative social change. Phenomenology, as employed here in continuation of Turino's work, guides this understanding in scholarship and in social life to help us make our ideas clear (Peirce 1878; Turino 2015). Turino points out that "with these seeds of understanding young people may be better equipped to believe in the possibilities of fundamental habit change and creation, and to take on the problems of sustainable futures for themselves" (Turino 2009, 16). As scholarship integrates theorizing with activism, a focus on habit change and the ways in which technologies such as music can be employed to realize change in specific ways is a necessary consideration for music scholarship and education. As Turino's scholarship reveals, musicking can change the world.

Chapter Summaries

Neither *community* nor *music* fully captures the breadth of the social dynamics discussed in this volume. Each can signify or exclude many things. But attending to specific cases at specific times and places reveals how reliably the music/community feedback cycle plays out across the globe. In demonstrating dynamic moments in the musical processes of shaping, reinforcing, undoing, and negating community projects, the contributors demonstrate the utility of Turino's toolbox for ethnomusicology.

As mentioned, Part I emphasizes processes of differentiation as music generates, shapes, and transforms community. The ruptures and migrations of history do not always forge new communities. Ioannis Tsekouras's work with Pontic Greek refugees reveals how music can be powerfully used to remember and connect, generating a kind of organic sociality but falling short of the musicked creation of community. The performance of *parakathia* brings cohorts together through moments of embodied memory and nostalgia; nevertheless, participants acknowledge the limits of these experiences and deny the possibility of recreating the "pure sociality" of their Pontic history.

Donna Buchanan demonstrates how the rigidity of past communities confronts the ambiguities of the present in the aftermath of violence and displacement. The tension between Armenian, diasporic, Bulgarian, Turkish, and scholarly agendas and understandings are negotiated in every gesture and melody in the dance performances of Bulgaria's bifurcated Armenian diaspora. Armenians living in Bulgaria struggle with balancing their need to assert their ethnicity with a genuine desire to collaborate and demonstrate inclusivity. As they dance, negotiating seemingly incommensurable participatory and presentational values within discursive contexts, a complex and unresolved Armenian cultural philosophy is performed.

Eduardo Herrera explores how in-group and out-group dynamics forged in heightened moments of fandom in soccer stadiums shape resilient ideas of community and belonging. He augments Turino's participatory models by foregrounding "inherent audiences" as essential to the sounded imaginings of soccer participants. The performance of fandom with clear and often violent pronouncements of group status exploits relationships of affective leverage to bring people together in the face of opposition and antagonism. His work shows how the fleeting moments of chanting during a soccer match can have long-term consequences for how Argentinians see themselves and others.

Music's lived reality as embodied knowledge does not easily fit within the legal structures left after the twentieth century's overwhelming colonial experiment. Veit Erlmann explores how political, legal, and indigenous actors negotiate the meaning of indigenous knowledge as social and legal institutions of South Africa struggle to represent indigeneity. Competing interests operate within seemingly incommensurate discursive frameworks to undermine the work of protecting indigenous knowledge within the legal framework of the state. Erlmann reveals how statist interventions reify a notion of "the indigenous community" that endangers the self-determination of indigenous peoples and exposes the challenge of decolonizing ossified cultural structures.

Part II prioritizes the dynamics of feedback as musical practice and social dynamics mutually form and inform one another. Joanna Bosse presents a case that is, initially, about pedagogy. For Bosse, a sustained and intentional classroom experience of collective musicking is essential to understanding how music works in social life. Participation teaches students how music is used in ways beyond what disembodied listening and reading can provide. This generates community among the students precisely as Turino's work suggests. Her students feel closer to one another than in their other classes, thus reinforcing the music/community feedback loop. Making music—even the music of "others"—forges social bonds and connections that endure beyond the act of musicking itself.

In examining musical competition in rural Bolivia, Thomas Solomon explicitly states that moments of performance are moments of community. It is remarkable how effectively past traumas and contemporary conflict can, through musical practice and participatory experiences, be forged into spaces of real belonging and avenues for social change. But depending on the factors involved, competition shapes community in multiple ways. He presents no fewer than seven different kinds of community fostered in competition that expose just how complex and unpredictable the music/community feedback cycle can be.

Sylvia Bruinders focuses on the Christmas bands of Cape Town, who perform their self-defined (and long-denied) citizenship by "parading respectability." After the brutality of apartheid, these competitions give marginalized communities a rare platform on which to generate musical sustainability and collective solidarity. When band members embrace both participatory and presentational values, their musical choices reveal motivations of citizenship, solidarity, and agency in the face of external expectations. Their presentational performance resists capitalist values in its constitution of community during competitions in which solidarity is often the unexpected outcome.

David A. McDonald presents a powerful case of Palestinian festivalgoers who strategically employ the reliable relation between music and participation to generate direct action and assert an anticolonial message in an environment where such assertions are dangerous and policed. In these bounded moments of participation during a festival, the possibility of an egalitarian aesthetic can emerge with important affective consequences. Joy becomes political as participatory performances carry the potential to transform the oppressive contexts in which they are bravely enacted.

Finally, Part III prioritizes the necessity of mutual indebtedness in the maintenance of just communities. Tony Perman expands on the power of music to forge senses of community and belonging outside of the contexts of its original purpose. By exploring "experiential schizophonia" among North American practitioners of the Zimbabwean mbira, he focuses on the consequences of music's social impact within contexts of racism and colonialism. Communities have been made because of mbira's participatory power, but without acknowledgment of mutual indebtedness, mbira practice risks reinforcing the systems of racism and colonialism that preceded these musical interactions.

Rick Deja addresses the way jazz's ethos of freedom can be employed in post-apartheid South Africa to generate more inclusive modes of social belonging. By comparing free and collective improvisation with pan-African jazz, Deja demonstrates that a sense of obligation can inspire greater inclusivity. Musical freedom is not enough to realize the ideals of social freedom in improvisation.

Inclusivity, ethics, belonging, freedom, and shared responsibility must be manifest in experience. Deja demonstrates how linking the values of improvisation to the knowledge of tradition effectively facilitates feelings of belonging and community to contribute to positive social change.

Stefan Fiol examines how efforts to safeguard "intangible cultural heritage" in a North Indian village festival involve both the making and unmaking of community. Forms of community engendered by ritual participation are undermined in part by the competing interests and goals of various actors involved in "heritagization." In order to be effective, heritage interventions require a "shift in consciousness" that foregrounds the vulnerabilities of the communities engendered through performance. Mutual obligation does not inherently lead to equity or inclusivity. Community is not utopian. Without centering differentiation and mutual indebtedness, competing value systems and knowledge systems risk undermining music's capacity to shape healthy communal practices.

As the contributors make clear, music is not a panacea that one can simply apply in contexts of social division and heal all wounds. Music can be used to exclude and include, to oppress and lift up. The goal is not to capture every nuance of the complexity of musical practice or social life but, instead, to identify, then harness, the elements that can be productively and collectively employed (see Healy 2015). There is a moral compulsion in our field to foreground the brutal and unfair dimensions of life as the most salient lens through which to both make sense of the world and to change it. This tends toward a structural critique of institutions and power as a means of improving those institutions. But critical thinking need not overshadow generous thinking (Fitzpatrick 2019). It is forever challenging to balance cynicism with naïveté or pessimism with optimism. By centering the value of difference in productive feedback dynamics of music and community while asserting the need for mutual moral indebtedness, we foreground music's potential to transform community for the better. Music provides hope, it helps imagine human ideals, and helps render those imaginings. And struggle is a necessary condition of hope and a foundation for ensuring that the musical helps make the social what it ought to be.

Notes

1. James Ferguson defends the social in his own centering of obligation when he says, "But without at least some concept of the social, we can hardly invoke something called 'social obligation'. . . . For the 'social' in 'social obligation' does not refer to a biological population, or a network of actants, or a set of economically interested agents linked by markets—it refers (as Durkheim rightly insisted) to a moral unity" (2021, 12).

2. The phrasing of this potential is inspired by Graeber and Wengrow (2021, 8), as quoted by Blum in the epilogue of this volume.

3. This decolonial vision should not imply fully decolonized projects; these are aspirational and laborious processes (see Nayatara Sheoran Appleton as cited in Figueroa

2020, 41). Ethnomusicology's colonial foundations are deeply entrenched and not easily overcome. Following the models provided by Tuck and Yang (2012) and Robinson (2020), in order to assure that "decolonial" language refers to substantive redress and structural change rather than powerless metaphors, the field itself needs to be partly given back, both epistemologically and ontologically.

4. Marx's dialectical materialism is a feedback loop. Bourdieu's "structured structures predisposed to function as structuring structures" is a feedback loop (1977, 72). In *The Anthropology of Music*, Alan Merriam asserts that "there is a constant feedback from the product to the concepts about music, and this is what accounts both for change and stability in a music system. The feedback, of course, represents the learning process both for the musicians and for the non-musicians, and it is continual" (1964, 33).

5. Novak's work on *Japanoise* provides one important exception (2013).

6. The others are genetic and environmental. In the spirit of Viveiros de Castro's multinaturalism (2004), Tomlinson's model may not fully account for all ontologies. In Ndau cosmologies, for instance, individuals are often born with spirits, offering a fourth spiritual inheritance system (Perman 2020).

7. In Turino's terms, "Firstness refers to an entity without relation to a Second, that is, an entity in-and-of itself. Secondness is the direct relationship between two entities without the mediation of a Third; it is brute force, or cause and effect, or contiguity. Thirdness involves the mediation of a First and a Second by a Third so as to generate something new, above and beyond the particulars of the First and Second" (2014, 190).

8. Beginning with "the world" also allows for the "many worlds" approach inherent in Viveiros de Castro's multinaturalism or Descola's approach to animism (Viveiros de Castro 2004; Descola 2013).

9. Peirce calls this the "commens"; "that mind into which the minds of utterer and interpreter have to be fused in order that any communication should take place" (1998, 477).

10. This emphasis on discourse and context as Thirdness shaping indexical experiences should not overshadow language's reliance on foundational processes of Firstness and Secondness (like all modes of Thirdness). Symbolism (in Peirce's sense) depends on indexicality and iconicity. As Silverstein (2003), Samuels (2006), Nakassis (2020), Lie (2021), and others have shown, understanding any semiotic system (music, language, or otherwise) in its own terms (such as the symbols of language) demands greater attention to contextual and "metapragmatic" considerations.

Bibliography

Agawu, Kofi. 2003. "Contesting Difference: A Critique of Africanist Ethnomusicology." In *The Cultural Study of Music*, edited by Martin Clayton, Trevor Herbert, and Richard Middleton, 227–37. New York: Routledge.

Amit, Vered. 2010. "Community as Good to Think With: The Productiveness of Strategic Ambiguities." *Anthropologica (Ottawa)* 52(2): 357–75.

Anderson, Benedict. 1983. *Imagined Communities: Reflections on the Origin and Spread of Nationalism*. London: New Left Books.

Bigheno, Michelle. 2008. "Why I'm Not an Ethnomusicologist: A View from Anthropology." In *The New (Ethno)musicologies*, edited by Henry Stobart, 28–39. Lanham, MD: Scarecrow.

Bourdieu, Pierre. 1977. *Outline of a Theory of Practice.* Cambridge: Cambridge University Press.

Brown, Danielle. 2020. "An Open Letter on Racism in Music Studies: Especially Ethnomusicology and Music Education." https://www.mypeopletellstories.com/blog/open-letter. Accessed January 18, 2021.

Cohen, Anthony P. 1985. *The Symbolic Construction of Community.* London: Tavistock.

Collins, Patricia Hill. 2019. *Intersectionality as Critical Social Theory.* Durham, NC: Duke University Press.

Csikszentmihalyi, Mihaly. 1990. *Flow: The Psychology of Optimal Experience.* New York: Harper and Row.

Csordas, Thomas J. 2008. "Intersubjectivity and Intercorporeality." *Subjectivity* 22(1): 110–21.

Deleuze, Gilles, and Felix Guattari. 1987. *A Thousand Plateaus: Capitalism and Schizophrenia.* London: Continuum.

Descola, Phillipe. 2013. *Beyond Nature and Culture.* Chicago: University of Chicago Press.

Feld, Steven. 2015. "I Hate 'Sound Studies.'" www.stevenfeld.net. Accessed January 18, 2021.

Ferguson, James. 2021. *Presence and Social Obligation: An Essay on the Share.* Chicago: Prickly Paradigm.

Figueroa, Michael A. 2020. "Decolonizing 'Intro to World Music.'" *Journal of Music History Pedagogy* 10(1): 39–57.

Finnegan, Ruth. 1989. *The Hidden Musicians: Music-Making in an English Town.* Cambridge: Cambridge University Press.

Fiol, Stefan. 2011. "Sacred, Inferior, and Anachronous: Deconstructing Liminality Among the *Baddī* of the Central Himalayas." *Ethnomusicology Forum* 19:191–217.

Fitzpatrick, Kathleen. 2019. *Generous Thinking: A Radical Approach to Saving the University.* Baltimore: Johns Hopkins University Press.

Fox, Aaron A. 2020. "Divesting from Ethnomusicology." *Journal of Musicology* 37(1): 33–38.

Gaunt, Kyra D. 2002. "Got Rhythm? Difficult Encounters in Theory and Practice and Other Participatory Discrepancies in Music." *City and Society* 14(1): 119–40.

Gourlay, Kenneth A. 1982. "Towards a Humanizing Ethnomusicology." *Ethnomusicology* 26(3): 411–20.

Graeber, David, and David Wengrow. 2021. *The Dawn of Everything: A New History of Humanity.* New York: Farrar, Straus, and Giroux.

Hamilton, Andrés Kaltwasser, et al. 2019. "What Makes Metalheads Happy? A Phenomenological Analysis of Flow Experiences in Metal Musicians." *Qualitative Research in Psychology* 16(4): 537–65.

Harney, Stefano, and Fred Moten. 2013. *The Undercommons: Fugitive Planning and Black Study.* New York: Minor Compositions.

Harris, Deonte L. 2022. "On Race, Value, and the Need to Reimagine Ethnomusicology for the Future." *Ethnomusicology* 66(2): 213–35.

Harrison, Klisala. 2012. "Epistemologies of Applied Ethnomusicology." *Ethnomusicology* 56(3): 505–29.

Healy, Kieran. 2015. "Fuck Nuance." *Sociological Theory* 35(2): 118–27.

Hesmondhalgh, David. 2013. *Why Music Matters*. West Sussex, UK: Wiley Blackwell.

Higgins, Kathleen Marie. 2018. "Connecting Music to Ethics." *College Music Symposium* 58(3): 1–20.

Jones, Jeffrey A. 2014. "Health Musicking in Skiffle Steel Orchestra: Thoughts on Collaboration Between Community Music Therapy and Medical Ethnomusicology." *International Journal of Community Music* 7(1): 129–44.

Kockelman, Paul. 2020. *Kinds of Value: An Experiment in Modal Anthropology*. Chicago: Prickly Paradigm.

Kohn, Eduardo. 2013. *How Forests Think: Toward an Anthropology Beyond the Human*. Berkeley: University of California Press.

Koskoff, Ellen. 2014. *A Feminist Ethnomusicology: Writings on Music and Gender*. Urbana: University of Illinois Press.

Latour, Bruno. 2007. *Reassembling the Social: An Introduction to Actor-Network-Theory*. Oxford: Oxford University Press.

Lie, Siv. 2021. *Django Generations: Hearing Ethnorace, Citizenship, and Jazz Manouche in France*. Chicago: University of Chicago Press.

Merleau-Ponty, Maurice. 1968. *The Visible and the Invisible*. Evanston, IL: Northwestern University Press.

Merriam, Alan P. 1964. *The Anthropology of Music*. Evanston, IL: Northwestern University Press.

Mitchell, Elizabeth. 2019. "Community Music Therapy and Participatory Performance: A Case Study of a Coffeehouse." *Voices: A World Forum for Music Therapy* 19(1): 1–18.

Nakassis, Constantine V. 2020. "Deixis and the Linguistic Anthropology of Cinema." *Semiotic Review* 9 (November 30). https://www.semioticreview.com/ojs/index.php/sr/article/view/65.

Nancy, Jean-Luc. 2000. *Being Singular Plural*. Stanford, CA: Stanford University Press.

Nettl, Bruno. 1993. *Community of Music: An Ethnographic Seminar in Champaign-Urbana*. Urbana, IL: Elephant and Cat.

Novak, David. 2013. *Japanoise: Music at the Edge of Circulation*. Durham, NC: Duke University Press.

Ortner, Sherry B. 2016. "Dark Anthropology and Its Others: Theory Since the Eighties." *HAU: Journal of Ethnographic Theory* 6(1): 47–73.

Pacherie, Elisabeth. 2014. "How Does It Feel to Act Together?" *Phenomenology and the Cognitive Sciences* 13(1): 25–46.

Palmer, Parker J. 2007. *The Courage to Teach: Exploring the Inner Landscape of a Teacher's Life*. San Francisco: Jossey-Bass.

Peirce, Charles S. 1878. "How to Make Our Ideas Clear." *Popular Science Monthly* 12 (January): 286–302.

Peirce, Charles S. 1955. *Philosophical Writings of Peirce*, edited by Justus Buchler. New York: Dover.

Peirce, Charles S. 1998. *The Essential Peirce: Selected Philosophical Writings*. Vol. 2, *1893–1913*, edited by Nathan Houser and Christian Kloesel. Bloomington: Indiana University Press.

Perman, Tony. 2020. *Signs of the Spirit: Music and the Experience of Meaning in Ndau Ceremonial Life*. Urbana: University of Illinois Press.

Rahaim, Matt. 2019. "Theories of Participation." In *Theory for Ethnomusicology: Histories, Conversations, Insights*, edited by Harris M. Berger and Ruth M. Stone, 219–32. New York: Routledge.

Rivera Cusicanqui, Silvia. 2020. *Ch'ixinakax Utxiwa: On Practices and Discourses of Decolonization*. Cambridge, UK: Polity.

Robinson, Dylan. 2020. *Hungry Listening: Resonant Theory for Indigenous Studies*. Minneapolis: University of Minnesota Press.

Robinson, Dylan, Kanonhsyonne Janice C. Hill, Armand Garnet Ruffo, Selena Coutoure, and Lisa Cooke Ravensbergen. 2019. "Rethinking the Practice and Performance of Indigenous Land Acknowledgment." *Canadian Theatre Review* 177:20–30.

Rukuni, Mandiyamba. 2007. *Being Afrikan*. Johannesburg: Penguin.

Salice, Alessandro, Simon Høffding, and Shaun Gallagher. 2019. "Putting Plural Self-Awareness into Practice: The Phenomenology of Expert Musicianship." *Topoi* 38(1): 197–209.

Samuels, David. 2006. "Bible Translation and Medicine Man Talk: Missionaries, Indexicality, and the 'Language Expert' on the San Carlos Apache Reservation." *Language in Society* 35(4): 529–57.

Scarry, Elaine. 1985. *The Body in Pain: The Making and Unmaking of the World*. New York: Oxford University Press.

Schiavio, Andrea, Damiano Menin, and Jakub Matyja. 2014. "Music in the Flesh: Embodied Simulation in Musical Understanding." *Psychomusicology* 24 (4): 340–43.

Schultz, Anna. 2020. "Still an Ethnomusicologist (for Now)." *Journal of Musicology* 37(1): 39–50.

Shelemay, Kay Kaufman. 2011. "Musical Communities: Rethinking the Collective in Music." *Journal of the American Musicological Society* 64(2): 349–90.

Silverstein, Michael. 2003. "Indexical Order and the Dialectics of Sociolinguistic Life." *Language and Communication* 23(3–4): 193–229.

Simpson, Audra. 2007. "On Ethnographic Refusal: Indigeneity, 'Voice' and Colonial Citizenship." *Junctures* 9:67–80.

Slobin, Mark. 1993. *Subcultural Sounds: Micromusics of the West*. Hanover, NH: Wesleyan University Press.

Small, Christopher. 1998. *Musicking: The Meanings of Performing and Listening*. Middletown, CT: Wesleyan University Press.

Solis, Gabriel. 2012. "Thoughts on an Interdiscipline: Music Theory, Analysis, and Social Theory in Ethnomusicology." *Ethnomusicology* 56(3): 530–54.

Steingo, Gavin, and Jim Sykes. 2019. "Introduction: Remapping Sound Studies in the Global South." In *Remapping Sound Studies*, edited by Gavin Steingo and Jim Sykes, 1–36. Durham, NC: Duke University Press.

Stokes, Martin. 2007. "Ethnomusicology IV: Contemporary Theoretical Issues." In *Oxford Music Online*. Oxford: Oxford University Press.

Strathern, Marilyn. 2006. "A Community of Critics? Thoughts on New Knowledge." *Journal of the Royal Anthropological Institute* 12(1): 191–209.

Straw, Will. 1991. "Systems of Articulation, Logics of Change: Communities and Scenes in Popular Music." *Cultural Studies* 5(3): 368–88.

Sykes, Jim. 2018. *The Musical Gift: Sonic Generosity in Post-War Sri Lanka*. New York: Oxford University Press.

Tomlinson, Gary. 2015. *A Million Years of Music: The Emergence of Human Modernity*. New York: Zone Books.

Tomlinson, Gary. 2018. *Culture and the Course of Human Evolution*. Chicago: University of Chicago Press.

Tuck, Eve, and K. Wayne Yang. 2012. "Decolonization Is Not a Metaphor." *Decolonization: Indigeneity, Education, and Society* 1(1): 1–40.

Turino, Thomas. 1993. *Moving away from Silence: Music of the Peruvian Altiplano and the Experience of Urban Migration*. Chicago: University of Chicago Press.

Turino, Thomas. 2008. *Music as Social Life: The Politics of Participation*. Chicago: University of Chicago Press.

Turino, Thomas. 2009. "Four Fields of Music Making and Sustainable Living." *The World of Music* 51(1): 95–117.

Turino, Thomas. 2014. "Peircean Thought as Core Theory for a Phenomenological Ethnomusicology." *Ethnomusicology* 58(2): 185–221.

Turino, Thomas. 2015. "On Theory and Models: How to Make Our Ideas Clear." In *This Thing Called Music: Essays in Honor of Bruno Nettl*, edited by Victoria Lindsay-Levine and Philip V. Bohlman, 378–90. Lanham, MD: Rowman and Littlefield.

Turino, Thomas. 2016. "Music, Social Change, and Alternative Forms of Citizenship." In *Artistic Citizenship: Artistry, Social Responsibility, and Ethical Praxis*, edited by David J. Elliott, Marissa Silverman, and Wayne D. Bowman, 297–312. Oxford: Oxford University Press.

Turner, Victor. 1969. *The Ritual Process: Structure and Anti-Structure*. Ithaca, NY: Cornell University Press.

Turner, Victor. 1974. *Dramas, Fields, and Metaphors: Symbolic Action in Human Society*. Ithaca, NY: Cornell University Press.

Viveiros de Castro, Eduardo. 2004. "Exchanging Perspectives: The Transformation of Objects into Subjects in Amerindian Cosmologies." *Common Knowledge* 10(3): 463–84.

Walker, Charles J. 2010. "Experiencing Flow: Is Doing It Together Better than Doing It Alone?" *Journal of Positive Psychology* 5(1): 3–11.

Waterman, Christopher A. 1990. *Juju: A Social History and Ethnography of an African Popular Music*. Chicago: University of Chicago Press.

Weiner, J. 2002. "Anthropology, the Law and the Recognition Space." Prepared for the session "Articulating Culture: Understanding Engagements Between Indigenous and Nonindigenous Life-Worlds," Australian Anthropological Society conference, Canberra.

Williams, Brett. 2002. "The Concept of Community." *Reviews in Anthropology* 31(4): 339–50.

Williams, Raymond. 1976. *Keywords: A Vocabulary of Culture and Society*. New York: Oxford University Press.

Wong, Deborah. 2019. *Louder and Faster: Pain, Joy, and the Body Politic in Asian American Taiko*. Berkeley: University of California Press.

PART I

Differentiation

1 Re-membering Pontic Sociality

Musical Longing as Community Surrogation

IOANNIS TSEKOURAS

In social sciences and the humanities, community has lost its analytical objectivity. Nevertheless, or exactly because of this ontological relativization, "community" remains a key concept in a multitude of discourses. In opposing political ideologies (e.g., conservative populism, neoliberalism, grassroots environmentalism, and anarchism), applied fields, and identity narratives, community remains a central idea, often contradictorily used both for new collectivities and as a remedy for modernity's alleged social decline (Bauman 2001; Creed 2006a; Delanty 2010). Inconsistencies and contradictions between academic and public uses characterize most enduring deconstructed "black boxes" (Bateson 2000), but community emerges most persistently across fields, theories, and ideologies.[1] In many of these uses the concept is taken for granted, escaping theoretical clarification or a common definition (Creed 2006b, 1–4).[2] The result is an obfuscating omnipresence.

This obfuscating omnipresence both results in and causes associations of facticity and positiveness. Community has been somehow both factual and good. These associations emanate from a persistent early sociological designation of community as pure and organic sociality, as "natural" everyday interpersonal socialization constitutive of the collective at large (Joseph 2002; Williams 1976, 75). In short, *community* has been used broadly to "account for the social" (Shelemay 2011, 349–50), often echoing Durkheimian reifications of society (Latour 2005).

Social science has recently distanced itself from these pre-assumptions. Community is now approached as a discursive category for organic sociality (Cohen 1985), through case-sensitive analyses that avoid a priori identifications between academic and native terms and uses and that account for genealogy and localization—whether and how discourses, policies, and practices of community localize cosmopolitan dogmas embedded in the Romantic and proto-modern sociological origins of the concept (e.g., Amit 2002; Joseph 2017; Kallimopoulou and Theodosiou 2020).

Ethnomusicology often substitutes organic sociality with musicality, identifying community with the musicking group. In this chapter, echoing the most recent trends, I offer an analysis of a musical negotiation of community narratives with a focus on the concept's Romantic legacy. I argue for an analytical separation between organic sociality, community, and musicality by demonstrating how musicking can offer experiences of organic sociality that do not form communities.

My case study is the Pontic Greek performance genre called *parakathi* or *muhabeti*, a practice of music socialization that enjoys special community status but is not recognized as forming communities. I analyze the dialectics between the ideal of community and the pragmatics of parakathi music performance and how these evoke representations of organic sociality and pure socialization. Ultimately, I employ Turino's distinction between formations and cohorts as a tool for a re-understanding of the negotiations between the pragmatics of social life and visions of organic sociality.

Community: A Short Overview

The conceptual history of community can be broadly summarized as a move from "traditional to elective" (Blanchot 1988). Community, initially approached as an objective geosocial collectivity, and therefore as a unit of anthropological, geographical, sociological, and historical analysis, has been reinterpreted as a collaborative fellowship emanating from visions of solidarity and belonging. These visions entail processes of identification with pure sociality that, ironically, recirculate the initial reifications (Delanty 2010; Joseph 2002). *Community* was first defined as the rural micro-collectivity of face-to-face socialization (*Gemeinschaft*) against the re-theorization of society as the civic macro-collectivity of the bureaucratic nation-state (*Gesellschaft*) (Tönnies 2001 [1835]). It signified the carving of a "third space" of pure sociality between the natural blood ties of family and the impersonal structures of society (Shelemay 2011, 356–57). Pure sociality was further interpreted as effecting an organic relation, a constitutive causality, between socialization and the group. The latter, in line with the sedentary bias of Herderian ethnology, was thought to reside on a specific territory. Hence, community was first conceived as the triptych socialization-group-locality (Creed 2006b, 4)—the sociological equivalent of culture.

Community as triptych was further connected with the Durkheimian dichotomy of mechanic versus organic sociality and to most related binaries: rurality-urbanity, center-periphery, tradition-modernity, indigeneity-colonialism, locality-translocality, subsistence-market economies, and so on. In ethnographic disciplines, community claimed organic sociality for the micro-social against modernization, offering a Romantic idealization of pre-modern rurality and reversing, and hence validating, Durkheimian evolutionism (Creed 2006a, 24–29).

Post-1930s research on ethnicity and urbanity (e.g., the Chicago School) and the post-1960 focus on displacement and identity led to the reinterpretation of community as "elective": as a choice formed within identity politics. This reconceptualization entailed an emphasis on fellowship—groups defined by collaboration—and the realization that organic sociality can be achieved without the sharing of locality and beyond face-to-face acquaintance.

"Elective community" liberated the concept from the rigidness of the micro-local but not from facticity and positiveness. Actually, these were intensified. Elective community has been celebrated as exceptionally communal, as an exemplary good, and as paradigmatically factual. The focus on the sentiments of groupness led to a reunderstanding of community as "imagined" (Anderson 1983) and "symbolic" (Cohen 1985), inviting a contrast with community as triptych. The traditional community with all its associations became the literal criterion for a contrasting and metaphorical definition of the elective community. A group united by a strong sense of groupness is defined as community in spite of or exactly because of the lack of other components of the triptych. This way, it emerges contrary to the traditional community as exceptional and exemplar: Grouping is all that has been left, an end in itself, amounting to a purer, self-referential, and hence more organic, sociality. In short, when the only facticity of the group is its groupness, it is interpreted as more of a community than is the traditional.

In other words, community as fellowship strengthened associations of facticity and positiveness, further intensifying the obfuscating omnipresence of the term. A celebrated example of the intensification of the obfuscating omnipresence of community is the phenomenon of communitarianism that characterizes political and identity discourses. In communitarianism, community has been elevated to an empty sign that allows conflicting conflations between its triptych and elective representations. Depending on the context, community can index any or all of the following: golden eras attached to exclusionary theories of ethnocultural origins; romanticized visions of premodernity tied to escapist consumerist habits; idealized representations of pure sociality as remedies to modern and postmodern traumas; revolutionary re-envisioning of equity and egalitarianism; or normalized conceptualizations of sociality that support governmentality and exclusion of nonprivileged groups (Bauman 2001; Rose 1999).

Still, the focus on the sentiments of groupness led to a turn to the insiders' discourses and eventually to the discursive character of community. The socialization-group relation has been reinterpreted from a unilinear causality into a case of dialectics, allowing a study of how community discourses, practices, and policies converse with social and power structures. Social sciences have now moved beyond definitions of community toward an espousing study of its complications and contradictions. Community is approached as a third space of sociality—neither individualized nor institutionally controlled—where relationships of unification, differentiation, reciprocity, and indebtedness are cultivated and negotiated (see Fiol and Perman, introduction to this volume). This flexible approach to community allows a reflexive and critical analysis of whether and how these relationships entail localizations of cosmopolitan influences, influences that may hegemonically effect exclusions and governmental processes that community is thought to oppose (e.g., Amit 2020; Joseph 2017; Rose 1999; Watts 2006).

Community and Ethnomusicology

Ethnomusicological scholarship has followed these broader trends. The "traditional community" of the triptych informed the pragmatics of "music's context" in the paradigms of "music in/as culture" (Shelemay 2011, 352–55). The elective community is represented by two overlapping and broad conceptualizations: "community as musical network" and "community as communitas." Community as musical network describes the social associations cultivated via music (e.g., Monson 1996, 12–14); it draws from Small's musicking (1998) and Giddens's social as recurrently performative (1986).

I use "community as communitas" for the examination of the social-building dynamics of participation in music. Such participation realizes and embodies social synchrony through ecstatic experiences of momentary equality and inclusiveness—communitas (Turner 1974)—that effect a merging between individual agency and collective action. These processes contribute to the forging of social cohesion and unity, experiences constitutive of sentiments of groupness and thus of community. When musical communitas co-articulates identity discourse, it indexes affectively the vision of the identity's collectivity, hence the centrality of music in religious ceremonies and political gatherings (e.g., Buchanan 2014; Turino 2008). Music provides the affective community, the Durkheimian jouissance (1915), of identity (Pegg et al. 2013).

These two overlapping and complementary ethnomusicological approaches—those of network and of communitas—have led to a tacit identification of organic sociality with musicality: a musical socialization constitutive of the group. The main contribution of ethnomusicology has been a demonstration of the fluidity between the real and the imagined. Music realizes the community as communitas, and vice versa, demonstrating the power of the community's metaphoricity. The liminality of musical experiences pushes the fluidity of the metaphorical toward the indexical immediacy of the sacramental (Bateson 2000) and hence provides realization of the imagined. In short, ethnomusicology has offered deeper understandings of the counterhegemonic dynamics of musical micro-social affectivity and of music's grouping dynamics, hence the applied field of community music (e.g., Higgins 2012).

Shelemay encapsulates and extends these developments with her concept of "musical community": "a social entity, an outcome of a combination of social and musical processes, rendering those who participate in making or listening to music aware of a connection among themselves" (2011, 365). According to Shelemay, musical community is a fellowship defined by the social reflexivity achieved via musical practices. The awareness of social connection offers an inclusive criterion that can accommodate different definitions. She suggests a typology of three processes: descent, dissent, and affinity. *Descent* refers to groups that claim historical continuity and institutional validity, *dissent* to counter-groups that question the status of a descent community, and *affinity* to groupings of affect. These processes are meant as coexisting and hence as vantage points of analysis.

In all these theorizations, the identification of community with organic sociality is taken for granted, leading to a reproduction of the proto-modernist definition and to a substitution of organic sociality with organic musicality. The danger is a reversal of the definition. A musical community is indeed a group that results from a musically ignited awareness of interpersonal relationships, but can we assert the reverse, that all such awareness groupings constitute communities? In this volume, by focusing on processes of differentiation, feedback, and mutual indebtedness, we push the inquiry further into the quality of the interpersonal relationships the community members are aware of. My analysis shows that awareness of interpersonal relations forms groups. Yet recognizing these groups as communities invites the negotiation of their ontology in relation to how the "traditional community" defines the qualities of the relations. Otherwise, paraphrasing Creed, every musical grouping is a musical community. I argue for an analytical separation between organic sociality and community that elevates issues of genealogy, localization, and their unintentional effects. I also demonstrate that musical interlocutors can be aware of these distinctions and define their relationships of obligation and feedback accordingly.

The Pontic practice of participatory dialogical singing known as *parakathi* or *muhabeti* is valued as an exemplar socialization, constitutive of interpersonal relationships. Practitioners of parakathi do not, however, identify the groups that are emerging and involved as communities. On the basis of Turino's distinction between formations (groupings that emerge from world-ordering processes) and cohorts (groupings voluntarily formed as responses to the world-ordering) (2008), I demonstrate how musicking can create cohorts of community post-memory: re-memberings of the memory of the community.

Community and Pontic Identity

In Pontic identity discourse, community, in Greek, *kinotita*,[3] is mediated through a nostalgia for a pre-modern rural past. Pontic nostalgia relates to two collective traumas: the 1920s Pontic exodus and the post-1950s urbanization of Greece. Pontians are the descendants of Greek refugees from the region of Pontos in the Turkish Black Sea. The Black Sea Greeks left their region and headed mainly for Greece between 1916 and 1923 to escape the "Christian genocide" (Hoffman et al. 2012; International Association of Genocide Scholars 2007)—the systematic annihilation of the Ottoman Armenians, Assyrians, and Greeks by Turkish nationalists. In Greece, they joined a larger Greek refugee population from Anatolia (Asia Minor). The 1923 Greco-Turkish population exchange agreement solidified the genocidal ethnic homogenization of both countries and verified the permanent loss of Asia Minor, Pontos included, for the Greeks (Hirschon 2006).

In Greece, most Pontians were issued a rural settlement in the regions of Macedonia and Thrace (Kontogiorgi 2006). The first years of settlement were dominated by the recollection of Pontos. The villages were places of Pontos nostalgia—a desire for an impossible return (Boym 2001) to the lost homeland. A systematic Pontic community narrative emerges in the context of post-1950s urbanization along with narratives of Pontic tradition and the development of a discourse of Pontic identity. Urbanization was part of a modernization process that entailed the mechanization of agricultural production, industrialization, and social mobility (Clogg 2000). By 1980 Greece had become more than 69 percent urban, with the countryside losing its (limited) self-sustainability. Urban migration was forced by poverty, unemployment, and political violence amounting to a "modern trauma" (Whitehead 2007) of social alienation and cultural shock. Rural nostalgia emerged as a remedy (Demertzis 2005).

In the Pontic case, rural and refugee nostalgias were combined in folkloric ideations, especially the *grande idée* of tradition. Pontic identity, a consciousness of belonging to the named collectivity of "the Pontians," was solidified in Greece as a realization of cultural difference from other Greek groups. On arrival in the new homeland, the Pontic refugees faced hostility from the locals and realized that, regardless of their common Greek identity, they were separated by visible differences of language, kinship organization, and music. Cultural difference does not define a non-Greek historical descent and thus a Pontic ethnicity. It is understood as historical and regional differentiation of a common ethnically Greek civilization. Pontic identity constitutes a case of "ethno-regionalism" (Vergeti 2000).

In this ideological scheme, Pontic cultural heritage ensured the social inclusion of Pontians as ethnic Greeks (Kailaris 2002), while it provided a re-membering of Pontic cultural particularity and of the memory of Pontos. Pontic folklore preserved this strategically essentialized cultural particularity as Greek tradition, further endowing refugee nostalgia with the anti-urban ideations of rural *kinotita* as the traditional community of the triptych.

After 1950 these ideations acquired extra momentum. Urbanization led to the idealization of rurality and provided institutions that elevated folkloric music practices into processes of Pontic sociality. These institutions are the Pontic cultural associations that evolved from refugee brotherhoods into rural immigrant clubs and folkloric centers. Ethno-regional folklorization entailed a "musicalization" of Pontic sociality via the systematic practice of folk dances. Folk dance enabled an urban reconstitution of the Pontic village, in its greatest inclusiveness, as the dancing social body of the rural festival. The inclusiveness of the dance practice verified urban nostalgia for the "traditional community." Folk dance connected urban Pontic sociality with the folkloric salvage agenda and ethnoregionalism. Finally, it promoted Pontic cultural difference by means of a medium familiar to the broader Greek society. By nurturing rural nostalgia, Pontic folklore verified the modernist dichotomy between tradition and progress, solidifying urbanization as an inevitable change and facilitating the Pontians' integration into the social whole. At the same time, it compartmentalized Pontic sociality in the cultural associations and their operations.

Since the 1980s, Pontic identity discourse has changed. Young Pontians, without direct experience of the traumas of exile and urbanization, cultivate a Pontic postmemory (Hirsch 2012). Narratives of loss have been re-appreciated as testimonies of Pontic cultural particularity beyond the folkloric salvage agenda. The focus has shifted from the salvation of cultural heritage to the rediscovery of the testimonial and affective remembering of the refugees' culture. In Pontic postmemory, the refugee settlements of Greek Macedonia are remembered as centers of Pontic structures of feeling, survivals of the affective recollection of Pontos. Hence, "Pontic community" is redefined as the sociocultural unit of refugee memory, and longing for the rural emerges as nesting nostalgias: a nostalgia for the life defined by the nostalgia for Pontos. Postmemory and nesting nostalgia validate the Romantic proto-modernist community by historicizing it as the era of the refugees. Pontic community thus becomes a model of affective sociality defined by nostalgia for the inevitable loss of Pontos. The cultivators of postmemory seek affective experiences of this traditional community away from the folkloric stage. Parakathi, or muhabeti, constitutes such a case.

Parakathi, or Muhabeti

Parakathi and *muhabeti* refer to an "around the table" gathering for social drinking and dialogic participatory singing. Thus, parakathi falls within a general category of socialization practices in the former Ottoman world that are characterized by ecstatically affective musicality, emotional intersubjective communication, comradeship, and homosociality. As testified by the Arabic term *muhabeti* (*muabbet*), used all over the former Ottoman lands for dialogical singing practices, *poetics* might allude to the syncretic aural cosmologies of Ottoman devotional Islam (Gill 2018; Markoff 2002).

In parakathi, music consists in an exchange of distichs (couplets) in rhymed fifteen-syllable iambs, sung to repeated tunes provided by a Pontic *lyra*, the Black Sea fiddle, also known as the *kemence*. Every distich entails two repeated verses. The first is complete grammatically but not semantically, thus introducing an expectation of meaning completion, which, intensified by the repetition, is satisfied by the second verse. The poetry can be improvised, but it usually comes from a known repertoire. There is no absolute correspondence between distich and tune. The singers choose the distich according to their desire, following conventions of style, repertoire, and dialogic flow. Parakathi music and poetry form the repertoire and style of the *epitrapezia* ("table songs").

The tunes, following a Pontic, and generally Greek, morphology (Baud-Bovy 1984; Kilpatrick 1980), are isomorphic to the distichs. The musical meter, usually in five (2+3), follows the iamb. A typical tune is eight meters long divided into two repeated phrases of four measures per verse. The tonic is reached at the end of the form, building tonal expectation supportive of meaning completion. The lyra textures of parallel polyphony or melody with movable drone support word painting. Parakathi communitas is described in relation to dialogic participation and empathic communication.

Dialogic Participation

The success of a parakathi depends on the inclusiveness of the singing dialogue: Everybody should sing. Hence, music performance is participatory, with music process being an end in itself (Turino 2009). The participatory ethos is encapsulated in the principle of "presence" (*parousia*), which, similar to the Aegean *ghlendi* (Kavouras 2005), means the presentation of one's self to the group through active engagement in the poetic dialogue by initiating distichs and contributing to the poetic flow. The exchange of couplets should form a poetic dialogue, with every new distich responding to the one just sung and leading to the emergence of fluid and semantically multidimensional poetic topics. An unrelated distich negates the dialogue, showing "lack of listening," a disrespectful behavior.

Participation etiquette also guides the role of the lyra. The demonstration of virtuosity is rejected as antisocial behavior, detrimental to participation. Loud, fast, and lengthy executions of complicated or unfamiliar tunes divert from the poetry, disturb the dialogic flow, and discourage participation. The lyra supports the singing and builds sonic constancy by neutralizing any tuning and rhythmic imperfections that could disturb continuity; it adjusts, thus, the tune to every participant's delivery. The reciprocity between lyra and voices leads to a dialectical emergence of a common rhythm. The lyra player guides without directing. Although (s)he controls the pace of the singing dialogue, (s)he leads the participants into believing that they are in charge.[4] All these factors result in a regular but non-canonic rhythm carrying a strong sense of (usually 5/4) anti-metronomic pulsation. The lack of metronomic regularity renders the rhythm fluid, but with an accentuated iambic meter. This contrast often creates rhythmic liminality.

Sonic constancy is also achieved via morphological fluidity. This is possible because of the manipulation of the relation between tunes and *kladhia*. *Kladhia* ("branches") refers to riffs: rhythmo-modal variations, summations, or condensations of tunes. The lyra player uses them as improvisational building blocks to prolong a tune, vary the melodic repetition, emphasize modality and rhythm, fill the pauses between the participations, and bridge sections (Marmaridis 2014).

In summary, dialogic interaction can be traced on three levels: semantically, between the distichs, synchronically-rhythmically, between lyra and singing; and diachronically-morphologically between tunes, kladhia, and singers. While the semantic dialogue is the essence of the poetic flow, the rhythmic and morphological dialogues build the malleable sonic constancy necessary for participatory continuity. Rhythmic and melodic fluidity define the style of the epitrapezia; they are both requirements and outcomes of the dialogic performance. They constitute participatory discrepancies that invite, inspire, and provoke the music process from which they emerge (Keil 1995).

The Poetics of Empathy

In optimal parakathi, poetic utterances express emotions by connecting singing and personal experience. Since most distichs come from a common repertoire, this connection is allegorical. Allegory is premised on the metaphoricity of the poetry, which captures a loosely defined poetic topic. For example:

> God, do not rain any more on the rocks,
> my tears suffice to water the grass.

The poetic image declares sadness. Metaphoricity consists in the hyperbole of the "rain of tears," which renders the poetic image representative of the topic of sadness.

Allegory means iconicity between the topic and the personal experiences of the participant. Every distich is a condensed personal parable. Singing a verse declares, "I feel like this poetic image." Hence, singing is interpreted as intersubjective communication of ineffable feelings. Afroditi Zamanidou explained: "When I sing [a distich], the only thing I have to do is to turn and look at a friend. I do not need to explain anything. . . . He knows" (interview, October 10, 2012). Pain, bodily and psychological, is designated the most important topic in parakathi, the most personal and thus most humanizing emotion. Therefore, singing is a dialogue of empathy. Every valid response is an empathic mirroring of pain (Ahmed 2004).

Parakathi as Community Commemoration

Dialogic participation and empathic communication define the optimal parakathi as exceptional socialization. The equality and inclusiveness of dialogical musico-poetic, "sequential" (Turino 2008) participation, supported by the undertaking of the leading role in singing—an agency celebratory of individuality—lead to communitas and thus to a merging of the individual and the collective. Communitas is further supported by the empathic dialogue. The allegorical expression of pain reveals a deeper, generically human self beyond social differences. In parakathi, multi-sensory representations of the self, subjectivities, are performed as sonic, kinesthetic, and symbolic expressions of a deeper self.

All these render the optimal parakathi a performance of organic sociality and accordingly of musical community. The intimate relationships necessary for the allegorical dialogue are forged through emotional intersubjective communication. The participants cultivate further personal relationships and the obligations of mutual understanding that result from dialogic confession. In this sense, parakathi makes the participants deeply aware of the connections between them.

This interpretation of musical community is further supported by the linguocultural specificity of the practice and the immediate feedback of dialogue. The Pontic framing of the empathic and emotional processes invites a designation of the performing group as the "affinity" or "affective" community of Pontic identity. Tunes and poetry emerging as devices and sedimentations (Gill 2017) of Pontic emotionality invite an interpretation of the parakathying tablemates as forming a grouping of differentiation. The element of feedback is not merely present as musical response but is the very essence of the dialogical flow. Every utterance is feedback to the utterance just performed.

A network definition of musical community is also applicable, supporting further the criterion of differentiation. In the allo-Pontic environment of the cities, parakathia (pl.) are among the few occasions dominated by the Pontic Greek dialect, while the poetry references landscapes and ways of life in Pontos. Participation necessitates knowledge of Pontic culture, language, and history, defining subgroups of connoisseurs. Hence, parakathi practices carve spaces and networks of Pontianness that can be interpreted both as dissent and descent communities. Dissent, because parakathia offer experiences of Pontianness versus the Greek majority and the mainstream Pontic folkloric practices; descent, because they mediate the Pontic tradition more truthfully than folkloric dance, validating Pontic ethno-regionalism and Greek nationalism.

All these interpretations of community are nullified by the fact that parakathi practitioners do not share them. Whenever I suggested a community-based interpretation, I faced either rebuttal or confusion. Although parakathi is not interpreted as forming communities, it is nevertheless valued as realizing the spirit of the pre-modern Pontic community. Paradoxically, parakathi realizes a community spirit but not the community itself.

This seeming paradox is resolved if we take into account the commemorative character of Pontic postmemory. Accordingly, parakathi makes present the absence of the pre-1950s Pontic community. The social reality that it references is understood as lost. This remark raises a series of questions. How does parakathi commemorate the lost community? How do Pontians understand contemporary gatherings? And what do all these mean for contemporary parakathi sociality? These questions lead to an examination of the particular ways in which parakathi practice evokes narratives of community commemoration.

The Lost Emergent Music Performance and the Longing for Holistic Sociality

Representations of the "Pontic community" are foregrounded in normative narratives. Usually these entail a folkloric representation of the Pontic village as the community of the triptych. Consider the following account by Dimitris Sotiriadis:

> Basic rule: The lyra should come out by itself! I experienced what I am telling you as a kid, at my grandpa's house. . . . There was no electricity, only an oil lantern. There were only men in the main room: the two neighbors, my grandpa, his older sons. The women and the children were in the other room. Now, look what happened: The children were playing, the women started talking: "I cooked this food today; tomorrow I have to milk the cow," and the men started doing the same regarding their own: "Today the sowing went well; we have to buy fertilizers. . . . Everyday things. Trivial issues. . . . And eventually, as if by itself, the lyra came out! You understand me? It was not a pre-required thing, the lyra. . . . So, when we say, "We are parakathying," . . . this does not mean that we sit around, we order some wine, and as we are there, we start singing! And I am totally adamant on this! There are cases when the lyra is not necessary. . . . Emotion did not prevail. (interview, May 29, 2012)

Sotiriadis offered a testimony of the pre-modern community. This, the authentic setting of parakathi, is described via folkloric representations—technological poverty, homosociality, family and neighborhood socialization—that emphasize locality and face-to-face sociality as defining the group. The community as triptych is dominant.

Sotiriadis referenced the loss of the traditional community indirectly, by commenting on the lost spontaneity of the emergence of music—what should be a "basic rule" of parakathi. In the pre-urbanized rural muhabeti, music (singing) emerged from unscheduled casual socialization and everyday reflections ("everyday things, trivial issues"), as spontaneous emotional expression. This emergent quality is declared with the common phrase "the lyra would appear by itself" (the rhetorical attribution of agency to the lyra makes the instrument a synecdoche of music). The lyra "appears by itself" in the sense that music should not be premeditated or scheduled; it should just happen. Emergence of music is contrasted to the contemporary musically framed practice, where people gather in order to make music (when people "order some wine . . . and start singing"). Emergent performance means a fluid connection between singing and social context that exemplifies parakathi as part of a way of life, not an exclusively musical event bounded in time and framed outside of the everyday but an occasional and casual social gathering. This fluidity defines music as spontaneous, not premeditated by a clear-cut change of frame from the verbal to the musico-poetic. The emergence of the singing should evolve from cues of emotional socialization and reflection. Hence, singing should acquire its exceptionality thanks to the preceding prosaic communication, emerging from the everyday. The positioning of these characteristics in the past suggests that their contemporary absence results from the loss of the community. The pre-modern village, represented as the community of the triptych, is commemorated through the contemporary absence of the emergent music performance.

Elder practitioners, experienced in rural life, verify Sotiriadis's descriptions. The lyra player Christos Tsenekidis remembered:

> As soon as it [parakathi] started it was unspecified how and when it would end. . . . For example, January 7, John the Baptist's day [name day of all people named Ioannis or Yannis]. . . . The lyra player with his friends would go with the lyra . . . to every Yannis's [house] in the village, singing and playing on the way as well. At one point, after midnight, they would be done with all the village's Yannises, but somebody would suggest, "Let's do it all again! Let's start all over!" And they would start from the very first Yannis. You see? When we were doing muhabeti we did not care about today, tomorrow, weekday, or weekend. (interview, May 2, 2012)

Here, muhabeti is described as an open-ended performance of excess: as spontaneous and undeterminable, framed by the socio-residential context of the village. The fluidity between music and the prosaic suggests temporal and social unity, realized through the mobility of the door-to-door muhabeti. The village again figures as the triptych.

In the same spirit, the singer and poet Lefteris Kokkinidis (Kokkinas) narrated:

> There would be one or two groups having muhabetia. At some point somebody might say, "You know what? I am fetching my wife, you should bring yours too," so their wives would come and they would start dancing. Village dances often started this way. (interview, October 26, 2012)

Here, there is a continuity between the gathering of the parakathi and the village as a whole.

In sum, the muhabetia (pl.) in the pre-modern villages achieved communitas because they were part of the wholeness of the pre-modern rurality: a sharing of temporality, place, and social space, characterized by the organic, group-defining sociality of intimate everyday relations. Pre-modern parakathi cultivated and forged these relationships by means of the excessive and affective experiences of a dialogical communitas. Parakathi was thus a socializing practice of organic importance for the triptych community.

Contemporary parakathi cannot have this organic role because there is no socio-temporal unity anymore. Instead, it commemorates community by revealing the absence of the socio-temporal unity as lack of musical emergence. Today, most parakathia are scheduled, albeit casually. Music is a definitional element, what makes them deserving of an allocation of time. Practitioners meet *in order* to have a muhabeti with the expectation of music, choosing it instead of other activities. Even when unscheduled, muhabetia usually appear in the context of other pre-arranged Pontic events such as dance festivals and nightclub performances. According to the Pontic lyra player and intellectual Dimitris Piperidis:

> We meet five [musicians] in a dance event and afterwards we say, "Why don't we play some music for each other, here, around the table, as we are sitting? Let's have a bottle of whisky." Is this really a muhabeti? I am not at all sure. (interview, March 12, 2012)

Piperidis described a reversal of Kokkinidis's reality: The parakathi, the private, emerges from the public. Its context is the scheduled dance event of the broader Pontic group, in accordance with the compartmentalization of Pontic sociality. Contemporary parakathi is not part of an everyday reality and a shared way of life. Similar to other practices of modernist leisure, it offers an exception, and thus escape, from the everyday. The nostalgic imagining of the community of the past is part of this escape. In other words, parakathi *o*ffers a heterotopia. Piperidis continued: "I believe that authentic muhabetia do not happen any more. They are just musical gatherings that imitate—mere efforts to perform what real muhabetia used to do" (ibid.). One leisure choice among many, parakathi *c*annot have the exceptional emotionality it used to. Piperidis went on:

> The muhabeti practitioner [of the past], for example, my grandpa, did not have any other way. . . . I watch TV, listen to radio, play CDs, and I might go to *bouzouki* nightclubs. Let's say that the next day I am having a muhabeti, can it really be the same for me as it was for my grandpa? How can I put the same soul in this process? (ibid.)

Younger practitioners attempt to counter these losses by emulating the so-socialization habits of the past. The singer and lyra player Polys Efraimidis told me:

> Our muhabeti is the way the elders conceive it. We do not say, "Let's bring a lyra, let's organize it, and put it also on Facebook." We have their mentality: "What are you doing this afternoon? Let's go have a coffee," and after the coffee, "How about a spirit?" and then things might get on their way. . . . I now feel it myself. If I drink a couple of glasses the first thing that comes to my mind is to take out my lyra and start singing. It is a way of life for me! It is the only entertainment for us. We do not do anything else. We do not even go to bars anymore. (interview, August 22, 2012)

Efraimidis claims the organic sociality of the pre-modern parakathi by turning it into the single choice for socialization, by a conscious elimination of other options. He verifies Piperidis's "imitation" interpretation. Efraimidis's practice emerges as meta-socialization defining a postmodern parakathi (a post-parakathi?). As with other cases of contemporary dialogical singing (Kavouras 2005; Sant Cassia 2000), parakathi performance comments on the frames and contexts of its performativity.

In conclusion, contemporary parakathi commemorates the pre-modern village by emphasizing its absence. This absence becomes present by means of a contrast between contemporary practice and elicited memories of past musical emergence and its temporal fluidity and socio-spatial unity—realities of a holistically communal life, before the privatization of the household and the division of time into quantifiably objectified units devoted to bounded activities (Giddens 1991). Memories of unity verify the community as triptych of the proto-modern European folkloric Romanticism, inviting a representation of the past parakathi as exceptional and as an excessive forging of existing organic relationships. Ecstatic musicality, remembered as organic sociality, indexes pre-modern wholeness. Yet not all memories elicited by parakathi verify communitarian socio-spatial and temporal unity. In reflections beyond normative narratives, the representations change.

Memories of Social Division, Performances of Unity

In memory narratives unfiltered by normative concepts ("community," "tradition," "parakathi"), representations of the unified socio-temporal space collapse. Parakathi emerges as characterized by patriarchy and affective music labor, revealing a divided social reality.

The most common setting for parakathi, the coffee house, involved only men. Women were excluded from these public spaces in ways typical of pre-modern Mediterranean patriarchy (Magrini 2003). In domestic parakathia women would sing, but under male control. According to the Pontic activist and intellectual Eleni Mentesidou,

> There were always some women who could sing and the men would expect them to do so and give them space. This was the case especially with women of an older age. A woman who could sing would find place in the muhabeti. (interview, March 9, 2012)

Participation in music was encouraged for women beyond reproductive age who enjoyed special symbolic capital and who could not be misunderstood as demonstrating sexuality.

Moreover, the men gave room and attention to women who knew how to sing. This music agency entailed particular repertoire. Women were expected to sing musical laments (*miroloya*) or "long tunes" (*makryn kayte*), unmetered tunes of large range that require special vocal skills and improvisatory abilities. The stylistic iconicity of these genres to actual dirges (regarding expressiveness and melodic patterns) placed them securely within the women's domain (Auerbach 1989; Seremetakis 1991). In other words, women were largely excluded from the singing dialogue. Their musicianship was treated with respect, but under conditions of age, gender, and music competence.

Women had their own muhabetia with singing and alcohol without men present. Such gatherings are testified by a rich repertoire of women's distichs and the fame of women versifiers and singers. The most celebrated case is the gatherings of the "pasture mothers." Until the late 1990s, on Pontic mountain areas of Greek Macedonia, elder women known as "pasture mothers" would move livestock to pasture lands for long periods to direct animal husbandry and dairy production. There, in an all-female environment, women's parakathia were regular occurrences, remembered today with intense nostalgia. The pasture mothers developed high musical competence that enabled them to defy gender norms by participating actively in public musical events. As Parthena Mentesidou and Symela Kousalidou recalled it:

PARTHENA MENTESIDOU: Wherever there was a wedding or a party I went. I
    drank and I sang! What a joy!

SYMELA KOUSALIDOU: I never have second thoughts about my singing! They
   used to make fun of us, "Ha! She went to a wedding and she sang!" I never paid
   attention. I did not care.
IOANNIS TSEKOURAS: Who was making fun of you?
SYMELA KOUSALIDOU: The other women who could not do the same. They were
   jealous. (interview, October 28, 2012)

Eventually, thanks to the folkloric elevation of music into a cultural value, the
pasture mothers gained a reputation as living folk treasures, attracting the admiration of professional musicians.

Overall, we can discern two separate gendered *parakathia* practices. Regardless of this duality, the society as a whole was hegemonically patriarchic,
as verified by some women's rejection of the pasture mothers' public musical
agency. These memories describe the unified social space of the fluid parakathi
as a male privilege. Memories of gender inequality trouble the representation
of the community triptych. There is no single organic sociality corresponding
to a single groupness. Homosocial socialization reveals a divided social reality.

Memories of gender inequality do not bring into question the parakathi poetics of empathic dialogue. Hence, parakathi communitas appears to have existed
in a gender-segregated fashion. Memories of music professionalism before 1950
draw a different picture. In pre-modern Greece music professionalism was assessed as affective labor, "work intended to produce or modify people's emotional experiences" (Hofman 2015, 4). The sensorial and emotional experiences
of music were often understood as neighboring seduction and so downgrading,
even stigmatizing, the musician.[5]

Pontic lyra players were divided into two broad categories: amateurs, usually
young male bachelors, who were playing for themselves and their friends, and
semiprofessionals who delved in coffee houses and taverns, performing for tips.
Amateur musical agency contributed to a high level of social capital praised
as performance of empathy and affective comradeship. (Semi-)professionals,
in contrast, were judged as low-income servicers who evoked emotionality for
material gain.

In other words, there could be a distinction between the lyra player as affective laborer and the parakathi practitioners as clientele. The musician, a servant,
performed for meager monetary gain; the participants, the patrons, performed
for emotional communication. This division often involved insulting behavior
toward the musician. Christos Tsenekidis remembered:

They even swore at me: . . ."Play! F*** your Virgin Mary!"[6] What would you do in
my place? . . . We suffered for our survival! Nowadays, nobody would dare tell you
such a thing, but back then . . . the lyra player was a lackey. . . . And we are talking
about the traditional muhabeti. . . . It took time for a refinement to happen. It was
after the elevation of the lyra that they started behaving. (interview, May 2, 2012)

Tsenekidis clearly speaks about refinement and the "elevation of the lyra" as processes tied to the folkloric recognition of Pontic music as art, defining cultural particularity. In relation to parakathi poetics, here we have a negation of the presence (*parousia*) principle as equality of participation and consequently of communitas for everybody in the parakathying group. The semiprofessional lyra player, regardless of their instrumental role, was excluded.

These parakathi-ignited memories do not verify solidarity and unity as inherent to a Pontic community. They reveal a social world characterized by divisions and hierarchies. Parakathi provided experiences of organic sociality, in the sense that the interpersonal relationships forged were constitutive of broader groups, but these groups did not unite into a single social body. In other words, the communitas of the parakathi was not representative of the social body as a whole, and the triptych's organic causality between sociality and group is problematized.

Contemporary parakathi contrasts with the memories of pre-modern rural practice. Today's groupings, both communitas and network, lie closer to the Romantic idealizations of community. The folkloric elevation of music into a cultural value has redefined lyra players' affective labor as art. Also, musicians do not receive money in parakathi, since music professionalism has moved to the spaces of dance events and nightclubs.[7] Hence, the musicians are venerated as leaders of the gathering, precisely because of their affective agency. In addition, the gradual erosion of gender segregation, rejection of explicit patriarchy, and the celebration of parakathi as Pontic traditional culture have reduced gender inequality. Homosocial parakathia are still frequent, with male gatherings often becoming racy. But mixed-gender gatherings are as frequent, with women treated more or less equally through participation in dialogical singing.

In many instances, contemporary gatherings offer exemplary experiences of communitas with spectacular performative eradications of social divisions and differences: Elders and youth engage in ecstatic parakathi dialogue, and young girls are idolized for their versifying and singing abilities. Similar inclusiveness emerges on the level of the network. Internet use has forged translocal parakathi networks that spread anywhere in the Pontic diaspora from the West Coast of the United States and Canada eastward all the way to Australia, with Greek Macedonia at the center. Contemporary parakathi network and performance groups still are not recognized as communities, however.

Conclusions: The Avowable Noncommunity

The parakathi *dialectics of the* Pontic community can be summarized in two contradictions. The first is that parakathi's celebrated dynamic of social bonding is premised on a de-identification with community. Parakathi affective, intersubjective, and ecstatic socialization stems from performing an absence of community. The second contradiction concerns the representations of Pontic community in parakathi memory. While normative narratives allude to proto-modern Romantic idealizations, narratives based on personal memory do not verify the sociality-single group causality of the community triptych.

These contradictions support a concept of community as an interpretation of governmentality. Accordingly, parakathi aficionados are willingly seduced by the Pontic folkloric idealization of the traditional community. Hegemonically allied with the *grand idée* of the Pontic tradition and with nostalgia for the Greek community, *parakathi* Pontians are seduced by the ecstatic affectivity of the musical experience into accepting the ideal of the traditional community, regardless of the memories of inequality and the current experiences of solidarity. By historicizing this ideal as the period of refugee settlement in Greece, they further extrapolate it into the past "as a foreign country"(Lowenthal 1985), negating the possibility of a Pontic community in the present and thus identifying with modernity against their Pontianness. The latter belongs to the past in rituals of commemoration that define Pontic heritage as an unattainable ideal, always and already conditioned by nostalgia—the impossibility of return.

In short, parakathi practices validate the idea that Pontic community is an impossibility, contributing to a modernist Greek governmentality. A psychologizing interpretation mitigates the accusation of governmentality by explicating the folklorically received traditional community as a remedy to the collective traumas of the genocide, the displacement, and post-1950 urbanization. Accordingly, parakathi is a practice of Pontic *jouissance*, ethnic escapism.

The contradictions are dispelled if we analytically separate musical communitas, pure sociality, organic sociality, and community. Parakathi calls into question both dominant significations of community—the traditional triptych and the fellowship—by juxtaposing contemporary celebrations of a chosen cultural heritage with the remembering of ecstatic performances of an unavoidable and flawed past sociality. The musical socialization of traditional parakathi is recognized as organic musicality, as music socialization constitutive of Pontic community, but it does not align with the idealization of a pure sociality, a natural, factual, and inherently good socialization. Face-to-face socialization does not lead to the forming of a single group. The triptych is nullified.

At the same time, the idealization of community as fellowship is also discredited. Contemporary parakathi realizes a purer sociality, but the relationships of solidarity and equality that define this sociality as purer are not organic; they are not constitutive of a community. In relation to the framework of community adopted in this volume, contemporary practices are characterized by both differentiation and feedback, but relationships of obligatory reciprocity are not always in evidence outside of musical performance. Contemporary parakathi groups are "inorganic;" they are self-referential gatherings without palpable connections to shared everyday life. The solidarity of fellowship is possible because of this de-materialization since there is less to share (and to divide), and so musicality can be obligation-free. The extrapolation of Pontianness to a transcendental sphere of tradition makes social solidarity and unity easier but does so in terms that, ironically, recall the idealized self-fashioning of Western society in classical concerts (Small 1998). In short, parakathi Pontians reject the inevitability of organic musicality; they do not designate every ecstatic grouping and musical network as community, and as a result they are also dismissive of the idea of elective community as a metaphor for traditional community.

All this leads to another conclusion. Parakathi nostalgia is not about the flawed social reality of the traditional community but, rather, about the excesses of this reality. Traditional parakathi is a model of Pontic sociality and of structures of feeling because it occasionally exceeded, in close relation to who was participating and how, the hierarchies and oppressions of the rural past. In Peircean terms, it was an instance of Secondness momentarily achieved against the First of the formation of pre-modern community, with benefits for the tablemates: relationships of cordiality and solidarity that extended beyond the performance occasion against the conflicts of pre-modernity. This excess, in agreement with the concept of communitas, was inextricably related to the conditions it had to exceed. The exceptionality of the everyday was related to the hardships of the unavoidable community of the pre-modern era. Parakathi practitioners address all these matters through a discourse of pained musicality, echoing broader Greek doxas. This is why, for the first generations, parakathi *was* "the only way." It was the limited opportunities, the lack of choices, resulting from the traditional community as a formation and a condition of Firstness that made parakathi so important. Many Pontians refer to the dialectics of suffering with stereotypical Greek phrases: "They [elders] have suffered, but for this reason they had stronger social bonds"; "they had suffered, so they could empathize; they could feel." Suffering is often described as necessary for musicality: "You would assume that today, being accepted and better off, we would be more active about our culture and music, but on the contrary, we make less music" (field notes, March 2012). In short, parakathi is remembered as community excess.

Following Roach (1996), contemporary parakathi practice can be described as an effigy of the excessive emotional wholeness and the framing dialectics of suffering of the pre-modern parakathi. Contemporary parakathi "fills by means of surrogation vacancy" (36); it carves a space for memory by acknowledging and framing the absence of what has to be remembered, both the flawed traditional community and its musically performative excess. Through this process of surrogation, community, both as traditional and elective, is deconstructed and parakathi emerges as the fellowship of Pontians without community. There is no revival of community but rather a revival of the feelings of excess of community.

In this sense, and in total agreement with postmemory (Hirsch 2012), the denial of the status of community to contemporary practices is the very condition of the surrogation's affective dynamic.

The modernist governmental interpretation still has merit. The historicized Pontic understanding of community is the result of the entrenchment of Pontic identity discourse in the idea of tradition and ethno-regionalism. Yet the psychologizing interpretation of parakathi as seductive, one that effects a false consciousness, does not hold truth. Contemporary Pontians take a critical stance toward their past, affectively attaching themselves to certain elements, while rejecting others.

I conclude with two theoretical points. First, resonating with the twenty-first-century critique, social science should avoid identifying community with organic and pure sociality. A heuristic application of the concept of musical community can be more obfuscatory than illuminating. Parakathi involves various socialities. The excessively ecstatic musical socialization of the traditional parakathi, the broader divided and hierarchical sociality of the pre-modern rural settlements, and the affective musical sociality of the contemporary optimal parakathi as effigy involve different understandings of interpersonal relations, different combinations of differentiation, feedback, and indebtedness. Designating them all as communities would be rather detrimental to understanding them.

Second, visions of community suggest also visions of identity and musical processes that provide significant insights into their emotional negotiations. Turino's distinction between formation and cohort can be particularly useful here (2008). Turino understands a formation as a collectivity formed by unavoidable factors of power relations, regardless of whether these factors are consciously addressed or doxically accepted. *Cohort*, on the other hand, refers to groupings of voluntary and elective identification. Pure sociality, which informs both traditional and elective community, suggests the emergence of community in between Turino's categories. Elective communities are cohorts that allude, directly or indirectly, to the vision of a community as ideal formation: a "natural" social reality of pure, organic, and unmediated sociality. The members of the parakathi cohort are deeply aware of the "cohortness" of their collectivity and of the excessive, partial, affective sociality of the formation they long for. In this sense, parakathia define cohorts of formation-nostalgia, to paraphrase Blanchot (1988), the avowable Pontic noncommunity.

Notes

Some of the key ideas presented in this chapter were first worked out in the context of the Greek publication *Music Communities in 21st Century Greece* (Μουσικές κοινότητες στην Ελλάδα του 21ου αιώνα). I express my gratitude to the editors of that volume, Eleni Kallimopoulou and Aspasia (Sissy) Theodosiou, for their insightful remarks, which have influenced how I understand the relation between community and parakathi. Also, this chapter would not have been realized without the hard work, insightful remarks, and inspiring and forming dialogue provided by the volume's editors, Stefan Fiol and Tony Perman. I am deeply indebted to them.

1. A keywords search in the University of Illinois online database with the term *community* in the title for 2018 only gave 189,874 results. The results for *nation*, *tradition*, and *ethnicity* were 15,652, 8,302, and 3,574 entries respectively.

2. A 1955 listing recorded more than ninety definitions (Creed 2006b, 7).

3. The word presents the same etymological logic as the English *community*. "*Kino* [*koino*] means "common.""

4. The lyra player has typically been a cisgendered heterosexual man, but this is changing fast. In the past few years I have noticed more and more women playing the lyra, and I have been told that their performance agency also involves parakathia.

5. This stigmatization relates to the deeply ingrained religious Manichaeism of spirit versus flesh; see Becker 2004.

6. Personalized blasphemy is among the most aggressive Greek insults.

7. There is indirect material gain. Musicians establish ties and reputations that translate into more gigs.

Bibliography

Ahmed, Sara. 2004. *The Cultural Politics of Emotion*. New York: Routledge.

Amit, Vered, ed. 2002. *Realizing Community: Concepts, Social Relationships and Sentiments*. London: Routledge.

Amit, Vered. 2020. "Rethinking Anthropological Perspectives on Community: Watchful Indifference and Joint Commitment." In *Rethinking Community Through Interdisciplinary Research*, edited by B. Jansen, 49–68. London: Palgrave.

Anderson, Benedict. 1983. *Imagined Communities: Reflections on the Origin and Spread of Nationalism*. London: Verso.

Auerbach, Susan. 1989. "From Singing to Lamenting: Women's Musical Role in a Greek Village." In *Women and Music in Cross-Cultural Perspective*, edited by Ellen Koskoff, 25–43. Chicago: University of Illinois Press.

Bateson, Gregory. 2000. *Steps to an Ecology of Mind.* Chicago: University of Chicago Press. First published in 1972.

Baud-Bovy, Samuel. 1994. *Δοκίμιο για το Ελληνικό Δημοτικό Τραγούδι.* Ναύπλιο: Πελοποννησιακό Λαογραφικό Ίδρυμα. First published in 1984.

Bauman, Zygmund. 2001. *Community: Seeking Safety in an Insecure World.* Cambridge, UK: Polity.

Becker, Judith. 2004. *Deep Listeners: Music, Emotion, and Trancing.* Bloomington: Indiana University Press.

Blanchot, Maurice. 1988. *The Unavowable Community.* New York: Station Hill.

Boym, Sveltana. 2001. *The Future of Nostalgia.* New York: Basic Books.

Buchanan, Donna A. 2014. "Introduction: Doing Ethnomusicology 'Texas-Style': A Musical (Re)Turn to Performance." In *Soundscapes from the Americas: Ethnomusicological Essays on the Power, Poetics, and Ontology of Performance*, edited by Donna A. Buchanan, 1–25. London: Ashgate.

Clogg, Richard. 2000. *A Concise History of Greece.* Cambridge: Cambridge University Press.

Cohen, Anthony P. 1985. *The Symbolic Construction of Community.* Chichester, UK: Ellis Horwood; London: Tavistock.

Creed, Gerald W. 2006a. "Community as Modern Pastoral." In *The Seduction of Community: Emancipations, Oppressions, Quandaries*, edited by Gerald W. Creed, 23–49. Santa Fe: School of American Research Press.

Creed, Gerald W. 2006b. "Reconsidering Community." In *The Seduction of Community: Emancipations, Oppressions, Quandaries*, edited by Gerald W. Creed, 3–23. Santa Fe: School of American Research Press.

Delanty, Gerard. 2010. *Community.* New York: Routledge.

Demertzis, Nikos. 2005. «Το τραύμα στη κοινωνία της διακινδύνευσης.» *Εκ των Υστέρων* 13:138–48.

Giddens, Anthony. 1986. *The Constitution of Society: Outline of the Theory of Structuration.* Los Angeles: University of California Press.

Giddens, Anthony. 1991. *Modernity and Self-Identity: Self and Society in the Late Modern Age.* Stanford: Stanford University Press.

Gill, Denise. 2017. *Melancholic Modalities: Affect and Turkish Classical Musicians.* London: Oxford University Press.

Gill, Denise. 2018. "Listening, Muhabbet, and the Practice of Masculinity." *Ethnomusicology* 62(2):171–205.

Higgins, Lee. 2012. *Community Music: In Theory and in Practice.* Oxford: Oxford University Press.

Hirsch, Marianne. 2012. *The Generation of Postmemory: Writing and Visual Culture After the Holocaust.* New York: Columbia University Press.

Hirschon, Renee, ed. 2006. *Crossing the Aegean: An Appraisal of the 1923 Compulsory Population Exchange Between Greece and Turkey.* Oxford, NY: Berghahn. First published in 2003.

Hoffman, Tessa, Matthias Bjornuld, and Vasileios Meichanetsidis, eds. 2012. *The Genocide of the Ottoman Greeks: Studies on the State-Sponsored Campaign of Extermination of the Christians of Asia Minor (1912–1922) and Its Aftermath; History, Law, Memory.* Athens: Aristide D. Caratzas.

Hofman, Ana. 2015. "Music (as) Labour: Professional Musicianship, Affective Labour and Gender in Socialist Yugoslavia." *Ethnomusicology Forum* 24(1): 28–50. http://dx.doi.org/10.1080/17411912.2015.1009479

International Association of Genocide Scholars. 2007 Resolution. http://www.genocidescholars.org/resources/resolutions.

Joseph, Miranda. 2002. *Against the Romance of Community.* Minneapolis: University of Minnesota Press.

Joseph, Miranda. 2017. "Community, Collectivity, Affinities." In *A Companion to Critical and Cultural Theory*, edited by Imre Szeman, Sarah Blaker, and Justin Sully, 205–23. Oxford, UK: Wiley Blackwell.

Kailaris, Giannis. 2002. *Τέταρτη Γενιά των Ποντίων. Κοινωνική Πρόσβαση.* Θεσσαλονίκη: Αφοί Κυριακίδη.

Kallimopoulou, Eleni, and Aspasia (Sissy) Theodosiou, eds. 2020. *Μουσικές Κοινότητες στην Ελλάδα του 21ου Αιώνα. Εθνογραφικές ματιές και ακροάσεις.* Αθήνα: Πεδίο.

Kavouras, Pavlos. 2005. "Ethnographies of Dialogical Singing, Dialogical Ethnography." *Music and Anthropology* 10: n.p. https://www2.umbc.edu/MA/index/number10/kavour/kav_0.htm

Keil, Charles. 1995. "The Theory of Participatory Discrepancies: A Project Report." *Ethnomusicology* 39(1): 1–19.

Kilpatrick, David Bruce. 1980. *Function and Style in Pontic Dance Music.* Athens: Pontic Archive, Committee of Pontic Studies. First published in 1975.

Kontogiorgi, Elisabeth. 2006. *Population Exchange in Greek Macedonia: The Rural Settlement of Refugees, 1922–1930.* London: Oxford University Press.

Latour, Bruno. 2005. *Reassembling the Social: An Introduction to Actor-Network Theory.* Oxford: Oxford University Press.

Lowenthal, David. 1985. *The Past Is a Foreign Country.* Cambridge: Cambridge University Press.

Magrini, Tullia, ed. 2003. *Music and Gender: Perspectives from the Mediterranean.* Chicago: University of Chicago Press.

Markoff, Irene. 2002. "Alevi Identity and Expressive Culture." In *Garland Encyclopedia of World Music.* Vol. 6, *The Middle East,* edited by Virginia Danielson, Scott Marcus, and Dwight Reynolds, 792–800. New York: Routledge.

Marmaridis, Serafeim. 2014. «Η παρατακτική τεχνοτροπία στη μουσική παράδοση του Πόντου. Το παράδειγμα του τικ». Πτυχιακή Διατριβή: Άρτα, ΤΕΙ Παραδοσιακών Μουσικών Οργάνων Ηπείρου.

Monson, Ingrid. 1996. *Saying Something: Jazz Improvisation and Interaction.* Chicago: University of Chicago Press.

Pegg, Carole, Helen Myers, Philip Bohlman, and Martin Stokes. 2013. "Ethnomusicology." In *Grove Music Online,* Oxford Music Online.

Roach, Joseph. 1996. *Cities of the Dead: Circum-Atlantic Performance.* New York: Columbia University Press.

Rose, Nikolas. 1999. *Powers of Freedom: Reframing Political Thought.* Cambridge: Cambridge University Press.

Sant Cassia, Paul. 2000. "Exoticizing Discoveries and Extraordinary Experiences: 'Traditional' Music, Modernity, and Nostalgia in Malta and Other Mediterranean Societies." *Ethnomusicology* 44(2): 281–301.

Seremetakis, Nadia C. 1991. *The Last Word: Women, Death and Divination in Inner Mani.* Chicago: University of Chicago Press.

Shelemay, Kay Kauffman. 2011. "Musical Communities: Rethinking the Collective in Music." *Journal of American Musicological Society* 64(2): 349–90.

Small, Christopher. 1998. *Musicking: The Meanings of Performing and Listening.* Middletown, CT: Wesleyan University Press.

Sugarman, Jane. 2004. "The Nightingale and the Partridge: Singing and Gender Among Prespa Albanians." In *Women's Voices Across Musical Worlds,* edited by Jane A. Berstein, 261–85. Boston: Northeastern University Press.

Tönnies, Ferdinand. 2001. *Community and Civil Society*. Edited by Jose Harris. Cambridge Texts in the History of Political Thought. Cambridge: Cambridge University Press. First published in 1835.

Turino, Thomas. 2008. *Music as Social Life: The Politics of Participation*. Chicago: University of Chicago Press.

Turino, Thomas. 2009. "Four Fields of Music Making and Sustainable Living." *The World of Music* 51(1): 95–117.

Turner, Victor. 1974. "Liminal to Liminoid in Play, Flow, and Ritual: An Essay in Comparative Symbology." In *The Anthropological Study of Human Play*, edited by E. Norbeck, 53–92. Houston, TX: Rice University Press.

Vergeti, Maria K. 2000. *Από τον Πόντο στην Ελλάδα. Διαδικασίες διαμόρφωσης μιας Εθνοτοπικής Ταυτότητας.* Θεσσαλονίκη: Αφοί Κυριακίδη.

Watts, Michael. 2006. "The Sinister Political Life of Community: Economies of Violence and Governable Spaces in the Niger Delta, Nigeria." In *The Seduction of Community: Emancipations, Oppressions, Quandaries*, edited by Gerald W. Creed, 101–43. Santa Fe: School of American Research Press.

Whitehead, Ann. 2007. "Introduction to Section 6. Trauma." In *Theories of Memory: A Reader,* edited by Michael Rossington and Anne Whitehead, 186–92. Baltimore: Johns Hopkins University Press.

Williams, Raymond. 1976. *Keywords.* New York: Oxford University Press.

2 Choreographic Participation of a Presentational Kind

Sound, Movement, and the Politics of Belonging in Bulgaria's Armenian Diaspora

DONNA A. BUCHANAN

Introduction

Scene 1

It is October 14, 2007, and, at the invitation of my Armenian Bulgarian friend Margarit, I am attending a concert honoring the composer and poet St. Mesrop Mashtots, who devised the Armenian alphabet in AD 404. We are seated in Sofia's Armenian *naroden dom* (literally, people's, folk, or national house, hereafter AND), a community center whose name is a holdover from the socialist era. Built in 1936, this multilevel facility houses Surp Asdvadzadzin (Holy Mother of God) Church, the archimandrite's apartments, the vestry offices, a social clubroom, and the Bulgarian headquarters of the Eparchial Council of the Armenian Apostolic Church and the Armenian Cultural-Educational Association "Erevan" (Yerevan), whose weekly newspaper is also edited here. It is in these offices that Margarit works part-time as secretary for the Eparchial Council and Erevan's board of directors. On the facility's third floor, a small single-level auditorium adjoins the club, whose movable wall partition opens to convert the entire space into a large hall. This hall, I would later find, frequently plays host to Armenian social events including parties, after-church social hours, music rehearsals, poetry readings, theatrical productions, benefits, and dinner dances. A compact wooden stage draped with a dusty red velvet curtain stands shuttered at one end. It is here, on the linoleum floor before the stage, that the concert occurs.

Anticipating an Armenian program featuring Armenian performers, I am mystified to find that but for an operatically trained soprano, none of the musicians is of Armenian heritage. Nor is the repertory that we hear. Rather, the concert mostly features well-known European art songs and arias by Debussy, Dvořák, Massenet, Puccini, Rossini, and Schubert with piano accompaniment. A Bulgarian conservatory student also performs a *haiduk* ballad set by the Bulgarian classical composer Dobri Hristov (1875–1941) in an enormous basso profundo to rousing applause.[1] The emcee remarks that this vocalist had asked the concert organizers to supply him with an Armenian piece so that he could feel closer to their community, but efforts to secure him a score from Yerevan had failed. The single exception is the song "Armenian Eyes" (Bulg. "Armenski ochi"), performed by the soprano. Composed by Sofia's Haigashod Agasyan (b. 1953) in 1979, this song, whose lyrics were penned by the acclaimed Bulgarian poet Vanya Petkova (1944–2009), is essentially embraced by the local diaspora as an anthem of their community. Its performance, together with Hristov's haiduk song, brings down the small house.

"Where were the folk songs and dances, the Armenian instruments like the *duduk, kanon, ud,* and *d'hol*? Does no one play them?" I quizzed Margarit later. "Not that I know of," she indicated. In fact, she was unsure what a kanon or a d'hol was.[2] But she had heard that a Bulgarian *kaval* player employed by Sofia's National Folkloric Ensemble "Philip Kutev" could play a little duduk, the double-reed aerophone whose plaintive timbre has become a poignant sonic icon of the emotional trauma associated with the 1915 Armenian genocide (Buchanan 2018, 151–55; Nercessian 2000).[3]

I began to suspect that what constituted "Armenian music" for this community differed markedly from my initial expectations, shaped as they were by my prior work with Bulgarian folkloric ensembles and the institutionalized discourses of authenticity and tradition they fostered (2006). In fact, Margarit's response would later be echoed by several of my interlocutors, who seemed unfamiliar with Armenian instruments but for the duduk and "some kind of drum," an oblique reference to the d'hol. To be sure, most were not musicians, yet recorded or live music of some sort was a component of most community occasions.

Masking my surprise, I tried again. "At an Armenian wedding, after the ritual, when you go to the restaurant for the reception, what kind of music is played?" "Recordings," Margarit replied, without elaboration. "Armenian music?" I asked hopefully. She shrugged. "Sometimes Armenian, sometimes Bulgarian—it depends."

Scene 2

It is mid-April 2008 and Margarit and I are having dinner at Ararat, a tiny, recently established Armenian restaurant in Sofia. The owner's son, Migel, an immigrant from Armenia in his thirties with dual degrees in law and economics, is also a multilingual singer who entertains patrons with live music after dinner. I survey the room, jammed with tables, wondering where the band will set up. At about 9:00 p.m., when Migel pulls out a microphone and attaches it to a small sound system, I realize that they are situated permanently in a boombox. Migel then proceeds, karaoke-like, to regale us with Alla Pugacheva's "Million Roses" and other Soviet Russian *estrada* favorites from the 1970s and 1980s, together with popular Bulgarian and Macedonian folksongs to a pre-recorded synthesizer soundtrack.[4] The crowd, including Margarit, responds enthusiastically, singing along with the Soviet and Bulgarian selections. When Migel begins an Armenian song a visiting Greek businessman stands up and joins in, singing Greek lyrics to the same melody in a spontaneous show of transregional affinity; Migel yields the microphone, inspiring the Greek's companions to dance the *hasapiko* near their table and throw money at the two vocalists.[5] Migel then invites Margarit to the microphone and she readily obliges, drawing on her years of experience as a member of the Surp Asdvadzadzin church choir and the Kirkor Kirkorov amateur Armenian mixed choir, which she joined in the early 1990s. They perform a second Armenian popular song in duet. The Greek men, now inebriated and in high spirits, exclaim at her vivacity and playfully paste a fifty-euro bill to her forehead.

I marvel at the multiple temporal, geopolitical, cultural, and demographic flows that converge in these interactions around the notion of a Bulgarian Armenian-ness, caught on the fractured shards of the Ottoman and Soviet ecumenes in the neoliberal environment of the postsocialist Balkans. In comparing diasporas to cosmopolitan formations, Turino (2004, 6) observes that "it is the multi-site nature of diasporas that gives them a special type of dynamism by providing cultural models and resources from a variety of places which cohere to a relative degree because of shared dispositions and experiences— dispersion and sometimes persecution key among them." Fair enough. Song is certainly such a resource. But to what extent did these Greek, Bulgarian, and post-Soviet Armenians really share dispositions and experiences, and how did these links, rooted as they are in different states, assist in maintaining "a common social identification" and shared "discursive emphasis on a central homeland" (5)? Did they all even espouse the same notion of "home"? Or was this a case of "multiple belonging," signposted and effectuated through the performance of music and dance at once participatory and presentational (Tölölyan 1996, 7–8; Turino 2008)?

Scene 3

Three years have passed since the concert commemorating St. Mesrop Mashtots. It is October 23, 2010, about 12:30 pm. I am once again sitting in the AND hall, pen and notebook in hand, strategically sandwiched between the grand piano and the stage, where I won't be in the way. I am here to observe the initial meeting of a new community group devoted to learning Armenian folk dances. Fifteen women and eight men between the ages of eighteen and twenty-five are waiting eagerly for the instruction to begin. Soon Emma Shahinyan, the group's twenty-three-year old choreographer, appears, and I introduce myself. A multilingual Sofia University senior double majoring in Chinese and Armenian studies, Emma was born in Yerevan but moved with her family to Plovdiv, where the largest community of Bulgarian Armenians resides, at age ten. She began dancing at age six, joining Plovdiv's folk dance group Garabner on its establishment in the early 1990s and becoming one of its featured soloists. Five years later she moved to Sofia to pursue her undergraduate studies. The idea to found a dance group here, the capital's first, arose among local members of Homenütmen, the Armenian scouts, in part to forge social bonds between the diaspora's young people. But for years, Emma told me, she had contemplated organizing something similar.

Emma begins by demonstrating line and semicircular dance formations in which all can participate. The instruction is bilingual; she counts steps and beats in Armenian but explains gestures in Bulgarian. The various choreographic components, when named at all, are also designated in Bulgarian. "Why don't you join us?" Emma soon proposes, noticing my avid interest. "There are no observers here," she adds laughingly, dismissing my half-hearted protests. "Just participants!"

Scene 4

It is March 3, 2011, both Bulgarian Independence Day and Armenian Vartanants, a holiday commemorating a fifth-century battle important to Armenian religious and political history.[6] I am costumed in the brand-new folkloric attire of the dance troupe Nairi, a multivalent girl's name that also signifies an ancient people and region of historic Armenia located in eastern Anatolia around Lake Van, which the Assyrians called the Sea of Nairi.[7] My small spherical cap, sewn from lightweight red, white, and black upholstery fabric patterned with provincial kilim motifs, matches an accompanying vest, short skirt, and soft, leather-soled slippers with upturned Aladdinesque toes, all stitched from the same fabric and worn with a black leotard. The men's pants and vests are similar in color but feature different motifs.

I am dancing in the troupe's premiere performance on the cramped, dilapidated wooden stage of the AND. As we spring from our left legs, right knees high in the air, I struggle to remember everything that Emma has taught us: posture erect; spine straight; toes pointed; shoulders down and back, blades pressed so tightly that a pencil can be pinched between them. I spot the Armenian ambassador and priest among other prominent community members in the crowd, and my courage almost fails me. Where is our dance line? Are we straight? Ordered appropriately by height? Equally spaced? Centered on the stage? Hands clasped at hip level, the dance line rocks and sways as we tilt our weight back, twisting slightly to the right while swinging our left legs diagonally across our bodies, and then repeat these gestures to the other side. We break into a new configuration and I strive to keep my arm movements supple and fluid as my hands sketch pliant curlicues in the air. Fingers terraced as if sipping high tea from a porcelain cup, thumbs and middle fingers positioned as if holding a thin cell phone between them, I marvel again at the intricate coordination demanded by even the simplest gesture, as each spiral of the hand is articulated with a pulsed flexing of the foot and ornamented with subtle head gestures. My eyes trail my fingers, following in their direction as I have been taught. Grace, elegance, modesty, restraint. Despite the physical exertion of the dance, and in sharp contrast to the men's expansive, athletic moves, as women we are never to display signs of strain. I look at Emma and she smiles encouragingly. "*Dance the gestures*," I hear her say in my head. "Don't just mechanically count them."

Our hands float and dip as birds in flight. We sway like trees. We dance the legacy of Soviet cultural policy. We embody the internal tension of a diaspora poised between ethnic assertion and assimilation. And our movements are choreographic metonyms of the mountains of Nagorno-Karabakh. But I don't really understand this until much later.

*   *   *

My chapter concerns sound, movement, and the politics of belonging in Bulgaria's Armenian diaspora. Like Turino (2004, 4), I am interested in how artistic practices "contribute to diasporic identity formation, maintenance, and transformation" and inform or express the subjectivities, sensibilities, and consciousness of diasporic actors. More specifically, building on the work of diaspora theorist Khachig Tölölyan, in this study I examine how artistic production, as facilitated by a "diasporic civil society" (2000, 109) of institutions founded or reestablished since Bulgaria's 1989 political transition, engenders the community's intricate internal dynamics and nurtures a unifying "diasporist discourse" of Armenian subjectivity in the face of potentially divisive forces (1996, 19). In Bulgaria these institutions include the Church, the Erevan Association, the Armenian Charitable Organization "H.O.M" (the Armenian Red Cross), the Armenian Elementary School Association "St. Hovagimyan," and the Armenian General Benevolent Union (AGBU) "Parekordzagan." Reestablished in Sofia in 1992, the AGBU is the greater diaspora's largest and wealthiest philanthropic organization, headquartered in New York and Geneva (Bohosyan 1999, 108;

Tölölyan 2000, 127). In Sofia, Erevan and Parekordzagan in turn sponsor many affiliated postsocialist groups and activities, including the Armenian scouts, youth organizations, language classes, a theater troupe, a Saturday morning daycare center, and three ensembles: the Sofia Chamber Orchestra (established 2006), the dance group Nur (Pomegranate, established in the spring of 2011), both associated with Parekordzagan, and Nairi. The community also sustains three Armenian newspapers, published in Burgas, Plovdiv, and Sofia, as well as the Parekordzagan monthly. Tölölyan points to the critical role played by key "ethnodiasporic figures," including scholars, intellectuals, and "above all, . . . writers, musicians, and other artists" in producing the discursive and "cultural commodities that underpin diasporic identity" (1996, 19).[8] It is such individuals, as creative agents and midwives of diasporic consciousness, that interest me here.

Armenians in Bulgaria: Diasporic Details

Bulgaria's Armenian diaspora is a temporally and culturally multilayered social formation with deep historical roots dating to the early medieval era. Since the 1991 dissolution of the Soviet Union and post-9/11 escalation of violence in Syria and Lebanon, this small Balkan state has become home to significant new numbers of Armenians seeking social stability, economic opportunity, professional advancement, or a foothold in Europe. Those emigrating from the Middle East are, like members of Bulgaria's older, more established diaspora, Anatolian or western Armenians. This sector includes survivors or descendants of refugees from Istanbul, eastern Anatolia, and Turkish Thrace displaced between 1894 and 1922 by the Hamidian massacres, the Turkish-Balkan population exchanges, or the 1915 Ottoman pogrom, whose centenary was commemorated worldwide in April 2015 and for which Armenians actively seek international acknowledgment as an indisputable act of genocide.[9] The newcomers emigrating from the Republic of Armenia are Caucasus or eastern Armenians whose older kin, if not they themselves, were Soviet citizens.

According to the 2011 census, of Bulgaria's population of nearly 7.4 million, a mere 6,552 self-identify as Armenian, a decline of about 4,000 from the 2001 census total of 10,832.[10] Informal sources, however, place the figure much higher—roughly 12,000 old diasporans and 25,000 to 40,000 newcomers—and remark especially on how the recent influx of eastern Armenians has swelled the minority's ranks.[11] The diaspora's two segments thus differ in size; they also dispersed from different parts of historic Armenia, for different reasons, in different generations.

One might assume a high degree of compatibility between the two factions, for Bulgaria's western Armenians share a Black Sea locus, a legacy of communist governance, and the ongoing experience of postsocialism with their eastern brethren.[12] Indeed, the mutual experience of state socialism has prompted the British sociologist Hratch Tchilingirian (2001) to term eastern European Armenians the "forgotten diaspora," because they disappeared from the larger diasporic map during the communist era. Significantly, however, post-Soviet Armenia, autonomous since 1991, does not occupy the heritage lands in Anatolia vacated by the older diaspora's families. Rather, for these westerners, the republic is what Razmik Panossian calls a "kin-state" in contradistinction to the locales that were ethnically cleansed in the late 1800s and early 1900s—a territorial metonym of the Armenian whole (1998, 149).[13]

The population's divergent geopolitical histories, situated on the faultline of the Ottoman Turkish and Russo-Soviet empires, wrought enduring differences in language and aesthetic disposition still relevant today. Eastern and western Armenians speak dialects that are almost mutually unintelligible; our dance classes were conducted in Bulgarian in part for this reason, and Armenian group members also often used this language to converse among themselves.[14] In some ways, the community remains fairly segregated. During the 1990s, when thousands of eastern Armenians flowed through Bulgaria on their way to other destinations, a discourse of heritage residents and new arrivals, "diasporans" and "Hayastanis," developed (Tchilingirian 2001). (*Hayastan* is the Armenian term for the Armenian state.) These ethnonyms belie an awareness of social difference within the Armenian minority, if not mutual alienation. The Armenian-Bulgarian case is thus compelling because its inherent dynamics challenge certain assumptions about the classical definition of a diaspora and the mechanics of homeland-diaspora interactions. Drawing on the work of William Safran, Turino identifies the diasporans' embrace of their ancestral lands "as their true, ideal home and as the place to which they or their descendants would (or should) eventually return—when conditions are appropriate" as a typological feature shared by most diasporic social formations (Safran 1991, 83–84, quoted in Turino 2004, 4). Yet the post-1991 exodus of easterners from the now independent homeland to Bulgaria represents a curious inversion of the conventional diasporan glance. Were these "Hayastanis," many of them fleeing an imploding post-Soviet economy exacerbated by the 1988 earthquake and the Nagorno-Karabakh conflict, initially embraced by hostlanders as genuine diaspora members? From the local perspective, the ethnonym suggests that perhaps they were not.[15]

Motivated by my concert experience in 2007, I had come to Sofia in 2010 curious about these sorts of fractures. What was going on in the musical margins between Bulgaria's eastern and western Armenians, and between this diaspora and ethnic Bulgarian Slavs, Armenians in Hayastan, and Armenians elsewhere in the world? Following Deborah Wong (2012, 15), I wondered how aspects of demographic movement, of diaspora and social transformation, were being performatively rendered in musical practice. I was intrigued by how community members understand "Armenian music," what remains of pre-1915 Armenian music making in Bulgaria today, and how the activities of Caucasus Armenian newcomers are influencing contemporary musical life. But as an ethnomusicologist who sought to learn from live musicians creating ethnically distinctive or inflected sounds, what I encountered confounded my aspirations. The community's key ethnodiasporic musical figures do not work in the folkloric realm.[16] New pop bands created by recent immigrants perform little that is inherently Armenian, preferring synthesizer-heavy socialist-style *estrada* instead. When I asked about Armenian music, I was pointed time and again to composer Komitas Vardapet (Fig. 2.1) and the duduk as quintessential emblems of musical practice.[17] When I inquired after other instruments, my acquaintances professed insufficient knowledge and remarked sadly on the absence of expert mentors. During the year of my fieldwork I was able to locate only two duduk players in the entire country, one of whom was the Kutev Ensemble *kavaldzhiya* mentioned above. For the annual April 24 ceremony commemorating the 1915 genocide, a duduk player from the homeland performed. A local elementary school music teacher, a Bulgarian married to an Armenian and fluent in his language, described her struggle to locate and learn Armenian children's songs for her pupils from books stored in the AND's disorganized library; in keeping with the literary emphasis of early folklore collection norms, there were books of lyrics but fewer with melodies. The eighty-person Kirkor Kirkorov choir, sponsored by Erevan for decades and known for performing Armenian and Bulgarian devotional, classical, and folk music repertory, had disbanded shortly before my arrival due to problems with its directorship and out-migration, which diminished its membership. Tölölyan points to music as one of five dominant modes of cultural production that shape diasporic consciousness in this Armenian transnation, whose ideological orientation shifted from "exilic nationalism to diasporic transnationalism" after 1991 (2000, 107, 124).[18] But my experiences in Sofia did not really support this statement—at least, not in relation to live music making. Clearly, I was asking the wrong questions, approaching the situation from the wrong angle.

With time, my research revealed five major findings, not all of which I can address fully here: (1) It is traditional dance, and not music, which is the locus of ethnodiasporan folkloric practice; (2) it is Armenian composers and musicians of conservatory training, together with choreographers, who are among the key figures cultivating a diasporist discourse; (3) this discourse, which is directed especially at transcending difference, pivots between ethnic assertion and assimilation, inclusion and exclusivity, entrenchment and exchange; (4) Bulgaria's top folkloric musicians have facilitated or responded to this discourse

Fig. 2.1. A 2019 stamp commemorating the 150th anniversary of Komitas Soghomonian in the series "Prominent Armenians."

by promoting collaborative musical ventures with Armenians in and outside the country; and (5) all of this is unfolding in an environment in which the younger generation of Armenians finds little relevance in the politicized differences of the past, and specific individuals, among them recent immigrants, are spearheading renewed attention to Armenian customs and holidays, thereby rejuvenating diasporan sensibilities.

Nairi

It was in this context that I began dancing with Nairi in October 2010. The group began as the amateur School for Armenian Dances, open to anyone, with no assumptions of regular attendance or formal performances. The focus was simply learning community line dances twice each week. Emma's goal was to enable Bulgarians to enjoy Armenian dances and to teach Armenians movements that would allow them to join wedding dances or similar celebrations with confidence. Within a month, however, it became clear that the Erevan Association's administrators envisioned something quite different, encouraging us to hold a staged inaugural performance as soon as December. The troupe then became a serious performance company of (initially) five men and sixteen women that trained three or four times a week for two to four hours at a time.

This was a significant time commitment, and the pace was physically and mentally grueling. Most of the group members were students or worked full-time jobs, including Emma. Those with small children and other obligations soon fell away. Although years of ballet training, figure skating, and competitive swimming had helped prepare me for the aerobic challenges to come, at age fifty I was twenty to thirty years older than the remaining participants and, as someone plagued by considerable performance anxiety, had zero desire to be onstage—in particular, to present choreographed Armenian folk dances to an Armenian public. I was snared firmly on the fence between Turino's participatory and presentational expressive fields, my ethnographic curiosity vying with an abiding discomfort concerning the ethics and politics of representation that these circumstances occasioned (Turino 2008, 23–65).[19]

But the dancing was also really fun, and my troupemates, warm and welcoming. For the most part, my apprehension loomed larger for me than it did for them. A few were also active themselves in Latin or Bulgarian dance ensembles, which had recently gained popularity as recreational alternatives to fitness centers; it was not unusual for younger group members to repair to dance clubs after our rehearsals. Emma reassured me that she believed dance can be enjoyed at any age and wanted the group to be age-inclusive. She had invited a Sofia diasporan in her sixties, whose lifelong dream was to learn her native dances, to join us; we also compared notes about an extraordinary eighty-year old woman whom I had seen dance a lengthy solo at an Armenian culture festival in Burgas a few weeks earlier. Moreover, I was not the only outsider; three ethnic Bulgarian Slavs, one of whom was married to an Armenian woman, were also core participants.

Nairi's choreographic models were the folkloric ensembles of Yerevan in which Emma had received her initial training, with all of the usual expectations concerning costumes and the stylized, balletic choreography that is the joint heritage of the Ballet Russe, the Moiseyev ensemble, and the Sovietized restructuring of local folkloric practice in cookie cutter collectives—a process with which I was only too familiar (Nercessian 2000; Shay 1999, 29–31). We worked hard to memorize a kaleidoscope of ever-changing choreographic figures and to develop synchrony as our routines evolved. Once we had conquered some basics, Emma introduced some of the ballet exercises of my childhood into our training. I felt like my life had come full circle.

My first hint of underlying tension concerned our choreographic aims as we transitioned to a concertizing formation. To begin we learned individual dance moves, extracted from tradition, which we would later combine into various configurations. But the regional origin, sociocultural and choreographic context, and meaning of these gestures—for example, their relation to labor or nature worship of the past, such as the miming of birds and trees—were not made explicit (see Khachatrian 1994, 134; Petrosian 1979, 2–5). "Can we please learn some standard Armenian folk dances?" a male dancer asked one evening. He said he would feel silly executing our footwork at Armenian social occasions without knowing what dance it derived from. The stylized choreography hindered rather than facilitated community engagement. Moreover, he questioned the gendered uniformity of our figures, given the significant differentiation that characterizes

Armenian dance. When would the men learn more masculine movements? Here Emma's pedagogical goal of initially teaching us "unisex gestures" that everyone could perform together collided with the gendered sensibilities of individual dancers. Although Emma retained an occasional emphasis on collective line dancing, shortly thereafter we began rehearsing men's and women's components, and gender-specific dances, separately.

Another instance of dissonance concerned our costumes. One of the troupe's women, a nurse and an exceptional artist, sketched gorgeous full-length traditional dresses for us and selected potential fabric in a rich dark green. We were very excited. Soon, however, a difference of philosophy became apparent; Emma preferred that our costumes distinguish us from other Armenian dance ensembles in Bulgaria, such as those in Plovdiv, Ruse, and Shumen. She wanted us to cultivate our own identity—visibly so. We were to purchase the outfits directly from a firm in Yerevan that supplied the ensemble circuit there. She explained that the elegant, heavy gowns were not appropriate for the energetic mixed dance that we would premiere and that she preferred a lighter, less conventional model that would better reflect the updated presentational aesthetic she wished to cultivate. She showed us sample kilim-like designs on the firm's Facebook page and we debated their relative merits. The men, in particular, wanted to know with which Armenian region the costumes were associated, while the women voiced concern about the above-the-knee wrap-around skirts, as conventionally, Armenian women's legs and feet are not visible when they dance. Emma explained that in Armenia troupes wear a wide variety of costumes, some national and some provincial. "And ours?" asked one of the men, anxious that their pants looked like pajama bottoms. "Ours have a maximum of national elements," she replied firmly.

I was intrigued by this nationalistic emphasis. Was it rooted in anticipated rivalry with other groups, the patriotic occasion of our premiere, or something else? The music to which we danced suggests an additional interpretive frame. Many of our original routines were executed to the soundtracks of YouTube videos amplified from a laptop. Our premiere was danced to "Menq enq mer sarere," the title track on the ethnopop album *Heartbeat of My Land*, released by the sister duo Inga and Anush Arshakyan (b. 1980, 1982) in 2009. Graduates of the Yerevan State Conservatory, the sisters captured tenth place for Armenia in the Eurovision contest with their song "Jan, Jan" in the same year. We christened our routine simply "Hayastan" because the word can be heard easily in the song's lyrics. But this was also an indexical summary of its contents. The lyrics and accompanying video teem with quintessential nationalistic, topographical, and cultural emblems signifying Armenian heritage. The production's color scheme is dominated by the red, orange, and blue of the Armenian flag. Dancers appear in traditional costuming and headdresses. Verses instruct them to "raise their hands up high" like the mountains and "blossoming apricot trees." We see snippets of calendrical rites: jumping the fire for fertility on February 14 to celebrate Dearintirach (Trndez; coincidentally, St. Valentine's Day), and the summer custom of Vardavar, when young people douse each other with water to celebrate life, love, the Transfiguration, and the ancient fertility goddess Anahid.[20] Both customs concern procreation and thus the social reproduction of the Armenian nation; this subtext, important to the song's overall meaning, is reflected in the following lines from the chorus: "[When] an Armenian sees an Armenian / There is life and love / We will make Armenia." Video imagery of a stork and toddler and young parents rocking their infants in cradles underscores the text's implications.

Much of the production is shot in the countryside, against mountains, a river, and a lake, possibly the iconic Lake Sevan. A literal translation of the song's title is "We Are Our Mountains." This phrase and its variant, "We are our land (soil)," are refrained a dozen times throughout the song, and it soon becomes evident to which mountainous land this refers. Toward the video's conclusion, Armenian strongmen wrangle Mount Ararat into the country with ropes slung over their shoulders. Ararat is a near sacred peak in Armenian belief; it appears on the state's coat of arms and is the nation's most vital topographical symbol. Once located in historic Armenia, the dual-peaked volcanic massif now sits just across the border, in eastern Turkey, a source of continuing anguish and antipathy for both homelanders and the diaspora (cf. Alajaji 2015, 6, 174n8). According to the Old Testament, it is the site where Noah's ark alighted; moreover, Noah's great-great-grandson Hayk, whose name came to signify Armenian (Hay) and Armenia (Hayastan) is, with Noah, a progenitor of the Armenian people (Abrahamian 2006, 37; Petrosyan 2001, 35–36). Visible on Yerevan's horizon, Mount Ararat therefore situates Armenia's ancient links to the Bible and the genesis of Christianity in the very earth.[21]

But in Inga and Anush's production Ararat is upstaged by the hills of Nagorno-Karabakh. The name of this contested region, which Armenians call Artsakh, means "Mountainous Black Garden." "We Are Our Mountains" is the region's motto (Kasparian 2001, 139). In the video, area peaks literally speak this titular phrase through animated mouths at the song's midpoint. Artsakh has been the site of armed conflict between Armenia and Azerbaijan since 1991 (de Waal 2003, 8). Legally located in Azerbaijan, the region and its predominantly Armenian population were controlled largely by Armenian forces until Azerbaijan reclaimed these occupied territories when war reerupted in the autumn of 2020.[22] Both states claim Nagorno-Karabakh as vital to their artistic and cultural heritage (de Waal 2003, 2010). In the video's opening frames, a cartographic outline of Armenia, Artsakh included, is projected in red on the participants' faces as they shout, "Hayastan!"

"We Are Our Mountains" is also the name of an iconic statue located above the airfield in Stepanakert, Artsakh's capital. Chiseled from pink volcanic tuff by sculptor Sarkis Baghdasarian in 1967, the monument depicts the effigies of an elderly man and woman wearing traditional headgear. The monument and its Armenian name, Tatik [u] Papik (Grandma and Grandpa), carry connotations of ancestor worship. Deep in Armenia's pre-Christian past, animist deities resided in stony peaks such as Mount Ararat. Megaliths called *vishap*s, or dragonstones, were erected to guard or mark water sources. These were the precursors of the Christian Armenian stone crosses, or *hachkar*s, awarded UNESCO Intangible Cultural Heritage status in 2010. Hewn from the same pink volcanic tuff, these gravestones are elaborately etched with elements of Christian theology, solar symbolism, and the world tree. Often raised in compound groups on the ground or on rocks themselves, hachkars visually suggest hills or mountain ranges and are microcosmic metaphors for Mt. Ararat (Azarian 1973, 29). In recent years new hachkars have been erected throughout the diaspora to memorialize those who perished in the Ottoman deportations and pogroms (Buchanan 2018).

For Armenians, then, stone is a potent cosmological element that marries the land and its residents to the sacred. In effect, the Artsakh monument suggests that the very ancestral spirits of Armenians have been embedded, since time immemorial, in the deified Nagorno-Karabakh landscape.[23] The monument is found on the unofficial republic's coat of arms and is overtly featured in the "Menq enq mer sarere" video and album cover, where the positioning of the vocalists' heads mimics the statue as it, in turn, emulates the dual but uneven peaks of Mount Ararat.[24] In fact, at the very point in the video where aerial footage of the statue appears, the sisters replace the words "We are our mountains" with "We are also Artsakh."[25] This is the "heartbeat" of the Armenian land, as the album cover suggests.[26]

The soundtrack reinforces these associations with strength, masculinity, and heroism. The video opens with a shot of several d'hols sitting on a rack, mountain peaks painted on their heads in blue. These are heard together with *zurna*s and *gos*, the large bass drum resembling the Turkish *davul* and Bulgarian *tŭpan*.[27] This aggressive combination of percussion and strident reeds traditionally accompanies dances such as the *kochari*, originally a militaristic men's dance from the Armenian highlands in which the dancers, in a socio-physical manifestation of community, build a fortress-like wall with their bodies. Indeed, as the sisters sing "The victories of our brave soldiers" (Armenia's initial territorial gains), the camera focuses on three male dancers performing a sword dance; this immediately precedes the line "We are also Artsakh." Our choreography, too, drew more on the figures of community line dances than the tip-toe, small-step, gliding footwork characterizing our later women's dances.

In village life of the early twentieth century the zurna and gos were also key components of wedding celebrations, making their use here, in association with "life and love," very appropriate. Because this instrumental combination appears in similar contexts throughout the Balkans, its sound simultaneously places Armenia inside the larger Black Sea region while choreographically defending its sovereign borders. This, plus the festive Balkan-style brass band heard throughout (also a wedding ensemble), made the song an apt choice for a multinational dance group emplaced where the Balkans and the Caucasus converge.

Our "Hayastan" routine might therefore be understood as a choreographic claim to Nagorno-Karabakh, our costumes a sartorial echo of nationalist sentiments, and it had the crowd on its feet every time we performed it. Whether this was because the audience appreciated our efforts (many were relatives of troupe members), were transported by the song's catchy appeal and joyous dynamism, recognized it from Armenian media or its association with Eurovision's Inga and Anush, or were sympathetic to its patriotic fervor is unclear. Since 1991, the Nagorno-Karabakh conflict and gaining official, worldwide recognition of the 1915 Ottoman pogrom as genocide have replaced Armenian independence as nationalist causes to which the diaspora cleaves (Panossian 1998, 160; Yazedjian 2004). Although no one ever discussed the song's extramusical associations in my presence, prior to our premiere, after a quiet conversation with one of the troupe's older members during a rehearsal break, Emma approached me to see if I knew how to strip the vocal tracks from YouTube videos so that we could dance to the instrumental mix alone. (I did not.) When I asked why, she replied that lyrics typically distracted audiences from focusing on the dance itself, and indeed, most of our other routines were accompanied only by instrumentals. Or was it that *these* words were particularly provocative? As Inga and Anush sing, "Wherever the road takes us / even into strange lands / regardless, we are Armenian! Armenian!"

Inclusivity and Exclusivity, Assertion and Assimilation

Whatever the case, the ethnic assertions of our choreography for "Hayastan" also occasionally existed in tension with the company's staunch embrace of collaboration and inclusivity, a third point of discord in the diasporan community. Shortly after the premiere, I learned that in a contentious three-hour meeting between representatives of the dance group, scouts, and Erevan's administration, a scout leader whose sister was a Nairi member argued vehemently against allowing non-Armenians to perform with the troupe. Although he did not dance with us, he had been instrumental in facilitating the group's establishment; indeed, some said the whole endeavor had been his idea. He had envisioned the troupe as a venue in which diaspora members could gather and socialize, and he insisted adamantly that all dance instruction should be monolingual—in Armenian—to help keep this key aspect of cultural identity alive. Apparently these matters, to which I am not unsympathetic, had been the source of heated discussion between select group members for weeks on Facebook, and the climactic meeting occurred while I was away attending a mumming festival. What this stance of exclusivity denies, however, is the large number of mixed marriages, romantic relationships, and friendships existing between Armenians and ethnic Bulgarians or other minorities (Georgians, Greeks, Karakachans, and Russians), including connections among the dancers themselves. Were the non-Armenian spouses and partners of diaspora members to be barred from participating in dancing—or in other AND initiatives?

Ultimately, the administration embraced the more inclusive philosophy that Emma advocated from the start. The company would remain open and diverse. As Solomon (2008, 78) found in his work on Turkish rap in Germany, however, this debate underscores that diasporas are not "coherent thing[s] out there in the real world that one can point to." Rather, they are "complex social formation[s] full of internal tensions and contradictions, with multiple intersecting histories, discourses, and practices." Solomon's observation is supported by the work of Gerald Creed (2006, 13–14), who, invoking Foucault, argues that "communities are constituted by and constitutive of different regimes of knowledge." The social relationships that comprise (diaspora) communities are thus inevitably shot through with "vested interests and configurations of power" holding "ideological significance" (ibid.). Friction and difference may be inherent in the community-building process; indeed, differentiation, whether as a function of democratization or of human ingenuity and imagination, can be socially valued even as it invites discord (Fiol and Perman, introduction to this volume).

Solomon thus cautions that diasporic analysis should not elide "the [hybridic] complexities of just exactly *who* is making the music," dance, or other artistic commodities around which diasporic social formations may coalesce and formulate a sense of belonging (2008, 78.). Later, when discussing the dispute with an Armenian acquaintance whose daughter danced with Nairi, I commented that the group's inclusive approach would build bridges. "An international formation," I said. "After all, everyone in it is a Bulgarian citizen." She looked at me in surprise and firmly asserted, emphasizing with her hands on her desk, "No, it's an *Armenian* ensemble. It performs *Armenian* dances." For her, it is the differential *content* of what is performed, not who performs it, that is the definitive factor. In this way, Nairi actively seeks to promote and sustain Armenian identity—western and eastern—while simultaneously inviting outsiders like its three Bulgarian members and this gangly, uncoordinated, inquisitive American woman of a certain middle age to participate.

Nairi is not alone in adopting this integrative approach. The philosophy of employing mechanisms of ethnic assertion to foster attitudes of openness underlies the majority of Armenian cultural productions that I witnessed in Sofia during 2010 and 2011. As Parekordzagan director Sonia Avakian-Bedrossian explained to me, the AGBU chamber orchestra was founded with a deliberately diverse personnel and repertory; it *includes* Armenian musicians and works but is also resolutely *inclusive* of others. For Avakian-Bedrossian, the social mission of the Armenian people is to reveal through their past suffering a peaceable alternative of tolerance and reciprocal exchange. Every concert featured standard classical works together with Armenian and Bulgarian compositions, as well as invited soloists from some other part of the diaspora. The March 2011 concert, for example, was patronized by the Lebanese ambassador, Micheline Abi-Samra, and featured the Lebanese guitarist Fadi Rachid and ud player Chadi Esber. The two joined the orchestra in an unusual arrangement of the well-known Andalusian *muwashshah* (a poetic Arab vocal composition) called "Lamma Bada Yatathana" (As he began swaying), popularized by the renowned Lebanese singer Fairouz in the 1960s and more recently by Syrian Armenian vocalist Lena Chamamyan. The same concert also included the premiere of *Musica Meditativa*, a work by Velislav Zaimov (b. 1951), president of the Bulgarian Composer's Union, and paid homage to the Soviet Armenian composer and conductor Aleksandŭr Spendiaryan (1871–1928), a key figure in establishing Armenian symphonic music and a national orchestra. Bulgarian kaval virtuoso Teodossi Spasov, one of the orchestra's first invited soloists, has continued to collaborate with prominent Armenian musicians such as the Greek-Armenian ud player and vocalist Haig Yazdjian. The Kutev Ensemble's director, composer Georgi Andreev, wrote his 2008 chamber symphony *Phoenix* for the AGBU orchestra; the work memorializes the 2007 murder of the Turkish Armenian journalist Hrant Dink, which occurred in Istanbul amid the political unrest surrounding international acknowledgment of the 1915 genocide. Beloved of the orchestra, it has become a standard part of their repertory (Buchanan 2018).

Highlighting the subjunctive quality of belonging-in-becoming, Turino writes, "Whether for a new nation, a new sub-culture, or an emerging diasporic cultural position, artistic forms can be used to make the imaginings of what the new subject position might look like, sound like, and feel like through a concrete, *coherently constituted* perceivable form" (2004, 11, original emphasis). In this regard, diasporas take work; they take time, energy, administrative savvy, material resources, creativity, foresight, and emotional fortitude to sustain. To raise diasporic consciousness and foster sentiments of belonging, the affective labor invested must also inspire diasporans to consume, develop an affinity for, identify with, and valorize the commodities produced (cf. Solomon 2015, 331, 333–36). As agentive artistic organizations constitutive *of* the diaspora performing *for* the diaspora, Nairi and the AGBU orchestra embody and actualize, in sound, personnel, and movement, the multinational reality of their local social formation. In doing so, they effectively harness lived difference as part of a community-building process that denies neither subjectivities of Armenianness nor "multiple belonging," for in today's diaspora, these are to some extent synonymous (Fiol and Perman, introduction to this volume; Tölölyan 1996, 7–8). Such an approach redirects the inhumanity of 1915 toward the common good; it does not dwell on the past but looks forward, beyond the anguish, to engage Armenian life in the present tense. That variance and challenges persist among Bulgaria's Armenians is undeniable. But in the spheres of music and dance, these sharper edges also seem to be giving way to vibrant instances of interlock.

Notes

For Tom, with affection, respect, admiration, and gratitude for decades of abiding friendship and collegiality; and for my dear friend Margarit Kerpitchian (1951–2022), without whom this study would not exist.

Previous versions of this chapter were presented at the 2011 joint meeting of the Society for Ethnomusicology and Congress on Research in Dance (Philadelphia, PA); at the 2012 conference "Music and Marginality in the Balkans: The Edginess of Edges," hosted by the University of Chicago Center for East European and Russian/Eurasian Studies; and for the June 2019 workshop "Teaching the South Caucasus," organized by the American Research Institute in the South Caucasus and Russian, East European, and Eurasian Center at the University of Illinois at Urbana-Champaign. I extend heartfelt gratitude to the Armenian dance ensemble Nairi, Sofia, and especially its director, Emma Shahinyan-Palova; the Institute for Art Studies, Sofia; as well as to Margarit Kerpitchian, Sophia Avakian-Bedrossian, Victor Friedman, Jonathan Hollis, Maureen Marshall, and Mari Firkatian for their gracious assistance with and contributions to various aspects of this project. Funding for my research was provided by a Fulbright-Hays Faculty Research Abroad Grant and the University of Illinois Campus Research Board and European Union Center, which I gratefully acknowledge.

1. The *haiduk* is a heroic male guerrilla fighter, romanticized in song and lore, who launched raids against the Ottoman Turks from the sixteenth to the nineteenth century to win Bulgaria's freedom.

2. The *d'hol* is a doubled-headed frame drum struck with the hands. Played principally by men, it resembles a tenor drum in size and is analogous to the Georgian *doli.* The *kanon* is the Middle Eastern seventy-two-string trapezoidal lap harp also found among Greek, Turkish, and Arab populations, called *kanonaki, kanun,* and *qanun,* respectively. In Armenia it is played principally by women.

3. Margarit was not wrong. *Kavaldzhiya* Lyubomir Zhelev plays *duduk* on the instrumental selection "Spomen za Ararat" (A memory of Ararat), from the Kutev Ensemble's 2003 production *Divi yagodi* (Wild strawberries), which showcases the country's several minorities (Buchanan 2015). See Turino 1999, 2000, and 2008, and Perman (2010, esp.

442–48) concerning the affective power of musical and choreographic icons and indices for shaping how the politics of identity, from the self to the nation, are felt, embodied, experienced, and agentively realized through performance.

4. Derived from the Russian and French words for "stage," *estrada* is a distinctively Soviet Russian genre of light popular music that arose in the 1960s in association with the state-sponsored "vocal instrumental ensembles" or professional "beat groups" that were one sanctioned answer to rock bands. Such songs draw on a variety of entertainment genres and are typically characterized by an anesthetized beat, submerged bass line, occasional folk elements, cheerful, optimistic, or nostalgic lyrics, and an orientation toward European art music in harmonization and accompaniment, which may feature symphonic instruments or a string orchestra. A related Armenian genre, *estradayin*, developed concurrently in the Lebanese diaspora but adopted regional characteristics: western Armenian lyrics, Armenian modality, vocal ornamentation, and "highly danceable" *baladi* rhythms shared by Turkish and other Middle Eastern ethnopop (Alajaji 2015, 122). See Alajaji 2013 and 2015 (chapter 4) for an extensive analysis of the *estradayin* movement.

5. I do not know whether the Greek businessmen were of Armenian heritage, but I suspect so. They were seated with Bulgarian Armenian and Bulgarian companions. The restaurant had few tables and was not downtown, leading me to surmise that it was probably known largely to an in-group who would also appreciate Migel's entertainment. The restaurant has since moved to a location closer to the AND.

6. The battle between Armenian and Persian forces occurred on the field of Avarayr in AD 451. The Armenian troops, led by Prince Vartan Mamikonian, fought to retain their Christian faith, while the Persians sought to convert them to Zoroastrianism. Although the Armenians lost the battle, they fought so ferociously that the Persian king rescinded his order, realizing that his conversion plans were futile. Vartan, who died in the battle, was later canonized and is celebrated as a hero of religious and national salvation.

7. The name's indexicality was important, Emma had told me. She didn't want something as obvious or territorially fixed as "Yerevan" or "Hayastan." By contrast, "Nairi" would resonate meaningfully in different ways for the entire community. To my mind, it also associated the group with Armenia's ancestral past, one shared by all living Armenians, whether in the Republic or the diaspora, thereby transcending local difference.

8. Ethnonational diasporas, as opposed to other kinds of transnational networks, have shared ethnicity as a basis (Sheffer 2006, 128). Gabriel Sheffer defines such diasporas as "cultural-social-political formation[s] of people . . . united by the same ethnonational origin and who reside permanently as minorities in one or more hostlands. Such diasporas emerge out of voluntary or forced migration, or out of both types of migratory waves, spreading from one ethnonational state or homeland to one or more host countries" (130–31). Ethnonational diasporans may "also experience secondary and even tertiary migration from one hostland to another" (131). Their "ethnonationalist identities . . . are based on non-essentialist primordial elements, myths, psychological factors, and interests related to their homelands," with which they sustain regular contact by creating "elaborate trans-state networks that permit and encourage multiple exchanges of

money, political support, and cultural materials" (ibid.). Such diasporas "seek to create, maintain, and promote communal solidarity" (ibid.).

9. The governments of Stamboliiski and Tsar Boris III opened Bulgaria's borders to Armenian refugees; according to Bohosyan (1999, 10), Bulgaria was the only European country to "legally and unreservedly" allow them within its borders, even though the country was teeming with refugees at that time, including Bulgarians from the Aegean, Thrace, and Macedonia. It was primarily Armenians from the Sea of Marmara, from Bandürma, Bursa, and eastern (Turkish) Thrace who came to Bulgaria through its southern border.

10. These are the most recent census data. According to Worldometer and United Nations estimates, the population of Bulgaria as of November 29, 2021, had fallen to 6.875 million.

11. Figures differ radically. Komitska et al. (2000–1, xviii) and Mitseva (2001, 19) suggest a total population of thirteen thousand Armenians at the millennium, while the Eparchial Council of Sofia's Armenian Apostolic Church estimates an unofficial figure of twenty thousand (Mitseva 2001, 19). Bohosyan (1999, 10–11) estimates an ebb and flow of about forty thousand eastern Armenian immigrants during the 1990s, not more than seventeen thousand of whom probably stayed. This would suggest a total Armenian population in the late 1990s of about twenty-five thousand. Armenia's Office of the High Commissioner for Diaspora Affairs (2023) maintains that thirty thousand Armenians currently reside in Bulgaria.

12. Panossian (1998, 150) describes the Armenian minority communities outside the Republic but inside the former USSR (e.g., in Azerbaijan and Georgia) as an internal diaspora that is now emerging as an autonomous entity but which has not yet been adequately researched, while other Armenian populations constitute an external diaspora. In my view, however, despite their Anatolian orientation, the western Armenian communities found throughout the former eastern bloc are bound to the internal diaspora by their mutual, albeit variable experience of Soviet socialist hegemony, postsocialist dynamics, and the lifestyles these have fostered. This "trans-state cultural formation," as Turino (2003, 61) might term it, is its own distinctive diaspora configuration involving broadly shared "processes of socialization" and "internalized dispositions" (ibid.).

13. Panossian reminds us that after 1915, "four-fifths of this historic homeland was depopulated of Armenians" and, although it comprised only 20 percent of the original landmass, only the Soviet republic remained a "tangible 'homeland'" for this nation until the 1990s. However, "this was not the only or the 'real' homeland of the diaspora.... The diaspora was not essentially *of this* homeland, but that of Western/Ottoman Armenia" (1998, 154, original emphasis).

14. In fact, many of the young adults in the group, born into families of western Armenian heritage, attended Saturday language classes.

15. Such conceptual cleavages have historical precedents. Panossian (1998, 156) observes that in the late 1940s, homeland Armenians referred to immigrants from abroad as *aghpars*. The term means "brothers" but acquired a derogatory cast.

16. Similarly, the anthropologist Evgeniya Mitseva (2001, 121) writes that, in the Bulgarian context, "as a consequence of the traumas inflicted by the genocide, both folklore

and the ritual-holiday system of the Armenians . . . were destroyed in their entirety. . . . Everything that could have resulted as a natural development of the traditions was interrupted," and any further "evolution of rituals among the Armenian immigrants does not exist."

17. Komitas Vardapet (Soghomon Soghomonian, 1869–1935), often simply called Komitas, was a priest, musical folklorist, composer, vocalist, and choir director critical to the development of Armenian classical music. His folksong collections comprise an essential record of pre-1915 musicianship among Anatolian Armenians. Together with more than 240 other artist-intellectuals, he was detained in Constantinople in 1915, deported to a prison camp, and later died as a consequence of the psychological breakdown he subsequently suffered (Alajaji 2015, 25–55; Paladian 1972). He is widely commemorated as a martyr of the genocide and a founding contributor to an Armenian national music style. As Alajaji observes, "In light of the continuing traumas of the genocide, the continued sense of loss of Home, and the disconnection" experienced within and between diaspora and homeland communities, Komitas has become "an increasingly rare shared symbol that not only connects the diasporic communities to each other, but, given his significance in Armenia, connects the diaspora to Armenia" (2015, 138).

18. The ability of musicians and musical artifacts to enhance feelings of belonging between widely dispersed diaspora populations is, of course, neither new nor limited to Armenians, even in the postsocialist moment. To cite but two examples, see Sugarman's groundbreaking scholarship concerning mediated musics and music videos in the Albanian transnation (2004), and Solomon's astute critique of diaspora theory and hybridity apropos his study of "Turkish rap" in Germany (2008, 2015).

19. The presentational and the participatory are two of the four fields of music making theorized by Turino in his *Music as Social Life* (2008). In my view, these fields are best understood as performance frames—as he himself describes them (29)—whose features, roles, habits, dispositions, values, and moral associations, as emergent within Turino's own fieldwork and typologized by him (e.g., 59, 90–91), represent nodes on a nuanced and variable culture-specific or context-sensitive spectrum. They are etic characterizations whose salience may be culturally differentiated. The way in which issues of presentationality and participation are locally conceptualized, contrasted (if at all), valued, and made and heard as socially real seems critical. In contrast to Turino's theorization, my musical experience suggests that the presentational and the participatory, as practices and even modalities of expressivity, are not always as discrete as his paradigm might suggest. In broad terms, there may be strong presentational dynamics characterizing a musical occasion that appears participatory, and vice versa—a commonsensical observation with which I do not think he would disagree (cf. 17 18). For me, the two modalities ebb and flow, are foregrounded and backgrounded, dialectically (and dialogically) intersecting throughout any music-making instance; the presentational and the participatory are never an either-or scenario. A string quartet performing onstage for a large audience may actually be playing principally for and *with* each other. In fact, I would argue that this ever-evolving, nonverbal interplay of participatory and presentational dynamics, and musicians' realization and "interki-

nesthetic" awareness of this interplay, contributes to intra-ensemble communication and music making's affective power—for both music makers and auditors, who can, of course, also be the same people (Salice et al. 2019; Fiol and Perman, introduction to this volume).

20. The fire jumping enacted on Dearintirach is a Zoroastrian legacy that became syncretized with the Christian observance of Christ's Presentation at the Temple. Vardavar was once linked to the Armenian goddess Astghik or Anahid, associated with water, fertility, and love. Although the Church correlates its occurrence fourteen weeks after Easter with the Transfiguration, it is of pre-Christian origin and today is an occasion for courtship and fun. *Vard* means "rose" in Armenian and is likely emblematic of the goddess. Water is an agent of purification. There are different legends about the custom's significance (see Aghajanian 2009; Abrahamian and Sweezy 2001, 217, 231).

21. Mount Ararat also carries profound pre-Christian cosmological significance. Among other associations, the peak's triangular shape is the center of the universe, from which the world tree grows (see Petrosyan 2001, 37).

22. On September 19, 2023, as this volume was being readied for press, Azerbaijan launched new hostilities in Nagorno-Karabakh, reoccupying the region and prompting more than 100,000 ethnic Armenians (ca. 80 percent of the enclave's population) to seek refuge in Armenia rather than submit to Azerbaijani governance. On September 28, 2023, Samvel Shahramanyan, the president of Artsakh, the unofficial Armenian Nagorno-Karabakh Republic, proclaimed that the entity and its institutions will dissolve on January 1, 2024, while on October 26, Armenian Prime Minister Nikol Pashinyan announced that a peace agreement with Azerbaijan was under discussion.

23. Compare Kasparian (2001, 139–40), who addresses the confluence of motto and icon, land and people, as a near primordial means of empowerment in the Artsakh conflict. He writes, "For Karabagh Armenians, the mere display or utterance of 'We Are Our Mountains' has been part-and-parcel of the act of reclaiming, of repossessing a history and territory that had been denied to them for many years."

24. The cover imagery can be viewed at the artists' Spotify page: https://open.spotify.com/album/oXU1A1UzlpjAZC3zM8KNk8, accessed October 24, 2022.

25. Sincere thanks to my PhD advisee, Armenian music specialist Jonathan Hollis, for originally bringing this connection to my attention.

26. One wonders whether the official album title *Heartbeat of My Land* was chosen to deflect attention away from "We Are Our Mountains." When the sisters competed for Armenia in the 2009 Eurovision contest with their song "Jan, Jan," released together with "We Are Our Mountains" on the same album, controversy erupted. Cartoonish line drawings of the statue appeared with those of other iconic sites in an introductory video trailer preceding the duo's semifinal performance. Azerbaijan protested, resulting in the images' deletion before the finals. Further complicating matters, however, at the Eurovision contest's conclusion, the previous year's Armenian entrant, Sirusho, displayed a photo of the monument on the audience-facing side of her clipboard when delivering Armenia's official vote (Krikorian 2009; Musayelyan 2009).

27. Later a clarinet replaces the *zurna*, emulating its timbre.

Bibliography

Abrahamian, Levon. 2006. *Armenian Identity in a Changing World.* Costa Mesa, CA: Mazda.

Abrahamian, Levon, and Nancy Sweezy, eds. 2001. *Armenian Folk Arts, Culture, and Identity.* Bloomington: Indiana University Press.

Aghajanian, Liana. 2009. "Vardavar: Celebrating an Armenian Water Festival." *Ianyan Mag: An Independent Armenian Publication,* July 19. Retrieved November 14, 2011. http://www.ianyanmag.com/2009/07/19/vardavar-celebrating-an-armenian-water -festival/.

Alajaji, Sylvia Angelique. 2013. "Exilic Becomings: Post-Genocide Armenian Music in Lebanon." *Ethnomusicology* 57(2): 236–60.

Alajaji, Sylvia Angelique. 2015. *Music and the Armenian Diaspora: Searching for Home in Exile.* Bloomington: Indiana University Press. Kindle.

Azarian, Levon. 1973. *Armenian Khatchkars,* edited by Varazdat Haroutiounian. By order of His Holiness Vasken I, Catholicos of all Armenians. Lisbon: Kaloust [Calouste] Gulbenkian Foundation.

Bohosyan, Mihran. 1999. *Armentsite v Sofiya: Istoricheski ocherk.* Sofia: Nastoyatelstvo na Armenskata Tsŭrkva "Surp Asdvadzadzii."

Buchanan, Donna A. 2006. *Performing Democracy: Bulgarian Music and Musicians in Transition.* Chicago: University of Chicago Press.

Buchanan, Donna A. 2015. "Beyond Nation? A Thrice-Told Tale from Bulgaria's Post-socialist Soundstage." *Anthropology of East Europe Review* 33(1): 1–29. https://scholar works.iu.edu/journals/index.php/aeer/.

Buchanan, Donna A. 2018. "Armenia Aeterna: Commemorative Heritage in Sound, Sculpture, and Movement from Bulgaria's Armenian Diaspora." In *Heritage of Death: Landscapes, Sentiment and Practice,* edited by Helaine Silverman and Mattias Friham-mer, 147–63. New York: Routledge.

Creed, Gerald W. 2006. "Reconsidering Community." In *The Seductions of Community: Emancipations, Oppressions, Quandaries,* ed. Gerald W. Creed, 3–22. Santa Fe: School of American Research Press.

Kasparian, John Antranig. 2001. "'We Are Our Mountains': Nation as Nature in the Armenian Struggle for Self-Determination, Nagorno-Karabagh." In *The Making of Nagorno-Karabagh: From Secession to Republic,* edited by Levon Chorbajian, 135–54. London: Palgrave.

Khachatrian, Genja. 1994. "Connection Between Folk Dance and Folk Costume in Ar-menia." In *Dance and Its Socio-Political Aspects, Dance and Costume: Proceedings of the 17th Symposium of the Study Group on Ethnochoreology, International Council for Traditional Music,* 133–34. Nafplion: Peloponnesian Folklore Foundation.

Komitska, Anita, et al. 2000–2001. *Armentsite v Bŭlgariya: Posveshtava se na 1700 god. ot priemaneto na hristiyanstvoto kato dŭrzhavna religiya v Armeniya.* Sofia: Etnografski Institut s Muzei pri BAN.

Krikorian, Onnik. 2009. "Ethnic Rivalry Wins over Kitsch in the Caucasus." *Front-line: Championing Independent Journalism,* May 15. Retrieved November 14, 2011. http://www.frontlineclub.com/blogs/onnikkrikorian/2009/05/festering-wounds -overshadow-eurovision-in-the-south-caucasus.html.

Mitseva, Evgeniya. 2001. *Armentsite v Bŭlgariya: Kultura i identichnost.* Sofia: IMIR.

Musayelyan, Suren. 2009. "Best Performance, Worst Place: Armenia Only Tenth at Eurovision-2009." ArmeniaNow.Com, May 17. Retrieved November 14, 2011. http://www.armenianow.com/news/9846/best_performance_worst_place_arme.

Nercessian, Andy. 2000. "A Look at the Emergence of the Concept of National Culture in Armenia: The Former Soviet Folk Ensemble." *International Review of the Aesthetics and Sociology of Music* 31(1): 79–94.

Office of the High Commissioner for Diaspora Affairs. 2023. "Armenian Diaspora Communities: Bulgaria." Retrieved September 3, 2023. http://diaspora.gov.am/en/diasporas/61/bulgaria.

Paladian, Sirvart. 1972. "Komitas Vardapet and His Contribution to Ethnomusicology." *Ethnomusicology* 16(1): 82–97.

Panossian, Razmik. 1998. "Between Ambivalence and Intrusion: Politics and Identity in Armenia-Diaspora Relations." *Diaspora* 7(2): 149–96.

Perman, Tony. 2010. "Dancing in Opposition: *Muchongoyo*, Emotion, and the Politics of Performance in Southeastern Zimbabwe." *Ethnomusicology* 54(3): 425–51.

Petrosian, Emma Kh. 1979. "Totemic Dances of Armenia." In *The Performing Arts: Music and Dance*, edited by John Blacking and Joann W. Kealiinohomoku, 1–6. The Hague: Mouton.

Petrosyan, Hamlet. 2001. "The Sacred Mountain." In *Armenian Folk Arts, Culture, and Identity*, edited by Levon Abrahamian and Nancy Sweezy, 33–39. Bloomington: Indiana University Press.

Safran, William. 1991. "Diasporas in Modern Societies: Myths of Homeland and Return." *Diaspora* 1(1): 83–99.

Salice, Alessandro, Simon Høffding, and Shaun Gallagher. 2019. "Putting Plural Self-Awareness into Practice: The Phenomenology of Expert Musicianship." *Topoi* 38(1): 197–209.

Shay, Anthony. 1999. "Parallel Traditions: State Folk Dance Ensembles and Folk Dance in 'The Field.'" *Dance Research Journal* 31(1): 29–56.

Sheffer, Gabriel. 2006. "Transnationalism and Ethnonational Diasporism." *Diaspora* 15(1): 121–45.

Slobin, Mark. 2012. "The Destiny of 'Diaspora' in Ethnomusicology." In *The Cultural Study of Music: A Critical Introduction*, 2nd ed., edited by Martin Clayton, Trevor Herbert, and Richard Middleton, 94–106. New York: Routledge.

Solomon, Thomas. 2008. "Diverse Diasporas: Multiple Identities in 'Turkish Rap' in Germany." In *Music from Turkey in the Diaspora*, edited by Ursula Hemetek and Hande Sağlam, 77–88. Vienna: Institut für Volksmusikforschung und Ethnomusikologie.

Solomon, Thomas. 2015. "Theorising Diaspora, Hybridity and Music." In *African Musics in Context: Institutions, Culture, Identity*, edited by Thomas Solomon, 319–60. Kampala: Fountain.

Sugarman, Jane C. 2004. "Diasporic Dialogues: Mediated Musics and the Albanian Transnation." In *Identity and the Arts in Diaspora Communities*, edited by Thomas Turino and James Lea, 21–38. Sterling Heights, MI: Harmonie Park.

Tchilingirian, Hratch. 2001. "The Forgotten Diaspora: Bulgarian Armenians After the End of Communism." *Armenian International Magazine* 12(3) [April]: 30.

Tölölyan, Khachig. 1991. "Exile Governments in the Armenian Polity." In *Governments-in-Exile in Contemporary World Politics*, edited by Yossi Shain, 166–87. New York: Routledge.

Tölölyan, Khachig. 1996. "Rethinking *Disapora*(s): Stateless Power in the Transnational Moment." *Diaspora* 5(1): 3–36.

Tölölyan, Khachig. 2000. "Elites and Institutions in the Armenian Transnation." *Diaspora* 9(1): 107–36.

Turino, Thomas. 1999. "Signs of Imagination, Identity, and Experience: A Peircian Semiotic Theory for Music." *Ethnomusicology* 43(2): 221–55.

Turino, Thomas. 2000. *Nationalists, Cosmopolitans, and Popular Music in Zimbabwe.* Chicago: University of Chicago Press.

Turino, Thomas. 2003. "Are We Global Yet? Globalist Discourse, Cultural Formations and the Study of Zimbabwean Popular Music." *British Journal of Ethnomusicology* 12(2): 51–79.

Turino, Thomas. 2004. "Introduction: Identity and the Arts in Diaspora." In *Identity and the Arts in Diaspora Communities*, edited by Thomas Turino and James Lea, 3–19. Sterling Heights, MI: Harmonie Park.

Turino, Thomas. 2008. *Music as Social Life: The Politics of Participation.* Chicago: University of Chicago Press.

Waal, Thomas de. 2003. *Black Garden: Armenia and Azerbaijan Through Peace and War.* New York: New York University Press.

Waal, Thomas de. 2010. *The Caucasus: An Introduction.* Oxford: Oxford University Press.

Wong, Deborah. 2012. *Speak It Louder: Asian Americans Making Music.* New York: Routledge.

Yazedjian, Ani. 2004. "Reconstructing the Armenian: The Genocide as a Cultural Marker in the Reification of Armenian Identity." In *Identity and the Arts in Diaspora Communities*, edited by Thomas Turino and James Lea, 39–50. Sterling Heights, MI: Harmonie Park.

3 Making a Jewish Neighborhood

In-Group/Out-Group Sonic Dynamics and
Affective Leverage in an Argentine Soccer Stadium

EDUARDO HERRERA

On a rainy Sunday afternoon I stood outside the Estadio Don León Kolbowski, home turf of Club Atlético Atlanta, a Division 3 team associated with the neighborhood of Villa Crespo, Buenos Aires. As I waited for the police to open the gates to the north section, where the most hardcore fans sit, I started talking to a group of young men carrying yellow and blue flags, equally colorful bass drums with a cymbal on top (*bombo con platillo*), a snare drum, and a trumpet. They asked me what my team was and looked perplexed when they learned I have liked several different soccer teams throughout my life. "I would change religion before changing clubs," one of them said. Soccer fandom in this city occurs at a much larger scale than in most places around the world. Buenos Aires has eight Division 1 teams (*Liga Profesional*) in the larger metropolitan area and dozens of Division 2 (*Primera Nacional*) and Division 3 (*Primera B*) teams that play in the sixty-nine stadiums located around the city. For most of these teams, fandom is closely tied to their home neighborhood and most prominently displayed by wearing team colors, tagging walls and neighborhoods with graffiti, and singing a vast repertoire of stadium songs that proclaim life-long love, encourage the team, and memorialize local histories, members of the community, and meaningful events. At the same time, many chants make fun of, bully, and even threaten fans and players of opposing teams using wit, slurs, and creative—and sometimes problematic—metaphors. For many fans, team alliance is a deeply engrained aspect of the self, a habit that is experienced as deep and perdurable, shared with people they interact with on an everyday basis and grounded mainly in the local neighborhood. A club like Atlanta is likely to elicit more passion and commitment than the country's national team, to the point where neighborhood

Fig. 3.1. Panoramic view of Estadio Don León Kolbowski, capacity fourteen thousand. Photo by the author.

soccer identity often trumps national. It is not uncommon for fans supporting the national team to foreground their neighborhood alliance.[1]

The neighborhood of Villa Crespo has long been associated with the Jewish community in Buenos Aires. The local soccer team, Club Atlético Atlanta, has been home to Jewish players, fans, and club executives throughout its history. Like other teams associated with Jewish communities around the world—Anderlecht, Ajax, Bayern Munich, Rome, and the Tottenham Hotspurs—rivals of Atlanta have used Jewishness as the basis for taunts, heckling, and outright violence.[2] The most salient of these practices are the chants that find vulnerability in this association with religion/ethnicity and mobilize it in the affective realm. On March 16, 2021, with COVID-19 restrictions in effect, fans of the team Chacarita Juniors were recorded on the streets singing a blatantly antisemitic chant before an encounter with the team Atlanta:[3]

> Aquí viene Chaca por el callejón
> Matando judíos para hacer jabón.
>
> Here comes Chaca, down the alley
> Killing Jews to make soap.

The terrifying connotations of those lyrics and the emotional response that they elicit are amplified if we consider, as Judith Butler suggests, that "vulnerability is enhanced by assembling" (Butler 2016, 12). Though most fans of Atlanta are not, in fact, Jewish, they experience the association of their neighborhood

with the Jewish community. Their vulnerability does not emerge from precarity but from history. As individuals, they might find themselves offended but not directly affected by antisemitic remarks. As a group, however, their vulnerability is dramatically augmented, and my intent is to understand the role that chants have in this increased emotional response.[4] Building on Ranaan Rein's ground-breaking book *Fútbol, Jews, and the Making of Argentina*, I claim that in-group/out-group sonic dynamics among the fans and rivals of Club Atlético Atlanta contribute significantly to grounding the relation between the neighborhood of Villa Crespo and Jewishness more broadly. The associations between Villa Crespo, Atlanta, and Jewishness are dialogically constructed by fans and rivals alike, so it is not only important to see how they are created and re-created by the repertoires shared with each other (their in-group), but also what others (the out-group) sing *at* them. The performance of fandom and its sonic components becomes a crucial aspect of this dialogue between in- and out-group, creating a lived experience that is hard to replace.

In brief, I start from a simple thesis: General soccer fandom, at its most basic level, functions much more as an affinity group than an identity group. A common interest allows people to connect and find themselves sharing emotions with each other, but this sharing takes place in what Scheve and Ismer (2013, 412), following Tuomela (2006), call an I-mode of shared emotions. Assembled individuals see themselves in others around them and have similar emotional reactions. I have an emotion and it is iconic of that of others. I-mode. But certain experiences can ground fandom in a different, perhaps more profound way, and strong in-group/out-group dynamics, especially those created by means of violence or the threat of violence, can transform the experience of those emotions from a collective I-mode—this affects me in a similar way as it affects others in my group—to a we-mode: this affects us.[5] There is a deliberate use of a vulnerability to generate a negative emotional response, what I call an *affective leverage*.[6] This affective leverage emerges from a perceived threat from an out-group so that it shifts this engagement from an I-mode to a we-mode emotional experience.

The first concept in this thesis that must be clarified here is my use of the words *collective emotion*. Following ethnomusicologist Tony Perman's definition of *emotion* as a "process of evaluation and response to signs that alter important ideas and habits of the self," we can consider that collective emotions not only alter *shared* ideas and habits but are interpreted on the basis of values that have been built on that very sharedness (Perman 2010, 434). At the basis of this process of emotion appraisal, individual values become secondary to group affiliation as the individual is precisely de-individuated (Herrera 2018, 489f.). Anyone's identification (or lack of same) with Jewishness as basis for that process of evaluation and response to the perceived threat then becomes secondary and substituted by the collective identification as (us) the Jewish team. These instances contribute to the formation of a collective memory that promotes a long-term emotional convergence and the basis for integration into an affective group.[7]

My argument is that Jewishness is used as affective leverage to insult, break, and degrade Atlanta fans who, perceiving a threat to their in-group, cling more tightly to a collective emotional disposition. In his examination of the phenomenological work of Edith Stein concerning communal experiences (2000 [1922]) and empathy theory (1917), the philosopher Thomas Szanto argues that when we experience shared emotions "there is a plurality [of individual] subjects 'constituting' a plural subject, and eventually constituting a supra-individual or 'communal experiential stream of experiences' of which the given emotion is an experiential part" (Szanto 2015, 506–7).[8] Atlanta fans, as individual subjects, experience being the target of out-group taunts and attacks (chants, hate speech, online posts, and actual physical confrontation). All of these are strengthened by association with instances of antisemitism in Argentina writ large. By being the targets of this mobilization of Jewishness as a type of vulnerability, fans transition from experiencing collective emotions as a plurality of individuals (I-mode) to experiencing them as plural subjects (we-mode) (von Scheve and Ismer 2013, 412). The sociologists Christian von Scheve and Sven Ismer describe how this kind of transition may occur in assemblies of individuals sharing certain beliefs and desires who then become aware of similar emotional reactions on the part of others. "For example," they write, "participants in the Arab Spring protest marches may initially have come together out of individual discontentment with the regime, collectively expressing 'I-mode' anger and indignation. Being assembled in large crowds and subjected to contagious face-to-face processes may then have heightened awareness of shared beliefs and desires and promoted the emergence of a common social identity, leading to the experience of corresponding 'we-mode' emotions" (ibid.). In a parallel way, the mobilization of Jewishness as a type of vulnerability to demean fans of Atlanta, whether Jewish or not, causes an experience of collective emotions grounded within the affinity space of fandom. The I-mode of appraising emotions ("I am not Jewish; therefore, this is not directly about me, even if I disapprove of antisemitism") is replaced by a we-mode ("this affront is against Us, regardless of ethnicity or religious affiliation") (Szanto 2015, 506).

Fandom

At the core of this study is what is known as fandom, an uneven social universe that may participate intermittently in both affinity and identity. On one hand, identity groups share situationally dependent constellations of habits that are foregrounded "to present ourselves to ourselves and to others, but also involve habits that others perceive in us as salient" (Turino 2008, 95). The dialogical basis of identity groups makes them inseparable from power dynamics in which outsiders can label us, name us for what they think we are. Name calling is ultimately a speech act, what Butler describes as finding out "how you are regarded[,] . . . summed up by a name that you yourself did not know and never chose" since we are "quite in spite of ourselves, vulnerable to, and affected by, discourses we never chose" (Butler 2016, 16, 24). On the other hand, fandom often resembles more what Kiri Miller has called affinity spaces. Miller suggests that affinity spaces are different from identity groups in that they create "a sense of connection across differences—not necessarily [an] 'imagined community,' but mutual understanding and common ground" (Miller 2012, 7). In other words, sometimes fandom cuts across identity groups (class, gender, ethnicity, race, social formations) and generates groupings irrespective of difference. The works of Pablo Alabarces, José Garriga Zucal, María Verónica Moreira, and Javier Bundio have positioned the concept of *aguante* (roughly translating to "resilience, courage, bravado, endurance, stoicism, and even fearlessness in physical confrontation") as a key element in understanding Argentine fandom, and I would add, at the center of the shared affinity (Alabarces, Garriga Zucal, and Moreira 2008; Alabarces 2012; Bundio 2012; see also Achondo 2022). Repeated performances of fandom, the reiterative and citational practice of going to the stadium, spending time with others, and engaging in collective synchronized moving and sounding result in embodied signs of *aguante* (Herrera 2018, 474–75). Techniques of the body, reiterative gestures, ways of singing, tattoos, scars, and even drinking to the limit all give fandom a concrete materiality that cuts across identity groups and is based on common ground.

Implicit Audiences

In previous work I have discussed how the participatory nature of sounding and moving in synchrony while chanting in the soccer stadium can lead to increased feelings of belonging that progress to states of de-individuation (Herrera 2018; see also Hiel, Hautman, Cornelis, and De Clercq 2007, 172). In this chapter I move away from the aspects of chanting that can be described as participatory—doing it together with others when having broad participation is more important than such other values as competency and quality—and instead consider the impact of soccer chanting as a practice directed toward opposing teams and fans. Visiting crowds and, in their absence, the ubiquitous television and cellphone cameras constantly remind audiences that they are being watched, heard, and recorded. Alice Rogers has suggested that this awareness during an essentially participatory activity adds a new role to those described by Turino as the roles of participants and potential participants (Turino 2008, 26). Rogers calls this new role that of *inherent audiences*, "people who are not potential participants, but are instead expected by participants to passively interact with the music" (Rogers 2016, 50). The usefulness of thinking about this new role is that it provides a way to understand that participatory practices may imply a potential listener who can be the object of the performance.[9] Just as in political protests, the target of a chant—the president of the rival club, the opposing fans themselves—might not be present. Still, mediation via YouTube, news outlets, or television broadcasts allows fans to imagine that their intended targets might one day be listening.

Whether the songs highlight the courage of the team, the unwavering support of the fans, and the cowardice of the opponents or whether they attempt to break, emasculate, or discriminate against the rivals, chants retell club histories and folklore, showcase their myths and their legends, and bring forth the best and the worst of stereotypes about their fans. Through chants and songs, the neighborhood, the region, and the nation are being presented and represented by both members and opponents.[10] But with Atlanta, something else is also at stake. Although in Buenos Aires there is a long tradition of soccer fandom being an informal expression of neighborhood identity, the association of soccer with Jewishness (or ethnicity, for that matter) is quite exceptional.[11] That forced identity grouping, imposed from the outside, creates a vulnerability that has historically made the team and its fans the targeted inherent audiences of antisemitism.

Atlanta, the Jewish Team

Numbering somewhere between 185,000 and 230,000, the Argentine Jewish community is the largest in Latin America and the sixth largest in the world outside Israel. Villa Crespo became a common destination for Jewish immigrants during the early twentieth century, so much so that it earned the neighborhood the moniker "Villa Kreplach" after the Ashkenazi and Sephardic dumpling. Yet it is worth noting that Villa Crespo is also home to Italian, Spanish, Arab, Armenian, Greek, Japanese, German, and French immigrants, while other neighborhoods in Buenos Aires such as Once have a significant Jewish population (Rein 2014, 10). Moreover, two other teams that began their history in Villa Crespo, Argentinos Juniors and Chacarita, were never associated with Jewishness and have in fact been some of the major perpetrators of antisemitic attacks. Marcelo Cosin, a longtime resident of Villa Crespo and fan of Atlanta, affirms that you cannot separate neighborhood, Atlanta, and Jewishness. Notice the centrality of singing in his account: "'In Villa Crespo one must be fan of Atlanta. You are born with a yellow and blue shirt. You walk to the stadium. You take Corrientes or Camargo [S]treet and eight blocks later you are in Humbolt, the street that sounds the most like Bohemians and Russians. They will sing at you 'the Russian's field, we are going to burn,' and you respond[,] 'The Russians, the Russians, the Russians will stick it up yours. . . . [The Jewish neighborhood of] Once smells like money. Villa Crespo smells like gefilte fish and sometimes pizza.'"[12]

Club Atlético Atlanta was founded in October 1904 by a young group of soccer fans from the Monserrat neighborhood, slightly east of Villa Crespo. At that time, football clubs became the main example of a large number of "civic associations" in Buenos Aires that were "trying to fill vacuums created by a rapidly expanding city and a weak government that could not or would not provide what the inhabitants wanted" in terms of social services and recreational activities (Horowitz 2017, 270). Like libraries or schools, amateur football clubs became part of everyday community life and were central to the social life of neighborhoods.[13] Promptly Atlanta became part of the organized amateur soccer activity in the city with its various categories. Moreover, the club became an important place for organizing social events; its tango dance parties became a significant source of income and provided young Jews "a possible avenue for meeting and dating young people of other ethnicities" (Rein 2014, 54, 80).

In spite of its growth, the club did not have a stadium until 1922, and the habit of wandering across Buenos Aires for games earned it the nickname *los bohemios*. It was also only in the 1920s that the neighborhood of Villa Crespo became an immigration destination for Central and Eastern European Jews. The linking of the Atlanta club with the Jewish community only began in the 1950s, however, when Atlanta started recruiting some Jewish players (not many) and developed a visible Jewish presence among its fans and administrators, most notably with the presidency of León Kolbowski from 1959 to 1969 (Rein 2018, 54). Under Kolbowski, Atlanta saw some of its most successful years. Still, Raanan Rein argues, Jewishness "was an identity imposed to the club by the fans of rival teams, and to a lesser degree, by the media" (Rein 2013, 70). The association stuck, and Atlanta's first international tour in 1963 was to Israel, where it played the national team and Maccabi Tel Aviv (69). In the collective imagination the Bohemios were now also connected with the notion of the "wandering Jew."

Atlanta joined the professional soccer league in 1931. In 1942 the club acquired a space for its headquarters, and during the following decades it added new teams in different sports such as handball and basketball. The club's new stadium, built in 1960, was renamed the León Kolbowski Stadium after its former president in 2000 (see figure 3.2). Today, Club Atlético Atlanta hosts competitions in indoor soccer, handball, boxing, roller skating, diverse martial arts, and ping pong, and provides the members with a swimming pool, children's music classes, childcare, activities for children with special needs, and dance classes (see figure 3.3). The flagship team, however, is still its male soccer team.

Whereas in the 1960s Atlanta was moderately successful for a team that was not one of the five major clubs in Argentina, between 1979 and 2008 the football club and its fans had little to celebrate. The team's performances became incredibly erratic, and the club failed to accomplish anything significant, having been relegated to Division 3 with sporadic periods in Division 2. The club's self-written history refers to this period as "tragic" and describes it as being "one step away from the abyss."[14] Euphoric moments were few and far between for Atlanta fans, and the players described as "not so much sleeping giants as

Fig. 3.2. "Estadio Don León Kolbowski (Club Atlético Atlanta)," screen capture from "100 años de Atlanta en Villa Crespo," Atlanta TV Oficial, https://www.youtube.com/watch?v=OrYcRcoXKbs&t=2s.

Fig. 3.3. Advertisement for multiple activities offered at the Club Atlético Atlanta (2019). Courtesy of Club Atlético Atlanta Sitio Oficial, https://www.caatlanta.com.ar/.

in a semi-permanent coma."[15] In 2016 the team was only one win away from achieving promotion when it lost at home before a full stadium, breaking the hearts of many hopeful fans. The next two seasons showed similarly frustrating results, but in the 2018–2019 season Atlanta reached second place in the league and celebrated once again having achieved promotion to Division 2. The streets of Villa Crespo exploded with joy, and spirits were high for months. As usual, chanting was a central way in which fans celebrated the advancement, both in small settings and in the streets.

> Veo, veo—¿qué ves?
> Una cosa—¿qué es?
> Que Atlanta ya se va de la B
> Para nunca más volver

> I see, I see—What do you see?
> One thing—What thing?
> That Atlanta is leaving the B League
> And is never coming back.

Atlanta's story, full of highs and lows, of collective euphoria and dysphoria, is the essence of the shared experience of fandom. The excitement felt in a

Fig. 3.4. Atlanta fans celebrating the promotion to the second division (2019).
Screen captures from a public post on "Universo Bohemio," Facebook, https://www.
facebook.com/UNIVERSO-BOHEMIO-230860560261060/.

season-defining goal, a save by a goalkeeper that avoids a last-minute equalizer,
a bad call from a referee that triggers the demise of a team member—all are embodied memories that emotionally ground fandom. These emotion-filled recol-
lections are continually relived as fans retell the stories of these moments with
pleasurable detail and similar experiences are sought after. Although the good
moments, the euphoric ones, form an important part of the bonding that takes
place, research concerning group psychology has demonstrated that dysphoric
moments, those of extreme unhappiness or sadness, lead to greater social cohesion than do euphoric experiences (Newson et al. 2018, 676). Within this logic,
antisemitism has been mobilized as a tactic to diminish and break Atlanta's fans.
The use of Jewishness as affective leverage by opponents becomes an instance in
which solidarity and community are sedimented in unwanted experiences.

Mobilizing Jewishness as Vulnerability

Among the ways in which Jewishness has been mobilized as affective leverage
is incorporating into song hurtful moments in the history of the Jewish community in Argentina. Of these, two stand out: the suicide bombing of the Israeli
embassy in Argentina on March 17, 1992, and the bombing of the Asociación

Mutual Israelita Argentina (Israeli-Argentine Mutual Association) on July 18, 1994 (Rein 2014, 146). Although yet to be solved, the attacks seem to have been organized by Hezbollah as retribution for stopping nuclear exchanges between Argentina and Iran. In the stadium, the story is embraced by rivals:

Señores voy a contarles
Lo que pasó en la embajada:
Pusimos un auto-bomba
Y no les ha quedado nada.

Hicieron una marcha, todos los israelitas
Para que no pongan bombas
Los hinchas de Chacarita.

Hay que matarlos a todos mamá.
Que no quede ni un judío.
Hay que matarlos a todos mamá
Que se mueran todos juntos.

—

Gentlemen, I'm going to tell you
What happened at the embassy:
We set off a car-bomb
And you have nothing left.

All Israelites organized a march
To stop the placing of bombs
By Chacarita fans.

We must kill them all, Mom.
No Jew shall remain.
We must kill them all, Mom.
They should all die together.

*   *   *

Les volamos la embajada.
Les volamos la mutual.
Solo les queda la cancha.
Se la vamos a quemar.

Les volamos la embajada.
Les volamos la mutua.
Les vamos a quemar la cancha.
Para que no jodan más.

Que cagada, que cagada.
No tienen hinchada,
No tienen embajada.

—

We blew up the embassy.

> We blew up the Mutual.
> All you have left is the pitch.
> We are going to burn that.
>
> We blew up the embassy.
> We blew up the Mutual.
> We are going to burn your pitch.
> So that you stop fucking with us.
>
> What a shame, what a shame.
> They don't have fans,
> They don't have an embassy.

Some sanctions have been imposed on teams whose fans have engaged in these kinds of practices, but historically there has been a systematic and latent antisemitism even at the highest echelons of the Argentine Football Association. Take, for example, Julio Grondona, president of the association from 1979 until his death in 2014, who, responding to a journalist who asked him why there had only been one Jewish referee in Division 1 matches, said:

> GRONDONA: Porque no creo que muchos judíos puedan ser referees.
> JOURNALIST: ¿Por qué?
> GRONDONA: Porque es difícil ser referee. Ellos nunca buscan lo difícil.
> JOURNALIST: [laughs uncomfortably]
> GRONDONA: Muchísimos amigos mios son judíos.
>
> GRONDONA: Because I don't think many Jews can be referees.
> JOURNALIST: Why?
> GRONDONA: Because it is difficult to be a referee, and they never go for what is difficult.
> JOURNALIST: [laughs uncomfortably]
> GRONDONA: Many of my friends are Jews.[16]

Collective demonstrations of antisemitism have been even more pervasive than individual discrimination. Atlanta's main rivals, Chacarita, Defensores de Belgrano, Platense, All Boys, and Argentinos Juniors, have used the word *Jews* as if it were an insult and have found multiple ways of using Jewishness as an entry point to break Atlanta fans' spirits. In 2000, for example, the core fans of the team Defensores de Belgrano received the team by throwing soap as players entered the field while hissing in imitation of the sound of gas chambers.[17] On November 30, 2002, fans of Club Atlético All Boys displayed a banner that took advantage of two near-homophones, the word *nací* ("was born") and the word *Nazi* (see fig.3.5).[18]

Antisemitic chants such as those quoted at the beginning of this section, though partly gone from the stadium, have continued circulating, mainly in social media or public places outside the field (e.g., the incidents mentioned at the beginning of this chapter in 2021). Fans of the team All Boys, for example,

Fig. 3.5. Fans holding a banner that says, "I was born in Floresta." In Spanish, *born* is "nací," a near homophone of *Nazi*. Published in *La Nación* (Buenos Aires), March 5, 2003, https://www.lanacion.com.ar/deportes/futbol/discriminacion-nid478419.

continue to use Jewishness as affective leverage when they post chant lyrics in which circumcision is brought up as an index of both Jewish cowardice and a supposed invasion only solved by their "return" to Israel:

> Ruso, ay que cagada,
> Vos sos judio porque la tenes cortada.
> ¿A que viniste? Hacé un favor,
> Si a la salida vos corres como un cagón?

> Ruso, naciste gallina,
> Y gallina moriras.
> Junto con los de Chicago
> Son la mierda nacional.[19]
> —

> Russian, what a fuckup,
> You are a Jew since you have it snipped.
> Why did you come, please,
> If when we exit you run like a coward?

> Russian, you were born a chicken
> And a chicken you will die.
> Together with [the team] Chicago
> You are the national shit.[20]

*   *   *

> Tienen la pija cortada no se por qué.
> Usan un gorrito raro no se por qué.
> Invadieron argentina no se por qué.
> Vállanse para Israel.

> Their dick is snipped, I don't know why.
> They wear a weird little hat, I don't know why.
> They invaded Argentina, I don't know why.
> Go back to Israel.

In the comments posted on a YouTube video featuring this chant as sung in the stadium, it is not uncommon to find comments such as the one posted by Fernando Serrano (online name):

> Ya deberias saber muy bien que las cargadas a los judios no es con intención de herir a los judios propiamente dichos, sino hacía los hinchas de Atlanta que les molesta ser llamados judios, es solo eso.
>
> ---
>
> You should know well that making fun of Jews is not with the intention of hurting Jewish people themselves, but fans of Atlanta who dislike being called Jews, just that.[21]

Despite the "we are just joking" dismissal of the antisemitic nature of the lyrics, antisemitic chants have been rapidly denounced and immediate actions have been taken to penalize the teams and fans responsible. Yet the apparent exile of the chants from the stadium does not mean that they have stopped circulating. Most frequently, these chants are brought up in social media sites or public places outside the field—after all, the incidents mentioned at the beginning of this chapter in 2021 happened on the streets.

Jewishness imposed by the out-group has been difficult to avoid, but to be sure, Atlanta fans themselves have to some degree embraced it and made it part of their identity. In 2012, when Atlanta won against the recently demoted River Plate, a traditional powerhouse in Argentina, Atlanta fans quickly took the opportunity to gloat on social media. River Plate fans are often referred to as "gallinas" (chickens or hens). In some instances, Atlanta fans used a picture of the Wailing Wall to make fun of the suffering rivals: "Chickens in the wall they deserve: the Wailing one." The same day, a famous Atlanta blogger cleverly posted the cover of a Kosher cookbook to explain what Jewish people could do with chicken (Rein 2014, 172).

Final Thoughts

That same rainy Sunday afternoon in which my lack of committed fandom had led to the statement "I would change religion before changing clubs," I had another memorable moment, one that I have documented elsewhere (Herrera 2018, 486). There must have been only about a thousand fans behind the Atlanta goal that night, and the cold, gloomy weather and the slowness of the match had lowered the energy. One of the rousers seemed quite annoyed that not everybody was singing. The rouser, as expected, started yelling, "Vamos, vamos, vamos!," and was visibly agitated. People got a little louder, but apparently not loud enough. The rouser then yelled at least three times, "Por que no se fueron a platea, judíos de mierda? (Why didn't you go to the seated stands, you fucking Jews?)," the assumption being that the more expensive seats would be more appropriate for the wealthier and less committed Jewish fans. With this, the crowd went significantly quieter. By screaming that question the rouser had crossed a line, behaving improperly in a space where there is usually very high tolerance. The lack of support for the rouser that was marked by the uncomfortable silence put him at odds precisely with common goals of the social participatory experience. By being singled out and left alone in his actions, the rouser became marked as a failure in a space where collective participation is the goal. The misuse of Jewishness as affective leverage to incite people to cheer had failed.

In Buenos Aires, soccer club and neighborhood are entangled; they are mutually constituted (Rein 2014; Frydenberg 2008). Topophilia, the love of place that many scholars have associated with football fandom, begins in the neighborhood and has its most important center in the stadium (Bale 2001, 92). But while neighborhood belonging is a common source of fan affinity and identity in Argentina, ethnicity is not. What is particular about this case is that the sonic attacks directed at fans mobilize Jewishness as a vulnerability even among those who, apart from being Atlanta fans, are not Jewish. It remains for further study that an underexplored aspect of this mobilization has to do with the intersectional nature of insults deployed at the stadium focusing on race, class, and sexual orientation. These aspects of identity become additional vulnerabilities that can be used through sound in a semiotically dense way to deploy offenses that would be unlikely uttered by lone individuals. What is certain is that whether fueled by antisemitism or by a more nuanced desire to "other" rivals, Jewishness is used as affective leverage, thus giving opponents the upper hand by exploiting a perceived source of vulnerability in the opposing team. Complementing this process is the embrace by Atlanta fans themselves of an imposed and often unwarranted Jewishness in order to sonically ground the experience of fandom.

This chapter foregrounds the way in which sounding together is a central factor in the social process of consolidating affinity (fandom). And while language is at the center of the sounding, this language still needs to be performed collectively in order to generate affective leverage. The creation of in-group/out-group dynamics among fans is the result of a social process performed most vividly through sound and movement, not as a solo experience but as a participatory, collective one. And in this sense, this soccer-centric experience resembles many instances in which shared emotion is constitutive of solidarity. But here, part of the collective subjectivity is constructed by listening, by being the target of the sonic event, the result of a dystopia built on vulnerability and otherness.

Notes

Thank you to the editors, anonymous reviewers, and those who provided feedback to an early paper version of this chapter at the 45th World Conference of the International Council for Traditional Music, Bangkok, Thailand, July 11–17, 2019.

1. For an example of thinking about soccer outside national or global communities, see Bale 2000.

2. Antisemitism in soccer around the world seems to be on the rise. In May 2021 the Belgian Football Association denounced Club Brugge's player Noa Lang for celebrating his team's title with a chant aimed at the fans of the team Anderlecht, singing, "I'd rather die than be a sporting Jew" (Agence France-Presse, "Brugge Star Investigated for Anti-semitic Chant," *WorldSoccerTalk*, May 22, 2021, https://worldsoccertalk.com/2021/05/22/brugge-star-investigated-for-joining-anti-semtic-chant/). Since 2015 the chant "My father was in the commandos / my mother was in the SS / together they burned Jews / 'cause Jews burn the best" seems to have quickly spread out from Netherlands and Belgium. Fans of the Dutch team Ajax, as well as other clubs associated with the Jewish community such as the Tottenham Hotspurs, Bayern Munich, and Roma have experienced an increased amount of discrimination from their rivals including Nazi salutes, antisemitic chants, and hissing sounds imitating gases and indexing the Holocaust (Cnaan Liphsiz, "Belgian Soccer Fans Sing Chant About Burning Jews," *Jewish Telegraphic Agency*, December 20, 2018, https://www.jta.org/quick-reads/belgian-soccer-fans-sing-chant-about-burning-jews). Ajax has frequently been harassed by fans of Anderlecht (Rotterdam), and Tottenham, nicknamed the Yids, has been attacked by fans of Chelsea, Liverpool, and West Ham.

3. See JPE, "Video: Los cantos antisemitas de la hinchada de Chacarita antes del partido con Atlanta," *Clarín*, March 17, 2021, https://www.clarin.com/deportes/video-cantos-antisemitas-hinchada-chacarita-partido-atlanta_0_MY7WAknmu.html. For a video see the tweet of @physicscastaway https://twitter.com/physicastaway/status/1371984350179364866.

4. Butler writes, "Vulnerability is not a subjective disposition. Rather, it characterizes a relation to a field of objects, forces, and passions that impinge on or affect us in some way. As a way of being related to what is not me and not fully masterable, vulnerability is a kind of relationship that belongs to that ambiguous region in which receptivity and responsiveness are not clearly separable from one another, and not distinguished as separate moments in a sequence; indeed, where receptivity and responsiveness become the basis for mobilizing vulnerability rather than engaging in its destructive denial" (Butler 2016, 25).

5. For parallels, see this volume's introduction, where Perman and Fiol expand on interkinesthetic affectivity and the ways music participates in creating a sense of responsibility for the sounds and actions of others.

6. I owe the concept of affective leverage to ethnomusicologist David McDonald.

7. See Scheve and Ismer (2013) for a discussion about the symbolic foundation of collective emotions.

8. Szanto is quoting Edith Stein (2000, 113f).

9. I am thinking of how street protests are directed at or against something, singing "Happy Birthday" at a gathering is directed at the celebrant, or religious participatory singing may be directed at a deity or deities.

10. Martha Newson has hypothesized that the aggressive behavior of some soccer fans might not be the result of social maladjustment, but may instead emerge from high degrees of social bonding and feelings of out-group threat that "embolden acts of hostility and self-sacrifice as efforts to defend one's psychological brothers-in-arms" (Newson et al. 2018, 677).

11. For similarities to the relation between neighborhood and fandom, see S. Stein 1988, 73.

12. Marcelo Cosin, "Villa Crespo," Letter to *La Nación* (Buenos Aires), January 2013, published on Facebook on September 8, 2017, https://www.facebook.com/notes/marcelo -cosin/villa-crespo/10151293777124999/.

13. According to the official history of the club, the name is supposed to refer either to the U.S. city that had recently suffered an earthquake or to a U.S. battleship that had arrived at the city of Buenos Aires. See Club Atlético Atlanta: Sitio Oficial, http://www .caatlanta.com.ar/historia-2.

14. Club Atlético Atlanta, "Historia," https://www.caatlanta.com.ar/historia-2.

15. In 1991 the Bohemios became the first AFA-affiliated club to declare bankruptcy. Dan Edwards, "Atlanta's Fairytale Run Comes to an End," *Buenos Aires Times*, October 21, 2017, https://www.batimes.com.ar/news/sports/atlantas-fairytale-run-comes-to-an -end.phtml.

16. For the interview see https://www.youtube.com/watch?v=YnTJ_DEEQpk, taken from the television show *El Sello* from TyC Sports, 2003. It is disturbing that the comments to this video are predominantly supportive of Grondona's statements.

17. Hernán Zin, "De cánticos y racism en las tribunas," *20 minutos,* August 28, 2011, https://blogs.20minutos.es/enguerra/2011/08/28/de-canticos-y-racismo-en-las-tribunas/.

18. Alejandro Rebossio, "Xenofobia en las gradas argentinas: Bolivia exige sanciones por cánticos racistas durante un partido del Independiente y el Boca," *El Pais*, Buenos Aires, March 10, 2009. See also Carlos Beer, "Discriminación." *La Nación* (Buenos Aires), March 5, 2009, https://www.lanacion.com.ar/deportes/futbol/discriminacion-nid478419.

19. See https://www.youtube.com/watch?v=o-j9sbFP3XI.

20. See ibid.

21. See https://www.youtube.com/watch?v=o-j9sbFP3XI&lc=Ugy7icOCwBCApCV _i1J4AaABAg.

Bibliography

Achondo, Luis. 2022. "Musical Messaging: The Social and Anti-Social Affordances of WhatsApp in the Football Culture of the Latin American Southern Cone." *Twentieth-Century Music* 19(3): 517–36.]

Alabarces, Pablo. 2012. *Crónicas del aguante: Fútbol, violencia y política.* Buenos Aires: Capital Intelectual.

Alabarces, Pablo, José Garriga Zucal, and María Verónica Moreira. 2008. "El 'aguante' y las hinchadas argentinas: Una relación violenta." *Horizontes Antropológicos* 14(30): 113–36.

Bale, John. 2001. "The Changing Face of Football: Stadiums and Communities." *Soccer and Society* 1:91–101.

Bundio, Javier. 2012. "Dinámicas de difusión del canto en un estadio de fútbol." *VIII Jornadas de Sociología de la Universidad Nacional de La Plata "Argentina en el escenario latinoamericano actual: Debates desde las ciencias sociales"* 1–8. http://jornadassociologia .fahce.unlp.edu.ar/vii-jornadas-2012/actas/Bundio2.pdf/view?searchterm=Bundio.

Butler, Judith. 2016. "Rethinking Vulnerability and Resistance." In *Vulnerability in Resistance*, edited by Judith Butler, Zeynep Gambetti, and Leticia Sabsay, 12–27. Durham, NC: Duke University Press.

Frydenberg, Julio D. 2008. *Historia Social del fútbol: Del amateurismo a la profesionalización.* Buenos Aires: Siglo Veintiuno.

Herrera, Eduardo. 2018. "Masculinity, Violence, and Soccer Chants: The Sonic Potentials of Participatory Sounding-in-Synchrony." *Ethnomusicology* 62(3): 470–99.

Hiel, Alain van, Lobke Hautman, Ilse Cornelis, and Barbara De Clercq. 2007. "Football Hooliganism: Comparing Self-Awareness and Social Identity Theory Explanations." *Journal of Community and Applied Social Psychology* 17(3): 169–86.

Horowitz, Joel. 2017. "Soccer Clubs and Civic Associations in the Political World of Buenos Aires Prior to 1943." *Soccer and Society* 18(2–3): 270–85.

Miller, Kiri. 2012. *Playing Along: Digital Games, YouTube, and Virtual Performance.* Oxford: Oxford University Press.

Newson, Martha, Tiago Bortolini, Michael Buhrmester, Silvio Ricardo da Silva, Jefferson Nicássio Queiroga de Aquino, and Harvey Whitehouse. 2018. "Brazil's Football Warriors: Social Bonding and Inter-Group Violence." *Evolution and Human Behavior* 39(6): 675–83.

Perman, Tony. 2010. "Dancing in Opposition: Muchongoyo, Emotion, and the Politics of Performance in Southeastern Zimbabwe." *Ethnomusicology* 54(3): 425–51.

Rein, Raanan. 2013. "Fútbol, etnicidad y otredad: El Club Atlético Atlanta de Buenos Aires." *Iberoamericana* 13(50): 65–78.

Rein, Raanan. 2014. *Fútbol, Jews, and the Making of Argentina.* Stanford: Stanford University Press.

Rein, Raanan. 2018. "El caudillo de Villa Crespo: León Kolbowski al frente del Club Atlético Atlanta." *Legado* 11:51–65.

Rogers, Alice. 2016. "'For the Union Makes Us Strong': Protest Music in the 1989–90 Pittston Strike." Master's thesis, University of Maryland, College Park.

Stein, Edith. 1989. *On the Problem of Empathy.* Washington, DC: Institute of Carmelite Studies. First published in 1917.

Stein, Edith. 2000. *Philosophy of Psychology and the Humanities.* Washington, DC: Institute of Carmelite Studies. First published in 1922.

Stein, Steve. 1988. "The Case of Soccer in Early Twentieth-Century Lima." In *Sport and Society in Latin America*, ed. Joseph L. Arbena, 63–84. Westport, CT: Greenwood.

Szanto, Thomas. 2015. "Collective Emotions, Normativity, and Empathy: A Steinian Account." *Human Studies* 38:503–27.

Tuomela, Raimo. 2006. "Joint Intention, We-Mode and I-Mode." *Midwest Studies in Philosophy* 30:35–58.

Turino, Thomas. 2008. *Music as Social Life: The Politics of Participation.* Chicago: University of Chicago Press.

von Scheve, Christian, and Sven Ismer. 2013. "Towards a Theory of Collective Emotions." *Emotion Review* 5(4): 406–13.

4 Assembling Indigenous Communities

The Making of South Africa's Intellectual Property Laws Amendment Act of 2013

VEIT ERLMANN

Much has been said over the course of the past two decades about the emergence of indigenous knowledge as a new subject matter of traditional intellectual property (IP) rights or sui generis rights germane to the special nature of indigenous forms of knowledge. In this chapter I seek to disrupt the prevailing narrative that indigenous knowledge represents something of a new frontier, a challenge to which the law merely responds and that, consequently, indigenous knowledge and intellectual property law share the same conceptual space as two stories neither of which can be told without the other being evoked in the same breath. In contrast to this narrative, I offer an account of how this coupling of indigenous knowledge and intellectual property law is part of a broader process in which various practices and forms of indigenous subjectivity are not a priori given but are the result of the qualities and capacities that are attributed to such subjectivities by various actors building and being entangled in complex assemblages of political power, scientific knowledge, and legal technicalities. In concrete terms, the chapter reviews the making of the Intellectual Property Laws Amendment Act 28 of 2013 in the Portfolio Committee on Trade and Industry of the South African National Assembly from 2010 to 2013.

Alternately hailed as pioneering or denounced as unworkable, the act unites what was a patchwork of international and regional instruments, covenants, doctrines, and statutes pertaining to copyright, trademark, design, and performer protection under an umbrella piece of national legislation by inserting a host of novel provisions into the country's existing intellectual property framework. Key to this effort and the focus of this paper is the fact that, apart from recognizing and protecting performances of traditional works, providing for the recognition and registration of indigenous designs, and the recognition of indigenous terms and expressions as trademarks, the act also vests rights of ownership in "traditional works" and "expressions of folklore" in "indigenous communities."

I narrate the work of the committee in chronological order, dividing the three-year process of passing the act into three phases: an initial period of about half a year in which the focus was on the government's proposed IP policy, followed by a prolonged phase of more than a year filled with hearings and workshops, and last, a relatively brief wrap-up period of redrafting. Drawing on the substantial body of documents and audiorecordings generated by the committee during this period and on several visits to its meetings and interviews with experts and other commentators, the chapter forwards an ethnographically informed theory of legislative practice in the context of the sticky encounter between state policy, democratic-representative politics, and the messy reality of cultural production on the ground. More particularly, it attends to the practices, techniques, and technicalities involved in the assemblage and representation of indigeneity.

In what follows I am using the terms *assemblage, representation*, and *indigeneity* to highlight the parallels, disjunctures, and slippages between legal, political, and anthropological forms of knowledge and the authority they afford to legal experts, politicians, and anthropologists to speak for or about indigenous people. A term such as *indigenous community* is less a descriptor of an existing social or cultural reality than it is a project of discursive bricolage. Excavated from the rubble of a ruinous history and combining the most disparate and unlikely of cultural and natural elements and circulating these elements through a variety of technologies of representation including law, the rules of parliamentary procedure, and expert knowledge, the concept reflects diverging epistemologies and serves different material interests. For instance, it allows the Portfolio Committee to constitute and legitimize itself as the representation of the indigenous body politic even where the views of the oldest and most vulnerable indigenous population, the Khoisan, are not taken into account. For the copyright expert, on the other hand, the indigenous community is little more than an anomaly that differs fundamentally from core tenets of the liberal imagination such as the rights-bearing, private property-holding individual. For the anthropologist, finally, the indigenous community is a painful reminder of its own long-standing complicity with colonial models of social being around which indigenous people were summoned to assemble in ways that negate indigenous views of what is in-born. At the same time, anthropologists frequently find themselves caught in a dilemma. On one hand, they desire to support indigenous people seeking redress for abuses of their traditional knowledge practices. But on the other hand, they are likely to insist on the anti-essentialist critique of the image of coherent communities that the act envisages as the basis for property claims, pointing to the attendant risk of reinscribing some of the very racial, ethnic, and cultural categories of colonial and apartheid ideology that have been used to subordinate indigenous people.

It is against this hypostatization of supposedly self-evident categories such as "indigenous community" that I reposition indigeneity as a fragile conglomeration of strategies, material practices, and rhetorical tropes that reflect as they enact a politics of belonging through which indigenous people may form various kinds of attachment to place, time, and expressive practices.

The Returns of Policy

Empirical inquiry, Jean-François Bayart reminds us in his pioneering *The State in Africa*, "passes through a narrow door" (2009, 271). My door, or rather, the first of several doors that I am inviting the reader to pass through, is policy. We are in room E249, one of several rooms in an annex to the Houses of Parliament in which portfolio and ad hoc committees are briefed on white papers, debate legislation on anything from forestry and the sugar industry to gambling, fine-tune legal definitions, and hold public hearings or question government officials. It is February 16, 2010, and the Portfolio Committee on Trade and Industry is holding its first meeting on what from now on will be referred to as the Intellectual Property Laws Amendment Bill (B 8B-2010). Members are seated in rows of benches facing each other, much as in the British Houses of Parliament. The governing African National Congress Party (ANC) occupies one block while the Democratic Alliance (DA), the largest opposition party, shares its block with smaller parties. Having settled, then, into our seats, we listen to officials from the Department of Trade and Industry brief MPs about the government's decision to introduce B 8B-2010. The presentation consists of four parts. In the first part the officials walk the committee through the bill's history from its origin in 1999 in the government's Policy on Indigenous Knowledge Systems to its eventual adoption by the cabinet in 2004. This is followed by a short discussion of the findings of a Regulatory Impact Assessment weighing the costs and benefits of the proposed legislation. In the remaining two, and for present purposes most crucial sections, the MPs are first given a rough overview of the international debates surrounding the protection of traditional knowledge by means of intellectual property systems, from the 1976 Tunis Model Law to the World Intellectual Property Organization (WIPO)'s Intergovernmental Committee on Intellectual Property and Genetic Resources, Traditional Knowledge and Folklore, established in 2000. The presentation ends—and my discussion begins—with eight policy goals:

To provide a legal framework for protection of the rights of traditional knowledge holder

To empower communities to commercialize and trade on indigenous knowledge

To bring TK holders into the mainstream of the economy

To improve the livelihoods of IK holders and communities
To benefit the national economy
To conserve the environment
To prevent misappropriation or bio-piracy; and
To prevent exploitation without recognition

At first blush, the list seems obvious enough. Surely, nobody would seriously object to protecting indigenous communities and their knowledge. And no South
African politician would put his or her career at risk by denying the need for
improvement in the living conditions of the country's marginalized citizens. Yet,
as the ensuing discussion demonstrates, the MPs transpose the policy goals to
quite a different discursive register. Rather than the international policy context
or the Regulatory Assessment, they home in on a flurry of colorful terms dotting
the slides: "tradition," "respect," "sustainability," "misappropriation," "benefit
sharing," "livelihoods" and, above all, "indigenous community."

How could it be determined, one MP asks, "who the originator of the indigenous knowledge was, whether this could be a person or a community?"
Another member is outraged that the meteoric rise to global stardom of Johnny
Clegg, one of South Africa's most popular musicians of all time, was allegedly
made possible because of his having "appropriated" Zulu *maskandi* street music
without permission from the community. "So Johnny Clegg would no longer be
able to write songs anymore," S. Marais of the opposition Democratic Alliance
counters, "but would have to refer to the community from which his songs may
have originated? Suddenly I cannot do what I am anymore, because I must go
to a community. Who is this community?"

"What about traditional music?," his party colleague Tim Harris chimes in.
Had the committee considered this important issue given that a lot of indigenous
music went to the West, where others made a fortune exploiting it commer-
cially? Had Solomon Linda's song "Mbube" not existed for centuries, and was it
therefore not an original work eligible for protection? And what is the meaning
of tradition anyway? Would it not be more appropriate to talk about indigenous
culture because it "succinctly captures the impact of colonial oppression?"

Yet other MPs take the conversation into patent law and the plant kingdom,
specifically *hoodia*, a succulent shrub that from time immemorial has served as
the source of water, food and energy in the country's arid northwestern region
and for a short while was touted as an appetite suppressor and anti-obesity
drug, and *rooibos*, a shrub that exclusively grows in the Cederberg region north
of Cape Town and is appreciated around the globe to make a tea rich in anti-
oxidants, calcium, and iron. "Whose intellectual property is hoodia?," one MP
inquires. "Unlike champagne, sherry and port," Alan Jeftha, a member of the
Standing Advisory Committee on Intellectual Property and an advisor to the
Department of Trade and Industry responds, "rooibos producers have been

on the receiving end, where rooibos had been registered as a trademark in the U.S.A. So, who really owns the rights to rooibos?"

"Communities and cultures are now mixed," someone on the opposition benches interjects. "Many items that the bill seeks to protect do not belong to a specific individual or group but rather to South Africa as a whole, for example, rooibos." No, another MP across the aisle retorts, "it belongs to the indigenous community of San who have inhabited the region for millennia."

Clearly, the government's attempt to frame its policy objectives against the backdrop of a coherent set of taken-for-granted parameters such as 'economy', 'environment', 'communities' and 'rights' does not immediately fit into the frame through which the MPs view their world. Theirs is more of an assortment of moral and cultural considerations and their valences in the unpredictable encounter with local ideas and sensibilities. But if in the minds of MPs the moral aspects of indigenous knowledge are beyond dispute, what about its legal valences? How can the moral be translated into the law? How can the state, in turn, stage itself as a moral authority through or despite the politics of lawmaking? What role do the technicalities of IP protection play within these processes? What theoretical models are available to think through the interplay of policy and parliamentary process beyond the obsession in conventional policy studies with efficiency and "smart" policy making?

In his book *Seeing Like a State* James Scott describes legibility and simplification as the central problems of modern statecraft (Scott 1998). By creating a standard whereby complex local practices can be monitored and transformed into a legible and administratively convenient format, he argues, the state is able to shape the social worlds in its care according to its agenda of "improvement." Scott identifies four conditions that account for the catastrophic failure of many of such "well-intentioned" projects of social engineering: the administrative simplifications enabling reordering of society and nature; a "high-modernist" confidence in science and technology as key elements in economic growth and the mastery of nature; an authoritarian state that uses its coercive power to put this ideology into practice; and last, a prostrate civil society that lacks the ability to resist this strategy (3–5). Of course, South Africa is not an authoritarian state, and civil society there is anything but docile. Nonetheless, some aspects of Scott's gloss of the developmental state as a great simplifier may well fit the fixation in South African state policies on grand transformative schemes—and their frequent running aground on the shores of global markets, local cultural sensitivities, and rampant corruption. At the same time, however, the idea that simplification is the central mechanism of state power by which state-initiated projects of social transformation can either succeed or fail is, well, too simple. The power of the state to shape social relations does not, or at least not primarily, reside in its ability to reduce the order of things to its lowest common denominator but in quite the opposite. Agency, the power to turn heterogeneity into homogeneity, uncertainty into predictability, a multiplicity of voices into a singularity of purpose, is never inherent in any one actor alone, be it the state or an obscure policy document. It requires the intertwining of a multitude of actors in a never-ending process of aligning competing prerogatives, interests, rationales, and moralities.

This premise, roughly modeled on science and technology studies and actor-network theory scholarship, calls for a different approach to the study of policy, one that rejects established rational-choice, instrumentalist paradigms that cast policy as a linear process leading from an analysis of a problem and the selection of a response to the implementation of a chosen course of action to the evaluation of the desired outcome (Shore, Wright, and Però 2011). Instead, here the focus is on the way policy making always revolves around itself; on how success and failure, order and disorder, method and madness are not dia-metrically opposed but co-produce each other in an endless loop. From this perspective, the disconnect between the government's presentation and the committee's impassioned albeit somewhat haphazard reaction might speak not to a failure of the policy so much as to a larger antinomy stemming from the nation-state's endeavor of accommodating difference within the framework of liberal governance and universal rights, on one hand, and the resurgence of the local and ethno-cultural, long believed to have been overcome since the transition to democracy, on the other.

The international debate about the protection of indigenous knowledge is a perfect illustration of these tensions. In the summary of the history of those debates the government appears to pursue two goals. First, it inserts its policy into a narrative of historical continuity and renewal. The policy, the officials seem to suggest, is part of a larger reform effort aimed at restoring the country's ties with the international system of policy diffusion that had largely been severed during apartheid. At the same time, it underscores the post-apartheid state's dual claim as the legitimate heir to the anti-colonial struggle and as the driving force of IP policy innovation in Africa. Second, despite the government's advocacy for the IP needs of the continent, the briefing also serves to garner parliamentary approval for what is ultimately a state-driven and, in part, global system of regulation. But it is precisely by positioning itself as a champion of both South African indigenous property rights and the international IP system that the government is caught in a bind. It must present a narrative in which difference does not undercut law's claims to universality, but at the same time, in foregrounding the material conditions under which indigenous knowledge and cultural expressions have historically been marginalized, the government must also take care to eschew questions about law's complicity in facilitating those very structures of marginalization (Anderson 2009, 114).

But there is more to these tales of global aspiration and national awakening. The history of indigenism and the struggle of indigenous peoples for the protection of their land and their natural and intellectual resources is shot through with subtle semantic nuances and translations that put a different complexion on the all-too-linear story of progress commonly told about that history. These translations appear to move back and forth along a continuum stretching from national interests at one end and indigenous claims at the other, from compartmentalized to holistic models of indigenous intellectual property and its protections, and from communal ownership to state trusteeship.

For example, early covenants such as the 1976 Tunis Model Law on Copyright and the 1977 Model Provisions drafted by a working group of UNESCO and WIPO share a fundamental tension between different types of entitlement. The Tunis Model Law casts the state squarely in the role of the guardian or "competent authority" that owns and is responsible for the regulation of "works of national folklore." But at the same time, it provides for exceptions for noncommercial uses by a public entity such as the state. By contrast, the Model Provisions offer national legislators the option of designating a "competent authority" to administer authors' rights while at the same time vesting ownership of what by then had come to be labeled "expressions of folklore" with the "aboriginal or other traditional communities." It was to take another two decades and the emergence of a broad coalition of indigenous and environmentalist movements for the interdependence of the restitution of ancestral lands, environmental protection, and cultural survival to be recognized in the seminal Convention on Biological Diversity of 1992. Although traditional cultural expressions are mentioned only in passing, the convention marks a significant moment in the shift from the compartmentalized, IP-centric Tunis Model Law and the ambiguities of the Model Provisions toward a more organicist view of indigenous culture as an integrated system of interwoven and mutually enabling practices that include "expressions of folklore" and distinct (and for the most part historically disparaged) forms of knowledge production.

By 2005 the drift toward merging folklore and traditional knowledge in some comprehensive system of protections entered its third and decisive phase, culminating in the Revised Provisions for the Protection of Traditional Cultural Expressions/Expressions of Folklore, also produced by WIPO. Apart from introducing the term *traditional cultural expressions*, the document breaks new ground in three ways. In contrast to the 1985 Model Provisions, it for the first time explicitly ties the regulation of folklore to customary law as the normative regulatory framework, regardless of whether the origin of such expressions is attributed to a community or an individual. Second, in addition to nation-states and traditional communities the Revised Provisions recognize indigenous communities as holders of traditional cultural expressions. Third, and perhaps most crucial, in referring to traditional cultural expressions as "expressions of traditional knowledge" instead of "expressions of folklore," WIPO with a scratch of the pen devalued the affective and aesthetic properties of folklore, casting such expressions as mere "carriers or embodiments of *information*" instead (Perlman 2011, 127, emphasis in original).

It is little wonder, then, that, hollowed out, made fungible, and put into circulation in global markets, these expressions merge seamlessly with several of the policy goals referred to above. The way expressions of folklore become legible to policy is through a series of dichotomies. For one, the desire to bring traditional knowledge holders into the mainstream of the economy and make them benefit the national economy is inherited from the largely discredited two economies doctrine developed by the country's second president, Thabo Mbeki. According to Mbeki the South African economy is divided into a developed, formal core, or first economy, and an underdeveloped, informal or second economy in the black townships and the rural periphery. On this logic, poverty can be eradicated by connecting the second economy to the first via a combination of market relations and sustained government intervention rather than by addressing the inequities that have been constitutive to the former ever since the first settlers set foot on South African shores and indigenous people became subsumed under what Peter Drahos, writing about indigenous knowledge in Australia, calls an "extractive property order" (Drahos 2014, 4; see also Cousins 2007; Terreblanche 2002).

A similar dichotomy is implied in the notion that the act is a key vehicle for preventing what the policy refers to as "misappropriation." Lacking historical, local, and indeed legal specificity, it does not offer any concrete prescription for legal or social action. Rather, like its cognate term "cultural appropriation," it is symptomatic of a deeper malaise troubling what Bruno Latour calls "political ecology" (Latour 2004) and its inability to speak to the larger concerns central to the social movements in South Africa and around the world. I refer to the science wars that are currently raging in South African academia. From the early twenty-first century, running parallel to the parliamentary debate about the present act and other measures addressing issues of science, culture, and cognitive justice, a universalist vision of science has struggled to assert itself against an aggressive science phobia framed as decolonial scholarship. The roots of this polarization are traceable to the late 1970s, when many Africanist historians and anthropologists, disillusioned with nationalist and socialist narratives of modernization and development, began to focus more on "history from below," rural communities, ethnicity, and cultural continuities.

In recent years, this legacy of critiquing science in the name of a decolonial politics has given way to a wealth of studies that unpack the entanglement of natural history, colonial history, and indigenous and scientific knowledge practices (Foster 2017; Ives 2017; Osseo-Asare 2014; Tilley 2011). "Colonial science," if it ever existed as a homogenous practice, in this scholarship resembles more a complex set of varied and often discordant interests, epistemologies, and methodologies intersecting with a great variety of political, economic, and historical factors playing out on a global scale at an ever-accelerating pace. It is these developments and the realities they have brought to the fore that both government and decolonial rhetoric fail to recognize, thus resulting in what one critic deplores as a "significant impoverishment of debate on the possibilities for postcolonial (or decolonial) scholarship in South Africa" (Green 2012, 1).

It is from this "identity politics of nature," then, that the term *misappropriation* derives one of its legal valences. Another valence derives from "cultural nationalism." Just as intellectual property law has become a key site for stabilizing traditional knowledge as a type of distinct knowledge, here the construction of this knowledge as the utterly incompatible and forever vulnerable "Other" of science serves to buttress intellectual property law's black-boxing of tradition as occupying a "neutral space, where history and politics informing the term remain in abeyance" (Anderson 2009, 9). As Jane Anderson argues, intellectual property statutes that seek to protect indigenous knowledge differ from intellectual property law in general in the sense that the latter does not distinguish any of its categories in terms of cultural identity. But in order to establish a connection between knowledge and identity and to specify certain forms of practice such as traditional knowledge as unique forms of property, the law must create a "special position." That position is a cultural one. Culture with a capital *C* becomes the "primary trope for identifying and explaining the unique concerns that are brought to intellectual property law by indigenous people" (2009, 10–11).

But as Rosemary Coombe has pointed out, the legal valence of cultural appropriation is a double-edged sword. While ostensibly lending credence to nationalist programs of the preservation and protection of a nation's cultural patrimony, the term also exposes the fallacy, pitfalls, and political counter-effects of this "special position." The rhetoric of cultural nationalism, Coombe tersely suggests, "bears traces of the same logic that defines copyright" (Coombe 1997, 85). As the West exported its concept of Culture to the rest of the world and nations or indigenous people were figured as authors of various cultures, this gesture of recognition was limited to objects of property such as prominent monuments or artifacts of superior or unique aesthetic value. Knowledge and forms of indigenous expression were not included. It has been stated many times but bears repeating: The history of indigenous struggle for empowerment has been a Janus-faced process offering few assurances for identity-oriented politics providing a stable foundation for intellectual property rights in traditional knowledge. On one hand, the very idea of indigeneity has become a tool of identity formation. By successfully coupling the idea to a variety of concepts such as "tradition," "community," "environment" or "ethics" and by contrasting them with the modernist nation-state's failure to formulate a universal vision of social order, indigenism was able to provide to indigenous movements a sense of "moral certitude" (Niezen 2003, 215). But on the other, by embracing the language of human rights and intellectual property to pursue its agenda of self-determination and cultural survival, the indigenous people's movement also had to reckon with another conundrum. With the prospect of national sovereignty having all but dwindled, in order to assert these rights indigenous people had to channel their demands through the labyrinth of international human rights organizations and its complex system of legal instruments, conferences, and NGO consultants, all of which in one way or another are committed to the principles of liberal individualism and its attendant property rights (Engle 2010).

The third dichotomy follows from the protectionism of the former stance against misappropriation. The idea that state policy should empower communities to commercialize and trade on indigenous knowledge assumes the prior existence of a divide in which indigenous knowledge is cocooned in some trade-free zone from which it, empowered by a state that sees itself as a custodian of cultural diversity, emerges into a free-trade one. This storyline obviously disregards the fact that South Africans have exchanged their knowledge and cultural expressions for thousands of years. More significant, however, it also overlooks a subtler dynamic at the heart of cultural processes in the twenty-first century, a dynamic that is about more than the intrusion of commerce into a sphere once glorified as that of the traditional, ideal, immaterial, or transcendent from which indigenous culture had to be protected. It is a dynamic, too, that has little to do with the picture of indigenous culture as somehow being destined to provide the raw material for the Western aesthetic imagination while at the same time condemning indigenous people to languishing in a state of cultural deprivation as passive consumers of Western cultural goods. Rather, as numerous scholars have pointed out, this dynamic culture in the global South is conceived as an open-ended process in which "human subjects and cultural objects produce, reproduce, and refashion each other" (Comaroff and Comaroff 2009, 29).

The call for commercializing indigenous knowledge and traditional cultural expressions also entails competing valences for indigenous subjectivity and agency. For one thing, it interpellates indigenous people to represent themselves to each other and the state in the terms set by the policy, thereby objectifying and ultimately domesticating them by once again containing them within the confines of their presumed collective identity, now legitimized by the act. But, ironically, the cultural commodity at the same time enjoins indigenous subjects to conceive of themselves as individuals. Indigenous producers are empowered to model themselves on the inspired, risk-taking "cultural entrepreneur" of the creative industries, while consumers find themselves forever engaged in a quest for individual selfhood mediated by ethnological knowledge and vernacular artifacts.

To summarize, the government's IK policy clearly generates its own discursive bubble, insulating it from the world around it. The policy not only constructs indigenous knowledge as a particular kind of object, but it also creates, to paraphrase James Ferguson, an epistemological frame around this object in terms of which it may be interpreted and rendered into its own language (Ferguson 1990). In this way policy becomes a prisoner of itself, trapped within its own narrow parameters and dichotomies and doomed to endlessly repeat the cycle of ambitious input and unsuccessful output. Steeped as it is in outmoded socioeconomic and cultural categories, it is virtually impossible to judge it by any criteria other than its own. A fragile assembly or "retrotopia," to use Zygmunt Bauman's apt phrase, of both retrogressive and forward-looking goals, it is unable to set out a practical agenda for transcending past and present injustices (Bauman 2017).

Expert Systems: Certifying Tradition

October 18 and 19, 2010. Parliament is now in its fourth term, and the committee, after months of buzzing with marginalia and trivialities, seems to have reached an impasse. With the ANC-led coalition coming out in support of the bill's communitarian gist and the oppositional Democratic Alliance taking a more conventional stance centered on copyright holders, the party lines are firmly drawn. But not only will the MPs have to come to an agreement about some of the key provisions of the bill, they yet have to engage with its finer points in more than a tangential fashion. With the ball thus squarely in their court, the critical question is how a bill can be molded into a statute that at once mirrors party politics and the interests of members' constituencies, stands up to judicial review, and is in line with South Africa's treaty obligations. For the ethnographer, however, who has patiently read countless minutes and silently followed hours of debate about tea, Zulu guitar music, and the cultural differences between Ndebele and Zulu-speaking knowledge holders, the larger question hovering about all this is less a moral, political, or normative one than it is one of technicalities. By what device, rhetorical gesture, protocol, or logic, he wonders, do all these divergent actors and interests become legible by and for the law? What technologies are needed to bring them into some form of association? And how might such associations be made durable enough to outlast the next meeting, the next term, the adoption by the full assembly, or simply the test of time?

Enter the expert. The committee had invited half a dozen legal experts, members of the National House of Traditional Leaders, and representatives of a broad spectrum of copyright-related trade associations, collection societies, and private individuals to speak to the documents they had submitted before the hearings began. The verdict is devastating. While acknowledging the urgent need to protect indigenous knowledge, speaker after speaker comes forward listing the bill's innumerable flaws. In the roughly fifteen submissions, four main areas of contention stand out: First, the bill does not provide for sui generis legislation; second, it is potentially unconstitutional; third, it is unworkable; and fourth, some of its definitions in regard to the subsistence of copyright are inconsistent.[1]

For instance, speaking for the 320-member Academic and Non-Fiction Authors' Association of South Africa (ANFASA), its chairman, Sihawukele Ngubane, worries that instead of providing protection for traditional knowledge and traditional cultural expressions by crafting new legislation, the bill inserts into existing "host acts" such as the Trade Marks Act, the Copyright Act, the Designs Act, and the Performers' Protection Act provisions that might be incompatible with the fundamentals of these acts' subject matter, thereby potentially compromising the integrity of those acts.

Meanwhile, Owen Dean, a leading authority on copyright and chairman of the law firm Spoor & Fischer, submits that by "clothing traditional knowledge as intellectual property and seeking to protect it as a species of intellectual property" the bill will encounter "serious and unacceptable problems in the context of South Africa's international treaty obligations, such as the national treatment requirement of TRIPS [Agreement on Trade-Related Aspects of Intellectual Property Rights], which provides that South Africa must give subjects of other member countries the same copyright protection as it gives to its own subjects." The bill, he states, "does not provide for this and thus places South Africa in breach of the TRIPS Agreement." Furthermore, he argues, there is a real chance that the bill will also run afoul of the South African Constitution, most notably the so-called property clause (sec. 25(1)). This clause prohibits "arbitrary deprivation of property" but the bill, Dean contends, does just that. It provides for the protection of traditional works that have been in the public domain to henceforth be "owned" by communities and for the commercial exploitation of these works to be controlled by a National Trust Fund, without any provision being made for the funds derived from such exploitation to be paid out to any community. Arguably, then, the bill wants to have it both ways. "Having in a sense granted rights in such property to a community, with the one hand," he notes, "the bill then removes such right from the community and places it in the hands of the Fund, with the other hand."

As the hearings wear on, others get into the practicalities of administering the legislation. Thus, representatives for the Southern African Music Rights Organization (SAMRO) and the South African Music Performance Rights Association

(SAMPRA), collecting societies for performance rights and sound recordings, respectively, decry the bloated administrative structures that must be established for dealing with the new subject matter. To wit, the bill provides for the creation of no fewer than four bodies: a National Council, a National Database for the recording of traditional knowledge and cultural expressions, a National Trust, and a National Trust Fund. On top of this, the behemoth section 28C(8) also provides that each community must formulate a protocol, preferably based on the UNESCO-WIPO Model Provisions, that identifies the community and sets out the terms under which indigenous works may be licensed to third parties. Noble as the ideas behind these institutions may be—from representing the indigenous communities and documenting and promoting the commercialization of traditional cultural expressions to administering funds flowing from such commercialization—they would create "complete and utter chaos," SAMPRA head Nicholas Motsatse cautions. Specifically, it is the provisions of section 9, which relate to sound recordings, that would complicate the negotiation of royalties at the heart of the modus operandi of collection societies the world over. These provisions would introduce into the process a swarm of parties that "clearly have no direct or indirect interest in a copyright in sound recording," in other words, the copyright owners and users of literary works, cinematographic films, broadcasts, published editions, and computer programs, he states.

Another stumbling block is the proposal for categories of eligible works. Here section 2(1) introduces the "traditional work" as a new category and defines it as "a literary work, an artistic work or a musical work which is recognised by an indigenous community as a work having an indigenous origin and a traditional character." As is well known, one of the most critical, globally recognized criterion for a work to be eligible for copyright protection is that such a work, in the phrasing of the South African statute, is "reduced to a material form" (section 2(2). But here is the rub. The bill does incorporate the materiality requirement for traditional works into section 2(2), but in subsection 2(2B) it adds the phrase "or communicated to the public." This right of communication to the public—which is, if not entirely nonexistent, is poorly defined under the current Copyright Act—is generally meant to include an exclusive right enabling authors to allow communication to the public of their works so that members of the public may access them from a place and at a time of their choosing, that is, primarily by online streaming. Hence, several scenarios may be envisioned for the subsistence of copyright in traditional works, one as quixotic as the other. The first situation would involve a work that has neither been reduced to a material form nor communicated to the public. While it seems reasonable to assume that a great number of traditional works fall within the first category, that of never having been reduced to a material form, and as such will continue to be denied protection, the proposed alternative path to protection via a right of communication to the public likewise will do little to make such works eligible for copyright. One of the reasons for this cul-de-sac is that even in the rare instance when such communication to the public were to occur, it is unclear who the "public" is. Assuming, ANFASA notes, that in South Africa's racially and ethnically divided climate the indigenous community from which the work in question originated, in addition to being the "author," frequently also constitutes the "public" the work is communicated to, the effect would be a situation in which author and public, absurdly, are one and the same, and where, accordingly, an author's "internal communication amounts to communicating with the public."

More than the technicalities, though, what draws the harshest criticism by far are the key requirements for the subsistence of copyright. Beyond originality and fixation, the definitions of authorship and ownership, speaking as they do to some of the most contentious issues of identity and belonging, are paramount. Predictably, most submissions waste no time in attacking the definition of the author head-on. Thus, the spokesperson of the collecting society DALRO (Dramatic, Artistic and Literary Rights Organization) takes issue with the concept of "traditional community" as the author and first and only owner of the copyright. According to section 1(1)(j), that community is

> any recognizable community of people originated in or historically settled in a geographic area or areas located within the borders of the Republic, as such borders existed at the date of commencement of the Intellectual Property Laws Amendment Act, 2011, characterized by social, cultural and economic conditions which distinguish them from other sections of the national community, and who identify themselves and are recognized by other groups as a distinct collective.

Not only are the terms indigenous and traditional used interchangeably to qualify the word community, the spokesperson says, they do not have the same meaning: "The Greek community in South Africa would arguably qualify as a *traditional* community, but obviously not an *indigenous* community." Organization member Gcina Mhlophe, the lone artist present at the hearings, adds another example:

> Let us assume an author wishes to write a book telling a traditional Zulu children's tale. Which Zulu community is entitled to lay claim to the story? The entire KwaZulu-Natal region? But what about the Zulu people in the Eastern Cape; do they have less of a claim? And what if the writer actually wrote the story as told by a Ndebele story-teller, which would then have slight Ndebele nuances when compared to the original Zulu version. Does this divest the Zulu people of their claim? And what if the Ndebele story-teller was from Bulawayo and not from Nelspruit?

Mhlophe's point is amplified by Anjuli Maistry, an attorney working for the Legal Resource Center, South Africa's largest human rights law clinic, founded in 1979. The definition of "indigenous community," she argues, as any community of people living within the borders of the republic or that historically lived in the geographic area located within the borders of the republic, is out of step with reality. Communities do not define themselves in spatial terms. Boundaries constantly expand and contract depending on many factors. In fact, in the Restitution of Land Rights Act *community* is defined as "any group of persons whose rights in land are derived from shared rules determining access to land held in common by such group, and includes any part of such group." In other words, Maistry notes, "communities define themselves through social and political organization at layered levels and through shared customary laws, values, identity and mutual recognition of culture."

But the lack of clarity in the definition of "traditional community" is more than the result of poor drafting. And it does more than brush aside established copyright norms according to which subsistence depends on a set of criteria linked to an individual author (such as the author's citizenship, domicile, or time of death) or juristic person (incorporation under South African law). Section 1(1) waters these norms down to the level of identity politics, or, as Nick Motsatse put it to the author, the bill amounts to little more than "populist sound bites."

After two days of hearings, countless inconsistencies and drafting errors have been pointed out, crucial terms have been shown to lack clarity, and the concept of the indigenous has never been more elusive. The chasm that had already opened between the members of the governing party and the opposition in the first months of sittings now has widened to the point where virtually the entire legal fraternity finds itself aligned with the opposition. Clearly, in this moment of what one might call constructive ambiguity, the fate of the bill is hanging in the balance.

To reiterate the main point of my argument, my interest is not in assessing the bill's conformity with established legal norms or how well it translates policy into an effective legal framework. Nor am I concerned with its inevitable failure. What I am interested in is the question of what the act does, irrespective of the fact that by 2023 it was still awaiting implementation. How might certain, usually unspoken a priori embedded in the concept of indigenous communities, and the knowledge they are seeking jurisdiction over, serve as podiums from which legal claims can be made not only about that knowledge itself but, more important, about law's interpretational sovereignty in defining it? How do these a priori enable or constrain specific understandings of the material, as it were, aspects of tradition, identity, citizenship, or even land? And how might the objects of such claims in turn react to some of those a priori of legal knowledge in ways that might upset such sovereignty?

June 7, 2011. The committee reflects on the blow the public hearings of October and November 2010 had dealt to B 8–2010, laying to rest the notion that it would move on to a vote in the full National Assembly anytime soon. For the past couple of weeks the committee has heard the parliamentary legal advisor review the critical comments offered during last year's hearings and the responses to those comments by the Department of Trade and Industry and the Companies and Intellectual Property Commission, the regulatory body within the Department of Trade and Industry overseeing the registration of intellectual property rights. Although these responses all acknowledged that the bill was breaking new ground, they agreed unanimously that there remain multiple areas of uncertainty and that, ultimately, the committee may be faced with but three choices going forward: to amend, redraft, or withdraw the bill entirely. While the last option meets with a rather lukewarm response, the decision about what further steps might have to be taken in amending or redrafting the bill will preoccupy MPs for several more weeks, laying bare the constraints and the productive force of expert systems in simultaneously masking and creating new realities.

The phrase "expert systems" is owed to the British sociologist Anthony Giddens. Inherent in the discontinuities of modernity, Giddens (1990) argued, are two conflicting mechanisms: the "disembedding" or "lifting out" of social relations from local contexts of interaction and the "reembedding" of these disembedded social relations in local conditions of time and place. Among the former, Giddens distinguishes two such mechanisms: "symbolic tokens" and "expert systems" (21–22). For the purposes of this chapter, it is the latter concept that is particularly useful in unpacking the subtleties of lawmaking in the second, the "definitional" stage of the committee's work. Following Giddens, I take expert systems to be forms of organized knowledge that structure our material, social, and cultural worlds in ways that remove us from our immediate experience of these worlds while simultaneously demanding that we have confidence in the ability of the experts to competently and accurately render a given state of affairs and to re-align it with that experience (34). Examples of such relationships of trust may include the belief in the reliability of the technologies we depend on for our daily lives; the expectation that the validity of expert knowledge is independent from the local, temporal, and personal circumstances in which it is produced or meant to become operative; the sense that the anonymity and alleged impartiality of statistics somehow provide a picture of reality that corresponds, at least in part, with the culturally encoded particulars of one's lived situation; the respect for scientific findings as an objective measure for managing the most intimate aspects of our lives; and last and most crucial for my argument, the confidence that the opaque terminology of lawyers is not some secret code but a means toward the ends of justice.

Of course, such relationships are never stable, especially in contexts of extreme volatility where the experts' say-so frequently clashes with deeply entrenched notions of truth, morality, and social order. These moments of instability and distrust therefore require constant monitoring, certification, and the availability of opportunities for engaging in and sustaining forms of direct communication, or what Giddens calls "facework" (80). The examples Giddens gives of such "facework"—such as people passing one another on a city sidewalk—have a certain scripted, performative aura and as such they are less helpful for my analysis. Although committee meetings are kept on track by a delicate balance of protocol and passionate engagement, I foreground the more improvisatory nature of the meetings, the shifting valences and ambiguities that drive the debate, such as in the following exchange, lightly edited for ease of reading:

> CHAIRPERSON: The committee has already decided to employ consultants, and some names of leading experts, including academics and figures in the industry, have already been put forward.
>
> HARRIS (DA): Everyone agreed that experts were needed on the technical matters; the committee is doing a disservice to the other experts who would advise the committee and who were not present.
>
> SELAU (ANC): It could become disastrous if every political party in this parliamentary committee meeting wanted to bring in experts, each with a different opinion.
>
> GCWABAZA (ANC): These experts are people the committee decided should consult the entire committee, regardless of party.
>
> VAN DER MERWE (PARLIAMENTARY LEGAL ADVISOR): Due to the complexity of the bill, and because of the variety of expertise that was needed, they might need a diverse panel to provide expert opinion.
>
> SELAU: Will any legal experts be among the selected experts? The committee needs to understand they are not in a meeting of lawyers, but in Parliament. Therefore, they should ultimately come up with a report that could go before Parliament for adoption.

The tug of war continues for another round of meetings, with the division between a pro-expert, disembedding-prone stance and a more "embedded" view reflective of South Africa's fractured political and cultural landscape remaining visible throughout. But by June 9, the committee finally resolves that the bill be redrafted by a task team involving the parliamentary legal advisor, the state law advisor, and the legal advisor to the Department of Trade and Industry, and that additional input will be sought from a select group of experts.

That list of experts is worth examining in more detail. In addition to five eminent law professors from universities in the Western Cape Province and one practicing lawyer, it includes the director of the Intellectual Property Division at the World Trade Organization, a member of Natural Justice, an NGO specializing in environmental and human rights law in Africa, and a representative for the Geneva-based (and now defunct) International Centre for Trade and

Sustainable Development. Several aspects of this selection stand out. First, there is, yet again, no practitioner of traditional knowledge. Although by 2010 South Africa had, for instance, become home to a vibrant, well-organized sector of traditional healthcare providers offering services in a wide range of fields from prenatal care and male circumcision to alternative medicine, the committee at no point bothered to invite a Khoisan or other indigenous person to share his or her experiences. In fact, none but one of the selected experts appear to have had any professional experience of working with and within indigenous communities in the first place. Finally, most experts are white males who have either graduated from or work at the University of Cape Town and, hence, may be assumed to reproduce the professional habitus and institutional structures governing it.

But the closed-shop atmosphere of this fraternity is not the only disembedding factor determining the bill's destiny. Fast forwarding another couple of weeks to July 25, 2011, we witness another key feature of expert systems: the attempt to gain incontestable sovereignty over competing knowledge claims by deploying what Karl Maton calls techniques of epistemological condensation (Maton 2015). Such techniques involve a variety of strategies such as the recontextualization of the voices of others, the incorporation of other voices into one's own speech by quoting or acknowledging the source of such voices, the open denial of alternative viewpoints, the endorsement of other positions as true, and emphatic forms ("I do believe"). These strategies may also use a wide variety of genres and formats such as bulleted lists, spreadsheets, glossaries, taxonomies, and flow charts. Taken together, these techniques and technologies allow experts to strengthen the "semantic density" of their knowledge claims by compacting a large quantity of seemingly unrelated and simple symbols into smaller units of meaning such as abbreviations, keywords, and definitions. Consequently, the more such symbols are condensed, the stronger the semantic density and epistemic authority of a claim and the smaller the chance that such a claim may be challenged by non-experts.

Law is, of course, no exception to this dynamic, condensation strategies being ubiquitous in a wide range of legal writing, but perhaps nowhere more prominently than in the definitions that frequently make up the first section of a statute. The significance of these naming conventions can hardly be overestimated. The drafting of legislation is a notoriously messy business, constantly shifting between time-honored conventions, the whims of the political actors involved, and the "cold" expertise of seasoned attorneys working in government departments and in Parliament. Yet even during the most unstructured of moments in the committee's deliberations it is the imperative of form that always asserts itself. And so, it bears reiterating what I have argued throughout: Form is what is at the heart of what it means to make law. The preoccupation with form, playing out over weeks and months of seemingly fastidious quibbling, is more than a mere sign of institutional inertia deflecting from the more substantive issues before the committee. Formal language, terminological precision, and procedural continuity are productive forces that have tangible effects on the distribution and the legitimation of power and the meanings people attribute to the web of relationships they find themselves in, often against their will.

To illustrate, let us turn to the series of further meetings held between July 25 and the middle of September of 2011 in which the definition of key terms such as "traditional" and "indigenous" moves to center stage. The former had figured prominently—and at times concurrently with "indigenous"—in the bill from the beginning as "traditional communities," "traditional knowledge," "traditional culture," "traditional context," "traditional music," "traditional cultural expression," "traditional work," and of course, "traditional intellectual property." Having just returned from a conference at the WIPO head office in Geneva, the task team (now rechristened, in the lingo of international politics, "working group") asks that the committee debate the legal advisors' suggestion to split the latter term into two categories: "hereditary" and "derivative" intellectual property. And to clear up the confusion around the simultaneous use of "traditional" and "indigenous," the working group further recommends that the latter term be used only in respect of an "indigenous expression of culture or knowledge," an "indigenous community," or "indigenous origin." But whence the need for a new terminology? The rationale of these amendments, the chairperson of the working group elaborates, stems from several issues that would arise if some of the provisions in the first draft pertaining to the basic requirements of copyright remained unchanged. For example, whereas in the first draft protection was only awarded to "recent" works, by introducing the category of "hereditary" IP, works that have been passed down from generation to generation would also be protected. Or take the example of ownership and transfer. Under the old draft, the National Trust Fund would be the owner of "traditional" knowledge, impeding the ability of communities to govern themselves. In order to mitigate this risk, the group advises that a tripartite distinction be made between hereditary IP owned by the community (or its representative), derivative IP owned by the author or creator, and in the case of IP with an unknown author or creator, owned by the trust.

Remarkably, although much of the foregoing defies ready comprehension, the committee does not feel the slightest inclination to debate this new wording in any depth, instead preferring to rehash some of the same points it had already gone over for more than a year. Rather than unraveling the terminological knot the MPs had tied themselves into, it might thus be more fruitful to examine how legitimation codes manufacture consent. One reason, for instance, for the committee's ready acceptance of the new classification of eligible works may lie in the way the working group pitched the proposed amendments to the meeting. The group framed its work in the form of what Matthew Hall calls "graphic ideology": a flow chart followed by a list of "minor issues" and "major issues" that are further broken down into "resolved" and "still unresolved" issues (Hall 2012, 14). Each of these is then put in relation to basic copyright requirements such as eligibility and ownership and placed within the relevant sections in the "host acts" that are affected by the new language. But what is so remarkable about something as mundane as a couple of PowerPoint slides? What distinguishes the group's way of getting its point across from all the diagrams and fancy fonts that academics or salesmen use to win over audiences at conferences and trade fairs? The way the group resolves the issue of the interchangeable terms "traditional" and "indigenous," I believe, rests on a number of subtle shifts whose logic is not rooted in some unmediated truth or the ability to condense such truth in a single concept but in a sequence of traceable steps. Put another way, epistemic authority in this instance is not achieved by inductively or deductively substantiating what is external to the method being used, but by foregrounding the method itself. The "content," if you will, of the slides is not an argument *for* or *about* something as much as it is a demonstration of the reliability of the argument itself. Beyond simply producing semantic density, the group's presentation rehearses the input-output mechanism underlying legislative work by self-reflexively opening, if only for a moment, the black box of bureaucratic rationality. And closing it again immediately afterwards. We have done our homework, the group seems to reassure the committee. We have gone through the hoops. Trust us.

To reiterate, in settings such as the portfolio committee meetings, expert knowledge is critical in foreclosing the possibility of working through a problem politically, ultimately leaving lawmakers with nothing but the "text" (in the deconstructionist sense where x means y and y is just another "text") as the only way to keep the legislative process moving forward, indeed, to have law. Yet the intertextual chain that ensues from and reproduces condensation also becomes subject to contestation at every turn.[2] In fact, the substitution of "traditional" with the heritage-derivative binary might simply be viewed as weakening semantic density and as an invitation to the committee to query expert knowledge through efforts at rarefaction. The discussion between the MPs and the drafters on July 25, 2011, illustrates the wave-like motion of law and politics, of alternating condensation and rarefaction pushing against each other:

HARRIS (DA): The draft is a vast improvement from what was previously produced. [Still, it] would require individuals to not only read the discrete sections in the four bills related to IK, but the entire body of intellectual property." [This might be complicated for the layman's understanding, especially for indigenous communities.]

LEGAL ADVISOR TO THE DEPARTMENT OF TRADE AND INDUSTRY JOHAN STRY-DOM: I am not a policy maker and reluctant to express myself on matters of policy. Nonetheless, I am concerned about the future process of the legislation, reminding members that it is important that a policy or political stance be adopted on the future approach to the bill.

VAN DER MERWE (PARLIAMENTARY LEGAL ADVISOR): If the committee decides to do further redrafts, the bill could not become a new principal act. The committee would need to reject the bill in toto and start a new one. In addition, the legislation is a continuation of a policy that had been approved by Cabinet. If this is rejected, the whole policy must also be reconsidered.

The specter of failure appears to steer the conversation into calmer waters: procedure ("continuation of policy"), form ("law is complex"), context ("understanding," "protecting people"), and transformation ("make history") are balancing each other out.

In the end, B 8B-2010 was adopted by both houses of the National Assembly and assented to by the president in December 2013. But as of this writing, the act is still waiting to become operative. Meanwhile, opinions about it remain divided, with some praising it as an example of the "positive protection of traditional cultural expressions by intellectual property rights" (Nwauche 2017, 97) and others decrying it as a "cumbersome and ineffectual way of achieving the objective of protecting TK" (Beharie and Shabangu 2014, 359). Yet whatever the flaws or merits of the act, the debate about the proper protection of IK and traditional cultural expressions will continue, and it remains to be seen what alternative models, if any, will eventually materialize. At the very least, such debate may have to look beyond either intellectual property law or some form or other of sui generis legislation by exploring concepts of belonging that transcend both reified notions of community and formal definitions of citizenship that underwrite liberal democracies. Some of the more promising of such concepts, for instance, are those that anchor the protection of indigenous creativity—and, indeed, cultural production globally—in models of socially responsible and ethical conduct. Whether as "artistic citizenship" in which the artist is not only good at his work but also does good (Martin 2006), as an "ethics of response" that calls on the audience to respect the artist and her work (Levinson 1998, 2), or as a non-deontic form of artistic practice that bears habits and values that serve goods that are "internal to the practice" (Bowman 2016, 71), it is these types of civic-ethic dispositions that may inject new energy into what has increasingly become a sterile system of bureaucratic, state-driven, and more often than not, patronizing measures that do more harm than good.[3]

Notes

1. For a comprehensive summary and evaluation of the final act, see Nwauche 2017, 110–43.

2. The term *intertextuality* is to be taken with a grain of salt. While it has little in common with the cross-references between sections of an act—and as such often rests

on prepositions such as "subject to"—it does not incorporate the entire range of meanings intertextuality has in literary theory and deconstruction. The sense in which I use it here is thus meant to convey more of a sense of the self-reproducing circularity of expert systems.

3. For more on this see Erlmann 2022, 156–73.

Bibliography

STATUTE

Intellectual Property Laws Amendment Act 28 of 2013. https://www.gov.za/documents/intellectual-property-laws-amendment-act-0.

SECONDARY LITERATURE

Anderson, Jane E. 2009. *Law, Knowledge, Culture: The Production of Indigenous Knowledge in Intellectual Property Law*. Cheltenham, UK: Edward Elgar.

Bauman, Zygmunt. 2017. *Retrotopia*. London: Polity.

Bayart, Jean-François. 2009. *The State in Africa: The Politics of the Belly*. 2nd ed. London: Polity.

Beharie, Tertia, and Tshepo Shabangu. 2014. "Traditional Knowledge, Traditional Cultural Expressions and Folklore." In *Dean and Dyer Introduction to Intellectual Property Law*, edited by Owen Dean, Alison Dyer, et al., 330–45. Oxford: Oxford University Press.

Bowman, Wayne D. 2016. "Artistry, Ethics, and Citizenship." In *Artistic Citizenship: Artistry, Social Responsibility, and Ethical Praxis*, edited by David J. Elliott, Marissa Silverman, and Wayne D. Bowman, 59–80. New York: Oxford University Press.

Comaroff, John L., and Jean Comaroff. 2009. *Ethnicity, Inc.* Chicago: University of Chicago Press.

Coombe, Rosemary. 1997. "The Properties of Culture and the Possession of Identity: Postcolonial Struggle and the Legal Imagination." In *Borrowed Power: Essays on Cultural Appropriation*, edited by Bruce Ziff and Pratima V. Rao, 74–96. New Brunswick: Rutgers University Press.

Cousins, Ben. 2007. "Agrarian Reform and the 'Two Economies': Transforming South Africa's Countryside." In *The Land Question in South Africa: The Challenge of Transformation and Redistribution*, edited by Lungisile Ntsebeza and Ruth Hall, 220–45. Cape Town: HSRC Press.

Drahos, Peter. 2014. *Intellectual Property, Indigenous People and Their Knowledge*. Cambridge: Cambridge University Press.

Engle, Karen. 2010. *The Elusive Promise of Indigenous Development: Rights, Culture, Strategy*. Durham, NC: Duke University Press.

Erlmann, Veit. 2022. *Lion's Share: Remaking South African Copyright*. Durham, NC: Duke University Press.

Ferguson, James. 1990. *The Anti-Politics Machine: "Development," Depoliticization, and Bureaucratic Power in Lesotho*. Cambridge: Cambridge University Press.

Foster, Laura A. 2017. *Reinventing Hoodia: Peoples, Plants, and Patents in South Africa*. Seattle: University of Washington Press.

Giddens, Anthony. 1990. *The Consequences of Modernity*. Cambridge, UK: Polity.

Green, Lesley. 2012. "Beyond South Africa's 'Indigenous Knowledge-Science' Wars." *South African Journal of Science* 108 (7–8): 1–10.

Hall, Matthew S. 2012. *Government of Paper: The Materiality of Bureaucracy in Urban Pakistan*. Berkeley: University of California Press.

Ives, Sarah. 2017. *Steeped in Heritage: The Racial Politics of South African Rooibos Tea*. Durham, NC: Duke University Press.

Latour, Bruno. 2004. *Politics of Nature: How to Bring the Sciences into Democracy*. Cambridge, MA: Harvard University Press.

Levinson, Jerrold, ed. 1998. *Aesthetics and Ethics: Essays at the Intersection*. Cambridge: Cambridge University Press.

Martin, Randy. 2006. "Artistic Citizenship." In *Artistic Citizenship: A Public Voice for the Arts*, edited by Mary Schmidt Campbell and Randy Martin, 7–26. New York: Routledge.

Maton, Karl. 2015. *Knowledge and Knowers: Towards a Realist Sociology of Education*. New York: Routledge.

Merlan, Francesca. 2009. "Indigeneity: Global and Local." *Current Anthropology* 50(3): 303–33.

Niezen, Ronald. 2003. *The Origins of Indigenism: Human Rights and the Politics of Identity*. Berkeley: University of California Press.

Nwauche, Enyinna. 2017. *The Protection of Traditional Cultural Expressions in Africa*. Cham, Switzerland: Springer.

Osseo-Asare, Abena Dove. 2014. *Bitter Roots: The Search for Healing Plants in Africa*. Chicago: University of Chicago Press.

Perlman, Marc. 2011. "From 'Folklore' to 'Knowledge' in Global Governance." In *Making and Unmaking Intellectual Property: Creative Production in Legal and Cultural Perspective*, edited by Mario Biagioli, Peter Jaszi, and Martha Woodmansee, 115–32. Chicago: University of Chicago Press.

Povinelli, Elizabeth. 2002. *The Cunning of Recognition: Indigenous Alterities and the Making of Australian Multiculturalism*. Durham, NC: Duke University Press.

Scott, James C. 1998. *Seeing Like a State: How Certain Schemes to Improve the Human Condition Have Failed*. New Haven: Yale University Press.

Shore, Cris, Susan Wright, and Davide Però, eds. 2011. *Policy Worlds: Anthropology and the Analysis of Contemporary Power*. New York: Berghahn.

Terreblanche, Sampie. 2002. *A History of Inequality in South Africa, 1652–2002*. Pietermaritzburg, South Africa: University of Natal Press.

Tilley, Helen. 2011. *Africa as a Living Laboratory: Empire, Development, and the Problem of Scientific Knowledge, 1870–1950*. Chicago: University of Chicago Press.

PART II

Feedback

5 Teaching Music as Social Life

Performance-Based Pedagogy in Ethnomusicology

JOANNA BOSSE

In the formative years of what is now contemporary ethnomusicology, scholars debated the very nature of the discipline and how to develop the research methods and methodologies that would contribute to our collective knowledge of music in cultural life while serving to distinguish the field from other types of music research. Cultural anthropology informed our reliance on fieldwork, participant observation, and the quest for musical fluency, or bi-musicality (Hood 1960), which became the centerpieces of our method, inspired by the conviction that the cultural fluency gained by performing musical traditions as well as by observing the performance of masters in a social context was crucial to understanding the role music plays in social life. The epistemological principle that knowledge is formed through embodied experience of performing music in its social context was central to the project of building this new discipline. Ted Solis, engaging the work of Leonard B. Meyer, suggests that performance is an effort to "shed the cognitive distance between ourselves and our 'subjects,' leading us to do what they do, and perhaps even be what they are" (2004, 4). In addition to enabling a stronger, more technical understanding of music and the people who perform it, Anne Rasmussen suggests that learning how to perform also elevates the status of ethnomusicologists from observer to participant in the very contexts that we are trying to understand and document and strengthens the subsequent ethnographic analytic writing by its reliance on the experience of performance (Rasmussen 2004, 215–16).

Over time, courses on ethnomusicological topics began making their way into the curricula of graduate and subsequently undergraduate programs. Once the National Association of Schools of Music (NASM) established a world music curricular accreditation requirement, ethnomusicologists eventually found a permanent place on music faculties across the United States and elsewhere.[1] Doing so required that ethnomusicologists align the newly formed discipline with the more established pedagogical conventions of instruction in Western European art music. In this context, geographical area studies found their place alongside music history courses on style periods, and in many institutions, world music ensembles took their place alongside orchestras, bands, and chamber groups. While the placement was intuitive and sensible from a number of vantage points, in the process an important disconnect was embedded into ethnomusicological instruction in American higher education.

The distribution of musical knowledge into individual performance instruction, ensemble performance, academic classes on music history and theory, and various repertory and technique classes seems sensible in large part because classical music students are required to move through all of these areas in the course of an undergraduate education. Over the course of four years, music majors learn the various intellectual and cognitive, experiential, and embodied ways of knowing classical music (and, increasingly, jazz) that we require of a college-educated musician, even if we generally fall short in the areas of integration and synthesis of that knowledge.

The creation of world music ensembles was originally proposed by Mantle Hood and others as a study group for graduate students in ethnomusicology. The impetus was to augment the more conventional academic study found in ethnomusicology graduate degree programs, which resembled Western classical music curricula at the undergraduate and graduate levels. The ensuing conversation about the role of music performance in ethnomusicological graduate studies and research that took place during the middle years of the twentieth century gave rise to the same observation I am making here, though in the context of undergraduate education: that academic study without performance is deeply flawed in that it runs contrary to the values of ethnomusicologists and the value of ethnomusicological study. In his preface to Hood's *Ethnomusicologist*, Charles Seeger distinguished between "speech knowledge," that is, "knowledge sought and expressed in terms of language," and "music knowledge," which is knowledge gained about music by the making of it (Hood 1971, vii), and suggested that the two are equally important. Given that there were no undergraduate ethnomusicology programs then, the role of performance for undergraduates remained outside the purview of the intense philosophical and practical pedagogical conversation that emerged (Trimillos 2004).

While we might interpret the commonplace role of world music ensembles in graduate ethnomusicology programs to indicate that we have all accepted the value of performance as expressed in those earlier discussions, we might turn to our pedagogical conventions at the undergraduate level to reveal our deepest intellectual habits. In undergraduate music programs (for there are practically no undergraduate ethnomusicology programs, a revelation in itself), students are not funneled through a variety of courses on the same topic, but rather choose one course (often a world music survey or area studies course) to complete their ethnomusicology "requirement."[2] The world music ensembles that have emerged in non-PhD programs have increased in number over the past several decades but provide something more akin to an extracurricular or co-curricular activity than an experience considered core to any degree (Solis 2004, 5). Similarly, the course often lies as an overload in a faculty member's teaching assignment (Rasmussen 2004, 216–17). In this educational context, students may be introduced to the topics of ethnomusicological inquiry, usu-ally framed as an area studies course—music of Africa, Native America, Latin America, and so forth—without the emphasis on experience/doing/performance that resides at the center of our research method; or they may learn to perform the music without necessarily learning anything more about the musical tradi-tion, the people who make it, or the context in which it is made. In short, we have separated the role of performance as an ethnomusicological research strategy from the knowledge about music of various cultural groups more commonly featured in our instruction. More often than not, the latter serves as the degree requirement whereas the former does not.

And so, while our ethnomusicological research method is embodied and engaged, the disembodied default (Kisliuk 2007) has driven the pedagogy of our core undergraduate curricular offerings. As Carol Muller (2011) has noted, the convention employs lectures on or even brief discussion of material deter-mined by the professor followed by listening to a piece of music before moving on to the next lecture topic. Assessments involve writing papers (including the classic ethnography of a concert) and taking tests and quizzes. Occasionally, some faculty may employ a tokenistic approach to participation with hand-clapping exercises, but rarely do they constitute a deliberate and sustained plan for increasing student understanding through performance (see Solis 2011 and Bosse 2011 for notable exceptions). The textbooks central to our field reflect these values—having innovated in the areas of promoting active listening and the sociocultural imaginary of our students—but have contributed very little to an experiential, actively engaged, performance-based ethnomusicological pedagogy.

I argue that the separation of musical knowledge, in the context of under-graduate Western art music studies, into courses about the sociohistorical con-text (musicology), courses in analysis (theory and composition), and courses of (performance), with little scaffolding between them, leaving it to students to generate their own cognitive connective tissue between these domains, is problematic on its own. It fails to take into account the extensive literature concerning college-level learning and the trends in higher education over the last several decades.[3] In the context of ethnomusicology, however, the reality is even more lamentable, for it suggests to undergraduates that the ethnomusicological contribution to collective musical understanding centers only on the academic content, that is, knowledge *about* the music traditions of "othered" cultural groups, rather than the more meaningful and perhaps revolutionary contribution of ethnomusicology to a different kind of theoretical and epistemological understanding of and relation to music itself.

Although we do not collectively discuss this as often as we should, ethnomusicology faculty across the academy (and our like-minded colleagues in related disciplines) are seeking to rectify the epistemological disconnect between our research and undergraduate teaching, forging creative solutions in the context of their local curricula to provide instruction in the various types of musical knowing that ethnomusicological inquiry can provide. Together with other ethnomusicological threshold concepts (Meyer and Land 2003; Timmermans and Meyer 2017), such as the importance of studying music in its cultural context and the value of a comparative approach, the methodological emphasis on *participant* observation, which has generally been understood to indicate experiential, embodied work in performance, is a transformative one that changes the way students understand the topic of musical knowing.

In this chapter I present my own efforts at ending this epistemological disconnect and laying bare the threshold concepts of ethnomusicological inquiry. It is not a perfect model without compromise, but rather a prompt for sustained discussion of how we can establish a greater sense of coherence between inquiry and method within ethnomusicological pedagogies. It is my hope that this conversation will also yield better advocacy for ethnomusicology within the music academy, NASM, and American undergraduate education more broadly.

There are a number of ways in which we might collectively achieve a better alignment of our research method, disciplinary values, and undergraduate pedagogy. A large-scale curricular approach linking various types of courses together might be fruitful. A College Music Society report leans in this direction (Shoehan Campbell et al. 2016). Another tack, one not at all incompatible with the first, is to explore options within the bounds of a single undergraduate course, that is, one course in which various types of learning would be synthesized. This article focuses on the course-based approach, suggesting a basic framework for better articulating our collective disciplinary valuation of experience as a fundamental element of music *as* social life (see, e.g., Barz and Cooley 2008; Berger 2009; Bosse 2015a; DeNora 2000; Friedson 1996;

Hagedorn 2001; Hahn 2007; Kisliuk 1998; Turino 1993, 1999, 2000, 2008; Turino and Lea 2004).

The undergraduate course in question depends on the idiosyncrasies of each institution and faculty appointment. It might be the conventional world music survey, an area studies course, a basic introduction to music, or other type of undergraduate course an ethnomusicologist might find herself teaching. Teaching such a course allows us to work in the curricular context in which we find ourselves, using the conventions of academic freedom in our individual classrooms to attempt disciplinarily grounded pedagogical change. In this chapter I suggest that course-bound options should be characterized by the following five elements, which align foundational elements of ethnomusicological inquiry with the best practices currently articulated in the more broad scholarship of teaching and learning: (1) the course must regularize and normalize performance by including it as a part of every class meeting; (2) measures must be taken to strike the appropriate balance of social safety and risk that your students need to overcome the technical and psychological challenges of performance; (3) student performance must be connected intellectually to the larger learning goals of the class in sustained and meaningful ways; (4) student performance must be assessed in some way, so as to communicate the value you place on the knowledge gained through performance; (5) individual and collective reflection on the lessons learned through performance must be built into the course activities in some way.

Detailing a performance-based approach implemented in a first-year undergraduate course on sub-Saharan African music for non-music majors, this article provides one model for closing the epistemological gap between knowledge *about* and knowledge *of* that I have described above. In addition to providing a more authentic mode of assessment, that is, one that is more closely aligned with what ethnomusicologists do in their research (Wiggins 1989, 1990, 1998; Koh 2017; Montgomery 2002, Svinicki 2005), this approach accomplishes several additional objectives. First, the kinesthetic, subjective, and experiential component of music making brings the topic of discussion and analysis literally into the bodies of students, making the topic more immediate and knowable. Second, through performance students internalize the modes of production under investigation, a move that enables them to reconsider the predominant Western preconception of music as an object (the "piece") to a social process resulting directly from and contributing to social relations (see Rasmussen 2004, 222–23). And third, it can make abstract concepts (theories of social structure, for instance) material by means of musical and social relationships embodied in performance that can then be reflected on via analytical reading, writing, and discussion. Their actual in-class experience teaches them how communities can be formed through performance.

Five Elements of a Performance-Based Pedagogy

Habituating Performance

The successful integration of performance with the more traditional academic modes of inquiry such as reading, writing, and discussion requires that they be placed on equal footing in the course content. The undergraduates with whom I have worked, whether music majors or not, are generally conditioned to consider experiential learning opportunities as the "fun" time that has little consequence for their learning or their grades. Although there may be some rationale for shaping course content in this way, I argue that doing so runs counter to ethnomusicological method, which usually places performance at the center of our research priorities as some of the most important, revelatory, and pleasurable work we do.

Bringing performance into our daily class habits is an important element in helping students regain a trust in their kinesthetic wisdom. It is important to keep this in mind even when working with music majors, who do not necessarily operate from an embodied sense of musical knowledge, in spite of (or perhaps because of) the type of instruction typical of Western European classical music performance.

In my own course, each class meeting was divided into three or four smaller time units. These "building blocks" included time for large-group performance (involving all the students together); a small-group activity of some sort in response to the required reading; group discussion following an additional related prompt like a musical recording, a film, or short in-class reading; and, time permitting, time for each small performance group to work on their projects.

The activities to which we dedicate class time are important indicators of our disciplinary values and articulate what we recognize as knowledge. Placing collective student performance on an equal footing with the discussion of recordings and readings, in-class writings, quizzes, and so forth is but one way I seek to communicate to students that performance is an important context for learning. In most instances, this took place at the start of our class and served as an effective centering device that disconnected students from cell phones and issues of the day. It became almost ritualistic in its constancy at the beginning of our time together.

Students entered the classroom and set about rearranging the tables and chairs to form a U-shaped space, with chairs around the outside of the tables and a large open space in the middle. We then met in the center of this open space and I began by setting the pace by walking and asking them to join me. We then layered various body percussion and vocal lines to create a rhythmic counterpoint that featured cross-rhythms of the sort that we would later find in the African music to be performed (see Solis 2004 and 2011 for a similar approach). In particular, I used this group activity to help prepare them for the performance of West African agbekor undertaken in the second half of the semester. I explained very little in this section of the class, relying on modeling, rote instruction, and repetition. We started with fairly simple interlocking patterns and slowly introduced more complexity as they became familiar with the patterns.

It took me a number of repetitions of this course to find the best way to step students through the various patterns and options in order to ensure that they were proficient in hearing, understanding, and performing cross-rhythms and the various iterations of the timeline of agbekor. In my first attempts I relied on Time Unit Box notation but slowly relinquished that approach for an aural rote method that was more successful.[4] After several times through this course, I have also come to realize the benefits of introducing the notion of a West African timeline very early in the course, breaking up its components and employing mnemonic devices to support their learning. We did not discuss West Africa, timelines, or agbekor until the second half of the semester, but when we did get to this material, students had some ability to at least recognize if not perform the basic elements of the genre. In addition to body percussion and rhythm work, we also made vocalization a part of our practice, and in particular, yodeling, focusing first on that found among the forest peoples of Central African Republic and then, at the close of the semester, with the yodeling found in Shona mbira performance.

Mitigating Risk

My experience with both music majors and non-musicians suggests that all students bring some resistance to the thought of performing traditions that are new to them—especially in front of their peers. Given that the majority of the students in my courses do not identify as musicians or performers of any sort, it is imperative to provide an environment that includes enough risk to make the activity worth doing, while providing enough social safety to ensure that they will feel confident enough to engage at some level, a context in which students feel they can commit to the performance and attempt new and more challenging (for them) things without risk of being punished, whether through grading or social standing.

I mitigated this risk in a number of ways. First, I often broke the larger group of twenty or so students into groups of three to five students and then gave them a part to perform. The reliance on group performance for the in-class work is important. I rarely singled out students individually, they did not perform juries, and the music/dance contexts were always collective in nature. The stronger students in the group were often interested in demonstrating their prowess and emerged to provide some guidance and cover for those who struggled; those who found performance more challenging receded a bit into the safety of the group.

Another element for mitigating risk and encouraging participation among all members of the class was introducing material incrementally, so the small, "doable doses" were easily available to almost all of the students. Even if they felt comfortable only walking in time, they were physically engaged, actively listening, and seeking an opportunity to join more heartily into the mix.

A final element is the lowering of expectations. Students enter music classes (and likely other arts classes) with anxiety about their own "talent" in the area. They often seek to lower my expectations early on in the course, and I also seek to lower their preconceptions about the level of performance required in a college-level course on music. One way to do this is by offering my own imperfections up as an example. Throughout the semester, and especially in the first few weeks as I am introducing the basic elements of music, I find a way to demonstrate a concept by performing myself. For instance, in a demonstration about ornamentation I will often sing heartily with my perfectly imperfect voice, lowering the expectations students might have about virtuosity and what it means to perform competently. Such demonstrations evoke laughter at my expense and give me an opportunity to convey that virtuosity and perfection are not the goal.

The mitigation of risk is not the same as the elimination of risk. To learn is to explore the limits of one's knowledge, which can be an intimidating venture. Eliminating risk entirely likely means that we have ceased to make ourselves vulnerable to what we do not know. But it does need to be mitigated to the degree that students will feel emboldened to take a chance. In the more conventional reading and writing, the risks students do or do not take are not necessarily public. But with performance, the students are more privy to each other's contributions, making it an even more intimidating prospect. The key is to create the right balance of risk so that students are challenged (and not bored) but not intimidated into not joining.[5]

The larger in-class performances allowed me to see who absorbed the material well and who did not. If necessary, I could then provide struggling students with additional support and perhaps one-on-one time. I do not subscribe to a belief in musical talent (as a capability that one is or is not granted at birth) that could prohibit students from learning the material; all can improve their capacity from the point where they start. Similarly, class performances also allowed me to identify potential student leaders and encourage them to assume that role, providing an additional challenge for them.

Periodically, we discussed our impressions of the group performance. These informal discussions were crucial to integrating performance into the learning by creating an opportunity for reflection (see below for more detail). Students frequently commented on the way the session started with timidity and how confidence increased through repetition, which, in turn, yielded higher energy. It was not uncommon for a student to single out the risk-taking of one of their peers, noting how she increased the volume of her singing or the size of her dance gestures, which then encouraged others to increase their own participation. I also generally asked them to discuss which elements of performance are more difficult and which are easier. These conversations were fairly free-flowing, but over the course of the semester, themes began to emerge that related to my overall learning goals for the course. I have found that if I provide plenty of silence and wait, student observations will become more detailed and more meaningful. It has been a challenge to resist my urge to fill silences with repeated and leading prompts, but it is worth the effort. I am not above cold-calling on students in this context, for I want them to learn that they all have powerful analytic skills for musical phenomena, regardless of their perceived individual musical abilities, but I do so gingerly and generally find a way to encourage and connect with any response a student offers.

In his work on flow states and optimal experience, in which music and dance contexts feature prominently, Mihalyi Csikszentmihalyi (1990) identifies the importance of appropriate levels of challenge. Striking a balance between challenge and comfort has proved to be an important factor in generating participation (and, one might argue, the first ingredient for the generation of a flow state). While my goal is not necessarily to generate flow states with every class performance, it is my desire that I can occasionally get students close enough that they see the potential of flow states, and the music/dance performance that can generate them, for transforming social relationships (Turino 2008).

Reflection

The literature on teaching and learning that has emerged in the past decades has indicated that the learning cycle is only complete—that we move beyond introducing an idea to the absorption of this idea in our students' understanding—when students are given an opportunity to reflect on their learning and then try again (Anderson and Adams 1992; Ash and Clayton 2009; Erickson, Peters, and Strommer 2006). This is especially the case for experience-based learning. Experiences alone, without the opportunity to reflect on them in a deep and meaningful way, fail to convey the lessons we hope our students will learn (Kolb 1994; Kolb and Kolb 2005).

Moving between the regularized performance outlined above and a few different types of reflective exercises became a standard element of my course. Some of these opportunities were informal in nature, whereas others were formal writing assignments submitted at certain points in the semester (see also Carol Muller 2011).

For informal reflection, I typically ask students to take a few moments and reflect in writing on an in-class experience, a concept from the reading, or a prompt. They then share some of what they wrote in small-group conversation with their peers, after which each small group might report out some of the themes that emerged in their conversation. The initial writing phase of this exercise is just to provide students with an opportunity to reflect and gather their thoughts; these impromptu writings are not submitted for grade.

This type of informal reflection begins on the very first day, when I ask the class to reflect on the lessons they have received about Africa in their lives. They then are given time to take inventory of the many messages they have received about Africa and how they have shaped their understanding of life on the continent. Given that few of my students have ever been to Africa, they generally understand from the outset that these messages are at best incomplete and at worst patent falsehoods created by a range of actors, interests, and contexts that are in need of interrogation. This sets out for us part of our agenda for the semester and, when successful, sets an expectation of such reflection throughout the course.[6]

Subsequent opportunities for informal reflection require students to think through their own experience performing together. I ask them to describe the emotional landscape for themselves: Were there moments of discomfort? Did something change for them throughout the experience? Did the actions that anyone else took surprise, discomfort, or embolden them? Was there resistance? If so, what might be the cause of such resistance? When asked on a daily basis, these questions form the beginning of a discussion about music, performance, and social life. Without singling out any individual, we discuss in general the feelings of discomfort that many of the students have about performing together, about their feelings of inadequacy, their lack of knowledge, worry about being judged, and times when they felt most comfortable.

Finally, we often use a similar technique when encountering movies, news reports, music recordings, images, and so forth. Beginning with the most immediate emotional responses and attempting to unravel them, working back from emotion to the concepts and experiences that drive them, helps students move beyond their visceral responses to African music and content. My goal is to help students develop a habit of reflecting on their initial emotional responses to unfamiliar music or new ideas, an invariable element of learning, and work through and beyond them to understand the resistance and received knowledge that might be impeding comprehension. The goal is to encourage a habit of reflection that will eventually yield a mind more open to learning.

Our final informal reflection takes place during our final exam period at the end of the semester. There, we return to the inventory of received knowledge with which we started the semester and reflect on the journey we have taken to fill in some of the gaps. We also discuss the journey they have taken as performers and our thoughts on how performing together regularly has changed them. Every semester, someone comments that they feel closer to this group than they do their peers in other courses. When that theme emerges we discuss what role performance might have played in creating greater social cohesion.

More formal opportunities for reflection occur through writing assignments that students submit on completing their unit performance project. These essays require students to discuss their performance, how it connects to what they have learned from the readings and recordings, and their own experience in performing with their group. These essays are required, and a grade for the performance will not be counted unless it is submitted.

Reflections, formal and informal, present an opportunity for students to supply the connective tissue between the range of experiences they encountered throughout the semester and the larger concepts and skills I hope they will learn. I find it helpful to provide the opportunities for students to do this themselves rather than making explicit the scaffolding myself. My job is to have created a context in which reflection is valued as a form of meaning making, to provide thoughtful prompts that will help set them in a fruitful direction, and to recede from the center of the discussion and allow students to fill the silences.

Performance as a Means of Knowledge Construction

If we want students to engage with performance seriously as a vehicle for constructing knowledge, then we need to demonstrate such potential for the performance in our class. It has generally been my experience that students are inclined to consider our time spent performing in class (and outside of class, for that matter) as fun time that is almost extracurricular in nature rather than a profoundly relevant and central moment of instruction. Even music majors, who recognize the value of performance in certain contexts, often struggle with this.

One powerful concept for helping convey the importance of performance in such a course is Wiggins and McTighe's backward design: a deceptively simple principle that suggests we start with the end in mind (2005, 1998). The design process starts with identifying our learning goals—what we want our students to be able to do as a result of this course. Working backward from our desired results, we determine what would serve as acceptable evidence of that learning and then design our learning plans with the aim of engaging students in the production of this evidence. This approach ensures alignment between course content, methods of instruction, and course assessments throughout the semester. This runs counter to a common practice of deciding first what topics one wants or thinks should be covered, mapping them across the semester, and only then deciding what students will actually do in the course. At first glance, the difference between the two approaches seems inconsequential, but once put into practice each will yield a very different outcome.

Backward design enables us to convey our serious interest in performance as a vehicle for gaining knowledge by connecting it to the learning goals and outcomes for the course. For example, my African music course provides students with various case studies of how contemporary music practice speaks to longer sociohistorical trajectories, and how music performance provides an opportunity to make sense of the past and imagine the future in the context of the present day. My goals, stated explicitly in my syllabus, are that students (1) develop some basic knowledge about the four cultural groups represented in the four units of the course and develop an awareness of some of the conditions that drive social life in various sub-Saharan African communities; (2) recognize the content of their own received (mis)perceptions of life on the African continent and are able to critically reflect on them and how they have been formed; (3) learn some basic musical elements and principles; and (4) awaken to the generative and reflective roles that musical practice plays in the creation of social realities across the globe.

Although a performance-based pedagogy addresses all of these learning goals, I employed it most specifically to address the latter two of them: to convey musical elements through performance (rather than listening) and to awaken students to the role that musical practice plays in the creation of social realities by having them experience (and reflect on) a shift in their own social reality via collaborative performance. It is one thing to ask undergraduates to read the theoretical literature on music and social life; it is another thing yet to ask them to reflect on previous experiences they may have had that provide some insight into music's role in social life and it is another thing altogether to create the context in which their own social life is made different by participating in music performance.

When students discuss our in-class performances and the change in dynamic and energy as various individuals contribute heartily to the performance, thus encouraging them to step up their own performance, they are touching on this notion. We can together integrate the theories we have read about music, cultural values, and social life. At the end of the semester, when students invariably convey their feelings of intimacy and closeness to their peers in this class as being more intense and qualitatively different than in other classes they are taking, we can once again talk about the role of music in generating and strengthening social relationships. Using the Kolb Learning Style Inventory (Kolb and Kolb 2005), we can integrate these conversations about sensorial feelings ("I really felt the groove just then") with emotional feelings ("I feel really connected to my classmates") with the abstract concept of music *as* social life.

Notice that I do not include in my goals an emphasis on acquiring virtuosic or even competent performance skills. One semester is not enough time for anyone to become competent, especially when divided into blocks of time spent developing a range of skills. Expecting competence runs the risk of producing what David Hughes calls "bad copies" of virtuosic musicians from around the world (Hughes 2004, 281). Vetter also notes that his students recognized the "educational merit of going through the process of learning a second musical language, even if fluency in that second language cannot realistically be achieved. Insights gained in this process will probably have greater application in my students' lives after college than will the specific performance skills they hone while in the ensemble" (2004, 119).

Performance as Authentic Assessment

Early in my experimentation with a sort of hybrid course blending performance and more typical academic activities, performance was introduced but not necessarily built into the course assessments. It was a fun and, at best, co-curricular opportunity. Students likely did learn something from it, but without the stakes of a grade attached to it, they were not inclined to consider it a moment of deep learning. In these contexts, my failure to tie performance to assessment conveyed that performance was not a high-value learning moment. Students know what we care about by how we use grades to apply value to the behaviors and products of their learning.

The literature on authentic assessment suggests that developing assessments that are aligned with what ethnomusicologists actually do in terms of our professional work ensures a higher degree of student engagement and investment in the outcomes (Wiggins 1989, 1990, 1998; Koh 2017; Montgomery 2002; Svinicki 2005). In order that our courses accurately reflect what ethnomusicologists do, we should seek opportunities to align our coursework and student activities with our professional research methods and professional activities. As Wiggins states, authentic assessment involves introducing students to

> engaging and worthy problems or questions of importance in which students must use knowledge to fashion performances effectively and creatively. The tasks are either replicas of or analogous to the kinds of problems faced by adult citizens and consumers or professionals in the field (1993, 229).

I confess that I feel some antipathy for grades. At times they can feel a callous, punitive, and overly institutional (read: neoliberal) way to approach learning. Were I to reinvent the academy, I might work hard to find another option. But I am required to evaluate my students' work in the form of a final grade. I also recognize that framed differently, grades can be understood to be an expression of the professor's values. The behaviors and activities through which students earn grades are those the faculty member values highly. Ensuring that the concepts and activities I value do align with the way I have distributed the points in my course assessments eases my discomfort about grades to a measurable degree.

It was in thinking about this alignment that I came to reconsider my teaching and embrace a performance-based pedagogy whenever possible. Test-taking, while seemingly efficient, was not an activity in which I placed great value. The concepts articulated through my exams and the behaviors I wanted to encourage through exam preparation—active listening to musical examples, connecting musical style to social phenomena and cultural groups—could be achieved by other means that were better aligned with my values and more authentic in that they better matched what I do in my research, thus contributing to students' understanding of what ethnomusicology is as a field of inquiry.

My course, then, had four units based on geographic areas, each culminating in a final assessment involving student groups performing for their peers a creation on which they worked independently throughout the unit. Each group performance project served as the culminating moment of a number of weeks spent on the musical genre in question. The performances were designed in such a way as to mandate repeated careful listening to the course reserve audio files. This was similar to the kind of preparation a more typical test would require while significantly improving their ability to identify musical examples. They offered the additional benefit of placing the work of listening in a small study group context to encourage more opportunities for peer mentoring. At the start of the unit, students were given a rubric for how their performance project was to be evaluated so that as they listened together and prepared their own performances they understood what I would prioritize in the grading of their project. These rubrics were originally designed in collaboration with a group of students in an early offering of the course. Students are invited to amend the rubrics before the start of each unit.

Every class period of the unit is meant to prepare students for their performance, whether through reflective writing, reading, discussion, or in-class performances. Other than Dennis Laumann's brief overview of African history (2013), the course relied on a compiled reading packet rather than a single text concerning world or African music. This packet drew on secondary source literature written by leaders in each area. These readings were chosen for the descriptive clarity of the performance practice, explanations they provide about the social context, and the degree to which they discuss the meaning derived from performance. A third of our class meeting time was invested in discussing these articles in small and larger groups and listening to musical or video examples similar to those discussed in the article. Students were urged to consider how the knowledge gained from the reading assignment could be performed in their final project and then given some time to break into their small performance project groups and discuss the possibilities, while the readings are fresh in their minds.

My reliance on peer mentoring and student-driven discussion of texts serves a number of purposes. It allows students to take an active leadership role in constructing their knowledge. Our earliest days of the semester are dedicated to excavating their assumptions and received (mis)perceptions about Africa, and my placing them in the role of driving our discussions places them in the position of actively correcting or augmenting what they know (or think they know) on the topic.[7] Doing so reinforces their own agency in the learning process and allows me to recede from what could be my role of cultural translator to serve as something more akin to a facilitator. In action, they become responsible for the quality of their learning rather than passive receivers of my knowledge. This move also allows for a more seamless connection between the out-of-class work on the performance projects and reading and the in-class discussions. Students move organically between the readings, the topic, and their performance projects in their small-group discussions, and supporting the development of a positive group dynamic is one result of the heavy reliance on group work in the class meetings. Finally, and most practically, doing so breaks up what is a long class period with more active modes of learning that prevent boredom.

A Note About the Dangers: Public Performance

The contributors to *Performing Ethnomusicology* (Solis 2004) present with candor the value and challenges of such student performance groups in what is otherwise a scant literature on ethnomusicological pedagogy. One particularly vexing element is the role of public concerts and the challenges they present in terms of the legitimacy of instruction and the ethics of representation.

My experience offering similar "world music ensembles" at institutions where I have previously worked matches closely that of the authors of *Performing Ethnomusicology*. It was my frustration with the model that drove me to seek an alternative that would more easily elide with institutional structures—avoiding any sort of overload in my work schedule or extracurricular designation for the content I teach, and avoiding professional activity that is undervalued in terms of promotion and tenure at my institution. This is not to say that ensembles cannot be made to work, and the authors of the Solis volume argue successfully for their value while making clear the challenges.

I have sought a different solution that also presents a compromise, one that jibes more easily with my institutional context, my own pedagogical and professional goals, and my vision of the role of ethnomusicology in the academy. This model does not rely on public concerts, and in fact I generally avoid them for all of the reasons made clear in *Performing Ethnomusicology*. The performances my students present are only for each other, fellow learners on the same journey who are aware of the challenges it presents. We talk together as a whole group, and I speak individually with each small group, about the issues of representation that are relevant for their choices.

That the politics of representation varies does not mean that it is eradicated. Students must wrestle with the ethics of their own performance. While they strive to match the stylistic qualities heard in recordings, they must also acknowledge the distance between their performances and what they hear. I do not use the word *authenticity* in class as a goal to which we should aspire, but avoiding the term does not prevent students from bringing preconceived notions of what "authentic African" performance looks and sounds like. Stressing more that our performances are learning opportunities first and foremost, I seek to create a dialogic form of intercultural performance similar to that proposed by Gage Averill for ensembles (2004): "The world music ensemble can thus be reconceived as a context in which students engage in dialogue and collision with musical and cultural codes other than their 'first-language' codes" (101).

A particularly troubling danger zone, whether the performance is public or not, is the potential for minstrel-like interpretations. Without guidance it is possible for uninitiated undergraduates, who often resort to humor when asked to wrestle with their discomfort with difference, to drift into problematic caricature. Like Locke, who suggests that teaching African performance is particularly challenging in a US context because of the legacy of slavery and Jim Crow, I try to avoid "mystification without underestimating difference" (2004, 175), focusing on technical abilities and reflecting on the practical, physical, emotional, and psychological resistance to musicking in an unfamiliar language. My students, most of whom are committed to social justice, are eager to be respectful in their work even if they are sometimes unclear about what that looks and sounds like. We discuss minstrelsy, as well as stereotypes about Africans and African Americans that they may have received without always recognizing it, and reflect on how we might take risks artistically without being disrespectful. This is difficult intellectual work but perhaps the most meaningful in terms of their habits as lifelong learners.

Conclusion

As intimated above, this course, with an emphasis on performance-based peda-gogy, is rooted in Turino's concept of music *as* social life (2008). It is driven by a desire to have students learn how music can build and shape community not through words, texts, and tests, but through their lived musical experiences. Rather than having them read theoretical literature about the relation between sound structures and social structures, I create a context in which they can actually hear and feel the relation between the two in their own experience and the community they build over the course of the semester. That students testify to feeling closer to the students in this course than in their other courses gives us an opportunity to talk about shared experience, the value of vulnerability in performance, and the relation between social structure and sound structure that they have lived for the previous fifteen weeks. Their understanding is not comprehensive or complete, but it is a powerful starting point for subsequent learning in the arts and humanities. There are limits to the model, of course, but it is certainly more consistently effective than the "talk and chalk" courses I have offered on the same content.

In addition to effectiveness, a performance pedagogy also shows students what ethnomusicologists actually do. Our research method is rooted in performance, augmenting performance with primary and secondary sources of all sorts, and interrogating the signs of performance as well as our own emotional responses from within it. Although most students will not progress to a graduate degree in ethnomusicology, it is my hope that they will continue to develop their criti-cal skills for analyzing performance *as* social life and that they will continue to seek performance experiences that bring them a sense of both artistry and community.

This course-based approach is just one of the many we might consider in an effort to articulate an ethnomusicological pedagogy in which our threshold con-cepts, intellectual premises, and methodological contributions to undergraduate music study are aligned and made explicit for our students. The goal need not be uniformity across the discipline but a more robust conversation about our teaching practices across educational contexts. It is through our undergraduate courses, more than our publications, that the world outside our ranks learns about the discipline—the contributions the field makes to broadening musical understanding, furthering understanding of music as a human behavior, and perhaps conveying a sense to all students that they carry within themselves the capacities to make music with others. As Turino has suggested, "The arts are a realm . . . where new possibilities leading to new lived realities are brought into existence in perceivable forms" (2008, 18). Creating educational opportunities for all types of students to experience the arts in this way is one of the most important contributions ethnomusicologists offer to the world.

Notes

I am deeply indebted to Tom Turino. As a professor, teacher, musician, and friend, his influence on my life is immeasurable. While certainly my scholarship has been profoundly shaped by his thinking about music and the reasons we make it, it is also in his teaching that he has made a lasting impression. Modeling the role of "co-learner," he shaped discussions on topics his students cared a great deal about and brought to the discussions an openness to and enthusiasm for learning from them. Now, almost twenty years later, I still enter my classroom with the goal of doing the same and will be forever grateful for the rewards the efforts have yielded. *Music as Social Life* (2008) was written for his students and served as the inspiration for a major shift in my own pedagogical method, outlined in this piece.

1. The term *world music* used throughout this chapter is drawn from ethnomusicological convention, especially in terms of survey courses and co-curricular performance ensembles popular from in the second half of the twentieth century. The phrase "world music" reflects the imperialist underpinnings of our field and our marginal position, as advocates for the equal study and representation of all musical traditions, in the American musical academy. In order to decolonize our curriculum we must eschew the "West and the rest" curricular model popular in most NASM-supported schools of music. One intermediate step that this article outlines is to develop courses that are more focused on single traditions or communities, or those that are in geographic and stylistic proximity, allowing the communities represented to stand on their own as important topics for study (Bosse 2015b). This is a small and perhaps unsatisfactory gesture, to be sure, but it is a step toward decolonization that requires less cooperation from our more reluctant unit colleagues and administrative structures.

2. Recently, the NASM leadership moved to eliminate this requirement in a peculiar move that indicates a step backwards in the movement toward greater representation, democratization, and racial awareness in the music curriculum in higher education.

3. A College Music Society report (Sheehan Campbell et al. 2016) voices this concern. Though I am not entirely convinced of the particularities of its suggestions for the future, I am in full agreement with the problem as they have named it.

4. I am particularly grateful to Dr. Cindy Taggart at MSU for encouraging me to eliminate the use of TUB notation and instead require students to rely more on their ears and physical memory. This was an important change in the development of my teaching, and it made a significant difference in student comprehension and satisfaction.

5. There is much discussion about turning our classrooms into safe spaces. This feels like an unrealistic bar to set for ourselves and an unfair promise to make to our students. Learning exposes our weaknesses. It is dangerous and subversive work. Furthermore, we cannot know how our students may be feeling unsafe in our classrooms and mitigate for all eventualities. For myself, I aim for respectful, compassionate, and "safe enough spaces" but make no claims that I could be capable of protecting my students from very much other than my own inconsideration.

6. I am particularly grateful to Kofi Agawu for his piece "The Invention of 'African Rhythm'" (1995). While specifically relevant for this course, we also discuss the wider implication that many ideas about Africa are inventions, and so a question we return to again and again is, "How has Africa been invented in this [movie, news report, musical example, our performance, etc.]?" This particular framing is challenging but obtainable for first-year undergraduates and invites them into constant reflection about their own perceptions of Africa, the general ways we generate meaning, and the challenge of veracity.

7. At various points in the semester we return to the theme of their received (mis) perceptions on African peoples. Clips from United States popular culture—feature films, documentaries from various time periods, children's television shows, music videos, and the like—provide them an opportunity to reflect on how these media have shaped perceptions in problematic ways.

Bibliography

Agawu, Kofi. 1995. "The Invention of 'African Rhythm.'" *Journal of the American Musicological Society* 48(3): 380–95.

Anderson, James, and Maurianne Adams. 1992. "Acknowledging the Learning Styles of Diverse Student Populations: Implications for Instructional Design." *New Directions for Teaching and Learning* 49:19–33.

Ash, Sarah L., and Patti H. Clayton. 2009. "Generating, Deepening, and Documenting Learning: The Power of Critical Reflection in Applied Learning." *Journal of Applied Learning in Higher Education* 1(1): 25–48.

Averill, Gage. 2004. "'Where's "One"?' Musical Encounters of the Ensemble Kind." In Solis 2004, 93–114.

Barz, Gregory, and Timothy Cooley. 2008. *Shadows in the Field: New Perspectives for Fieldwork in Ethnomusicology.* Oxford: University of Oxford Press.

Berger, Harris M. 2009. *Stance: Ideas About Emotion, Style, and Meaning for the Study of Expressive Culture.* Middletown, CT: Wesleyan University Press.

Berliner, Paul. 1993. *The Soul of Mbira.* Chicago: University of Chicago Press.

Bosse, Joanna. 2011. "Bridging the Divide Between Pedagogy and Epistemology: A Performance-Based Pedagogy for Undergraduate Ethnomusicology Courses. Paper presented at the annual meeting of the Society for Ethnomusicology, Philadelphia.

Bosse, Joanna. 2013. "Sound Understandings: Embodied Musical Knowledge and 'Connection' in a Ballroom Dance Community." In *Bodies of Sound: Studies Across Popular Music and Dance,* edited by Sherril Dodds and Susan Cook, 39–54. London: Ashgate.

Bosse, Joanna. 2015a. *Becoming Beautiful: Ballroom Dance in the American Heartland.* Urbana: University of Illinois Press.

Bosse, Joanna. 2015b. "Beyond NASM." In The President's Report, "A Multivocal Response to the College Music Society Task Force on 'Transforming Music Study from Its Foundations: A Manifesto for Progressive Change in the Undergraduate Preparation of Music Majors.'" *SEM Newsletter* 49(3): 4–5.

Bosse, Joanna. 2019. "Performance-Based Pedagogy: In Search of Epistemological Alignment in Ethnomusicology Undergraduate Coursework." Paper presented at the annual meeting of the Society for Ethnomusicology, Bloomington, IN.

Charry, Eric. 2000. *Mande Music: Traditional and Modern Music of the Maninka and Mandinka of Western Africa*. Chicago: University of Chicago Press.

Chernoff, John. 1979. *African Rhythm and African Sensibility*. Chicago: University of Chicago Press.

Csikszentmihalyi, Mihalyi. 1990. *Flow: The Psychology of Optimal Experience*. New York: Harper and Row.

DeNora, Tia. 2000. *Music in Everyday Life*. Cambridge: Cambridge University Press.

Erickson, Bette LeSere, Calvin Peters, and Diane Weltner Strommer. 2006. "Learning Styles." In *Teaching First-Year College Students: Revised and Expanded Edition of Teaching College Freshmen*, 35–45. San Francisco: Jossey-Bass.

Friedson, Stephen. 1996. *Dancing Prophets: Musical Experience in Tumbuka Healing*. Chicago: University of Chicago Press.

Hagedorn, Katherine. 2001. *Divine Utterances: The Performance of Afro-Cuban Santeria*. Washington: Smithsonian Institution Press.

Hahn, Tomie. 2007. *Sensational Knowledge: Embodying Culture Through Japanese Dance*. Middletown, CT: Wesleyan University Press.

Hood, Mantle. 1960. "The Challenges of 'Bi-Musicality.'" *Ethnomusicology* 4(2): 55–59.

Hood, Mantle. 1971. *The Ethnomusicologist*. New York: McGraw Hill.

Hughes, David. 2004. "'When Can We Improvise?' The Place of Creativity in Academic World Music Performance." In Solis 2004, 261–82.

Kisliuk, Michelle. 1998. *Seize the Dance! BaAka Musical Life and the Ethnography of Performance*. Oxford: Oxford University Press.

Kisliuk, Michelle. 2007. "Wrestling with Some (Em)Body: A Family Research Trip to Jewish Ghana and Beyond." Paper presented at the annual meeting of the Society for Ethnomusicology, Columbus, OH.

Koh, Kim H. 2017. "Authentic Assessment." *Oxford Research Encyclopedias: Research and Assessment Methods*, edited by George W. Noblit. Accessed on Sept. 13, 2019. https://oxfordre.com/education/view/10.1093/acrefore/9780190264093.001/.0001/acrefore/9780190264093-e-22.

Kolb, Alice Y., and David A. Kolb. 2005. "The Kolb Learning Style Inventory—Version 3.1, Technical Specifications." Boston: HayGroup, Hay Resources Direct.

Kolb, David A. 1994. "Learning Styles and Disciplinary Differences." In *Teaching and Learning in the College Classroom*, edited by Kenneth A. Feldman and Michael B. Paulsen, 232–55. Needham Heights, MA: Ginn.

Laumann, Dennis. 2013. *Colonial Africa, 1884–1994*. New York: Oxford University Press.

Locke, David. 1980. "Improvisation in West African Music." *Music Educators Journal* 66(5): 125–33.

Locke, David. 1982. "Principles of Offbeat Timing and Cross-Rhythm in Southern Ewe Dance Drumming." *Ethnomusicology* 26(2): 217–46.

Locke, David. 2004. "The African Ensemble in America: Contradictions and Possibilities." In Solis 2004, 168–88.

Meyer, J. H. F., and R. Land. 2003. "Threshold Concepts and Troublesome Knowledge: Linkages to Ways of Thinking and Practising." In *Improving Student Learning: Theory and Practice Ten Years On*, edited by C. Rust, 412–24. Oxford: Oxford Centre for Staff and Learning Development. Available online: "Enhancing Teaching-Learning Environments in Undergraduate Courses: An Introduction to the ETL Project," Occasional Report 4, May 2003, last accessed September 25, 2023. https://journals.sagepub.com/doi/10.7227/IJEEE.42.1.2

Montgomery, Kathleen. 2002. "Authentic Tasks and Rubrics: Going Beyond Traditional Assessments in College Teaching." *College Teaching* 50(1), 34–40, DOI: 10.1080/87567550209595870. Accessed September 13, 2019.

Muller, Carol. 2011. "Becoming Music to My Ears: From Sound/Noise to Music as Students Listen Closely to World Music." Paper presented at the annual meeting of the American Folklore Society, Bloomington, IN.

Rasmussen, Anne K. 2004. "Bilateral Negotiations in Bimusicality: Insiders, Outsiders, and the 'Real Version' in Middle Eastern Music Performance." In Solis 2004, 215–28.

Seeger, Charles. 1971. Preface to *The Ethnomusicologist* by Mantle Hood. New York: McGraw Hill.

Sheehan Campbell, Patricia, David Myers, and Ed Sarath. 2016. "A Manifesto for Progressive Change in the Undergraduate Preparation of Music Majors." *College Music Society*. https://www.music.org/pdf/pubs/tfumm/TFUMM.pdf. Last accessed October 9, 2020.

Solis, Ted, ed. 2004. *Performing Ethnomusicology: Teaching and Representation in World Music Ensembles.* Berkeley: University of California Press.

Solis, Ted. 2011. "Moving Experiences: Dancing as a Pedagogical Strategy in the Music Classroom." Paper presented at the joint meeting of the Society for Ethnomusicology and Congress of Research in Dance, Philadelphia.

Svinicki, M. D. 2005. "Authentic Assessment: Testing in Reality." In *Alternative Strategies for Evaluating Student Learning*, 23–29. San Francisco: Jossey-Bass.

Timmermans, J. A., and J. H. F. Meyer. 2017. A framework for working with university teachers to create and embed 'Integrated Threshold Concept Knowledge' (ITCK) in their practice. *International Journal for Academic Development.* Available online 17 Oct 2017; DOI: http://dx.doi.org/10.1080/1360144X.2017.1388241 (October 8, 2020).

Trimillos, Ricardo D. 2004. "Subject, Object, and the Ethnomusicological Ensemble: The Ethnomusicological 'We' and 'Them.'" In Solis 2004, 23–52.

Turino, Thomas. 1993. *Moving Away from Silence: Music of the Peruvian Altiplano and the Experience of Urban Migration.* Chicago: University of Chicago Press.

Turino, Thomas. 1999. "Signs of Imagination, Identity, and Experience: A Peircian Semiotic Theory for Music." *Ethnomusicology* 43(2): 221–55.

Turino, Thomas. 2000. *Nationalists, Cosmopolitans, and Popular Music in Zimbabwe.* Chicago: University of Chicago Press.

Turino, Thomas. 2008. *Music as Social Life: The Politics of Participation.* Chicago: University of Chicago Press.

Turino, Thomas, and James Lea. 2004. *Identity and the Arts in Diaspora Communities.* Warren, MI: Harmonie Park.

Turnbull, Colin. 1987. *The Forest People.* New York: Touchstone.

Vetter, Roger. 2004. "A Square Peg in a Round Hole: Teaching Javanese Gamelan in the Ensemble Paradigm of the Academy." In Solis 2004, 115–25.

Wiggins, Grant. 1989. "A True Test: Toward More Authentic and Equitable Assessment." *Phi Delta Kappan* 70(9): 703–13.

Wiggins, Grant. 1990. "The Case of Authentic Assessment." *Practical Assessment, Research and Evaluation* 2(2). https://www.pareonline.net/getvn.asp?v=2&n=2.

Wiggins, Grant. 1993. *Assessing Student Performance: Exploring the Purpose and Limits of Testing.* San Francisco: Jossey-Bass.

Wiggins, Grant. 1998. *Educative Assessment: Designing Assessments to Inform and Improve Student Performance.* San Francisco: Jossey-Bass.

Wiggins, Grant, and Jay McTighe. 2005. *Understanding by Design.* Expanded 2nd ed. Alexandria, VA: Association for Supervision and Curriculum Development.

6 Musical Competition as Community in Highland Bolivia

THOMAS SOLOMON

Musical performance in the Andean highlands of Bolivia and southern Peru frequently takes the form of competition. The aural image of (apparent) cacophony resulting from multiple musical groups (most often performing on panpipes or other kinds of flutes) competitively playing different tunes simultaneously in the same performance space is a staple of Andeanist musical ethnography.[1] Interaction between performers in musical competition can be formally organized in many different ways, depending on the social setting and performance context. Musical competition can take the form of song dueling, in which participants in the performance alternate with improvised couplets, either in a predetermined order or in an order that emerges during the course of the performance. Performance interaction can also take less obviously structured—and to the outsider unfamiliar with such performance practices, apparently chaotic—forms, as when different musical groups sharing the same performance space play different musical pieces simultaneously, each group trying to play louder and longer than the other. The choice of winners and losers of musical competitions may be formally determined and announced by event organizers or left to be debated among the performers and audience after the performance event is over. There are thus many local variations on the general theme of competition.

In this chapter I explore some examples of musical competition I observed and documented during ethnographic fieldwork in highland Bolivia in the early 1990s. The examples serve as a starting point for an exploration of how interaction in such competition-based performance creates different kinds of social relationships that constitute musical communities. I argue that, in the Bolivian contexts I describe, the idiom of competition provides a flexible means for performing social relations that can instantiate many different approaches to building community through music. The many different ways in which performers may musically interact with each other in competition can construct community as an intimate conviviality among friends, as a union of complementary forces, as the interaction of anonymous urban subjects, and as colonial relations of domination, among other possibilities.

My theoretical point of departure is Christopher Small's argument that musical performance in itself constitutes or creates a set of social relationships. Small suggests that the social relationships of performance *model* those in society at large, and that the different social configurations in different kinds and instances of performance (such as genres, situations, or physical arrangements) thus provide different *models* of how society might be organized. As Small explains, "When we perform, we bring into existence, for the duration of the performance, a set of relationships, between the sounds and between the participants, that model ideal relationships as we imagine them to be and allow us to learn about them by experiencing them" (1998, 218). Thomas Turino takes broadly the same approach when he refers to "the community being brought forth through performance" (2008, 157). A related argument—or a different way of stating it—might be that different ways of configuring social relationships in performance construct different subject positions that people may inhabit, such that musical performance becomes a catalyst for generating social identities, both individual and collective.

I explore the implications of these arguments in a series of seven ethnographic vignettes describing musical performance from my fieldwork in various times and places in highland Bolivia, focusing in particular on the patterns of social relations created in and through those particular moments of performance. I argue that, rather than being a single principle that works in the same way across different performance contexts, the general idiom of competition lends itself to a number of ways of structuring performance and that competition thus provides a flexible way of performing many different kinds of community. In Small's terms competition instantiates different "models" of and for community. But, moving beyond the modeling metaphor, I suggest that rather than simply serving as a means to model social relationships that will be re-created in other times and places outside of musical contexts, concrete moments of musical performance are themselves self-contained *moments of community*, bringing people together in different kinds of social formations.

My approach is broadly comparative, so I will not be providing much ethnographic context for the examples I discuss, but instead will focus rather tightly on the specific social relationships constructed in specific performances between different performers, and between performers and audiences (and other kinds of participants when relevant). If competition in itself as an abstract category implies a highly structured way of interacting, I want to focus on *how* what might be called different "modes" of competition construct different ways for performers to socially relate to each other. The approach is thus consistent with the theoretical and methodological approach that emerged in ethnomusicology in the late 1970s known as the ethnography of musical performance (McLeod and Herndon 1980).[2]

Although I describe some of these ways of socially relating as more constrained and others as more open-ended or emergent, at a larger level all of the musical practices I describe can be considered to be emergent in the act of performance. Following Judith Butler's (1988, 1993, 1999) theorization of how performative acts constitute gendered subjects, I thus take a broadly performative approach. By *performative* I mean that instances of performance do not simply enact pre-existing norms and structures but that social relations are created in and through the act of performance. This is a commonplace argument nowadays, so there is, of course, nothing new in this approach. This does not mean, however, that performers do not creatively use existing idioms for social expression in performance. Society is not remade from scratch in every event of performance. The general idiom of competition provides a wide repertoire of practices that performers may draw on when they find them useful, and performers, of course, draw on their previous experiences participating in similar or analogous events.

The seven examples that I present give some idea of the great variation in the way competitions may be socially organized. Some of the parameters of contrast between the different examples I discuss include rules or conventions for turn taking, which range from flexible and emergent to rational and rigidly enforced; the number of participants involved and their organization in performance as individuals or musical groups; the level of intimacy between performers themselves and between performers and audiences; the presence or absence of a stage manager or master of ceremonies who directs the performance; and formal or informal means of evaluating the competition and selecting winners and losers. These and other variables come together in performance to construct both social relationships and the social space in which those relationships are acted out.[3]

Example 1: Song Dueling Among Friends in a Provincial Town

The first example I discuss is an instance of informal music making among frends in the small provincial town of Mizque in the Bolivian department of Cochabamba. This performance took place in November 1990. The performance idiom of competition employed in this example is known in the Quechua language as *takipayanaku*, which can be translated as "song duel." The verb root *taki-* in Quechua means "to sing." The suffix *-paya* indicates a repeated action performed with special interest (Soto Ruiz 1979, 429). The suffix *-na* indicates "that the subjects of the sentence are acting on each other in a reciprocal fashion" (Bills et al. 1969, 150), while *-ku* is the reflexive suffix. The term *takipayanaku* thus literally means singing back and forth between two or more people, each one doing so for his or her own benefit or interest. The term thus succinctly describes what happens in a song duel (Solomon 1994, 380).

In this performance, the verses were in the genre known as *coplas* (couplets), in this case the subgenre *coplas de Todos Santos* (coplas for All Saints Day), since the performance occurred in early November. To the accompaniment of a guitar played by one of them, the performers engaged in song dueling by both drawing on a stock repertoire of pre-composed coplas and improvising new verses appropriate to the occasion. Turn taking in this performance was emergent; all persons present could enter and drop out of the performance as they wished. In this performance, which lasted about eleven minutes, four people participated by singing between them a total of fourteen coplas. In this case, the decision *not* to sing should also be considered a participatory choice. Others present who did not sing also participated, however, by clapping during the instrumental interludes between verses. The space of the performance can be characterized as intimate, as the performers were mostly sitting around a table in a small rural bar (actually the front room of someone's house, used as a serving area, figure 6.1). The performers

Fig. 6.1. Performers in a song duel in the town of Mizque, November 1990. Photo by the author.

were all from the same small town, and all knew each other well. There were no formal judges to decide winners and losers in the competition, but there was a set of informally recognized conventions by which most were in agreement as to who won and who lost the duel; people would also discuss such duels afterwards. Such informal music making among friends that I observed was generally well lubricated by the consumption of alcohol, in this case *chicha* (corn beer) served by the woman who owned the house (who also joined in singing a verse in between serving customers). The performance can be characterized as an intimate ritual, with conviviality among friends the primary goal. The sometimes strong insults exchanged in the verses were not taken personally, and the performance was punctuated throughout by laughter from the performers themselves and others present.[4] The kind of community constructed via this performance was thus one of friends who enjoyed each other's company and enjoyed making music together. The competitive aspect assumed the participants' competence in the performance idiom of the song duel (being able to sing correctly formed coplas appropriate to the occasion), but the highest priority was having a nice time among friends.

Example 2: An Urban Festival of Song Dueling

My second example is also a performance of Quechua-language song dueling, but on a much larger scale than the previous example. This was a public event held in the Félix Capriles soccer stadium in the Bolivian city of Cochabamba in March 1993, advertised as a Festival de Takipayanakus (festival of song dueling). The event was organized annually during the 1980s and early 1990s by the radio station Radio San Rafael, operated by the Catholic Church in the city, and in 1993 was also sponsored by a Bolivian beer company, Taquiña, which had a large banner hanging in front of the stage to promote it (at least, until a strong wind blew the banner away during the course of the afternoon). The event I attended was billed as the twenty-third annual festival of this type, so it had a long institutional history.

Cochabamba is a fairly large city, with a population in 1993 of about 520,000. Because this was a large-scale public event with significant expenses incurred in its staging, the organizers charged admission. As I entered the stadium gate, I paid my entrance fee (5 Bolivianos, around US$1.14 at that time) and was given a printed ticket stating the name of the event and the date, with a stamp indicating the entrance fee had been paid (figure 6.2). The ticket taker kept the other half of the ticket stub for accounting purposes. The elevated platform serving as a temporary stage was set up near the center of the sideline of the soccer field on one side of the stadium; the attending public was small enough to fit on that side of the stadium, directly facing the stage (figure 6.3), so the opposite side and the two curved ends of the stadium were empty throughout the event.

Fig. 6.2. Ticket from the 23rd Festival de Takipayanakus in Cochabamba, March 1993. Photo by the author.

In this event, performers participated not as individuals but as members of small groups (*comparsas* in Spanish) of generally five to seven people, including singers (with some groups having only men, others only women, and still others being mixed-sex) and accompanying musicians who played a variety of instruments including guitars, *charangos* (a small stringed instrument), accordions, and *bombo* (a large drum). The festival was arranged annually around the time of Carnival (mid-to-late February), so the genre most groups performed was *coplas de Carnaval*. Because of the large number of participants, the organizers used a bureaucratized procedure whereby performing groups who wished to participate had to register beforehand. The sequence of the performances was announced at the start of the event, which was organized in heats of semifinals and finals wherein groups were either eliminated or advanced to the next stage. The various performing groups styled themselves as representing different provincial towns or villages in the region surrounding the city, the names of some groups also made reference to their occupations such as mining or bus driving and ticket taking on a particular bus route in the city. Some groups wore costumes, such as the aforementioned miners, who wore hardhats, rubber boots, and waterproof yellow slickers. Many groups held up handmade signs with their group name on them, helping the audience keep track of which groups

Fig. 6.3. View of the soccer stadium in which the Festival de Takipayanakus took place. Photo by the author.

were performing at any given time. Within each group there was generally a designated soloist who improvised the sung verses, accompanied by the other members, who played instruments and sang during the repetitions and refrains. The various groups did not know each other from before, because they came from different provincial towns or different parts of the city, and had registered separately to participate in the festival.

For the song dueling itself, pairs of groups chosen arbitrarily by the organizers were juxtaposed onstage and made to compete by trading three verses each, back and forth. A master of ceremonies (hereafter MC) and two stage managers, all identifiable by their identical white T-shirts with the same logo, were present onstage to coordinate the event; the whole performance was thus heavily stage-managed (figure 6.4). Technological mediation was visible during the performance, which was amplified by the use of a public address system; the microphone used by the MC was subject to heavy reverb, and the whole event was simultaneously broadcast live by the organizing radio station. Interaction between the performing groups was also heavily mediated and regulated by the MC, who strategically stood between the groups and moved the single microphone present onstage back and forth between them in order to keep any one group from going on too long, thus ensuring a relatively brisk, efficient pace in order to get through the long list of groups signed up to perform.

Fig. 6.4. Participants onstage during the Festival de Takipayanakus. One performing group (*comparsa*) is on the left, the emcee and stage managers (with white tee shirts and microphone) are in the middle, and another comparsa (in miners' costumes) is on the right. Each group holds up a sign with its name. Photo by the author.

This performance can be characterized as an urban folkloric ritual, a public display of culture on show. The performers stood on a stage in front of an audience, the ongoing commentary by the MC emphasized and contributed to the spectacle aspect of the event, and the sequence of performers followed an orderly procedure whereby different groups came to the stage to perform and left it once they were finished. The judges used a bureaucratized procedure to formally determine winners and losers, whom the MC announced after each round and at the end of the event. The audience could, of course, have its own favorites.[5]

In this event the different performing groups came together briefly onstage in a formalized competition organized and sponsored by external entities (the radio station and a beer company), according to rationalized bureaucratic procedures. Although internally the individual groups were generally made up of friends or co-workers, members across the different groups would otherwise be anonymous to each other in everyday life in the city. The competition thus itself constructed an instance of the fleeting social encounters characteristic of urban life, in which one may create a sense of identity within one's small social group, while otherwise being anonymous within the urban space as a whole.

The organization of the competition was also itself an instance of the large-scale social organization typical of densely populated urban areas, in which the sheer number of people involved is institutionally managed by the use of bureaucracy and other rationalizing procedures. Also an element in this particular performance was the ongoing friendly rivalry between the different provincial towns that some of the groups represented (even if their members actually lived and worked mostly in the city). The kind of community constructed here was that which typically comes about in urban areas—a short-term sharing of space between people who otherwise remained anonymous to each other and went their separate ways once the event that briefly brought them together was over.

Example 3: Singing at a Wedding Party in a Provincial Town

My third example of musical competition is singing performed at a wedding celebration in April 1993, referred to in Quechua as *kasamintu takiy* (from Spanish *casamiento,* "wedding," "marriage"). This event occurred in the provincial town of Chayanta in the province of Bustillo in the region of Norte Potosí, where I was doing long-term fieldwork during most of 1993. The setting was the front room of a person's house, which doubled as a bar (similar to the venue in the first example above), loaned for the occasion. The singers were all female relatives of the bride and groom: various aunts and cousins, mostly married and middle-aged, who had come from their home communities to Chayanta (the closest church with a regularly stationed parish priest) to celebrate the wedding. The were accompanied by a young man, unrelated to the newly married couple, who played charango. As the afternoon passed, the female relatives of the bride and the groom took turns singing verses, some improvised for the occasion, others drawing from a deep well of existing formulaic verses in the genre that everybody knew. As they sang, the women danced in a circle around the young man playing the charango (figure 6.5). The verses included some mild teasing: the relatives of the bride sang in support of her and teased the groom and his family; the relatives of the groom correspondingly sang in support of him while sending a few gentle verbal barbs at the bride and her family. The teasing was good-natured, however, and nobody took offense. Some of the verses also had a somewhat didactic aspect because they indicated the seriousness and importance of the occasion, referring to the new "alliance" that had been formed between the two families by the marriage, and reminding the young couple of the responsibilities they had now taken on as they entered the social institution of marriage. Although the performance thus resembled in formal terms the song duels discussed above, a cooperative, celebratory spirit prevailed, and

Fig. 6.5. Performers at a wedding celebration in Chayanta, April 1993. The singers dance in a circle around the young man who plays the charango. Photo by the author.

there was no need to identify winners and losers. The singing was carried out by the female relatives of the newlyweds, but all present could join in by dancing and clapping their hands during instrumental interludes between verses.

Like the performance of coplas in Mizque described above, this performance was characterized by intimacy and conviviality. The participants all knew each other, and everyone present was encouraged to participate in celebrating the occasion—an important rite of passage for the newlyweds but also a chance for the older women to express themselves in song. In this intimate ritual, the close community ties of family were the center of attention, and the competitive aspect, though somewhat muted, emphasized the union of complementary parts (the bride and groom and their respective families) to establish the social whole.

Example 4: Carnival in a Village Community

My fourth example of musical competition comes from the celebration of Carnival in the Indigenous village community of Irupata, the main site of my fieldwork in 1993. In the Indigenous communities of Bustillo Province in northern Potosí, Tuesday and Wednesday of Carnival week (typically in mid-February) when I was there were the days for *wisitas* (from Spanish *visitar*), visits to other villages. On these days *kumparsas* (from Spanish *comparsa*, as used above), small bands of four or five unmarried boys and girls in their teens and early twenties, roved from one community to another to play music and visit with friends. Roles in musical performance were gendered: boys played stringed instruments while girls sang verses in Quechua. On arrival in a community, each kumparsa headed to the house of friends or relatives. The residents invited them inside or to the house's back patio, where the group played a song genre called *wayñu* especially associated with Carnival. The owner of the house offered the players *chicha* and the group performed again for a while before moving on to another house within the village. After visiting several houses in this way, the group then moved on to another village, usually one within a walk of an hour or two. Wherever they happened to find themselves at nightfall, they stayed, usually playing music all night in someone's house until they set off for another village in the early morning, eventually returning to their home village by Wednesday evening.

During these Carnival visits, two or more musical groups from different village communities could encounter each other while visiting the same house. In these situations, the groups simultaneously performed different songs competitively. In such cases, each group tried to play louder and longer than the others. In this context each group could limit its singing to one or two formulaic verses repeated again and again, typically verses naming their home community or describing its landscape.[6]

I witnessed such a performance in Irupata during Carnival in late February 1993. As evening fell, two performing groups from different communities found themselves in the main room in the same house. Each group performed their own song. The stringed instruments played by the two groups were not tuned to the same tonal center, and the playing and singing of the two different songs simultaneously with two different keynotes went on for about twenty minutes. In order to not get disoriented and lose their place in the song, each group sang and played progressively louder, trying to drown out the other. Eventually both stopped at about the same time (though my field notes are somewhat sketchy on this point) and left the house to move on separately to other places and continue to perform. Because the verses consisted largely of the repetition of the names of their communities and descriptions of their landscapes, in textual terms, the competition was explicitly constructed in terms of collective identities at the village community level.

In this competition there was no formal duel with procedures for turn taking. The competition was emergent in the moment owing to the happenstance meeting of the two groups. The participants spontaneously engaged in competition when they, by accident, happened to find themselves in the same performing space. Because of the ephemeral nature of this short event, I did not get any information as to whether it was considered that either of the groups had "won" the competition, but I suspect that, owing in part to the fluidity of the situation, each group would claim that they were the "winner" as a matter of pride.

In this example the "performance of community" was literal, since the two musical groups came from two different village communities, and that identity was the primary motivator of the performance. The performance can thus be described as an emergent ritual of community identity.

Example 5: A Pan-Community Music Festival

My fifth example of musical competition occurred in the same Indigenous community, Irupata, as the previous example, about three weeks before it in early February 1993. In this case, however, rather than a *fiesta* in the agricultural-religious calendar of feast days, the event was a music *festival* sponsored and organized by the NGO Taypikala, which worked closely with Irupata and other Indigenous communities in the region in projects of "cultural development" (*desarrollo cultural*). This specific event was a festival to celebrate the third anniversary of the radio station Mallku Kiririya, for whose construction the NGO had obtained funding from European donors in order to provide communications infrastructure to be operated by and for Indigenous people in the region. The festival began outdoors but was quickly moved into the large indoor meeting space adjacent to the radio station's studio after it began to rain.

The sponsoring organization coordinated all aspects of the festival and paid most of the expenses. There was no admission fee. All who wanted to attend could do so, though the remoteness of the community meant that the vast majority of those attending were from other Indigenous villages in the surrounding countryside within walking distance of a few hours at most. There were also a few visiting dignitaries, such as politicians and peasant union leaders, specially invited by the organizers. The sponsoring organization carefully planned the festival to proceed according to a timetable with a specific sequence of events. Performing groups were invited to participate and scheduled to play in a given order; failure to be ready to take the stage when called could be grounds for disqualification. The musicians performed in groups of four to six on a designated stage area in front of an audience (figure 6.6). A master of ceremonies with a microphone introduced each performing group by the name of its community and called on the next scheduled group to prepare to take the stage after the current one finished its performance. While members of performing groups from different communities could interact unofficially offstage, there was no onstage interaction between them, and groups were discouraged from continuing to play offstage within earshot because it interfered with the orderly progression of the festival and distracted attention from the groups still playing onstage.

The festival was organized explicitly as a competition, with prizes awarded to named winners of first, second, and third place. The panel of judges (*jurado*

Fig. 6.6. Performers from the community of Berenguela at a music festival in Irupata, February 1993. Photo by the author.

calificador) was made up of outsiders who were thought to be impartial. The prizes awarded included tools used in agriculture (for example, hoes and pick-axes), large bags of fertilizer, small bags of coca, the sandals made from discarded automobile tires that were the preferred footwear in the region, and acrylic yarn used to knit traditional caps, scarves, and belts. The groups who won the competition were invited to take the stage again and perform an encore of their winning songs.

Because this was an organized competition with named winners and prizes to be awarded, musical groups were keen to participate and provide a winning performance. New pieces with texts praising the sponsoring NGO were com-posed especially for the festival. Whereas in performance during the fiestas of the agricultural-religious calendar (for example, saint's day feasts) musicians might play a single song or tune throughout the entire fiesta, the festival format required performing groups to prepare two different pieces, each about four to five minutes long, in order to show a breadth of repertoire. Groups could be penalized if they only had one song or tune prepared.

Because the site for festival performance was literally a stage toward which all attention was directed, each group tried to do things that would distinguish it from the others. Musicians thus developed new performance strategies so that their ensembles stood out from those of other communities. Performers also dressed up to play in the festival. On top of the usual festive dress they would also wear for a fiesta, both boys and girls also wore as many knitted pieces and weavings as they had available in a manner that could be described as "piling it on." Girls wrapped around themselves and draped over their shoulders several *lliqllas* (woven carrying cloths) and brightly colored scarves. Boys hung down their backs or along the backs and sides of their legs woven scarves called *chupa* (lit. "tail"), and hung brightly colored *ch'uspas* (small knitted pouches for carrying coca) from cords around their necks (Figure 6.6). The performers knew that they were being judged in part on this display of traditional textiles, and so they played up to the judges' expectation of a colorful display with this over-the-top presentation of Indigenous weaving and knitting. This kind of self-presentation amounted to what can be called "strategic auto-essentialism," a kind of self-conscious acting out of the folkloric stereotypes that outsiders had of Indigenous culture.[7]

In this event the competition was not merely for its own sake as a performance idiom but, rather, was directed toward a specific goal: winning prizes and gaining the prestige that comes from winning. While the majority of the audience was made up of Indigenous villagers from the same communities as the performers, the performances were actually directed largely toward outsiders—the sponsoring NGO, the judges, and other visiting dignitaries. The performances at this festival thus constructed a community that brought together Indigenous villagers and representatives of the world outside their villages in a kind of hierarchical patron-client relationship; here competition took the form of a folklorized version of Indigenous culture tailored for the consumption of outsiders.

Example 6: Ritual Musical Battling in a Ceremonial Center

The sixth example I present is part of a large ritual complex involving pilgrimage and a ceremonial battle (called *tinku*) between moieties, based on a cosmological mapping of large-scale ecological zones in the province of Bustillo. I focus on only one specifically musical part of this ritual complex, the simultaneous performance of different community-based troupes (*wayli*, from the Spanish word *baile*, "dance") from rural villages who played a pentatonic type of panpipes locally known as *julajula*. The event I describe here occurred during the Fiesta de la Cruz (Feast of the Holy Cross) in early May 1993. For the celebration of this feast day, each wayli band of pilgrims made the journey by walking from their home communities to Chayanta, the regional ceremonial center (mentioned above as the site of the wedding celebration). Throughout the journey of several hours, the men of each wayli played the julajulas continuously. Leading each wayli was a pair of unmarried girls who continuously waved white flags. The central plaza in Chayanta, next to the church, was the focus of activity, and the different waylis arrived there throughout the day, each playing their own emblematic melody on the julajulas while doing a serpentine dance around the plaza (figure 6.7). Often several groups arrived and performed simultaneously, sometimes with each group's instruments tuned to a different tonal center, thus creating a kaleidoscopic multitonal texture as different melodies in different tonalities intertwined with each other. The sundry groups made no effort to coordinate with each other. There was no formal turn taking; each group tried to play louder and longer than the rest, according to their stamina and ability to stay organized. Although the general parameters of the ritual, including the simultaneous performance of the various groups, were familiar to all the participants, the specific articulations of different groups at any one moment were emergent, even accidental, depending on when the groups happened to arrive in the plaza at any given moment.

Although the performing groups were all concentrated within the plaza, there was a certain flexible use of space there. Each group, coming from different directions in the territory surrounding the town, entered the plaza via a particular street that corresponded to a mapping of regional ecological zones onto the geography of the town; each group marked out its temporary space

Fig. 6.7. A wayli troupe arrives playing panpipes in the plaza of Chayanta during the Fiesta de la Cruz, May 1993. Photo by the author.

in the plaza via movement and sound, with the street running alongside the church on one side of the plaza being particularly prized territory. There were no judges and no formally named winners or losers of the competition, but groups that played weakly or only for a short period of time could be commented on later. Police officers tried to keep order, making sure to break up any fistfights that broke out between members of rival groups, in order to keep such fights from escalating into a large-scale riot. But the event was not extensively stage-managed.

In spatial terms this performance can be characterized as a regional communal ritual. The competition was at multiple levels: the level of individual village communities, the level of the nine Indigenous groupings (*ayllus*) to which the communities respectively belonged, and the level of the two moieties based on complementary ecological zones among which the ayllus themselves were distributed. Depending on how many village communities decided to participate in the ritual on a given occasion, the competition could potentially be between dozens of communities. The social relationships between these communities were that of equality and complementarity; the individual parts came together in the same social, physical, and sonic space to embody a social and cosmological whole. Each group was always mindful of the presence of the others but insistently, even obstinately, constructed its own community's coherence and local identity through music and movement that marked out the space it temporarily occupied in the plaza. The simultaneous performance of the different communities, however, also constructed and embodied the more encompassing social groupings that included all the communities in a large-scale regional structure. The community constructed in this ritual complex, including the musical performance on the julajula panpipes, was thus articulated at several levels (typical of the segmentary organization of Indigenous societies in the Andes), the most locally specific of which was the individual village community (each with its own band of pilgrims playing its own emblematic tune) and the most encompassing of which was the cosmologically based moiety, expressed in terms of the ecological complementarity between upper and lower zones, which provides the basis for moiety membership.[8]

Example 7: Panpipes Versus Brass Band at a Saint's Feast Day Celebration

The seventh and last example I discuss comes from a saint's day feast in another Indigenous rural village in northern Potosí. During the early 1990s the community of Wayt'i celebrated annually the fiesta of the Virgin of Guadalupe. This celebration was primarily by and for the local community, but visitors were welcome. I attended the celebration of the Virgin of Guadalupe in Wayt'i in

September 1993.⁹ That particular year, the fiesta sponsors in the village invited two different musical groups to perform: a panpipe group (*sikuras*, another type of panpipe distinct in construction and playing technique from the julajula panpipes mentioned above) from the village itself, and a brass band hired from a community a few hours away. The two groups alternated playing throughout the day. But at various points during the afternoon and evening, when one of the groups was already playing, the other also started up, and both groups continued to play simultaneously for a while (figure 6.8). The simultaneous performances created a sonic duel on decidedly unequal terms, since the brass band was much louder than the panpipe group, and for the most part the brass instruments drowned out the panpipes. When I asked participants in the fiesta about the juxtaposition of these two very different musical groups, I was told that the brass band was recruited from a village that had become (as my interlocutors put it) more "civilized" (they used the Spanish word *civilizado*) in its customs. Locally, the brass band was discursively associated with urban culture. The panpipe group, on the other hand, was discursively associated with Indigenous culture and village life—"our custom," I was told.

The space for this performance was an open area adjacent to the community's main cluster of houses that served as a sort of makeshift plaza, though the physical settlement itself was not based on the Spanish town plan with a grid of streets surrounding a square plaza in the middle (like, for example, the

Fig. 6.8. A panpipe group and a brass band perform simultaneously during a fiesta celebration in the community of Wayt'i, September 1993. Photo by the author.

town of Chayanta mentioned above). In this competition, there were no judges and there was no formal organization for turn taking. As in the examples of the Carnival kumparsas and the arrival of the wayli pilgrimage groups in Chayanta, the competition was emergent, based on who could play the loudest and longest. But as I have already suggested, the competition was from the start on unequal terms, for the brass band tended to overpower the panpipe group. The interaction between the two groups was not stage-managed during the performance itself. But the whole event was to a certain extent orchestrated ahead of time by the fiesta sponsors, since they had invited both performing groups and would have known that the two groups would probably end up playing simultaneously during the fiesta, given that this was already a common practice in the region.

This performance in Wayt'i in September 1993 can be characterized as a local village community ritual, since it was carried out on a feast day when the village was known to host a celebration. The specific musical dynamic between panpipes and brass band, however, articulated within the village what might be called "colonial space." By drowning out the panpipe group, which was specifically associated with Indigenous culture and village-community life, the brass band, associated with urban culture, in effect colonized the sonic space of the ritual, enacting the unequal power relation between colonizer and colonized.[10]

Conclusion: Competition as Community

A once-common ethnomusicological methodology for analysis of the place of music in society was to identify patterns or structures in musical sounds and/or the actions of people during musical performance and then search for analogous patterns or structures in other realms of culture or social behavior. This kind of analysis was thus based on a search for homologies (Solomon 2008) or what Turino (1989) calls "the coherence of social style and musical creation." Emerging in the early 1970s under the banner of "music as culture," this approach had its heyday in the late 1970s and early 1980s, but traces of it can still be found in more recent work. Small's (1998) argument, as discussed at the beginning of this chapter, regarding the way musical performance models social relationships outside of performance, shares some DNA with the "music as culture" approach. And when Turino evokes "the community being brought forth through performance" (2008, 157), he seems to be updating that approach by melding it with the practice theory that began to influence ethnomusicology beginning in the late 1980s. The brief analyses above also demonstrate the use of homology as explanation, as in my suggestion that the social relations of the stadium performance of song dueling in the festival format was homologous with social relations more generally in urban environments.

A crucial theoretical and methodological question to be considered in this theorizing is how what happens specifically during musical performance affects or relates to experience and action in other social domains that are not specifically musical. Given their heavy intellectual (and presumably personal and even emotional) investment in music, it is perhaps natural that ethnomusicologists would want to privilege music and attribute to it a significant role in shaping social life and experience. But I would prefer a more cautious approach that, while affirming the importance of music and the communities it engenders, does not take music to be primary in the formation of other social and cultural domains. It is one thing to say that a general social style or set of predispositions to think and act in certain ways can inform musical thought and action. It is quite another to say that music comes first, prefiguring or structuring other domains of social life.

In their introduction to this volume, Fiol and Perman offer a broadly pragmatic and phenomenological definition of *community* as "the composite relations grounded in similarity and difference among agents who act on their interdependence or mutual indebtedness." In their theorization, *feedback* and *mutuality* are key aspects of the relations that create community. In the examples of musical competition discussed here, there is feedback not only between musical performance and community in the abstract but also directly between the different performers themselves as they set themselves in competition with each other, either as individuals or as groups functioning as teams. Interdependence and mutuality are necessary for competition to function and are thus the basis for both structuring performance and structuring community. Performance and community become one and the same. The musical give and take between competitors is the sonic stuff of community, both as a set of individuals coming together as a single community through their shared dueling in an intimate context (with dueling thus being internal to the community) and as larger groups that form rival communities that compete with each other. Feedback thus simultaneously constructs both similarity and difference. Here difference is not a matter of an internal-external dichotomy but is incorporated within musical communities themselves. Mutuality also constructs both similarity and difference—similarity in that the competitors (individuals or groups) set themselves up against each other via singing or playing within a shared idiom that makes them intelligible to each other, and difference in the fact that within that shared idiom an individual becomes a member of a given musical "side." The idea of mutuality is even made discursively explicit in the Quechua-language term *takipayanaku* that designates dueling in song. The ubiquity of competition as performance idiom in this part of the Andes means that competition is habit in the sense that it is iterative within and across performance genres and occasions and thus a building block for community in any particular iteration.

When describing the examples of musical competition discussed above as instances of musical community, I am not arguing that the various social relationships of community created in these moments of performance consistently and predictably determine, cohere with, or even model social relationships in other realms *outside* of music. Rather, I make the somewhat less ambitious claim that moments of musical community are their own entity as bounded, identifiable moments of performance and thus worthy of study in and of themselves as cultural and social phenomena, without necessarily giving them primacy in ontologies of culture and society. As I stated in the introduction, rather than simply serving as a means to "model" social relationships that will be re-created in other times and places outside of musical contexts, concrete moments of musical performance are *themselves* self-contained moments of community, bringing people together in different kinds of social formations. Rather than join in debates about the extent to which, as Fiol and Perman put it in their introduction, "the social bonds made when musicking can coalesce into communities that last beyond the time constraints of musicking itself," I instead advocate for a rather less ambitious understanding of the role of music in community-making that recognizes music as producing what might be called contingent, emergent, and self-contained *moments of community*.

In the case of the examples discussed above, one can thus speak of musical competition *as* community—as a way of bringing people together, however briefly, in social relationships. Moments of performance are moments of community, bounded in space and time. Specifically, in regard to the ethnographic vignettes discussed above, I suggest that the idiom of competition flexibly lends itself to engendering many different kinds of social relationships in performance.

In this chapter I have approached musical competition as a flexible idiom by means of which social relations that express community are created and performed. I have presented seven examples of musical competition from fieldwork in highland Bolivia and explored how those events bring people together in different kinds of community. The diversity of these examples suggests that musical competition in the Bolivian Andes does not simply "model" one type of agonistic social relationship but can, depending on the specifics of the performance context, bring people together in many different kinds of communities, ranging from an intimate gathering of friends or family members, through the anonymous encounters of urban life, to the complementarity of equally balanced forces or hierarchical relationships of power.

Notes

Field research in Bolivia during 1990 and 1993–1994 was made possible, respectively, by a grant from the Tinker Foundation and a Fulbright Hays Dissertation Research Abroad Fellowship. An early version of this chapter was presented at the annual conference of the British Forum for Ethnomusicology, March 29 to April 1, 2012, in Durham, UK.

1. See, e.g., Abercrombie (1998, 389), Bigenho (2002, 178–79), Rasnake (1986, 671; 1988, 248), Rockefeller (1999, 139), Sallnow (1987, 160–61, 187, 195, 202), Stobart (2006, 193–96), and Turino (1989, 19–20; 1993, 65–67).

2. See especially Herndon and McLeod's chapter on song dueling in Malta, which maps out variations in performance style in different kinds of occasions in which song dueling can be performed (Herndon and McLeod 1980).

3. My approach here can be fruitfully compared with Bruinders's discussion in this volume of how "communities might be sustained through competition."

4. I provide a complete transcription and translation of the text of this performance, as well as further analysis, in Solomon (1994).

5. For comparison, see Bruinders's discussion in this volume of what she calls "the contestable nature of musical assessment" in which debates about who deserved to win a competition may continue long after the adjudicators' decision is announced.

6. The material in this section is adapted from Solomon (2000), which also discusses the larger ritual context and provides more details of the song texts performed on the occasion described here.

7. For further discussion of festivals, see Solomon (1997, chap. 4, and 2014). Some of the material in this section draws on the 2014 article.

8. For more on the ethnographic context of the events described in this section, see Solomon (1997, chap. 8, and 2020).

9. Attentive readers may note that the well-known Mexican feast of the Virgen de Guadalupe is celebrated on December 12, not in September. In northern Potosí, however, *Guadalupe* refers not to the famous Mexican apparition of the Virgin but is another name of Mamita Pitunisa, a local image of Mary whose fiesta falls on September 8.

10. For more detailed description and analysis of this event, see Solomon (1997, chap. 9).

Bibliography

Abercrombie, Thomas A. 1998. *Pathways of Memory and Power: Ethnography and History Among an Andean People.* Madison: University of Wisconsin Press.

Bigenho, Michelle. 2002. *Sounding Indigenous: Authenticity in Bolivian Music Performance.* New York: Palgrave. https://doi.org/10.1007/978–1–137–11813–4.

Bills, Garland D., Bernardo Vallejo C., and Rudolph C. Troike. 1969. *An Introduction to Spoken Bolivian Quechua.* Austin: University of Texas Press.

Butler, Judith. 1988. "Performative Acts and Gender Constitution: An Essay in Phenomenology and Feminist Theory." *Theatre Journal* 40(4): 519–31.

Butler, Judith. 1993. *Bodies That Matter: On the Discursive Limits of "Sex."* New York: Routledge.

Butler, Judith. 1999. *Gender Trouble: Feminism and the Subversion of Identity.* New York: Routledge. First published in 1990.

Herndon, Marcia, and Norma McLeod. 1980. "The Interrelationship of Style and Occasion in the Maltese *Spirtu Pront.*" In *The Ethnography of Musical Performance*, edited by Norma McLeod and Marcia Herndon, 147–66. Norwood, PA: Norwood.

McLeod, Norma, and Marcia Herndon, eds. 1980. *The Ethnography of Musical Performance.* Norwood, PA: Norwood.

Rasnake, Roger. 1986. "Carnival in Yura: Ritual Reflections on 'Ayllu' and State Relations." *American Ethnologist* 13(4): 662–80. https://doi.org/10.1525/ae.1986.13.4.02a00050.

Rasnake, Roger. 1988. *Domination and Cultural Resistance: Authority and Power Among an Andean People*. Durham, NC: Duke University Press.

Rockefeller, Stuart Alexander. 1999. "'There Is a Culture Here': Spectacle and the Inculcation of Folklore in Highland Bolivia." *Journal of Latin American Anthropology* 3(2): 118–49. https://doi.org/10.1525/jlca.1998.3.2.118.

Sallnow, Michael J. 1987. *Pilgrims of the Andes: Regional Cults in Cuzco*. Washington, DC: Smithsonian Institution Press.

Small, Christopher. 1998. *Musicking: The Meanings of Performing and Listening*. Middletown, CT: Wesleyan University Press.

Solomon, Thomas. 1994. "Coplas de Todos Santos in Cochabamba: Language, Music, and Performance in Bolivian Quechua Song Dueling." *Journal of American Folklore* 107(425): 378–414. https://doi.org/10.2307/541690.

Solomon, Thomas. 1997. "Mountains of Song: Musical Constructions of Ecology, Place, and Identity in the Bolivian Andes." PhD diss., University of Texas, Austin.

Solomon, Thomas. 2000. "Dueling Landscapes: Singing Places and Identities in Highland Bolivia." *Ethnomusicology* 44(2): 257–80. https://doi.org/10.2307/852532.

Solomon, Thomas. 2008. "Music as Culture? Reflections on an Ethnomusicological Moment." *Studia Musicologica Norvegica* 34: 68–90. https://doi.org/10.18261/ISSN1504 -2960-2008-01-05.

Solomon, Thomas. 2014. "Performing Indigeneity: Poetics and Politics of Music Festivals in Highland Bolivia." In *Soundscapes from the Americas: Ethnomusicological Essays on the Power, Poetics, and Ontology of Performance*, edited by Donna A. Buchanan, 143–63. Farnham, UK: Ashgate.

Solomon, Thomas. 2020. "Dancing the Landscape: Music, Place, Collective Memory, and Identity in a Highland Bolivia Pilgrimage." In *Cultural Mapping and Musical Diversity*, edited by Britta Sweers and Sarah M. Ross, 123–44. Sheffield, UK: Equinox.

Soto Ruiz, Clodoaldo. 1979. *Quechua: Manual de Enseñanza*. Lima: Instituto de Estudios Peruanos.

Stobart, Henry. 2006. *Music and the Poetics of Production in the Bolivian Andes*. Aldershot, UK: Ashgate.

Turino, Thomas. 1989. "The Coherence of Social Style and Musical Creation Among the Aymara in Southern Peru." *Ethnomusicology* 33(1): 1–30. https://doi.org/10.2307/852167.

Turino, Thomas. 1993. *Moving Away from Silence: Music of the Peruvian Altiplano and the Experience of Urban Migration*. Chicago: University of Chicago Press.

Turino, Thomas. 2008. *Music as Social Life: The Politics of Participation*. Chicago: University of Chicago Press.

7 Sustaining Musical Collectivities Through Competition

Christmas Bands in Cape Town

SYLVIA BRUINDERS

Members of the St Joseph's Christmas Band arrive at the clubhouse at 8 a.m. one Sunday for the City and Suburban Christmas Bands Union's annual competition. They put the final touches to their dress: Ties have to be knotted in exactly the same manner for the "best-dressed band" category in the competition, so Chris Petersen, the captain, is placed in charge of knotting everyone's tie. Their uniform consists of gray trousers, gray shoes, gray hat, a white shirt with a teal blazer, and a yellow tie. Some musicians pick up their instruments and play through problematic passages trying to perfect them; others shine their shoes yet again. There is excitement in the air as they wait for everyone to arrive. The men joke with each other, wondering which band they will "put to shame" this year; they boast about their prowess at competitions and their unbroken record of winning the "solo" (musical) category for nine consecutive years in the union competitions. The children are restless, playing with each other, running around; the men shout at them to stop running about and to keep their uniforms clean. Members are slow in arriving, but in the air the promise of a day of sociality, friendship, and the tension that accompanies competitions is palpable. Just before leaving in the bus for the stadium where the competition takes place, they gather at the gate of the clubhouse to perform the solo one last time.

The Christmas bands, located in the Western Cape of South Africa, are seemingly founded on respect for each other and cohesion among the bands; however, rivalry is quite a strong feature as well. There are two performance contexts: the annual competitions in which the bands compete for various trophies for aspects of their performance practice, and the street parades, which include house visits to their members and longstanding supporters. Unlike the Belfast marching bands, they do not skirmish in the street parades (see Ramsey 2009), or "road marches," as the bands refer to them. Here the bands display solidarity of purpose and community as shown through the respectful acknowledgment of the passing band. For instance, a band that has entered a neighborhood before another will form two lines as a guard of honor through which the second band passes. Members of the first band remove their hats and place their right hands with hats over their hearts (see Bruinders 2017, 35). At the competitions, however, the rivalry is more palpable among the band members as well as their cheering supporters; emotions are viscerally displayed. While there is "ritualized friction" (see Boonzajer Flaes 2000, 49, on Ghanaian police bands) within individual bands (as I suggest in Bruinders 2017, 50–51), it also occurs between bands, as exemplified annually on competition days. Similarly, in the preceding chapter, Solomon discusses the "ongoing friendly rivalries between the different provincial towns" in Bolivian urban festival song dueling. In this chapter I discuss how the Christmas bands as musical collectivities are contested yet produced and sustained via competition. I engage Thomas Turino's notions of participatory versus presentational performance and show that in this cultural practice these performance formats are not so clearly distinguished. In the case of the Christmas bands (as in many other cultural practices in South Africa), competition, being an example of presentational performance, drives sociability and community in multiple ways rather than reinforcing capitalist values (Turino 2009, 95).

What Are the Christmas Bands?

Christmas bands are heterogeneous wind bands that usually have been founded by related families and friends within certain neighborhoods in the Western Cape Province in the early to mid-twentieth century. They wear uniforms comprising colorful jackets and ties, shirts, dull-colored trousers with matching socks and shoes, and a hat with a feather placed dashingly on the right-hand side. A small string section consisting of one or two cellos, guitars, banjos, and sometimes violins as well as an accordion often support these wind bands. This accompanying section fills in the harmonies (accordion), supports the bass line (pizzicato cello), and provides an upbeat rhythm (guitars, banjos, and pizzicato cello). The instrumentation depends on the kinds of instruments owned by the families or band members. Thus, each band, though similar in form, is quite different from the next in content and can range in membership from thirty to two hundred people. They perform Christian hymns and marches as well as light classical and popular pieces. Their members belong to a marginal racialized Creole grouping referred to as coloured in South Africa. They are people of mixed descent who came from various parts of the Indian Ocean world (Indonesia, India, Mozambique, and Madagascar) as slaves to the Cape Colony between 1652 and 1806 as well as the autochthonous groups and Europeans who settled in the colony. Since emancipation in 1838, they have experienced the erosion of their citizenship, especially since the mid-twentieth century. It is a social grouping that has existed in the unenviable interstitial space between the economically powerful white and numerically powerful black African groups in colonial and apartheid South Africa, and it still experiences this marginal status in present-day democratic South Africa. Although their original neighborhoods have been decimated by apartheid policies of forced removals, bands have remained together as extended family bands, reconstituting themselves after their removal to far-flung places across the Cape Peninsula.

There have been some attempts to recruit members who are not from this ethnic, class, and religious grouping (working-class coloured Christians), but they have not been successful. I suggest that their shared history under colonialism and apartheid as well as their Christian ethics (although most are not staunchly religious) connect them in a particular manner that inadvertently excludes others who do not share this history and ethics. For instance, Cape Muslims have a very similar history but not the Christian ethics, and although many of them have been supporters of the Christmas bands for years because they live in the same neighborhoods, they have not joined the bands, or if they have, not for long. Cape Muslims are mostly involved in the Cape Malay choirs

Fig. 7.1. St. Joseph's Christmas Band on a road march in 2011. Photo © Paul Grendon.

as well as the minstrel troupes, which attract both Muslims and Christians. Similarly, a few black African Christians joined some bands for a short while, they were not enticed to stay because their lived experiences are quite different, which disrupts the easy bonding at band activities.

Christian organizations such as the Salvation Army and Church Lads Brigades, which subscribe to notions of order and discipline, as can be witnessed in the strict execution of their marches, have influenced the Christmas bands. The Christmas bands' parade season opens with a road march in one of the communities on December 16, a national holiday that kick-starts the summer vacation season in South Africa, or, more customarily, on Christmas Eve in the central city of Cape Town, their ancestral home. Bands march in platoon formation of three or four abreast and aspire to execute the marches precisely (figure 7.1), though this exactness in marching is more obvious in the competitions. Christmas Eve also starts off the road marches to different neighborhoods where the bands visit their members and supporters in an annually renewed rite of reciprocation. Here they share *'n tafel* (a table of foods, of local delicacies), performances by the band, exchanges of speeches, and prayers. This renewal rite continues on Sunday afternoons into February or March until the band has visited all or most of its membership as well as the sick and aged members of their communities. During this time the bands participate in the competitions, which occur from February through early April. There are two levels of competition: the Union and Board competitions. Christmas Bands Unions are federal structures consisting of a number of bands, whereas the Christmas Bands Boards are federal structures consisting of a number of unions. The two board competitions include the bands that have gained the first six places in the union competitions, with the bands that have gained the first three places competing in "Board Competition A" and the rest in "Board Competition B." In some years they hold a championship competition in which the best bands in the two board competitions compete again.

Contestation at Competitions

The judges of the competitions adjudicate three important aspects (among others) of their performances: the "solo," the prescribed musical piece; "best-dressed band," the uniform review; and the "grand march past," the parade around the competition arena, usually a sports stadium. Whereas I have written elsewhere about the different categories of competition (see Bruinders 2006, 2006/7, 2012, 2017), I focus solely on the musical item, the solo, in this chapter. Although this category seems to create the most tension in the competition, musical performance also adds to the sense of camaraderie and social cohesion. The solo is a piece of either religious orchestrated music or light classical music that each bandmaster, a member of the band, or a capable musician who is not a member of the band arranges for its particular instrumentation. Even this arrangement, I was to learn, entails an element of surprise and competitiveness on competition morning when it is first revealed during its performance. Professional musicians, often music teachers or professors at the local universities, usually adjudicate the solo.

The word *solo* is appropriated from Western art music and reflects the sense of aspiration to an elite cultural practice. All the most competent band members usually participate in the solo because it would be devastating to be left out of this significant performance. The union or board officials give the band a copy of the score a few months before the competitions. It is often an arrangement for solo voice or choir and piano that is appropriately rearranged, most often for two sets of wind quartets (or more parts if the accompaniment is complex). The instrumental parts are doubled, tripled, or quadrupled, depending on the number of performers on an instrument. This kind of arrangement can lead to an unbalanced sound, but the bandmaster has to carefully weigh the desire for a balanced sound against the prestige of performing in the competitions. Anyone left out will feel severely snubbed, so this decision is always a difficult one for the bandmaster to negotiate. Thus, there are constant threats from the bandmaster and captain (in charge of discipline of the entire band) to not include anyone in the competition who does not show up regularly for rehearsals. The threats are hardly ever carried out, but the warnings continue at every practice. Having all the capable instrumentalists perform at the competition, though not necessarily ideal for the bandmaster, ensures high spirits and camaraderie on competition day.

The trend, these days, is for the bands to overwhelm their rivals with an exciting arrangement for a large ensemble. Such an arrangement would include a dense harmonic structure with several musical lines performed by different wind instruments, foregrounding sections of the wind ensemble at different points in the music. The larger bands are more spectacular in their performative effects, appealing to the audiences' aesthetic sensibilities by foregrounding the sounds of unusual combinations of instruments such as sousaphones and bass tubas contrasted with flutes and clarinets, and by excessive contrasts in dynamics. The bands clearly model themselves on the symphony orchestra (or perhaps military and paramilitary bands), adhering to strict discipline at rehearsals, with the conductor being the unquestioned authority. Unlike a symphonic performance, however, the emphasis is on the spectacular nature of the visual or sensory experience along with the auditory. The audience may erupt into applause at any moment to show their appreciation of the timbral and dynamic contrasts, almost drowning out these carefully staged effects.

The unique arrangement of the solo, provided most often by the band director, is a matter of pride for the band. In 2007, at a South African United Christmas Bands Board annual general meeting, the board's musical director gave each band a pre-arranged score of the 2008 solo rather than have individual band directors arrange it as usual. Many bands opposed this idea strongly. I failed to understand why, so I supported the director in his endeavor at musical uniformity.[1] My reasoning was that each band would be given a fair chance to perform a good arrangement, as I have heard arrangements that vary in standard considerably over the years; I thought that this would be an ideal way to level the playing field. The band members' reasoning, I learned later, was that they wanted to arrange the music to suit their particular bands, rather than have it arranged for an anonymous ensemble that might not include their peculiar instrumentation. In this way they could imbue the piece with their band's unique identity rather than have this decided by someone else. I realized my naïveté after a conversation with Chris Petersen, captain of the St. Joseph's Christmas Band (hereafter St. Joseph's), in which he clarified this reasoning to me. This band had a particular musical identity for which it was known due to the unusual arrangements of its bandmaster, the late Wally Witbooi. Besides, the bands' arrangements only emerge in their performance on the morning of competition and is an aspect of the spectacular and competitive nature of the performance. Saint Joseph's was particularly vehement in its opposition to the board's musical director's newfangled ideas and decided not to participate in the solo category. This sparked heated discussion in both the union and the board, and in the end the City and Suburban Christmas Bands Union, the federal structure to which St. Joseph's belonged, took a decision to boycott the solo category in the board competition of 2008. A principled decision like this obviously jeopardizes the band's and the union's final position in the competition tremendously, but the point they were making seemed far more important than the goal of winning. For band members, the notion of providing some kind of equitable situation while using a musical arrangement decided on outside the individual band was not a favorable solution at all. In fact, this idea disrupted its competitive edge, which was increased by the musical arrangement itself. Besides, this attempt at uniformity undermined each band's identity as a discrete musical collective.

Nevertheless, band members often express considerable resentment of competition results. Stories abound to substantiate their claim that certain bands always win, not necessarily because they are good or play the music correctly. "Playing the music exactly as it is written" or representing an authoritative score is a matter of serious contention to many band members. Often there are complaints that certain bands render a piece that has been substantially altered from the "original score," and questions are raised as to how they can win the solo with such an altered score. This gives rise to speculation about corrupt adjudicators who advise these bands on how they expect the piece to be performed and who are paid off to ensure that they win first prize. These serious allegations are quite likely unfounded, but it is very hard to convince the members of the professional integrity of adjudicators. I believe this situation may be due to the lack of musical skills among band directors who apply a crude interpretation to the music without the contextual knowledge base that accompanies the transmission of Western art music. Thus, the band may play all the correct notes, with a semblance of phrasing, but fall short of rendering an appropriate interpretation of the piece overall, literally interpreting dynamics such as crescendos and decrescendos without consideration of the musical context or dynamic effect. Nor is this the only problem; difficulties with tuning and embouchure are perennial, and the instruments are often very old and worn-out. The frustration the directors and other members feel when they consistently fail to win a prize after many months of hard work is understandable. I believe that the contestable nature of musical assessment at the competitions arises because band members and adjudicators use different assessment criteria: For band members the score is the absolute authority and is read literally; their aim is to present the unmediated authority of the text. For the adjudicators the score is merely a representation of the music, and they expect musicians to interpret it within the acknowledged aesthetic and performative parameters of Western art music. One year the City and Suburban Christmas Bands Union drew up criteria and distributed them to the solo adjudicators, who are mostly outsiders to the cultural practice of the Christmas bands. The idea of presenting the adjudicators with the bands' own criteria was, I suggest, an attempt at controlling a musical practice that they perceive as uniquely theirs, performing the classical repertory, with its own cultural and musical complexities, their way. Perhaps this need to take ownership of their aesthetic practice relates to their sense of occupying a marginal sociopolitical status: A measure of satisfaction and dignity is maintained even when people outside the practice adjudicate the music. Similar measures of control exist in other cultures (see, e.g., Turino 1997; Hagedorn 2001). Nonetheless, there remains a tension between performing rather difficult classical pieces acceptably and producing a Christmas band sound.

The Christmas Band Sound

The importance of music as a social connector and marker of identity has been the focus of many ethnomusicological research studies (see Austerlitz 1997; Pacini Hernandez 1995; Turino 1984, 1993). This is especially the case when these musical practices are an inherent part of social organizations. Thomas Turino (2008) argues that the goal underlying participatory practices is to enhance social bonding, and various features of sound such as rhythmic repetition and dense sonic textures function to reach this goal (e.g., Zimbabwean mbira music and Aymara panpipe music in Peru). Furthermore, he suggests that dense overlapping textures, wide tunings, and loud volume provide a "*cloaking function* that helps inspire musical participation" (2008, 46, italics in original). The focus of attention is therefore not on sound as an end product but, rather, on the heightened social interaction integral to the performance activity. Although Christmas bands draw on the repertory and musical practice of Western hymnody and light classical pieces rather than create a new repertory, and their music is often performed in a presentational way, they constitute large social organizations of musical and related performance where music functions to connect people in very special ways. Band members and their local supporters bond as a community: in this case, by adhering to a particular cultural practice and Christian ethics. Although an extrinsically presentational format, intrinsically the participatory values embedded within the musical practice communicate the notion of collective identity.

Thus, at important occasions such as the annual ritual house visitations and competitions, members of these communities experience a deep social engagement and solidarity in which music plays a crucial role. They experience a *communitas* (Turner 1969) in which petty differences disappear and they unite through their common humanity. St. Joseph's demonstrated this communitas during its parade season when the membership disagreed with a last-minute decision by the executive committee to include a visit to a sick elderly supporter on one of the road marches. The members reacted to this high-handed decision by the executive committee in a heated discussion about the correctness of entertaining late requests. The meeting was dismissed without resolving the matter; then, somewhere along the route, the decision was taken to do the right thing and to visit the elderly supporter, and nothing more was said about it. The players performed together in the bus and on the road marches, displaying their ethics of respectability and solidarity as if there had been no disagreement earlier.

Through participation in the band's activities, members learn what it means to be a member of a Christmas band, but ultimately these practices, with their enduring notions of discipline, order, and morality, involve a performance of citizenship via their parading of respectability, since the notion of citizenship was such an elusive one for this community throughout the nineteenth and twentieth centuries. I suggest that the Christmas bands' embodiment of respectability in neat uniform dress, performing "respectable" music on Western instruments, precise marching, and moral constitution of their collective selves is an enactment of their desire for the recognition of their inalienable right to citizenship. Though the democratic elections of 1994 changed the political situation for South Africans, the working-class coloured people among whom I did my fieldwork did not necessarily feel that much has changed for them. This embodiment of respectability fulfills dual notions of their own and their idea of outsiders' views of their identity.

Although Christmas bands consist of a variety of wind instruments, the overall sound of these bands is quite unlike the sound of a typical wind band. This is due to a range of factors that may be perceived as unconventional performance practices in comparison with cosmopolitan practices and band styles. First, as mentioned above, the bands are quite heterogeneous in their constitution: No band has instrumentation exactly like another's. Each Christmas band is thus unique in some way, because each one is constituted with whichever wind and string instruments are at hand. Second, the preference for certain sound qualities such as wide tuning, a predilection for breathiness on the saxophones, and relaxed phrasing and embouchure are passed on generationally, leading to a locally distinctive sound. Third, the saxophones, though sweet-sounding, are played with a pinched reed, which gives the timbre a rather nasal quality. Fourth, the distinctive sound of the Christmas bands is due in part to their choice of harmonic progressions. I describe the harmonic progressions of the arrangement of the hymn "Great Is Thy Faithfulness,"[2] which renders progressions typical of the Christmas bands to deliver that characteristic sound, in figure 7.2. The hymn, unusually, is arranged in five-part harmony, with the most common chords used being the primary chords I, IV, and V, chord ii, and occasionally chords iii and vii. The fifth part is created with the sixth added to the primary chords I and IV and the seventh, ninth or eleventh, or a combination of these, added to chords V, ii, and iii. These harmonizations lend the music a jazz feeling, especially when used in succession. Although the hymn is based on chordal progressions of the common practice period, the arranger of the music is unaware of the rules associated with the practice and makes liberal use of consecutive fifths and octaves and enharmonic clashes, and he does not resolve the progressions at the ends of phrases with the usual cadence progressions but instead may end a phrase on chord V with the added seventh or on chord I with the added sixth. Finally, the arrangements are often in close harmony, giving these bands quite a unique sound. The outcome is similar to the "heterogeneous sound ideal" (Wilson 1992) of New Orleans second-line brass bands. These factors, along with individualistic interpretations and practices within the ensemble, are responsible for the production of a dense sound, which indeed can be seen to epitomize in many ways the sound of Cape Town and the entire Western Cape region. The sound of these close jazzy harmonies is considered typical of the Christmas bands. Although Wally Witbooi was self-taught and absorbed most of the harmonic structure of Western art music, his music had a unique expressive quality. He was recognized for this quality, and some younger bandleaders who had formal

Great is thy faithfulness

Fig. 7.2 The hymn "Great Is Thy Faithfulness" as arranged for Christmas band by Wally Witbooi.

training up to university level were eager to maintain this sound for some of the hymn repertory. This typical Christmas band sound is therefore valued as part of the Cape's musical heritage.

Another characteristic of this regional sound is the *ghoema* rhythm, a syncopated underlying rhythm found in several Western Cape musical practices,

Fig. 7.3. The ghoema rhythm can be heard in various genres of the Western Cape.

usually played on a single-headed barrel drum with the left hand marking the beat and right hand playing the syncopated rhythm. The banjos and guitars drive this underlying rhythm in the Christmas bands, because they do not usually incorporate drums. The rhythm can be transcribed as shown in figure 7.3.

These are essential sonic ingredients for the ghoema musical complex:[3]: the three parading "disciplines" in Cape Town in which the Christmas bands have played an integral role. A representation of this characteristic sound and rhythm occurs in what is often referred to as the "Cape Jazz" style brought to international attention by Abdullah Ibrahim in such works as "Manenberg Is Where It's Happening" (on the label The Sun, 1974).[4] I argue that the ensuing sound density masks individual performers and allows members at various skill levels to participate in the ensemble, particularly when the bands are performing on road marches and at community events. When the band plays in the community, this typical "Cape" sound is not only desired by the community but also allows individual members to perform comfortably without feeling self-conscious about their competence. Band members learn to play confidently within the ensemble relatively quickly. Having had to learn to play the clarinet very quickly in order to play with the band on its road marches, I really appreciated this relaxed attitude, which allows for deep embodied social experiences of feeling and playing music together.

Musical Communities

The notion of community music as a field of study emerged in the United Kingdom in the 1970s (Schippers 2010, 92), though, according to Shelemay (2011, 352), the focus of early ethnomusicological research was often on geographically bounded communities. One of the earliest articles about community music is by J. Lawrence Erb (1926), titled "Music for a Better Community." The article is concerned with (among other things) the role of the educational system in furthering the music education of individuals and the edifying role of music in the lives of adults, in particular. It is probably this last point about the "edifying role of music" that has given rise to many community music organizations and practices, particularly for the working classes in previously colonial societies such as South Africa.[5] Shelemay (2011, 354) claims that the study of musical communities has been ongoing—"music historians have for decades given attention to collectivities of all types"—and that large participatory groups, such as Ghanaian drum ensembles and Indonesian gamelan, have engaged scholarly interest owing to the close social relationships they engender because of performance. Nevertheless, she suggests that critical discussions about the concept of community or even the definition of a musical community are sorely lacking in musical scholarship (2011, 354; see also Schippers 2010, 92). She proposes that "rethinking the notion of community opens opportunities . . . as an integral part of processes that can at different moments help generate, shape, and sustain new collectivities" (Shelemay 2011, 350). The Christmas bands, though not new collectivities, have certainly been generated, shaped, and sustained as a particular cultural formation (Turino 2008) by means of music and notions of community such as group participation and social bonding. This corresponds with the suggestion by the editors of this volume that "community emerges from the moments of intersubjectivity (as in musical performance) that put sentient beings in relation to one another" (Perman and Fiol, introduction).

In her article "Sounding out the City: Music and the Sensuous Production of Place," Cohen (1995, 445) suggests that "music . . . plays a unique and often hidden role in the social and cultural production of place and, through its peculiar nature, it foregrounds the dynamic, sensual aspects of this process emphasizing . . . the creation and performance of place through human bodies in action and motion." I suggest that group participation by amateurs, community bonding, and social engagement, along with notions of place related to a particular musical practice, give coherence to our understanding of community music. The Christmas bands, by means of the physicality of their parades, both as a presence in their communities and their embodiment of the practice in uniform dress and military-style marching, evoke notions of place for the Creole communities of the Western Cape. This *place* is often the city of Cape Town itself, from which many of the earliest bands emerged. The forced removals of the Creole communities from their erstwhile neighborhoods by the apartheid regime during the 1960s and 1970s contributed toward the contestation of place for these communities and their parading practices in Cape Town. Although not an overt contestation, it is nevertheless enacted annually in three different parades (one by each "discipline": the Christmas bands, the Minstrel Carnival, and the Malay choirs) in the (formerly forbidden) city center. These parades, in which "human bodies in action and motion" appropriate the business-oriented city center with a carnivalesque array of colorful uniforms, movement, and music, allow for bonding and social engagement with a much larger community, now including their supporters. The yearly participation in the parades engenders the renewal of communities that otherwise still feel quite marginalized politically, economically, socially, and culturally.

Sustaining Musical Communities

The notion of music and sustainability has been given much prominence recently, for instance, in *World of Music* (2009, 2015) as well as in *Sustainable Music*, a research blog on the subject of sustainability, sound, and music curated by Jeff Todd Titon (see https://sustainablemusic.blogspot.com/.). The concept also emerges in many other instances, such as the article by Titon (2015) in the *Oxford Handbook of Applied Ethnomusicology* and the article by Schippers (2018) in the *Oxford Handbook of Community Music*. Indeed, community music and sustainable music practices seem to complement each other: one cannot exist without the other. Titon (2009, 6) posits a simple truism that people sustain music and music sustains people, and therefore sustaining music means sustaining collectives of people making music. The idea that communities might be sustained by competition seems like a contradiction, yet there are plenty of places in South Africa alone and in other parts of the world (see, e.g., Goertzen 2018; Gunderson and Barz 2000; Stillman 1996) where this is the case. In his study of Peruvian music, Turino (1993, 67) reinforces this idea with his assertion that "the competitive nature of musical performance is closely linked to the strong value of community solidarity," although the competitive display in this case is not formalized as it is elsewhere. Solomon, in this volume, suggests the idea of "musical competition *as* community" and states that "moments of performance *are* moments of community" (emphases in original). Likewise, in South Africa, the Rieldans[6] competition not only sustained this rural dance form but also revived it through the attraction and participation of a significant number of young people rather than the elderly who had been its custodians and sole practitioners. The competition was initiated in 2006 by the ATKV (Afrikaanse Taal en Kultuurvereeniging, Organisation of Afrikaans Language and Culture) in an effort to preserve the dying art form (see Britz 2019). Communities of performers and audiences are sustained by the practice, revived by the competition. Another example of a thriving competition in South Africa is the national choral competition, which has several knockout rounds at the local and regional levels prior to the national competition. Big businesses such as Old Mutual (an insurance and investment company), Telkom (a government communications parastatal organization), and South African Breweries support these competitions. All these competitions stimulate and sustain large communities, including participants and supporters, in South Africa. Goertzen (2018, 129) suggests that "music competitions are curiously egalitarian: they offer lesser musicians space and time on stage they might not otherwise receive because the eventual victors must beat someone." I would add that they also provide a platform for ordinary people, often those marginal to society, to show and give their best to their larger communities of supporters. Opportunities such as these in which ordinary people have a platform on which to (re)present themselves, often in their finery and after months of honing their skills, are very rare for black working-class communities in South Africa. They simultaneously challenge and confirm individuals and communities in ways that society customarily does not. Although rife with tensions and conflict, the process of preparation for the competitions and the actual competitions draw these musical communities together in sociability and solidarity.

Conclusion

In his article about music making and sustainable living, Turino (2009, 95) posits the four fields of music making: participatory performance, presentational performance, high-fidelity recording, and studio audio art recording. Furthermore, he suggests that "presentational performance and high fidelity recording fit best with the profit goals and competitive values of capitalist societies" and that "participatory performance provides a powerful experiential model of alternative values and ways of being for people in capitalist societies. Repeated involvement with participatory performance creates a special social space for habit change necessary for developing alternative, sustainable ways." I argue that the Christmas bands do not fall so easily into either the presentational or the participatory performance category.[7] The band members are in the presentational performance mode when they perform on stage at an event or at competitions when they are being adjudicated for their performances and "competitive values" are at stake. But during their many hours of practicing and playing, solely as a musical band or accompanying the road marches, they slip into a participatory performance mode in which every member is involved in some kind of performance together, whether playing an instrument or marching to a strident rhythm. The camaraderie expressed in their bodies, moving together in time to the music, and their facial expressions of deep satisfaction and pleasure in experiencing this kind of cohesion as a band, are extremely infectious. Even after one of the ritual conflicts in the St. Joseph's Christmas band, when they are out marching in the streets or performing at an event, this camaraderie envelops the band and tensions dissipate. My sense is that much of it had to do with the mischievous disposition yet firm guidance of the band father, the late Johannes September, who started St. Joseph's in his late teens with his cousin Andrew September in 1936. Johannes September had a wonderful sense of humor that he used as part of his repertory of leadership skills, and he usually managed to persuade everyone to come together in unity for the greater cause of the band. Probably the close-knit community of relatives and friends that forms a band is another factor in this creation of a sustainable musical community. With minimal funding from government or business, Christmas bands have sustained themselves for many decades through the performance of music and related activity: the bands sustaining the music and the music sustaining the bands.

Notes

1. I had joined the St. Joseph's Christmas Band in order to complete my doctoral research on the Christmas bands movement and was a delegate to the meeting.

2. The obvious inaccuracies prevalent in the score are sometimes resolved during rehearsals, but the score was transcribed exactly as I received it.

3. I coined the term *ghoema musical complex* when I first wrote about the three parading disciplines, which include the minstrel troupes and Malay choirs, for my PhD dissertation in 2012. See Bruinders 2019 for more concise writing about the term.

4. In a radio interview on Fine Music Radio (February 15, 2013), Abdullah Ibrahim credited the Christmas bands with inspiring his compositions.

5. The formation of the Eoan Group, a cultural organization performing opera, ballet, and drama for coloured people founded in 1933 by Helen Southern-Holt, a white woman, is one such example. The Eoan Group formed the first operatic company in South Africa in the 1950s with amateur singers, many of whom struggled to read music. The company traveled to the United Kingdom in 1975 to perform their operatic repertoire in London and Scotland (see Eoan History Project 2013).

6. Literally "reel dance" from the Scottish dance form, but it is more of a locally conceived dance in the rural Western Cape in which the choreography is based on rural activities and gender normativity. Considered to be the oldest indigenous dance form in southern Africa, reached international attention when the group from Wupperthal, Nuwe Graskoue Trappers, won several medals in different categories and the open dance category in the World Championship of Performing Arts competition in Los Angeles in 2015.

7. Turino does not necessarily suggest that the four fields framework is a complete or closed system for analysis (2009, 97).

Bibliography

Austerlitz, Paul. 1997. *Merengue: Dominican Music and Dominican Identity*. Philadelphia: Temple University Press.

Boonzajer Flaes, Robert M. 2000. *Brass Unbound: Secret Children of the Colonial Brass Band*. 2nd ed. Amsterdam: Royal Tropical Institute.

Britz, Engela. 2019. "Songs in the Dust: *Riel* Music in the Northern and Western Cape Provinces, South Africa." Master of Music thesis, University of Cape Town.

Bruinders, Sylvia. 2006. "Grooving and Learning with a Christmas Band." In *The Transformation of Musical Arts Education: Local and Global Perspectives from South Africa*, edited by Hetta Potgieter, 106–23. Potchefstroom, South Africa: North-West University.

Bruinders, Sylvia. 2006/7. "This Is Our Sport! Christmas Band Competitions and the Enactment of an Ideal Community." *South African Music Studies* 26/27:109–26.

Bruinders, Sylvia. 2012. *Parading Respectability: An Ethnography of the Christmas Bands Movement in the Western Cape, South Africa*. PhD diss., University of Illinois, Urbana-Champaign.

Bruinders, Sylvia. 2017. *Parading Respectability: The Cultural and Moral Aesthetics of the Christmas Bands Movement in the Western Cape, South Africa*. Grahamstown, South Africa: NISC.

Bruinders, Sylvia. 2019. "Ghoema Musical Complex." In *Bloomsbury Encyclopedia of Popular Music of the World*, Vol. 12, *Genres: Sub-Saharan Africa*, edited by David Horn and John Shepherd, 153–57. London: Bloomsbury Academic.

Cohen, S. 1995. "Sounding out the City: Music and the Sensuous Production of Place." *Transactions of the Institute of British Geographers* 20(4): 434–46.

Eoan History Project. 2013. *Eoan: Our Story*. Johannesburg: Fourthwall Books; Stellenbosch: DOMUS.

Erb, J. Lawrence. 1926. "Music for a Better Community." *Musical Quarterly* 12(3): 441–48.

Goertzen, Christopher. 2018. "Music Contests and Communities: A Small Competition Powwow and a Complex Fiddle Contest." In *The Routledge Companion to the Study of Local Musicking*, edited by Suzel A. Reily and Katherine Brucher, 129–37. New York: Routledge.

Gunderson, Frank, and Gregory Barz, eds. 2000. *Mashindano! Competitive Music Performance in East Africa*. Dar es Salaam, Tanzania: Mkuki na Nyota Press.

Hagedorn, K. J. 2001. *Divine Utterances: The Performance of Afro-Cuban Santeria*. Washington: Smithsonian Institution Press.

Pacini Hernandez, Deborah. 1995. *Bachata: A Social History of a Dominican Popular Music*. Philadelphia: Temple University Press.

Ramsey, Gordon. 2009. "Music, Emotion and Identity in County Antrim Flute Bands." PhD diss., Queen's University, Belfast.

Schippers, Huib. 2010. *Facing the Music: Shaping Music Education from a Global Perspective*. Oxford: Oxford University Press.

Schippers, Huib. 2018. "Community Music Contexts, Dynamics, and Sustainability." In *The Oxford Handbook of Community Music*, edited by Brydie-Leigh Bartleet and Lee Higgins, 23–41. New York: Oxford University Press.

Shelemay, Kay Kaufman. 2011. "Musical Communities: Rethinking the Collective in Music." *Journal of the American Musicological Society* 64(2): 349–90.

Stillman, A. 1996. "Hawaiian Hula Competitions: Event, Repertoire, Performance, Tradition." *Journal of American Folklore* 109(434): 357–80.

Titon, Jeff Todd. 2009. "Economy, Ecology, and Music: An Introduction." *World of Music* 51(1): 5–15.

Titon, Jeff Todd. 2015. "Sustainability, Resilience, and Adaptive Management for Applied Ethnomusicology." In *The Oxford Handbook of Applied Ethnomusicology*, edited by Svanibor Pettan and Jeff Todd Titon, 157–96. Oxford Handbooks Online.

Titon, Jeff Todd. 2019. *Sustainable Music: A Research Blog on the Subject of Sustainability, Sound, Music, Culture, and Environment*. Accessed September 25, 2020. https://sustainablemusic.blogspot.com/.

Turino, Thomas. 1984. "The Urban-Mestizo Charango Tradition in Southern Peru: A Statement of Shifting Identity." *Ethnomusicology* 28(2): 253–70.

Turino, Thomas. 1993. *Moving away from Silence: Music of the Peruvian Altiplano and the Experience of Urban Migration.* Chicago: University of Chicago Press.

Turino, Thomas. 1997. "Music in Latin America." In *Excursions in World Music*, edited by Bruno Nettl, Charles Capwell, Philip V. Bohlman, Isabel K. F. Wong, and Thomas Turino, 223–50. Upper Saddle River, NJ: Prentice Hall.

Turino, Thomas. 2008. *Music as Social Life: The Politics of Participation.* Chicago: University of Chicago Press.

Turino, Thomas. 2009. "Four Fields of Music Making and Sustainable Living." *World of Music* 51(1): 95–117.

Turner, Victor. 1969. *The Ritual Process: Structure and Anti-Structure.* London: Routledge and Kegan Paul.

The World of Music. 2009. Vol. 51, no. 1, Music and Sustainability.

The World of Music, n.s. 2015. Vol. 4, no. 1, Sound Futures: Exploring Contexts for Music Sustainability.

Wilson, Olly. 1992. "The Heterogeneous Sound Ideal in African-American Music." In *New Perspectives on Folk Music Traditions: Essays in Honor of Eileen Southern*, edited by Josephine Wright and Samuel A. Floyd Jr., 328–38. Warren, MI: Harmonie Park.

8   Affective Assembly and Participatory Politics at the Palestine Music Expo

DAVID A. MCDONALD

Standing backstage at the Palestine Music Expo (PMX) in April 2019, Tamer Nafar quietly admitted, "I think I may have crossed the line this time." As he paced anxiously among an assemblage of press and festival delegates, crowds of young Palestinians swelled in anticipation of his upcoming performance with the hip hop collective DAM. A seasoned performer on the front lines of political controversy, Tamer Nafar rarely shies from scrutiny. Rather, he thrives on it. For nearly twenty years, his unapologetic voice has captured the hearts of a generation of Palestinians. But on this April night in Ramallah he was noticeably anxious about confronting the crowds at the Grand Park Hotel.

Three days earlier Nafar had released a music video, "Tamer Must Vote," wherein he urged Palestinian citizens of Israel (colloquially called '48s) to vote in the upcoming national elections.[1] His logic was sound: By participating in Israeli electoral politics Palestinians stood the best chance of preventing a fifth term for Prime Minister Benjamin Netanyahu and, perhaps, increasing their political influence in the Knesset. But his perspective was toxic: Amid a hostile campaign that featured openly racist calls for expulsion and annexation by both candidates, any plea for participation in Israeli elections reeked of normalization (*tatbīa'*). For many, voting would sever political ties between privileged, enfranchised '48s in Israel and those without civil liberties living under occupation in the West Bank and Gaza Strip, all while reinforcing the fallacious image of Israel as the Middle East's one shining democracy (Pappe 2017, 205–10). For them, to vote is to give the occupier the gift of recognition, while it disregards the disenfranchisement of millions.

Within hours of its release, the video went viral. The *Guardian*, CNN, and the *New York Times* all ran dedicated articles.[2] It was clear that international news media loved the optics of Palestinians voting as Israeli citizens. But back home, Nafar knew that he may have alienated his base right before his biggest performance of the year.

Making my way into the festival, I was confident that the crowd would rally behind their superstar. "No worries," I said to him. "The video will get people talking. And who knows? Maybe it will be enough to show Bibi [Netanyahu] the door." My logic was sound, for no artist of the past twenty years has had a greater impact on the pursuit of Palestinian self-determination than Tamer Nafar. But my perspective was naïve. Tempers were high in the run-up to the election. And even Palestine's favorite rap collective could not escape the crowd's frustration. As the group was announced, celebratory chants spread throughout the theatre, "Abū Nafar! *clap clap clap!* Abū Nafar! *clap clap clap!*"[3] But just as quickly, the chanting changed. A group of fans equipped with signs made their way to the front of the stage chanting, "*Yusqūt Tatbīa*'!" (Down with normalization). This was a modified version of the familiar slogan "*Yusqūt al-Nazām*" made famous during demonstrations at Egypt's Tahrir Square in 2011. The rhythm and cadence were well known, the signs provided the text, and the chant spread easily through the crowd. Security moved in to confiscate the signs, but the chants persisted. A circle of protesters emerged, redirecting attention away from the stage inward toward the chanting. Nafar stood motionless at center stage, microphone down by his side, noticeably affected. He surrendered the moment and once the chants subsided, he began a set of new songs from DAM's album *Ben Haana wa Maana* (2019). The crowd had made its point. The atmosphere during the first few songs was tense, but within minutes the crowd had resumed its enthusiastic support, singing along, dancing, and taking pictures of the artists on stage. Following the performance DAM signed autographs and posed for selfies with their many fans. Nafar waved off my attempt at an interview, noticeably frustrated. The crowd did indeed come around, but Nafar got the message.

It is within these brief performative moments that the affective power of sound to shape bodies and the body politic becomes most obvious. Indeed, music is powerful not merely in its capacity to solicit participation, but also in its capacity to transform communities; to guide them through a multilayered process of confrontational, deliberative, and pragmatic social action (Mattern 1998). In this brief moment, familiar sung protest chants, drawn from the collectively remembered past, proved to be an effective tool for demanding recognition, asserting presence, and rewriting normative codes of legibility. At first confrontational, the chants soon took on a deliberative character, and later moved toward pragmatic social transformation. Voices raised in solidarity created feelings of solidarity. Bodies moving together in coordinated action shaped the contours of the body politic. Competing notions of community, nation, and citizenship were given opportunity for growth and transformation. Within the audience,

nested intersectional groups each made claims to the nation, demanding recognition and acceptance. And from that demand, the community reemerged,
motivated to move forward in new ways.

I focus on this particular moment, brief as it was, to begin a conversation
about the activist potential of sounded thought and behavior. Although in previous work I may have focused entirely on the content of the songs performed and
their efficacy in reflecting and generating anticolonial sentiment (McDonald
2009, 2010, 2013b), in this chapter I investigate the affective dimensions of sound
and assembly as tools of direct action and anticolonial politics. In particular, I
am interested in exploring the idea of festivals as a form of affective assembly
and coalitional performance. For example, how do festivals, as opposed to traditional concerts and street protests, constitute sites of activism and forms of
social and political intervention? What potential does this performance and the
larger PMX festival have for advancing Palestinian efforts at self-determination?
Attending to the activist turn in ethnographic research, I seek to explore festivals as potential forms of direct action and anticolonial politics (Wong 2004;
Hayes 2010; Snyder 2022; Paramaditha 2018; Shao 2021). Specifically, how can
a critical ethnographic study of festivals reveal the ways in which organizers,
performers, and other participants encounter and challenge the myriad forms
of violence that frame their world?

As Turino eloquently demonstrates, participatory action, and in particular
coordinated sonic and gestural action, are among a variety of activities that can
be potential resources for social change, alternative citizenship, and long-term
political transformation (Turino 2016, 298). According to Turino, participatory
music making and dance are key to social change because they operate according
to values and practices diametrically opposed to the dominant capitalist ethos,
they engender a kind of egalitarian consensus building, they are pleasurable, thus
leading to a continuity of involvement, and they become "the basis for special
social cohorts (voluntary social groups drawn together by enthusiasm for the
activity and by shared, pre-existing tendencies toward the broader values that
underlie the activity)" (ibid.). In participatory contexts cohort members support
each other in the practice of alternative habits of thought and action. Flow states
and profound feelings of *communitas* positively reinforce these new habits as the
basis for community and connection (V. Turner 1969; Csikszentmihalyi 1990).
And when these new habits contrast with and challenge the status quo, the activity exhibits a kind of performativity whereby participants both imagine and
enact new aspirational models of citizenship and belonging (Snyder 2022). Over
time, as these habits and values are socialized across generations, new forms of
belonging, new citizenship, and new political realities emerge (Turino 2008).

While Turino's case studies focus on the subtle long-term effects of participatory music making, I believe that this model proves useful as a starting point for

theorizing more direct (immediate) activist interventions such as those exhibited at the PMX festival in 2019. Indeed, festival scholars have long attended to the ways in which participatory dynamics elicit feelings of *communitas* necessary for a successful festival experience (Rutherdale 1996; Van Heerden 2009; E. Turner 2012). Roxy Robinson goes further, demonstrating that the tensions between participatory and presentational dynamics have a direct impact on the activist potential of any festival event (Robinson 2016, 11). According to Robinson, participatory models elicit a more meaningful mode of social celebration in that they allow audience members a level of direct control, hence becoming part of the performance. In the moment I describe above, political impact was dependent on direct, physical, and sounded audience control. Whether such control is solicited by artists or taken from them, when barriers separating performers and spectators dissolve a more egalitarian ethos emerges. This emergence, I argue, is crucial to understanding how such festivals as PMX can become tools of direct action, activism, and anticolonial politics.

Moving from the more intimate spaces Turino describes to larger political contexts, it is worth considering how these same dynamics operate. If we imagine festival participants (and festivals themselves) as attempting to claim direct physical and sounded control over public spaces, as interventions into the spheres through which bodies may appear and be seen and heard, we notice a similar process brought to scale. Insofar as participants find pleasurable the emergence of egalitarian modes of interaction, so, too, might we imagine festivals as a means for historically marginalized groups to feel and act as if they are "part of the performance" (Robinson 2016, 11). In this way, festivals gather and mobilize participatory assembly toward strategic coalition building. They are forms of direct action that operate as moments of affective assembly and coalitional performance. Coming together, moving rhythmically, acting in concert—all are aspects of an affective assembly, a strategic form of political performativity that marshals desire for a more livable life (Butler 2015, 18).

And yet, the politics of participation is not enough. Specifically, I argue that although participatory dynamics are an important resource for social and political transformation, any theory of festival activism must attend to the contested spheres of appearance through which any political demand can be made (context); the role of media (gaze) in the politics of legitimation; and the precarity, vulnerability, and exposure of those assembled (violence). Context, gaze, and violence are key variables. Using PMX as a case study, I argue that the signifying effect of festival activity is not merely to facilitate feelings of solidarity or belonging among participants. Nor is it to enable the articulation of transgressive ideas. Rather, the activist potential of festivals lies in the constitution and legitimation of transgressive bodies, the manipulation of external gaze on those bodies, and the reclamation of public spaces on behalf of those bodies. The signifying effect of PMX lies in its capacity to define communities and legitimize their presence within conflicting (often violent) spheres of appearance (Arendt 1958; Rancière 1999; Butler 2015).

If settler-colonial states are premised on the absence or erasure of indigenous populations, anticolonial politics must always entail some kind of intervention into the fields of visibility and audibility that enact and enforce such erasure (Arendt 1958; Rancière 1999). As many scholars have argued previously, where Palestinians are rendered invisible, where demands for rights and recognition are always and already foreclosed, the struggle for self-determination is at its base a struggle for appearance (Butler 2009; Peteet 2017; Hammami 2016, 174). How and under what conditions might Palestinians, then, begin to appear, to be seen and heard as subjects worthy of empathy and recognition (Butler 2009, 2–5)? What role might music festivals such as PMX have in advancing this process?

For its many participants, and at various levels, PMX makes a direct and embodied intervention into the visual and aural spheres of appearance through which Palestine and Palestinians become known and meaningful. As this bois-terous group assembled to protest various forms of colonial erasure, they exer-cised a performative right to appear and be heard, a right to insert their bod-ies into confrontational environments, and in that appearance, enact "a more livable set of economic, social, and political conditions" (Butler 2015, 11). This moment aptly demonstrates Judith Butler's notion of the "embodied and plural performativity" of assembly (58), whereby precarious bodies redeploy spaces of appearance in order to contest and negate existing forms of political legitimacy. The performative means by which these demands are made, what I label here as affective assembly and coalitional performance, are essential components for theorizing festival activism.

Palestine Music Expo

The Palestine Music Expo was initially conceived by Rami Younis, Martin Goldschmidt, Mahmoud Jrere, and Abed Hathout as a means of providing valuable performance opportunities to Palestinian musicians. Their idea was to bring leading music industry professionals to Ramallah for a three-day festival where they would interact with local musicians in a variety of contexts: panels, workshops, and performances. International delegates were also invited to lead professional development sessions, provide feedback, and work with musicians on cultivating their craft. In his interview with *PBS News Hour*, Rami Younis explained:

> We are connecting Palestine to the rest of the world using music. That is [how] I would describe PMX with one sentence. That is what we do. This is us, trying to tell the world that Palestine isn't just Gaza, occupation, soldiers, checkpoints, and

that. Palestine is also music. Palestine is also cinema. Palestine is all of this stuff. People don't see that. And we are not victims. We're not victimizing ourselves.[4]

In a meeting with the artists before the 2016 festival PMX co-founder Martin Goldschmidt stated:

> Basically, as you all know it is not easy being a musician anywhere. It is more than doubly not easy being a musician in the West Bank. So, we are trying to find ways to help. The first thing we are going to do is bring people from international festivals. We are going to bring people from international festivals to Ramallah and Haifa. We are going to bring booking agents [who] book tours in Europe and America to Ramallah. And we are going to be able to meet them, you'll be able to present your music. And you'll have a chance to ask their advice, see what they are looking for. . . . And you can learn a lot about what to do and what not to do. It can save you a lot of time. Just meeting them can create opportunities. You will have the opportunities to hang out, and talk one-on-one. Some of them will give workshops. You will realize that they are real people. The other side of it is *they will realize that you are not a bunch of terrorists*. [laughter] You are stable musicians. It's quite frightening to come here. We will create that sort of one-to-one opportunity. And the ways to learn how it works. But we want to do more than that. *We want to do things that [create] long-term healthy infrastructure.* We are not sure what they are, what we need. We also need to raise a lot of money to do it. Maybe. Hopefully this event is something that grows bigger. *Ways of connecting you with each other, so you learn from other Palestinian musicians what works and what doesn't work. Ways of connecting you with the international community. And to connect international community with you.*[5]

Each of these comments articulates a sincere desire to build infrastructure, develop musical acts, and connect Palestine to international audiences. It is also important, however, to point out a parallel desire to change the ways in which international audiences view or otherwise interpret Palestine. Both Goldschmidt and Younis expressed the desire to humanize Palestinians through popular music and culture. Insofar as the festival provides essential performance opportunities for young Palestinian musicians, it also provides the outside cosmopolitan world with a new lens through which to see (and hear) Palestine.

The overall production of the festival reflected these goals. The event was held in one of Ramallah's finest resort hotels, the Grand Park. Festival delegates and artists were provided with delicious catered meals, refreshments, and concierge services. Merchandise tables offered T-shirts, CDs, posters, and other pop music paraphernalia. The stage, sound, and lighting were state-of-the-art, akin to major world music festivals in Europe and North America. Documentary film crews circulated among the crowd, interviewing performers and audience members alike, while nightly performances were live-streamed online. In my two decades of attending music festivals throughout the region, PMX was by far the most impressive in its production and execution.

In just its first three years PMX drew more than fifteen thousand visitors. Sixty percent of them were between the ages of eighteen and thirty-four. PMX 2019 featured seventy-five invited delegates from ten different countries, with twenty-one different bands performing for a total crowd of more than five thousand attendees.[6] And all of this occurred amid an ongoing humanitarian crisis and military occupation. An event of this size presents considerable logistical challenges. As Rami Younis pointed out to me, "The biggest challenge [for us] is always getting people to where they need to be. At times it's impossible. But that is the whole point, showing the world that the occupation can't prevent us from putting on a great show."[7] Indeed, the infrastructural and technological accomplishment of producing an event of this magnitude was itself a kind of victory against the occupation. One performer, Apo, noted, "It's definitely an escape to have fun. We enjoy, we see, we do, and it's great stuff, but alas I'm going to pass these checkpoints again. I'm going to have to talk to these soldiers so I [can] go back to my home. [It] doesn't feel good but that is life."[8] Before his performance at PMX 2019, Bashar Murad said:

> It was amazing. I played in PMX 2017, two years ago. And this is my second performance. This [is] one of my favorite events that has happened in Palestine ever. So, I think everyone that is watching this should come. . . . It was a really cool feeling. People were into it. And the feeling on stage, the lighting, the production is huge. So, I think it was one of my favorite performances I've ever done.[9]

These comments highlight the at times insurmountable obstacles of producing a music festival in Palestine. Immobility, vulnerability, and escape were important mechanisms for creating social meaning. Each indexically pointed toward the violent carceral geographies that Palestinians must navigate in their daily lives. Indeed, the occupation was the (not so) subtle context within and against which festival participants assembled. By this I mean that the occupation was more than mere backdrop for PMX; it was a determining condition and therefore central to its signifying effect.

The Matrix of Control

Although Ramallah possesses the trappings of any cosmopolitan city in the Arab world, it exists as an "enclave" of provisional life under military occupation (Peteet 2017). In these enclaves, the local population lacks any form of nationally or internationally recognized citizenship or legal protections. Governed by the Israeli military, Palestinians in the West Bank and Gaza Strip live under the ambiguously defined jurisdiction of the Israeli state, yet they are by no means citizens of that state. They are subjected to Israeli military law but are refused the legal means to contest that law via the democratic process. Lisa Marie Cacho effectively adopts Orlando Patterson's (1982) notion of "social death" to describe such groups. "Ineligible for personhood," these populations "are excluded from the ostensibly democratic processes that legitimate law, yet they are expected to unambiguously accept and unequivocally uphold a legal and political system that depends on the unquestioned permanency of their rightlessness" (Cacho 2021, 6).[10]

The rightlessness that Palestinians experience is rooted in a settler-colonial project that seeks to ensure the mobility and security of Israeli Jews at the expense of the indigenous Palestinian population (Wolfe 2006; Weizman 2012; Peteet 2017). Patrick Wolfe labels this a "logic of elimination," whereby indigenous bodies, histories, and presence must be eliminated in the act of constructing a new colonial society (Wolfe 2006, 389). The fundamental premise of the settler-colony, Wolfe argues, rests on an empty landscape. So goes the Zionist trope *"a land without a people, for a people without land"* (Said 1979, 9; Khalidi 1997, 101; Pappe 2017, 31–35). The settler-colonial regime thus relies on and produces differential visibilities by means of which the settler-colony can be instantiated and legitimized while the native's presence is erased (Shalhoub-Kevorkian 2010, 10). This erasure is enforced via various forms of colonial governance that criminalize Palestinian presence as an existential threat to the state and its founding narrative. Where Israeli law presumes, requires, and enacts their erasure, Palestinians are denied the option to be law-abiding. Simply being Palestinian can be a criminal act (Berda 2011, 45; Peteet 2017, 21).

The ongoing military occupation of the West Bank and Gaza Strip is the most visible (though by no means the only) mechanism of Israeli settler-colonialism. Justified by twin discourses of Israeli security and Palestinian criminality, in practice, the occupation exerts a "matrix of control" over Palestinian life (Halper 2006). Israel's spatial occupation seeks to control the land by building Jewish settler colonies and their constitutive bypass roads, military bases, surveillance towers, checkpoints, closed military areas, and airpower. To do this, the Israeli military oversees a complex network of laws, permits, architectural planning systems, and home demolitions designed to severely constrain Palestinian mobility and limit growth (Weizman 2012). Both of these fields, spatial and legal, impose divisions that separate and transform Palestinian spaces and further implement a hierarchy of access to natural resources. In addition to reducing space, the occupation enforces temporal hardship, disrupting the rhythms of everyday life via forced closures, circuitous routes, bureaucratic delays, and long, debilitating lines (Peteet 2017). Routine closures, confinement, searches, and arrests constitute choreographed conditions of disorder and unpredictability, a kind of "calibrated chaos," that serves as a form of colonial governance and collective punishment (Peteet 2017, 18).

For Palestinians living in these enclaves, where unpredictability, disorder, and the threat of incarceration are strategically calibrated for maximum effect, daily life involves a perpetual state of anxious anticipation, trepidation, and waiting. As Peteet writes, "Discipline and anti-discipline are partnered to simultaneously produce visibility and invisibility, chaos and order, predictability and unpredictability, a Palestinian body that must switch gears constantly, undercutting planning and sociality—a body perpetually on edge" (2017, 19). Across these diverse fields operates a slow-moving ethnic cleansing engineered to encourage the settlement of Palestinian land by Israeli Jews and the elimination of Palestine's indigenous population by means of collective punishment.

Within a settler-colonial discourse in which millions of exiled and dispossessed Palestinians are not only unrecognized but profoundly unrecognizable, and simply being Palestinian is, therefore, a transgressive (if not criminal) act, such festivals as PMX not only provide a powerful means of being Palestinian but create essential pathways to being heard and seen as such (McDonald 2020). As an act of affective assembly, PMX laid bare the incarcerative effects of the occupation, and in denying and defying its precepts, took direct action against it. International delegates were given the chance to experience Palestinian life first hand on solidarity tours of Bethlehem, Hebron, and Jerusalem. These tours were both strategic and effective, educating delegates on the history of the Palestinian crisis, providing direct experience of life under occupation, and soliciting empathy for Palestinian artists. Invited artists and ticket holders faced even greater hardship travelling to Ramallah. Simply appearing at PMX was an act of transgressive politics.

This message became clear when the Gaza-based Sol Band took the stage. Since its establishment Sol Band had struggled mightily against censorship and harassment by the local Islamist (Hamas-dominated) municipal government. Sol Band's rock-infused approach to Palestinian folk songs and Arab pop classics ran counter to local Islamist politics, putting the group at great risk of arrest and harassment. To make matters worse, the Israeli military refused to allow key band members to leave the Gaza Strip, forcing the group to find last-minute replacements ("Anybody know a good bass player?"). Despite these difficulties Sol Band appeared on stage to one of the largest ovations of the night. Everyone in the audience seemingly knew the difficulties the group had faced in making it to the stage: first, in creating a rock band with such limited resources; second, in withstanding the threats of local Islamist authorities; and third, in successfully navigating the Israeli occupation. Their celebrated appearance signified an incredible victory against conservative Islamism and colonial occupation. After the performance, lead singer Hamada Nasrallah was astounded by the crowd's reaction. "We never expected such a supportive audience," he told me. "We are just so happy to have made it here at all. We had no idea there would be so many people."[11]

Sol Band's appearance at PMX was also heralded as a victory for Palestinian unity and community building. Following their thirty-minute set festival organizer Abed Hathout was quick to point out that PMX represented a unique national collaboration. "PMX is about supporting [Palestinian] musicians, wherever they can be found," he explained. "We got over 300 applications [to perform], and we took the best musicians no matter where they were [from]. By far, this is the best representation of contemporary *Palestinian* music."[12] Hathout's declaration speaks to a victory of mobility and further illustrates the potential for PMX to be a tool for community building. Drawing musicians from Israel ('48s), the West Bank, the Gaza Strip, and the diaspora under a single banner of Palestinian music makes a powerful statement: that despite efforts to eliminate or segregate Palestinians, they remain one indivisible community. Through a complex interplay of performance, image, acoustics, and various technologies of representation, PMX indexically staged a unified national community for international consumption.

Optics and Legitimation

And yet, any act of self-fashioning holds severe consequences for those omitted, excluded, or left unseen or unheard. By marking the event as "Palestinian," PMX laid claim to the nation and its various humanitarian demands. For musicians who were not included in the event, those who perhaps performed folk, classical, or religious musics, PMX was particularly damaging, not only by its denial of international exposure and opportunity, but more important, by its essentializing of Palestinian music for international consumption. Indigenous folk poet-singers and dancers (*zajjal īn*), for example, were not considered for inclusion. Likewise, performers of Islamic repertoires (*inshād din īya*) were excluded (or self-excluded) by virtue of the festival setting, which included mixed audiences and alcohol consumption. In the field of Palestinian art music only one group, Le Trio Jubran, has ever performed at PMX. I assume that their inclusion was a result of their international reputation and pop fusion style. Insofar as this was a pop music festival intended to better position Palestinian artists in the international pop music marketplace, those left out were not only denied exposure but legitimacy. Composer and virtuoso instrumentalist Issa Boulos expressed serious concern that PMX will have a negative effect on artist agency and creative control.[13] In his conversations with participating artists, Boulos learned that many revamped their set lists to appeal to international audiences. Other musicians were offended that a large portion of the participants communicated in English and were drinking alcohol, using profanity, and dressed inappropriately, with piercings and tattoos. According to Boulos, one instrumentalist said, "[PMX] is not for us, it's intended for a different crowd. The festival is tailored to a younger generation and not for *serious* musicians. It embraces hip-hop and rap more than anything else." Boulos finished his critique by stating:

I am concerned that one of the last scenes that was untouched by the commercial industry or by any other platforms . . . will lose its edge, artistic engagement, expression, integrity, and identity. I am concerned that such platforms can easily turn into a space/time capsule for local communities that are already alienated within their own culture and picked up by Westerners, because what these communities do seems to be consensual to Western values. The notions of cultural colonialism, alienation, decolonization, cultural values, and identity seem to induce some discussions about where Palestinian national discourse is heading.[14]

Former Ministry of Culture official Nader Jalal publicly opposed the festival during one of the workshops, pointing out that "presenting Palestinian music solely for international audiences does little to support and preserve an independent Palestinian culture. . . . What message are we sending young musicians? That in order to succeed you must become a DJ or perform hip-hop." Instead, he inquired, "Why isn't the festival working to celebrate and support Palestinian artists who know their culture and history?"[15]

At the heart of both Boulos's and Jalal's comments is an important cultural anxiety that events such as PMX unintentionally further orientalist readings of Palestine by appealing to the "compassionate gaze" and cosmopolitan sensibilities of international audiences (McDonald 2020, 41). While showcasing pop music is perhaps the most efficient means of facilitating opportunities for Palestinian artists abroad, the signifying effect of this or any public assembly lies in its capacity to define communities and, by the nature of their size and visibility, legitimize their appearance. Performed before an audience of international music industry delegates and streamed across multiple online platforms, PMX is more than a mere stage for appearance; it is a mechanism of self-fashioning and control. And as much as I enjoyed the festival, marveled at its production, and celebrated its reception, this was not a representative showcase of Palestinian music. Rather, PMX presented an image of Palestine strategically crafted for international consumption and beholden to the demands of neoliberal market forces: familiar, comfortable, safe (yet exotic), stylish, victimized, and above all, worthy of support and recognition.

This struggle over legitimation invariably takes place in the play between public performance and media representation, where festival organizers, performers, and participants each lay claim to the event and its significance. If Palestine is constituted through the interplay of these performative materials, sounds, and technologies, then the media does more than simply report these claims. Rather, they play an essential role in the process by which the community is defined and its demands are made.

Without question PMX made the occupation visible to international audiences. And further, it demonstrated that Palestinian musicians are on the cutting edge of pop music production. Yet it did so by appealing to the compassionate gaze of international audiences. The effect of such a solicitation is rarely eman-cipatory. Rather, it positions Palestinians as objects of international consump-tion. This is an appeal that essentializes and reinforces victimization. Playing to the compassionate gaze has proved lucrative for festival organizers and artists alike. But, at the same time, such appeals create an expectation, a demand that these musicians conform to cosmopolitan aesthetics, values, and politics. The Palestinian cause was framed similarly: Palestinians are worthy of recognition and support on the basis, not of their humanity but of their cosmopolitanism. Both Boulos and Jalal express the desire for Palestinians to develop, innovate, and reclaim the agency to define themselves on their own terms. They seek to move beyond the standard trope of victimization and bring into visibility a situation in which Palestinians are not merely those who suffer but those who create (Faulkner 2014, 160). Celebrations of cosmopolitanism as a means of political resistance often neglect these points. Legibility and the accommoda-tion of difference are equally tools of colonial dominance and oppression.

Direct Action

While fully recognizing these points with regard to improving inclusivity and representation, to produce an event of this magnitude, under such difficult condi-tions, is nevertheless an extraordinary accomplishment, and not merely in building infrastructure and connecting Palestinian musicians with international audiences. Palestine Music Expo's greatest impact, I argue, is as a form of direct action against the occupation. The *Midwest Academy Manual for Activists* defines *direct action* as when "the people directly affected by the problem take action to solve it" in ways that alter power relationships and give them a sense of their own power, defined on their own terms (Bobo 2001, 11). David Graeber (2009) similarly defines *direct action* as a kind of "insistence, when faced with structures of unjust authority, on acting as if one is already free. . . . One does not solicit the state. One does not even necessarily make a grand gesture of defiance. Insofar as one is capable, one proceeds as if the state does not exist" (203). Graeber further explains that direct action is "a way of actively engaging with the world to bring about change, in which the form of the action—or at least the organization of the action—is itself a model for the change one wishes to bring about" (206).

In PMX we find all of these elements. Festival organizers were clear about their desire to take action against the occupation and the underlying "logic of elimination" that sustains it. They did so by imagining and enacting a desired political alternative without regard or deference to the Israeli state. Festival organizers strategically crafted a pop music experience intended to disrupt and displace the overdetermining effects of the occupation. The festival was in part about staging Palestine and Palestinian music as it one day might be, as it one day should be. Akin to what Ghassan Hage conceives as "alter-politics," PMX offered a desire-based enactment of a political alternative rather than a demand-based performance of political opposition (Hage 2015, 2). Not a protest, per se, PMX was an enactment of an alternative Palestine richly desired by its participants.

As Graeber suggests, PMX actively endeavored to bring about change in a manner that modeled the change one wished to bring about. As both a means and an end, PMX imagined Palestinian sovereignty through its enactment. Andrew Snyder describes this as "pre-figurative politics, in which the action is a performative manifestation of new social and political relations, as well as an explicit and targeted petitioning of power" (Snyder 2022). In my conversations with festival participants it was common to hear exclamations like, "I can't believe we are sitting in Ramallah right now!" "Who knew we could do this?" or "This festival is exactly what we are fighting for." In an interview with *al-Jazeera*, Palestinian activist and journalist Basem Tamimi explained:

> What we can do now is *cultural* resistance. We have a new audience, not the political people, but music and others, poetry, sports. And this is a new way, not war but through culture. The idea is not just to scream against occupation, but to show that this is a place of joy. *Joy is the best revenge.* You are supposed to be a repressed people. But if you show it's a place of life, it's a great thing.[16]

Tamimi's reference to joy is particularly important because it further affirms how political potential is further aggregated by means of affect. More than a protest, parade, or speech, PMX is an affective assembly.

Alter-politics is a form of direct action that resists occupation via pleasure and the desire for an alternative future (Hage 2015). The idea of resistance through creative participatory politics and the pleasure that ensues reorients our thinking away from activism based in anger and refusal. Celebratory forms of resistance such as these may not directly end the occupation, but they certainly impede its normalization. Moreover, they offer Palestinians an opportunity for some sense of dignity and self-fashioning. Festival performer Jasmine explained, "The beautiful thing is that we are not coming here and going back and saying, 'Yeah, it's so hard and everything.' I go back and say it was amazing. I met these amazing ladies, we had the best time ever, and it was just beautiful. *It brings beauty to me.* That is the magic that I experience."[17] Watching thousands of young Palestinian fans scream and dance without concern for the awaiting violence outside, I am reminded of the importance of pleasure, joy, and beauty in any political endeavor. It's moments of joy such as these that make possible the continued struggle against seemingly insurmountable odds.

Palestine Music Expo explicitly enacts a redistribution and reinvention of bodies, affects, and sensorial politics. Even in the brief moments described above, when festival participants attempted to take control of Tamer Nafar's performance, we witness a kind of experimental exercise of political freedom. Within the festival, participants could learn how to move politically, how to activate, explore, or experiment with a kind of agency unavailable in everyday life. As a form of direct action, PMX countered the occupation by acting on the premise that the Israeli state has no legitimate authority to determine, sanction, or control modes of popular dissent and political engagement.

Conclusion

As an act of countervisibility PMX creates spaces for seeing and hearing Palestinians beyond the "logic of elimination" (Wolfe 2006, 389). The festival seeks to mobilize Palestinians as visible, legible, knowable subjects for various internal and external audiences. Indeed, each panel, workshop, and performance might be considered a strategic act of intervention against the incarcerative mechanics of the occupation, against Israeli efforts to segregate Palestinians from each other, and against the colonial spheres of appearance through which Palestinians have historically been erased (Arendt 1958, 50). In all of these spaces, festival participants deployed countervisibility as a means of advancing emancipatory goals.

But what makes PMX unique is its use of a festival as a means of direct action and anticolonial politics. For many of its participants PMX was an affective assembly, a coalitional performance of emancipation and sovereignty. And though the kind of escapism it afforded was ephemeral, I would argue that this kind of direct action is not trivial. Indeed, this kind of work has both immediate and long-term effects. In making Palestinian life a bit more livable PMX can be a major force in political transformation, not merely in the chants, slogans, or lyrical critique performed but as a coalitional performance that sustains enthusiasm through boisterous celebration. As Turino reminds us, musical experiences such as these foreground the crucial interplay between the possible and the actual (Turino 2008, 16–17). This festival offers a multisensorial opportunity for the impossible, the nonexistent, or the ideal to be imagined and enacted, leading to new lived realities. These performance experiences draw our attention to what is possible, they wake us from habit, and they provide "a temporary sense of a life more deeply lived" (Turino 2008, 18).

To this, I would add that in contexts of extreme vulnerability, participation in events such as PMX have a greater activist potential. The stakes are different. The escalation of risk heightens the potential for political transformation in that, by their appearance, participants indexically demonstrate a profound sincerity in their demands. Although each of the participants at PMX explicitly vocalized an opposition to Israeli occupation, they also, by virtue of their assembly, posed their challenge in corporeal terms. That is to say, simply by their presence these Palestinian bodies signified prior to, and apart from, any musical gesture. The intervention occurs in the very act of assembly, in the demand for appearance, and in the resulting exposure and vulnerability to state violence. To assert that Palestinians live, create, dance, and celebrate is already a politically significant form of countervisibility that implicitly challenges the underlying tenets of the occupation. Appearing together in a kind of coalitional performance where Palestine is reimagined, seen, heard, and felt through desire and joy, PMX participants enact a kind of affective assembly that by means of its resonance aggregates and extends conventional political demands. In this way PMX offers a fascinating case study in the ethnomusicological study of activism, not merely in its presentation of politically engaged artists or in its connecting those artists to the outside world, but as an act of affective assembly wherein Palestinians come together in embodied participatory action, and in that act lay claim to the nation and its desire for self-determination.

Notes

1. Tamer Nafar, "Tamer Must Vote." https://www.youtube.com/watch?v=TtMFjKYZ6bA.
2. Oliver Holmes, "Rapper Tamer Nafar Urges Palestinians not to Boycott Israel Poll," *Guardian*, April 6, 2019; David M. Halbfinger, "Boycott Israel's Election? A Palestinian Rapper Says No," *New York Times*, April 4, 2019; "Popular Palestinian Rapper Releases New Song Urging Arab-Israelis to Vote amid Calls for Election Boycott," *i24News*, April 4, 2019.
3. The chant "Abū Nafar" (Father of Nafar) is an example of a *kunya*, or teknonym, that expresses respect and bestows honor by referencing Tamer Nafar's position as head of household.
4. *PBS News Hour*, June 13, 2019.
5. PMX, "What Is PMX?" December 22, 2016, emphasis added.
6. PMX 2019 attendance statistics are from the PMX website.
7. Personal communication with the author, April 5, 2019, Ramallah, Palestine.
8. Televised interview with *al-Jazeera*, April 8, 2017.
9. Televised interview, *Night in Palestine*, June 7, 2019.
10. While Cacho's research is directed at the United States, her argument is pertinent to other settler-colonial environments.
11. Personal communication with the author April 5, 2019, Ramallah, Palestine.
12. Personal communication with the author, April 5, 2019, Ramallah, Palestine (emphasis added).
13. Personal communication with the author, May 14, 2019, Chicago, Illinois.
14. Personal communication with the author, May 14, 2019, Chicago, Illinois.
15. Public comment during the PMX 2019 festival panel on the history of Palestinian music and culture, April 6, 2019, Ramallah, Palestine.
16. Televised interview with *al-Jazeera*, April 8, 2017 (emphasis added).
17. Televised interview with *PBS News Hour*, June 13, 2019 (emphasis added).

Bibliography

Arendt, Hannah. 1958. *The Human Condition.* Chicago: University of Chicago Press.

Berda, Yael. 2011. "The Security Risk as a Security Risk: Notes on the Classification Practices of the Secret Service." In *Threat: Palestinian Prisoners in Israel*, edited by Abeer Baker and Anat Matar, 44–56. London: Pluto.

Bobo, Kimberley A. 2001. *Organizing for Social Change: Midwest Academy Manual for Activists.* Santa Ana, CA: Forum.

Butler, Judith. 2009. *Frames of War: When Is Life Grievable?* London: Verso.

Butler, Judith. 2015. *Notes Toward a Performative Theory of Assembly.* Cambridge, MA: Harvard University Press.

Cacho, Lisa Marie. 2021. *Social Death: Racialized Rightlessness and the Criminalization of the Unprotected.* Durham, NC: Duke University Press.

Csikszentmihalyi, Mihaly. 1990. *Flow: The Psychology of Optimal Experience.* New York: Harper and Row.

Faulkner, Simon. 2014. "On Israel/Palestine and the Politics of Visibility." In *Immigrant Protest: Politics, Aesthetics, and Everyday Dissent*, edited by Katarzyna Marciniak and Imogen Tyler, 147–68. New York: SUNY Press.

Graeber, David. 2009. *Direct Action: An Ethnography.* Edinburgh: AK Press.

Hage, Ghassan. 2015. *Alter-Politics: Critical Anthropology and the Radical Imagination.* Carlton, Victoria: Melbourne University Press.

Halper, Jeff. 2006. "The 94% Solution: Israel's Matrix of Control." In *The Struggle for Sovereignty: Palestine and Israel, 1993–2005*, edited by Joel Beinin and Rebecca L. Stein, 62–74. Stanford: Stanford University Press.

Hammami, Rema. 2016. "Precarious Bodies: The Activism of 'Bodies That Count' (Aligning with Those That Don't) in Palestine's Colonial Frontier." In *Vulnerability and Resistance*, edited by Judith Butler, Zeynep Gambetti, and Leticia Sabsay, 167–90. Durham, NC: Duke University Press.

Hayes, Eileen M. 2010. *Songs in Black and Lavender: Race, Sexual Politics, and Women's Music.* Urbana: University of Illinois Press.

Khalidi, Rashid. 1997. *Palestinian Identity: The Construction of Modern National Consciousness.* New York: Columbia University Press.

Mattern, Mark. 1998. *Acting in Concert: Music, Community, and Political Action.* New Brunswick: Rutgers University Press.

McDonald, David A. 2009. "Poetics and the Performance of Violence in Israel/Palestine." *Ethnomusicology* 53(1): 58–85.

McDonald, David A. 2010. "Geographies of the Body: Violence and Manhood in Palestine." *Ethnomusicology Forum* 19(2): 191–214.

McDonald, David A. 2013a. "Imaginaries of Exile and Emergence in Israeli Jewish and Palestinian Hip-Hop." *Drama Review* 57(3): 69–87.

McDonald, David A. 2013b. *My Voice Is My Weapon: Music, Nationalism, and the Poetics of Palestinian Resistance.* Durham, NC: Duke University Press.

McDonald, David A. 2020. "Junction 48: Hip-Hop Activism, Gendered Violence, and Vulnerability in Palestine." *Journal of Popular Music Studies* 32(1): 26–43.

Pappe, Ilan. 2007. *The Ethnic Cleansing of Palestine*. Oxford: Oneworld.

Pappe, Ilan. 2017. *Ten Myths About Israel*. New York: Verso.

Paramaditha, Intan. 2018. *Apple and Knife: Stories*. Jakarta, Indonesia: Lontar.

Patterson, Orlando. 1982. *Slavery and Social Death: A Comparative Study*. Cambridge, MA: Harvard University Press.

Peteet, Julie Marie. 2017. *Space and Mobility in Palestine*. Bloomington: Indiana University Press.

Rancière, Jacques. 1999. *Dis-Agreement: Politics and Philosophy*. Minneapolis: University of Minnesota Press.

Robinson, Roxy. 2016. *Music Festivals and the Politics of Participation*. London: Routledge, Taylor and Francis Group.

Rutherdale, Robert. 1996. "Canada's August Festival: Communitas, Liminality, and Social Memory." *Canadian Historical Review* 77(2): 221–49.

Said, Edward. 1979. *The Question of Palestine*. New York: Times Books.

Shalhoub-Kevorkian, Nadera. 2010. "Palestinian Women and the Politics of Invisibility: Towards a Feminist Methodology." *Peace Prints: South Asian Journal of Peacebuilding* 3(1): 1–21.

Shao, Oliver Y. 2021. "How Is That Going to Help Anyone? A Critical Activist Ethnomusicology." In *Transforming Ethnomusicology*. Vol. 1, *Methodologies, Institutional Structures and Policies*, edited by Beverley Diamond and Salwa El-Shawan Castelo-Branco, 87–100. New York: Oxford University Press.

Snyder, Andrew G. 2022. "Music Is Liberation: The Brass Liberation Orchestra and Direct Action." In *At the Crossroads of Music and Social Justice*, edited by Brenda Romero, Susan Asai, David A. McDonald, Andrew Snyder, and Katelyn Best, 239–58. Bloomington: Indiana University Press.

Turino, Thomas. 2008. *Music as Social Life: The Politics of Participation*. Chicago: University of Chicago Press.

Turino, Thomas. 2016. "Music, Social Change, and Alternative Forms of Citizenship." In *Artistic Citizenship: Artistry, Social Responsibility, and Ethical Praxis*, edited by David J. Elliott, Marissa Silverman, and Wayne D. Bowman, 297–312. New York: Oxford University Press.

Turner, Edith. 2012. *Collectivity: The Anthropology of Collective Joy*. London: Palgrave Macmillan.

Turner, Victor W. 1969. *The Ritual Process: Structure and Anti-Structure*. London: Routledge and Keegan Paul.

Van Heerden, Esther. 2009. "Liminality, Transformation and Communitas: Afrikaans Identities as Viewed Through the Lens of South African Arts Festivals: 1995–2006." PhD diss., Stellenbosch University.

Wolfe, Patrick. 2006. "Settler Colonialism and the Elimination of the Native." *Journal of Genocide Research* 8(4): 387–409.

Weizman, Eyal. 2012. *Hollow Land: Israel's Architecture of Occupation*. London: Verso.

Wong, Deborah. 2004. *Speak It Louder: Asian Americans Making Music*. New York: Routledge.

PART III

Mutual Indebtedness

9 Love and Debt

Performing Difference on the Mbira

TONY PERMAN

In memory of Chartwell, who built the bridge I traverse.
I am indebted.

Mukwasha mukuyu, haaperi kudyiwa.
(The son-in-law is a fig tree, he never stops being eaten.)
—Shona proverb

Learning the mbira is like falling in love, at least in Mary Catherine Bateson's terms, in which love depends on recognizing commonality and valuing difference (Bateson 2015). When my research students asked a white mbira player from California why she played mbira music from Zimbabwe, she suggested love—of the music, the people, and the place from which they came. Whether I'm talking to Zimbabwean spirit mediums, American students unexpectedly absorbed by the instrument, or lifelong members of West Coast marimba bands, explanations for why one plays the mbira often come down to love. Similarly, in his book *Love and Theft* Eric Lott (1995) interprets the musical practices and desires of white Americans who mimicked Black performance as minstrelsy in antebellum America through a lens of love. This is not to suggest equivalency between these practices; far from it. I play the mbira, and I bristle at my comparison. Rather, this provocation is intended to highlight the stakes involved when performing difference. When it comes to musicking in practices embedded within centuries of social inequality and oppression, love is not enough.

How might performing difference productively generate empathy to unsettle the boundaries of cultural fixity or intersect with creative, semiotic, or neoliberal freedoms? How should it shoulder burdens of moral responsibility? Perhaps Bateson's definition of love is incomplete. Love may recognize commonality and value difference, as she suggests, but it is also indebted, forever feeding back in relation to a sense of obligation. Fred Moten and Stefano Harney rely on the

Fig. 9.1. Tony Perman with Chartwell Dutiro in London, 1996. Photo by Lucy Duran.

concept of debt, which one acquires via interaction and historical inheritance that must be acknowledged (2013, 159), is mutual (61), and can never be repaid or forgiven (63). In order for love to be just, this recognition of debt must "become activated as a principle of social life" (154). Perhaps love, in the sense that can redeem mbira playing like that described here, also means the willing acquisition of interminable debt. Commonality, difference, and debt inform the love that is a prerequisite for righting historical wrongs, much like the son-in-law in a Shona family in Zimbabwe, the proverbial fig tree, ever bearing fruit that never ceases to be eaten. *Mukwasha mukuyu, haaperi kudyiwa.*

This essay focuses on the North American mbira community as "one" context of performing difference, although this multifaceted collection of participants and their motivations is difficult to summarize. What progress I have made owes much to collaborative work with three former Grinnell College students—Anne

Rogers, Sunny Zhao, and Luke Jarzyna—who helped shape this project and conducted their own ethnographic work with communities of American mbira enthusiasts. Together we worked with musicians from multiple backgrounds from both Zimbabwe and the United States.

The mbira has profoundly shaped communities that would not exist without it but that inevitably carry the traumas of racialized social inequality and the violent legacies of entrenched colonial injustice with them. This does not distinguish the mbira or its allure, but the historical complexities that tether its sounds to the ancestral spirits for whom they are ideally sounded render the mbira an instructive locus for exploring how the potential for difference to become self comes with the risk of violence and erasure. Unless we carefully consider past injustices, the love that binds these musical communities together reveals the theft that is a constant risk. When the important extramusical associations and contexts surrounding the mbira are detached, reducing music to mere sound in a more profound form of what R. Murray Schafer calls schizophonia (1977), theft and erasure threaten to define musical practice. Absent an acknowledgment of indebtedness and a ceaseless effort to do justice to that mutual and unpayable debt, performing difference and becoming the other risks erasing difference and consuming the other.

The mbira is the most widely heard of several related instruments from Zimbabwe on which metal keys are struck by the player's thumbs and forefingers. Beyond some structural similarities, the purposes with which these instruments are played, core repertoire, and expectations of performance vary from one instrument to the next. The primary purpose of this particular mbira (known as *nhare* or *mbira dzavadzimu*) is to serve ceremonies during which mediums are embodied by spirits of the dead as one component of a vibrant multisensory event. Whereas it seemed possible at the height of British colonialism to physically count the number of players, in 2022 there were hundreds of players in Zimbabwe and abroad that form a robust interconnected community organized around a single sacred musical tradition and homeland, often respectfully referred to by players abroad as "the source."

Mbira as Stranger. Anecdotally, based on decades of conversations with American players, the mbira's initial appeal for non-Zimbabwean players is often its sonic connotations of mystery and implication of otherness as songs oscillate between seemingly major and minor tonalities. Exposing a kind of "hungry listening," as Dylan Robinson calls it (2020), that emerges from a state of consumption built on perceptual habits and biases that treat sounds separately from their purposes and practices, this attraction to otherness is not always the motivating factor, because the musical elements typical of mbira coincidentally resemble those found in much-loved musical styles abroad (see Turino 1998), but white mbira performers have been criticized for simplistically appropriating the sounds of the African other.[1]

Sara Ahmed worries that this kind of "stranger fetishism . . . invests the figure of the stranger with a life of its own insofar as it cuts the stranger off from the histories of its determination" (2000, 5). Shallow performances of difference such as this risk erasing histories and complexity in the service of consuming exotic difference. The desire for mysterious music risks overshadowing the peoples and histories behind it. But this is not a given, and accusations of appropriation often paint with a broad brush. Unfortunately, initial encounters are always shallow. Accessing the depths of the mbira's meaning is a necessary burden (an obligatory debt) of experiencing the mbira's transnational and transhistorical intimacy.

Mbira as Self. Music is, after all, only fully accessible when it becomes less strange, less exotic. The distances signified during initial encounters of wonder and mystery are soon narrowed by the investment of time, energy, and humility needed to learn how to play, thus domesticating difference and celebrating commonality. Loosely akin to language learning, invested bi-musicality changes how performers of difference frame their senses of self and assert their senses of identity,[2] but there is a constant danger of artificially distinguishing between "the one who becomes" (Ahmed 2000, 118), that is, the ever-evolving self (Ahmed writes "consumer"), and "the one who merely is" (118), the stranger.

But not all players learn to identify with the mbira as self *after* encountering it as a stranger. For Zimbabwean players like Musekiwa Chingodza and Chartwell Dutiro, or American players who learn as children, relating to the mbira as a core part of self happens long before it is understood. Musicking as a child is deeply habit-forming. But foreign players are often expected to acknowledge that the mbira is, or should be, a stranger to them. Ironically, numerous players abroad in such places as the Pacific Northwest *do* identify the mbira as self before learning of its story and embeddedness in the fabric of Zimbabwe's history. In the marimba bands and mbira gatherings that have emerged in the decades since Dumisani Maraire first traveled to Washington State in the 1970s (Matiure 2008), dozens of children learn to music in Americanized spaces of Zimbabwean performance. It is who they are because they were socialized into it at a young age. Phenomenologically speaking, the contexts (Thirdness) of their shared experiences (Secondness) are often radically different from those that define performance in Zimbabwe (see the introduction).

Racism and colonialism loom large in this discussion, or they should. Whereas inequality in the United States is largely due to unresolved racism and the legacy of trans-Atlantic slavery, in Zimbabwe inequality is more directly traced to the exploitative history of British colonialism. These interrelated histories reveal the intractable legacies of white supremacy in different ways. In the United States in particular, celebrations of a shared humanity that don't acknowledge discourses of race and racism risk whitewashing the histories of oppression and inequality that lead to these kinds of attractions and anxieties. In Zimbabwe, mbira gatherings that bring foreigners of means together with locals burdened by the struggles of life in a failed state risk reinforcing and exploiting the racist and classist hierarchies that have remained in colonial Rhodesia's turbulent wake. Yet Chartwell Dutiro suggests that white mbira performers who learn to play beyond Zimbabwe's borders have a responsibility to travel to Zimbabwe. Acknowledging how Zimbabwe's colonial history implicates the mbira, he says,

> In Zimbabwe, the white people were the ones who came and told us the *mbira* wasn't good. They convinced us that the bible was right, and told us to throw away the *mbira* and sing hymns. Now, white people come back to Zimbabwe and tell us that they now like the *mbira*, and my people listen. We need to use education in the process of decolonization; we have to be emancipated from mental slavery. This is why I do what I do, in order to inspire my people, and this is why it is important for white people who like *mbira* to go to Zimbabwe.[3]

The centrality of debt emerges from these histories. As Harney and Moten suggest,

> There is this debt at a distance to a global politics of blackness emerging out of slavery and colonialism, a black radical politics, a politics of debt without payment, without credit, without limit. This debt was built in a struggle with empire before empire, where power was not with institutions or governments alone, where any owner or colonizer had the violent power of a ubiquitous state (2013, 64).

For Kathleen Higgins, performance can promote cross-cultural understanding and forge bonds of sympathy but may also reinforce ethnic and sectarian division (Higgins 2012). As explained in the introduction, music can productively connect people, facilitate empathy, and build community, but it isn't an inherent good. Music has been exploited for nefarious political projects of division often enough that ethical musical engagement can't be assumed. It's a conundrum that is difficult to reconcile.

There are too many voices in the mbira-playing community to generate consensus. There are Zimbabwean ex-pats in the United States who are deeply ambivalent about American, especially white American, appropriations of their culture that continue old colonial hierarchies, foreign performers of the mbira who have transformed their lives in deference to their respect for the traditions they love; mbira players from Zimbabwe who ceaselessly teach and share their traditions; North American academics who celebrate the strength of the American mbira and North American academics who rebuke it; and finally, the spirits, whose voices are perhaps the most obscured but which carry the weightiest moral authority for those who choose to listen. My students and I have spoken to mbira players resident in the United States who identify as Black, white, and otherwise; men, women, and otherwise; Zimbabwean, American, and otherwise; agnostics, atheists, and followers of spirits. I have worked with mbira players in Zimbabwe, the United Kingdom, and the United States; I've spoken with the spirits, who are the owners of the music for some but markers of backwardness, conservatism, and otherness for others.

Whose voices matter most? Zimbabweans disagree; North Americans disagree. No conclusion satisfies all perspectives. Historically, past chiefs and powerful *makombwe* and *mhondoro* spirits should matter most. But their voices are perhaps the hardest to hear in a rural Iowa classroom. The pages to follow include ethnographic work among Zimbabwean performers in Zimbabwe and the United States, as well as performers of multiple racial and national identities within the United States. My students and I have worked with at least one representative of each of the categories crudely listed above. In the search for an equal music, not all voices should be considered equally, but "should" is difficult to determine a priori. A voice only operates as such when it is acknowledged and intently heard.

Community and Empathy

When I ask American mbira lovers why they play, explanations quickly move to the community that exists because of the instrument. Tom in Santa Cruz says, "You're sort of participating in something that you're creating together so there's a connection." Musekiwa Chingodza, a renowned Zimbabwean player, says, "As mbira brings people together it also helps to build the community." This is not surprising, since it is a prototypical participatory genre integrating multiple parts requiring varying degrees of skill. One reading of the literature on the mbira by Paul Berliner (1993), Tom Turino (2000), Jennifer Kyker (2019), and others is that the raison d'être of mbira is the building of community (through the Secondness of collective flow). Spirit possession is important because it builds community in ways that transcend death itself. One common trope compares the mbira to a telephone, analogous in that it exists to provide a channel of communication to nurture a relationship with an ancestor that is a building block of community (Berliner 1993). Briannah, who grew up playing Zimbabwean music in Boulder, Colorado, says, "I like playing because it brings a sense of community that I don't think is found in other aspects of the culture I grew up in in America." But there are perhaps also reasons why people in the United States look to perform difference with the mbira rather than embrace a local participatory practice such as old-time music or shape-note singing. Its connection to a distant place with spiritual responsibilities does not seem incidental.

Community from Unhu

How do place and race categories define how community can be understood and *felt* among the myriad performers of the mbira who recognize the instrument as belonging to them or to somebody else? *Community* is a slippery term, frequently used uncritically. Following the introduction to this book, I define *community* as the composite relations grounded in similarity and difference among agents who act on their recognition of interdependence or mutual indebtedness. Community benefits from its flexibility, accommodating nations, ethnicities, and families as much as clubs, enthusiasts, and "affinity communities" (Shelemay 2011), but "affinity" ignores the centrality of mutual obligation in community. Mbira enthusiasts who celebrate the community that emerges from playing the mbira without acknowledging the fraught identity histories that lie beneath the surface risk inadvertently exploiting those histories.

Community can accommodate both kin and "oddkin" (Haraway 2016). In his theory of social formations, Thomas Turino (2008) distinguishes between cultural cohorts and cultural formations, and the mbira community discussed here is productively disciplined by this model. For Turino, partial sets of shared habits characterize cultural cohorts, whereas more comprehensive sets define cultural formations (2008, 112). The mbira community is a cohort (linked by habits of mbira playing) that cuts across formations of religion, diaspora, race, and nationality in ways that can be empowering, liberating, or threatening, depending on one's perspective.

Ethnomusicology has effectively demonstrated that music is a powerful means of generating community. But participants in ceremonies in Zimbabwe already knew this. Mbira as a mode of knowledge and a tool for fostering healthy relationships has long been reliably employed and transmitted from one generation to the next. Without indigenous ways of knowing and the embodiment of theory in practices such as this, ethnomusicology centered in Europe and the United States could never have reached the conclusions that are now so consistently taught.

In a Zimbabwe-centric theory of community, what is learned and craved during encounters such as those enabled by the mbira is *unhu,* which Jennifer Kyker defines as "a moral sense of personhood" (2016, 17). As she and others make clear, what defines this moral sense is a person's connection to others and modes of relating in generous ways, or "being a person among others."[4] It can even mean humanity itself (Serpell 2019). Unhu carries responsibility and, in Harney and Moten's terms, debt. Mandivamba Rukuni argues that "being a good human being by embracing these values, and leading your life along these pathways, is the trusted way of thanking your ancestors and of communicating with your Creator" (2007, 112). Without debt, there is no unhu. Without unhu, there is no community. If there is, the shallow community that remains risks sustaining the injustice of inequality.

Empathy

Mbira generates care, concern, and connection with distant people who would otherwise remain unknown: empathy. Although theorized in multiple ways, empathy has the potential to generate intimacy among strangers, eliding differences to connect people across barriers that divide them. Racism, nationality, religion, age, education, ethnicity, and gender can each prevent an American mbira enthusiast raced as white and a Zimbabwean performer raced as black from feeling like anything other than strangers. But "music can bridge entrenched boundaries" (Higgins 2018, 5). Creative acts of community building, the admiration and responsibility that emerge with mbira-generated empathy, and the active processes of what Chartwell and Musekiwa call "building bridges," are central to the music's appeal, power, and transmission (Dutiro 2007).

Of course, as Saidiya Hartman so powerfully illustrates, empathy generated through one's own imagination and experience risks placing "the self in the other's stead" and can obliterate that other (1997, 19–20). Empathy without an acknowledgment of mutual debt is merely pity. When I asked Musekiwa if he felt that these bridges went in both directions or if he was just feeding mbira-hungry Americans, he said, "Yeah, I feel the bridge is going to Zimbabwe because some people, some students, some of my friends who I have taught . . . they are helping other Zimbabweans back home, not just me. Myself, when we look for help, we are both humans. We share almost everything in common. . . . I want to treat people how I feel, the way I want to be treated also. I don't want to take advantage."

But the desires behind the love that shapes the empathy that builds these communities can also be rooted in dissatisfactions with home and their accompanying anxieties. This is true whether you are a young Zimbabwean caught in the country's post-colonial decline or an American seeking spaces to generate community and develop an unnamed sense of unhu. Briannah's words suggest as much. This love of mbira, giving focus to a desire for otherness, can mask an anxiety tied to self and identity. Mbira becomes an index for a desire that the world in which one finds oneself was different. For Zimbabweans, it offers links to a past freed from the unshakeable burdens of colonialism and its stubborn aftermath. For Americans, the sound of the "other" becomes a hopeful panacea for the ills at home. When responding to an ad for a performance by Musekiwa at Grinnell College in 2019, one person exposed frustration with their own community and the utopian desires represented in his music (see fig. 9.2).

Humility and hope are proffered as paths to a better future in America. But the shift from obligation to aspiration risks constraining the agency of the musicians it celebrates, who are now praised for ostensibly representing idealized values rooted in an idyllic past. They recall an uncomfortable moment for me as

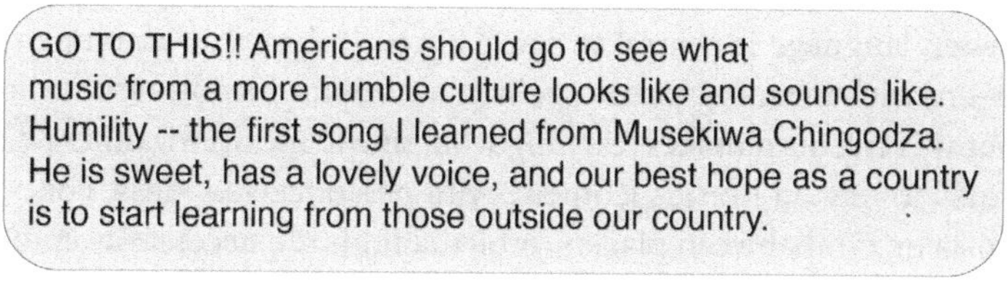

> GO TO THIS!! Americans should go to see what
> music from a more humble culture looks like and sounds like.
> Humility -- the first song I learned from Musekiwa Chingodza.
> He is sweet, has a lovely voice, and our best hope as a country
> is to start learning from those outside our country.

Fig. 9.2. Facebook post celebrating Musekiwa Chingodza in 2019.

a novice mbira player accompanying Chartwell Dutiro to Zimfest on Vancouver Island, Canada, in 1998, when an American mbira player rebuked Chartwell for his longstanding practice of performing with guitars and saxophones instead of playing it the real way. That person congratulated him for only using mbira on that 1998 tour.

Empathy is difficult (Hartman 1997, 18); it is precarious (19). By dictating the values to be musically celebrated, people risk reducing others to the shallowest of characteristics that will likely only be entrenched if the music remains a veneer on pre-determined habits unencumbered by investment and education, that is, knowledge. Knowledge, as embodied in performance and contextualized by study, conversation, and a consistent reminder not to mistake one's own experience for another's, is a prerequisite for a lifelong commitment to empathic performance.

Knowledge

One step toward understanding one's motivation or the music being embraced is simple: education. Chartwell argues, "We need education as a process of decolonization. People have got to learn" (Levay 2007, n.p.).[5] He sees hope despite the entrenched legacies of colonial inequalities. In his interview with Levay, Chartwell quotes a Shona saying: "Just because the baboons have gone to eat maize in your field, you don't abandon the field and say 'I am not going to the field anymore because the baboons have eaten my maize'" (ibid.). Whether in formal institutions of higher learning such as the college where my mbira classes take place, or in informal spaces underneath these institutions as what Jack Halberstam calls "study" in his introduction to *The Undercommons*, as "a mode of thinking with others separate from the thinking that the institution requires of you" (2013, 11), this "thinking with others" is implicitly acknowledged as the key space in which mbira's meaning can be gleaned, especially when done with an acknowledgment of indebtedness to players from Zimbabwe and their spirits.

But what can music mean? Can meaning be learned? To answer the second question first, of course it can . . . at least in part.[6] The first is more complicated.

Musical sounds are often liberated from the semantic predictability of language. Even when language is central to musicking—in lyrics or accompanying discourse—music's meanings are not reliant on language's power or its limits. It is free. But this freedom makes learning what music means for others difficult. It is too easy to rely on music's iconicity with preconceived ideas. For ethnomusicologists or Zimbabwean players, mbira sounds are necessarily embedded in deeper histories and contexts (Thirdness). Music is a way of knowing;[7] mbira music thus is a kind of indigenous knowledge that ought to be centered in these conversations.

What is this knowledge? For Musekiwa, it is necessarily spiritual. He, Chartwell, and Tute Chigamba all embody deeply understood theories of mbira as collaborative, communal, and instrumental in transcending the boundaries of life and death. The instrument itself carries the weight of this knowledge.[8]

Ethnomusicology has embraced music as a vehicle for encountering and experiencing difference. But whether this encounter becomes social knowledge is rarely certain; it requires communication. The communicative power of musical signs remains elusive, given their avoidance of linguistic predictability and generality. In explaining the impact of a sign in the mind of the utterer relative to the sign's impact in the mind of the hearer, Peirce offers the idea of the commens: "that mind into which the minds of utterer and interpreter have to be fused in order that any communication should take place" (Peirce 1998, 477). It is that which is shared between two minds and makes communication, even community, possible: shared knowledge. When mbira is played in Zimbabwe, there exists a commens between players (as utterers) and spirits (as interpreters) that makes communication possible. As I begin to teach mbira to my students, mediating between them and Zimbabwe, no such commens exists. There is only sound. I demonstrate for students, as my teachers demonstrated for me. By the time players in Zimbabwe first strike the mbira, however, they have often heard the songs countless times and confronted the spirits that they call. Learning sequences on the mbira is rarely the first step in the process. Conversely, my students begin in almost total ignorance. Over time, repetition and practice solidify these sequences into models for performance and improvisation, but the structure of a typical college musical ensemble constrains me. When students get but a single credit, I am loath to ask too much of them. We rarely read or write. We simply play. An inclusive spirit-centric commens may eventually emerge, but that is a distant possibility during those initial moments in the classroom. At first, there is only mimesis and alterity.

Without context, sound taught to people with no commens can lead to a sound-centrism stripped of its indexical associations, what David Samuels calls "semantic purification" (Samuels 2006), in a process akin to schizophonia: "the split between an original sound and its electroacoustic transmission or reproduction" (Schafer 1977, 90; Feld 1994). These authors focus on recordings, but the consequences may be more pronounced when addressing musical processes rather than musical products. The rewards of participatory experience conveniently avoid contextual complexity. The "semantic purification" discussed by Samuels is political since the indexical associations of specific terms are deliberately erased to modify the meanings of the words uttered (2006).

Some, like the Bay Area mbira player Casey, recognize knowledge as the path to respect: "You're going to learn how to respect. . . . We barely know what we're doing but we're all so in it together." But it's hard to acknowledge something not yet known. While there is sincere devotion to "the source" and acknowledgment of a teacher's authority, students can unwittingly dismiss a song's depth of meaning, potentially accepting music's status as mere content. For Musekiwa, "mbira songs are humans," agents of the spirits. This can seem metaphorical or exaggerated, but, as Robinson highlights in his exploration of settler-indigenous engagements in Canada, "the meeting that takes place between listener and listened-to is bounded by a Western sense orientation in which we do not feel the need to be responsible to sound as we would another life" (Robinson 2020, 15–16). Taking Musekiwa seriously means taking the songs that he offers seriously, too. Community seemingly comes before knowledge or informed respect, but community is only possible when there is a sense of commens, of shared knowledge. There is a feedback relation that, it is hoped, builds productively into something bold and inclusive. It is arguable that white mbira play is indeed a colonial appropriation, but learning to listen to affect and agency in sound can decolonize the normative listening habits of privileged subjects and bring marginalized communities closer to the center of one's attention (see Robinson 2020, 38).[9] Without this feedback loop, music remains merely sound, detached from the depths to which Musekiwa alludes, its agency dismissed and obliterated.

Freedoms

Freedom is such a slippery word. Used widely, it is hard to separate from the assumptions or values of its user, ever tied to secularism, liberalism, and political sovereignty. For the mbira, freedom can't be fully secular without erasing its spiritual foundations. It can't be liberal without imposing attitudes about freedom tied to the "West" and neoliberalism. What are the consequences of musical freedom or the dangers of experiential schizophonia? This species of schizophonia detaches the sonic from the social, separates potential signs from long-established semiotic objects, and reimagines sounds to reflect the new performers' values.

This semiotic liberation is appealing to musicians attracted solely to the mbira's sound as an autonomous field. Art for art's sake. Chartwell Dutiro worried that "sometimes it is a kind of tokenism, when students have studied many different musics and think that the mbira will provide one more to their list" (quoted in Levay 2007, n.p.). As Saba Mahmood made so clear, agency need not imply resistance to or freedom from social norms (2005, 14). Freedom from the social contexts and histories that the mbira carries with it (Secondness without Thirdness) is not inherently liberatory but potentially irresponsible.[10]

It may not be bold for an ethnomusicologist to argue that music is always meaningful, but not everyone agrees. Music is not always seen as a form of knowledge. When I interviewed Musekiwa for this project and explained my purpose, he quickly sighed and said, "It's a pain in the butt actually. . . . When I share my songs, I'm giving my heart also. My heart is there, all my love is there. I have been keeping it for all these years, for you. Until now, I'm giving it to you the way I do it, I'm not taking anything out. I would appreciate if you can also keep it the way I keep it." Later, he added, "Because you gave yourself opportunity, or you gave yourself power, [saying,] 'I can change this and do what I want.'"

Musekiwa's perspective encourages reflection on two robust legacies of ethnomusicology: first, a conviction that music is meaningful *because* of its context and history (Thirdness), and second, the transmission of music as embodied knowledge through ensembles like the mbira or the gamelan that unavoidably alter that context: bi-musicality (Secondness). It can be difficult to meaningfully sustain the first with the spread of the second. Regardless of their value, college "world music" ensembles are exercises in strategic schizophonia that can undermine the insistence that the mbira is meaningful because of its spiritual and historical associations. Because these contexts are typically absent from collegiate ensembles, the sound must inevitably mean something different. When Danielle Brown called out ethnomusicology for being embedded in histories and structures of racism and colonialism (2020), it is likely these kinds of entanglements that she had in mind.

When performing difference, there is a tension between creatively expressing one's own experience and respectfully acknowledging the authorities with whom it is inextricably tied. Indexing the self and mimicking the other are quite different. Michael Taussig says mimesis can be a mode of becoming other, and indeed spirit possession, the primary purpose of mbira performance, powerfully illustrates how processes of mimesis can transform into acts of becoming (Taussig 1993; Perman 2020). But a medium giving way to an ancestral spirit is a different bridge to build than a white American enthusiast becoming Zimbabwean, not least because mediums acknowledge their debt to the spirit.

Schizophonia creates semiotic and artistic freedom, the freedom from responsibility. If sounds have no indexical associations, or if these connections aren't hard-wired as "truth" but merely suggestive of possibility as "belief," the freedom to interpret as one desires is attractive. My students often get frustrated with the conservatism with which I approach mbira education, but the creative freedom that Musekiwa and Chartwell feel emerges *from* the reality of spirits, not in spite of it. Freedom is rarely the value most celebrated in Shona mbira performance, and debt prevents it from overshadowing responsibility or obligation. For Jennifer Kyker, as a mbira player and academic (and commentator on this essay), debt suggests itself as a deeper form of love. Without it, freedom twists itself into a manifestation of neoliberal triumph. The effort to resist schizophonia, and to bear the burden of debt that is acquired through building the connections across time and space that define the network of mbira players and spirits, is essential.

The spread of the mbira abroad can seem detached from the economies in which it spreads, especially as so many of the North American communities that embrace it identify as anti-capitalist. The mbira values that resonate and attract devotion are social, communal, and collective, its motivations credited to love and respect. But capitalism finds a way, whether in the temptation to monetize newly acquired cultural capital or the acknowledgment that respect necessitates remuneration. Appreciation becomes payment, giving back means creating commodities—CDs, digital downloads, instruments, T-shirts. For Zimbabweans brought to North America to teach, this is necessary. Even if Zimbabwe's economy hadn't collapsed, it is hard for musicians to make a living. Potentially monetizing these skills is a powerful motivation for Zimbabwean mbira players who take repeated trips away from their families. Building community abroad is nice, but securing the family at home is essential. As Zimbabwe's economy continues its decades-long collapse, compounded by COVID, the need to make a living and earn more than simply appreciation is real. To be fully modern is to be free from poverty (Ferguson 2006). At a minimum, acknowledging one's debt to these histories as a foundational principle of continued engagement is essential. Otherwise, the desire to expand the self and become other becomes either an act of consumption of the exotic other or the purchase of artistic freedom and cultural property rights. In his meditations on blackface in American history, Hanif Abdurraqib writes, "The thing I find myself explaining most vigorously to people these days is that consumption and love are not equal parts in the same machine. To consume is not to love, and ideally love is not rooted solely in consumption" (Abdurraqib 2021, 83). Unless players recognize their debt to this history of colonialism and its racist underpinning, and understand that this debt is unpayable, exchange becomes the ethic, liberating payers and players from the burdens of history and social inequality.

In the United States, learning mbira has become more transactional than in Zimbabwe. In the market for mbira knowledge, the only trade barrier is the opportunity of privilege, and the mbira economy is fraught with opportunities for exploitation or anxiety. Histories of inequality and injustice shape those opportunities. Consumers who acquire mbira knowledge often feel a sense of ownership or entitlement. This may be accompanied by a sense of responsibility, respect, stewardship, obligation, or anxiety, but those do not necessarily come tethered to knowledge. Musekiwa says, "I'm not selling it, because if I'm selling it you will ask how much do you charge? This music, when we teach, it's more like we plant a tree which is going to grow some fruit that everyone is going to enjoy. The seed will not die." He doesn't want a payment that would imply the end of a transaction or the resolution of debt. He wants the debt itself. As his student, the more indebted I am to him, the deeper our connections become and the more likely his work in my life will continue. He is indebted to me as well, although a power imbalance obviously exists. As Harney and Moten write, "We owe each other everything" (20). "Debt [is] a means of socialization" (61).

Moral Responsibility, Debt, and the Legacy of Inequality

These three freedoms—artistic, semiotic, and neoliberal—compete with a moral responsibility that shapes one's very humanity, community, and unhu. From a capitalist perspective, there are two camps: those who feel they have purchased freedom and those who feel it is anathema to the mbira's spiritual purpose. The first approaches mbira as a commodity to be purchased or sold. Questions and debates arise regarding ownership and regulation. The second treats the mbira as an agent of spiritual power, beyond transactional ethics and immune from market values. That there are members in both camps from Zimbabwe and abroad muddies the waters. The mbira maker Albert Chimedza lambastes those with an anti-capitalist perspective, saying, "How is it possible that the very people who are profiting the most from our culture [white people] simultaneously cry from the mountains that we must not make the mbira a capitalist product?" (quoted in Mark 2017, 162). As someone whose career has been built in part on the mbira, I take his words seriously.

As Jennifer Kyker suggested to me, debt offers a third space beyond the blunt cost-benefit analyses of cultural commodification or the utopian blinders that ignore the consequences of colonialism. In communities such as the mbira-playing one discussed here, questions of responsibility rarely lead to easy answers. It is perhaps odd to be identified so strongly with practices that have nothing to do with genealogy, spirituality, or even language. For Donna Haraway, "making kin as oddkin rather than, or at least in addition to, godkin and genealogical or biogenetic family troubles important matters, like to whom is one responsible" (Haraway 2016, 2). Rights and responsibilities are so intertwined that the lack of obvious responsibility often raises questions about one's rights. But perhaps the gap between spiritual genealogy and world music exploration only exists for players who lack a commens with the spirits. Musekiwa argues that the spirits acknowledge that foreign players (like me) who may initially feel separate from the spiritual and racial lineage of the mbira are also connected to this genealogy.

Addressing his ensemble, which is rooted in the Ewe traditions of Ghana, David Locke writes, "Global relations of power and issues of social justice simmer beneath the optimistic humanistic surface" (Locke 2004, 168). Among the divergent voices that belong to this community, some would question my legitimacy to play this music or speak about it, euphemistically calling it weird (see fig 9.3). Reinforcing the sentiment of #africaforafricans, I've had students argue that I, as a white musician, should have less freedom than Black musicians because of the freedoms denied them over generations and the structural inequalities that emerged.

Musekiwa dismisses these voices, saying, "When you are outside the scene, you can't actually give a comment or say anything because you are not part of it. . . . They just say these words to us but we will just keep going with what we are doing because we love this and we know the history of this. This is part of our life." Jonono, a Zimbabwean musician living in California, agreed, telling my students, "I know some people who say, Oh, you are stealing our culture, things like that. . . . They don't really know, you know? So that's why you see the teachers, you know the spiritual people from Zimbabwe, they are willing to teach anyone who is willing to learn . . . it's got nothing to do with your color, with your skin, with your background."

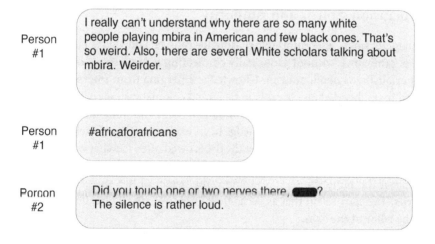

Fig. 9.3. Facebook conversation responding to a post about Zimfest.

But there are divergent voices. Chartwell cautions that "many ethnomusi-cologists have recorded lots of music from different cultures: how many have done justice to the people whose music was recorded[?]" (Levay 2007, n.p.). The Zimbabwean American rapper Tendai Maraire, or Chimurenga Renaissance, makes his perspective explicit in his song "Boom."

> I don't give a damn about they emotional feelings.
> They say they love the music but I know they're just stealing.
> Y'all been stealing since Rome, it's in your nature, you can't stop.
> If you touch my music, you're gonna get socked. (Chimurenga Renaissance 2016)

His anger takes on added resonance when you acknowledge that his father, Dumisani Maraire, was central to the growth of the Zimbabwean music scene in North America. He's lived this story.

Appropriation is a complicated term, simultaneously slander and a call for justice. The failures within utopian projects of multiculturalism or racial equality lead to demands that one stay in one's lane or #africaforafricans as often as they lead to calls for diversity, empathy, or knowledge-inducing exploration. Recall my student, for whom musical freedom should be limited to the disenfranchised lest it reinforce social inequality and erase marginalized practices. The banjo's shift from exclusively African American performers with visible roots in the Caribbean and Africa to European American performers as the very embodi-ment of whiteness gives incontrovertible evidence of the potential consequences of this kind of appropriation. Theft can be an act of love. If students ignore the spirits as they jam on African instruments, where do those spirits go?

Conclusion: Spirits and Authority

I am increasingly uncomfortable sharing the musical knowledge I have acquired from Zimbabwe without indexically connecting it to histories of spirituality, imperialism, or neoliberalism. Knowledge emerging from interpersonal rela-tionships embedded inextricably in racial and colonial systems of inequality and oppression carry ever-deepening burdens of debt and obligation. This seems particularly true when that knowledge bears explicit spiritual indebtedness. The impetus is rarely transactional, but the debts owed often feel that way. Musekiwa argues that "when we talk about bad things, we should also think about good things at the same time. . . . You know, the owner of this music, they are the spirits. The spirits said that as far as they know, we are all one, despite the fact of the color of the skin."[11]

If learning the mbira is like falling in love, for people like Musekiwa it's filial love for an infallible parent, the ancestor. For people like me, who came to the mbira later in life, the love is different. It is perhaps worth "staying with the trouble" induced by these "odd" kinship communities (Haraway 2016). After all, "we become-with each other or not at all" (4). This love is more freely given. If I didn't love it, I could stop playing, free from the burdens of responsibility, at least in theory. Realistically, I doubt I could stop. Musekiwa would likely credit that to the spirits. But even if I stopped, my love for the mbira is rooted in a debt that I would still owe. Freedom from responsibility is an illusion. An outsider's love for the mbira can be idealized or romanticized, limited to the similarities and differences Bateson mentions, but only if the debt is refused. That refusal must itself be refused. *Mukwasha mukuyu, haaperi kudyiwa.* I am the son-in-law, a term of kinship, acceptance, and never-ending indebtedness.

When my students asked how it feels to teach mbira music to outsiders, Musekiwa described his pedagogy as a process of cutting parts of himself off and sewing them onto others, painting a vivid picture of violent, willing, and resilient interpersonal connections. He gives himself away in these seemingly innocuous pedagogical encounters. Musekiwa's commitment to risking his own sense of bodily integrity for the sake of spiritual truth is one I deeply admire and one to which I am indebted. As the Cameroonian philosopher Achille Mbembe says when summarizing Hegel, "Spirit attains its truth only in finding itself in absolute dismemberment" (2019, 69). Musekiwa risks his life for the truth of the music he lives by.

But what do the recipients of this gift offer in return? At a minimum they must offer an acknowledgment of receipt and the debt it carries with it. But that is not enough. For many students the anesthetic of privilege presumably numbs them to the reality of just what Musekiwa is doing as their teacher, but mbira connects them nonetheless. What knowledge is necessary for this connection to have shared value, purpose, and consequence? If it is spiritual for one and escapist for another . . . what is actually shared?[12] To channel a description the Canadian poet Cecily Nicholson uses about indigenous-settler relations in Canada (Nicholson 2020), Musekiwa is reaching out, generously sharing something so important that it is akin to severing a limb. My students and I are reaching in, hungrily consuming what he shares. One feeds, the other is fed. As a gesture toward reciprocity, equality, or emancipation from this reality, I offer acknowledgment, friendship, money, occasional employment. I pay a debt, but it isn't enough. I don't complete this payment; I can't.

This debt is mutual, but Musekiwa obviously risks more than I do in the exchange. For him, it is a risk worth taking. The spirits and the music compel him. The Oakland-based Zimbabwean dancer Julia Chigamba thinks similarly, saying, "[Music and dance] make you open your heart and make you see other people. . . . Sometimes other people or normal people we pretend. And music doesn't pretend. . . . The music dictates who I share with. Don't hold it back. You gotta share." When debt is shared, and willingly received as a demonstration of the love that many players express for the community they have entered, community is expanded, enhanced, and strengthened. It can offer one small window into a path toward undoing the world in which these legacies of racism and colonialism define so many encounters. But acknowledging this debt does not absolve responsibility. It takes tremendous work to pay back the unpayable.

The gifts I have been given by Chartwell Dutiro, Tute Chigamba, Musekiwa Chingodza, and many others have defined my personal and professional life for more than twenty-five years. In his reflections on unhu and the path it offers to the world, Rukuni ends by saying "It starts with you" (2007, 118). Despite being a professor and a father, within the community of the mbira I am a student. When I teach mbira at Grinnell, generating debts among my own students, my student status is obscured, but my student debt—to my teachers, their teachers, their spirits, and their sistren and brethren buried in the balance sheets of a failed post-imperial economy—is the driving force and looming shadow veiling our interactions. When foregrounded, I work to repay my unpayable debts in these moments. When the ethic of indebtedness determines my actions I teach more honestly and honorably. When it slips my mind, hubris and hunger can seep in, unfettered by obligation.

As a mbira player raced as white on the privileged side of the racist and colonial systems of injustice that plague both sides of the Atlantic, recognizing myself as such is but the first step in making this debt the principle of social life in which musicians such as Julia Chigamba, Musekiwa Chingodza, and Chartwell Dutiro share their musics and their art through violent acts of musical suturing. Questlove frames creativity as "taking the existing world and making something new from it" (2018, 156), which offers a hopeful lesson in obligation as well. When acknowledging structures of inequality in the existing world, do engagements with that world creatively contribute to something new?

Beyond acknowledgment, what are my responsibilities as a guest listener and player in the mbira ecumene? How can listening and musicking be anti-racist? Situating myself within theories of decolonization only rings true if I live them in practice (Rivera Cusicanqui 2020, 56). Mbembe approaches decolonization as "a praxis of self-defense and as an experience of emergence and uprising" (2021, 224). "Guests" should support this praxis rather than disrupt it and should develop indebted relationships with this "decolonized community" (224). If my participation supplants or decenters the communities to whom I am indebted, I have failed (Rivera Cusicanqui 2020, 57).

The initial steps are easy: listen, enter with humility, accept and acknowledge the spaces in which guests may be unwelcome, and be the bridge that Musekiwa and Chartwell have worked to build. Beyond that, I offer this essay as a "productive impasse" against the easy way out (Berlant 2011, 199), which would be simply playing music because I like how it feels, ignoring the complex morass of implications for the communities around me. An equitable exchange grounded in genuine empathy and an acknowledgment of indebtedness is a precarious thing. Mbira ought not to be fodder for my own hungry consumption. As the Zimbabwean dancer and educator Rujeko Dumbutshena told a group of American students during an online mbira class organized by Jennifer Kyker in 2021, we would always be guests to this music, and guests ought to relinquish their claims of power or control. These practices of listening, acknowledging, and serving should reveal the steps to follow. By privileging the voices of the ancestors and the musicians through whom they communicate, by challenging the politics of difference that reinforce resilient structures of racism and colonialism, it is possible for mbira communities to help "confront the hegemonic projects of the North with the renewed strength of our [their] ancestral convictions" (Rivera Cusicanqui 2020, 70). When Musekiwa sews parts of himself onto others through his vulnerable act of education he binds the binaries of these communities-in-formation—self and stranger, colonized and colonizer, white and Black—into the nascent possibility of creating something better.

Fig. 9.4. Tom Turino, Stefan Fiol, and Tony Perman in Claremont, California, November 14, 2010.

Notes

This essay carries many debts. I am indebted to Tom Turino, whose mentorship and friendship have defined much of my career; Chartwell, Musekiwa, Sekuru Chigamba, and my other mbira mentors in Zimbabwe for bridging me to these communities; Stefan Fiol for the labor and resilience that made this book happen; Jennifer Kyker for suggesting Moten and Harney's work and helping me find a language for these obligations; my former students Sunny, Luke, and Anne for the work and reflection that contributed greatly to this essay; and my students in "Race and Musical Taste" and "Performing Difference" at Grinnell College for taking the journey with me.

1. See Tanyaradzwa Tawengwa's critique of the Google doodle (https://www.google.com/doodles/celebrating-mbira) about the mbira on May 21, 2020 (Tawengwa 2020).

2. Bi-musicality was central to ethnomusicological training in the middle of the twentieth century (Hood 1960). Although understandings of self and other seem not to have been overtly theorized, "[Mantle] Hood's focus on the mastery of students of a second musical language reinforced the move away from comparative studies and toward in-depth explorations of single musical cultures" (Averill 2004, 96).

3. Chartwell Dutiro, quoted in Levay 2007, n.p.

4. This (*kuva munhu pane vanhu*) is how the musician Oliver Mtukudzi framed unhu in his work with Jennifer Kyker (Kyker 2016, 17).

5. Chartwell also says, "What we are talking about today, though, could so easily be looked upon as an imperial idea because it is not understood properly. Lots of music students have been going to Zimbabwe, to visit my village, ever since I came to Britain in 1994, and in the village they don't have any problem. But in the city, where there are few academics, you have problems with people who feel that ideas from outside shouldn't be accepted. This is because of the environment, where people were once colonized, who feel that accepting outside ideas might lead to colonization again" (Levay 2004).

6. *Meaning* here captures the relation between the object a sign represents and the effect of that representation.

7. In his quest for epistemic freedom Ndlovu-Gatsheni says, "Recognition of various forms of knowledge and knowing is called for in decolonization" (2018, 5).

8. This is succinctly captured in Turino's story of meeting Henry Chigamba in the crowded Mbare Township only to learn that Henry had successfully protected the belongings he'd left behind by placing his mbira (and its spiritual gravitas) on top of them (Turino 2000, 41).

9. I acknowledge Tuck and Yang's admonition that decolonization is not a metaphor (2012), while also accepting the potential limits of this assertion (Garba and Sorentino 2020). Their argument is specific to the indigenous-settler relations of North America, but acknowledging multiple "scapes" on which power is learned, employed, and exploited (soundscape, landscape, and so on) reveals metaphor to be a powerful process through which new ideas and realities can be made manifest (see Appadurai 1996; Samuels et al. 2010). I hope I honor Ngugi wa Thiong'o's call to "decolonize the mind" with that suggestion (Ngugi 1981). Chartwell's desire for emancipation from mental slavery recognizes the impact of colonization on the mind in the specific context of colonial and post-colonial Zimbabwe (see also Ndlovu-Gatsheni 2018).

10. Unfortunately, I utterly misrepresented Professor Mahmood's point in my book, mistakenly crediting her with the very argument she opposes: the attribution of agency to resisting customs and traditions (Mahmood 2005, 8, quoted in Perman 2020, 201).

11. Biology and the science of human evolution have long corroborated this indigenous claim, grounded in spiritual knowledge, that skin color masks an inherent human unity (see Saini 2019).

12. Honestly, much is shared: community, communitas, rhythmic entrainment, social groove, joy. But the question is still essential.

Bibliography

Abdurraqib, Hanif. 2021. "Sixteen Ways of Looking at Blackface." In *A Little Devil in America*, 68–88. New York: Random House.

Ahmed, Sara. 2000. *Strange Encounters: Embodied Others in Post-Coloniality*. London: Routledge.

Appadurai, Arjun. 1996. *Modernity at Large: Cultural Dimensions of Globalization*. Minneapolis: University of Minnesota Press.

Averill, Gage. 2004. "'Where's One?' Musical Encounters of the Ensemble Kind." In *Performing Ethnomusicology: Teaching and Representation in World Music Ensembles*, edited by Ted Solis, 93–114. Chicago: University of Chicago Press.

Bateson, Mary Catherine. 2015. "Composing a Life." *On Being with Krista Tippett*. October 1. https://onbeing.org/programs/mary-catherine-bateson-composing-a-life-aug2017/. Accessed May 14, 2019.

Berlant, Lauren. 2011. *Cruel Optimism*. Durham, NC: Duke University Press.

Berliner, Paul. 1993. *The Soul of Mbira: Music and Traditions of the Shona People of Zimbabwe*. Chicago: University of Chicago Press.

Brown, Danielle. 2020. "An Open Letter on Racism in Music Studies: Especially Ethnomusicology and Music Education." https://www.mypeopletellstories.com/blog/open-letter. Accessed November 10, 2020.

Chimurenga Renaissance. 2016. "Boom." *Pungwe*. Chimurenga Renaissance (sound recording).

Dutiro, Chartwell. 2007. "Chosen by the Ancestors." In *Zimbabwean Mbira Music on the International Stage: Chartwell Dutiro's Life in Music*, edited by Chartwell Dutiro and Keith Howard, 1–8. Aldershot, UK: Ashgate.

Feld, Steven. 1994. "From Schizophonia to Schismogenesis: On the Discourses and Commodification Practices of 'World Music" and 'World Beat.'" In *Music Grooves*, edited by Charles Keil and Steven Feld, 257–89. Chicago: University of Chicago Press.

Ferguson, James. 2006. *Global Shadows: Africa in the Neoliberal World Order*. Durham, NC: Duke University Press.

Garba, Tapji, and Sara-Maria Sorentino. 2020. "Slavery Is a Metaphor: A Critical Commentary on Eve Tuck and K. Wayne Yang's 'Decolonization Is not a Metaphor.'" *Antipode* 52(3): 764–82.

Halberstam, Jack. 2013. "The Wild Beyond: With and for the Undercommons." In *The Undercommons: Fugitive Planning and Black Study*, by Stefano Harney and Fred Moten, 3–12. New York: Minor Compositions.

Haraway, Donna J. 2016. *Staying with the Trouble: Making Kin in the Cthulucene*. Durham, NC: Duke University Press.

Harney, Stefano, and Fred Moten. 2013. *The Undercommons: Fugitive Planning and Black Study*. New York: Minor Compositions.

Hartman, Saidiya V. 1997. *Scenes of Subjection: Terror, Slavery, and Self-Making in Nineteenth-Century America*. New York: Oxford University Press.

Higgins, Kathleen Marie. 2012. *The Music Between Us: Is Music a Universal Language?* Chicago: University of Chicago Press.

Higgins, Kathleen Marie. 2018. "Connecting Music to Ethics." *College Music Symposium* 58(3): 1–20.

Hood, Mantle. 1960. "The Challenges of Bi-Musicality." *Ethnomusicology* 4(2): 55–59.

Kyker, Jennifer. 2016. *Oliver Mtukudzi: Living Tuku Music in Zimbabwe*. Bloomington: Indiana University Press.

Kyker, Jennifer. 2019. "Zimbabwean *Hosho* Playing in *Mbira* Ensembles, Possession Ceremonies, and Popular Songs: A Preliminary Assessment." In *Proceedings of the Symposium III.4, Mbira Music/Musics: Structures and Processes*, edited by Klaus-Peter Brenner. Fifteenth International Conference of the Gesellschaft Für Musikforschung, Göttingen, September 4–8, 2012. Hildesheim: Olms.

Levay, Rachel, with Chartwell Dutiro. 2007. "Music Management, Copyright, and Music Education." In *Zimbabwean Mbira Music on an International Stage: Chartwell Dutiro's Life in Music*, edited by Chartwell Dutiro and Keith Howard. London: Ashgate. Formerly at www.soas.ac.uk/music (now deleted).

Locke, David. 2004. "The African Ensemble in America: Contradictions and Possibilities." In *Performing Ethnomusicology: Teaching and Representation in World Music Ensembles*, edited by Ted Solis, 168–88. Berkeley: University of California Press.

Lott, Eric. 1995. *Love and Theft: Blackface Minstrelsy and the American Working Class*. Oxford: Oxford University Press.

Mahmood, Saba. 2005. *Politics of Piety: The Islamic Revival and the Feminist Subject*. Princeton, NJ: Princeton University Press.

Mark, Andrew. 2017. "The Sole Mbira: An Ecomusicological Critique of Singularity and North American Zimbabwean Music." *Topia: Canadian Journal of Cultural Studies* 37:157–88.

Matiure, Sheasby. 2008. "Performing Zimbabwean Music in the United States: An Ethnography of Mbira and Marimba Performance Practice in the United States." PhD diss., Indiana University.

Mbembe, Achille. 2019. *Necropolitics*. Durham, NC: Duke University Press.

Mbembe, Achille. 2021. *Out of the Dark Night*. New York: Columbia University Press.

Ndlovu-Gatsheni, Sabelo J. 2018. *Epistemic Freedom in Africa: Deprovincialization and Decolonization*. London: Routledge.

Ngugi wa Thiong'o. 1981. *Decolonising the Mind: The Politics of Language in African Literature*. Harare: Zimbabwe Publishing.

Nicholson, Cecily. 2020. Roundtable on Intersectional Listening Positionality at the Sixty-fifth Meeting of the Society for Ethnomusicology, October 29, 2020.

Peirce, Charles S. 1998. *The Essential Peirce: Selected Philosophical Writings*. Vol. 2,

1893–1913, edited by Nathan Houser and Christian Kloesel. Bloomington: Indiana University Press.

Perman, Tony. 2015. "A Tale of Two Mbiras." *African Music* 10(1): 102–26.

Perman, Tony. 2020. *Signs of the Spirit: Music and the Experience of Meaning in Ndau Ceremonial Life*. Urbana: University of Illinois Press.

Questlove. 2018. *Creative Quest*. New York: HarperCollins.

Rivera Cusicanqui, Silvia. 2020. *Ch'ixinakax Utxiwa: On Practices and Discourses of Decolonization*. Cambridge, UK: Polity.

Robinson, Dylan. 2020. *Hungry Listening: Resonant Theory for Indigenous Studies*. Minneapolis: University of Minnesota Press.

Rukuni, Mandivamba. 2007. *Being Afrikan*. Johannesburg: Penguin.

Saini, Angela. 2019. *Superior: The Return of Race Science*. Boston: Beacon.

Samuels, David. 2006. "Bible Translation and Medicine Man Talk: Missionaries, Indexicality, and the 'Language Expert' on the San Carlos Apache Reservation." *Language in Society* 35(4): 529–57.

Samuels, David W., Louise Meintjes, Ana Maria Ochoa, and Thomas Porcello. 2010. "Soundscapes: Towards a Sounded Anthropology." *Annual Review of Anthropology* 39:329–45.

Schafer, R. Murray. 1977. *The Tuning of the World*. New York: Random House.

Serpell, Namwali. 2019. *The Old Drift*. London: Hogarth.

Shelemay, Kay Kaufman. 2011. "Musical Communities: Rethinking the Collective in Music." *Journal of the American Musicological Society* 64(2): 349–90.

Taussig, Michael. 1993. *Mimesis and Alterity: A Particular History of the Senses*. New York: Routledge.

Tawengwa, Tanyaradzwa. 2020. "Cultural Vampires: White Exploitation of Zimbabwean Mbira Music." *Daily News*. May 26. https://dailynews.co.zw/cultural-vampires-white -exploitation-of-zimbabwean-mbira-music/. Accessed November 10, 2020.

Tuck, Eve, and K. Wayne Yang. 2012. "Decolonization Is Not a Metaphor." *Decolonization: Indigeneity, Education and Society* 1(1): 1–40.

Turino, Thomas. 1998. "The Mbira, Worldbeat, and the International Imagination." *The World of Music* 40(2): 85–106.

Turino, Thomas. 2000. *Nationalists, Cosmopolitans, and Popular Music in Zimbabwe*. Chicago: University of Chicago Press.

Turino, Thomas. 2008. *Music as Social Life: The Politics of Participation*. Chicago: University of Chicago Press.

10 Sounds and Social Belonging in Southern Africa

Collective Improvisation Versus Pan-African Jazz

RICK DEJA

Navigating belonging in contemporary South Africa continues to be a salient issue decades after the 1994 political transition from a system of institutionalized racial segregation to one of democratic majority rule. The university environment, in conjunction with the local music scenes it intersects, offer both opportunity and challenge in addressing this issue. The notion of decolonizing the curriculum has been especially present in South Africa following the Fees Must Fall movement in 2015 and later the Rhodes Must Fall campaign in Cape Town. The former was in response to rising student fees and a demand for increased access to universities by marginalized groups. The Rhodes Must Fall campaign was in response to the statue of Cecil Rhodes and, moreover, to emblems of institutional racism and white supremacy associated with him. In many South African institutions there is a sense of obligation to create a more inclusive environment, encouraging fruitful discourse and engendering new ways of being in the world within a local context. Some forms of music making offer useful tools to foster both individual expression and inclusivity, the effect of which depends on specific musical and social factors.

In order to unpack this, the discussion that follows is informed by several theoretical frameworks developed in Tom Turino's work, especially those regarding Peircean semiotics or phenomenology (e.g., signs *of* as opposed to signs *about* experience), participatory musics, and cultural cohorts and translocal cultural formations. Ultimately, I suggest that by exploring the mobility of free improvisation in contrast to more stable conventions of musical genres (such as Afro-jazz), one may better understand subjective positioning and how musicking may contribute to fostering equitable social relations on a broader scale.

Music: Collective Free Improvisation and Afro-Jazz

In my performance career, the opportunity and ability to improvise across genres has long been a point of entry to expand into new musical terrain and ultimately participate in new social milieux. Frequently, improvising has been a major unifying element in situations where musicians of diverse backgrounds come together to simply jam, drawing freely from different genres, aesthetic preferences, and social values. For many musicians involved in ethnomusicological fieldwork, musical performance is a staple activity for getting acquainted with new cohorts and locations (Flood 2017).

Since my arrival at the University of Cape Town (UCT) in 2018, I have been interested in how collective free improvisation and Afro-jazz may help bring musicians of varied backgrounds together as a means to encourage interchange across disciplinary lines (Western classical music, jazz, and African music) and other boundaries (gender, race, nationality, language, and ethnicity). These particular genres are ones I have been involved with regularly throughout my career. Both collective free improvisation and Afro-jazz are embedded in broader cosmopolitan contexts, but there are local scenes in South Africa in which both of these genres are performed to varying degrees. My decision to work with these particular practices at UCT was a matter of pragmatics, but the contrast between them has proved illuminating in pedagogical and social terms.

Collective free improvisation is a creative context in which the music is composed during the course of performance, drawing freely from different musical styles and generally not bound by a particular set of aesthetic preferences. As a discursive practice, it brings about a variety of stylistic trends and social values that emerge from local and translocal interchanges. That said, often the overarching goal is to be as inclusive and equitable as possible by removing limitations of musical conventions. Afro-jazz is discursively understood as a combination of jazz and indigenous sub-Saharan African musical practices. The cosmopolitan aspect of jazz is driven by the enduring power of North American models, but there are clear indexes to African traditions, some widely practiced and others more geographically particular. These two practices emphasize some form of manipulating musical structures and performance conventions, exemplified most by free improvisation. Cultural associations related to place, cultural groups, and social practices tend to be foregrounded in Afro-jazz and minimized in free improvisation. Exploring these two genres provides useful insight into the ways individual musicians navigate senses of group belonging in the multifaceted and often politicized soundscape in South Africa and beyond.

Free Improvisation: Attributes and Labels

I use the phrase *collective free improvisation* to refer to a musical activity in which all participants compose the music during the course of performance. They do so in a sonic dialogue in which predetermined musical parameters are few to none. There are no formal schemes governing the organization of sounds other than the decisions of the individual participants within the ensemble, and the range of acceptable sounds is as wide as the participants are willing and able to conceive it. The notion of right and wrong notes is removed, and practitioners may choose the conventions of any number of genres, or they may discard the notion of genre entirely. This often results in performance practices that push the parameters of conventional musical aesthetics, but this is not necessarily a defining characteristic. Because of these flexible attributes, this activity shows promise as an effective means for fostering inclusivity and perhaps creating a space for generating a sense of group belonging. In practice the reality tends to be a bit precarious.

This instability is mirrored in the terminology. The phrase *free improvisation* implies a freedom of musical expression at the discretion of the individuals involved. Some scholars and practitioners, however, employ labels other than free improvisation, some to avoid various connotations and others to reframe the practice in a useful manner. Derek Bailey uses the term *non-idiomatic improvisation*, and Jesse Stewart prefers *pan-idiomatic improvisation*. Bailey distinguishes between idiomatic improvisation (e.g., jazz improvisation) and non-idiomatic improvisation ("free"), explaining that the latter is not tied to a particular idiomatic identity even if it is highly stylized (1993, xii). Drawing from this, Stewart uses the term *pan-idiomatic improvisation* because participants are free to draw from any existing genre or stylistic convention (2016, 35).

This array of labels illustrates the various experienced realities that collective improvisation offers. The goal of some performers may be to draw freely from any genre, whereas for others it may be to avoid conventional genres altogether, thus creating an ethos of experimentation and new possibilities. I use the term *free improvisation* as it is colloquially understood among musicians I have worked with in South Africa and the United States. This underlying semantic debate, however, is important because it highlights the role of decentering of predetermined convention and the reliance on negotiation and consensus of individual participants in the moment of performance.[1]

This internal negotiation among the practitioners is one of the fundamental aspects of improvisation described by Scott Thomson. Thomson poses the question, "What elements make group improvisation identifiable to the majority of listeners in contrast to composed or genre-based music?" (2008, 2). His response is that those elements lie in the "pedagogical imperative" of improvisation. Every performance must involve adaptive learning in order to be successful. Thomson explains that "an environment in which collective aesthetics are cultivated and human and musical difference can be reconciled demands an ongoing, collaborative process of pedagogy that is the mark of a responsive, responsible improviser" (4).

It is largely because of this, Thomson argues, that such a context of music making reduces hierarchy in favor of an egalitarian inclusive ethos: "Without preordained aesthetic and technical criteria to which the members of an ensemble attempt to adhere, there is no standardized, explicit hierarchy through which authority is bestowed upon improvisers within a particular group" (Thomson 2008, 5). This decentering of authority could situate collective free improvisation as a potentially valuable musical practice to counteract damaging social hierarchies related to race, class, and gender found in many South African contexts.

In many regards this resembles the ethos of participatory music frequently discussed by Turino (1993, 2000, 2008). The acceptable range of individual contributions may stand in slight contrast to traditions discussed in Turino's work. The absence of commitment to a single paradigm contributes to this, for as Bailey explains, "The characteristics of freely improvised music are established only by the sonic-musical identity of the person or persons playing it" (Bailey 1993, 83). Individual agency is driven by and responds to collective goals of group creation and performance and thus accommodates variety. Fischlin, Heble, and Lipsitz (2013) describe this as "dialectical synthesis," stating, "Improvisation turns opposites into dialectical syntheses. It balances competing claims and interests. Improvisers need to counterpoise imagination with discipline, ego with empathy, and self-assertion with self-effacement" (xiii).

These references all speak of an egalitarian ethos in relation to musical inclusivity, but to what extent might improvisation contribute to forming a sense of belonging? In her research on free improvisation and performance anxiety, Kathryn Ladano presents a useful strategy for addressing individual performance within the collective group:

> Evidently, performance anxiety manifests as a profoundly individual problem: those afflicted feel unable to perform *as individuals* in front of *groups*. In a carefully cultivated pedagogical or performative space, however, free improvisation can become a means of integrating individuals—even those (perhaps especially those) who may be isolated or alienated by performance anxiety—into the collective, making the community a potential space for empowerment and healing. (Ladano 2016, 47, emphasis in original)

The expressive possibilities for the individual within the collective, as described here, may offer insight into community: According to Fischlin, Heble, and Lipsitz (2013), improvisation "calls into being an experimental, alternative community in which individualism does not have to degenerate into selfishness and where collectivity does not have to dissolve into conformity" (xiii). Both instances refer to a beneficial relationship between the individual and the collective that is facilitated by some sort of group improvisation. Nonetheless, the practice has its limitations.

In theory, the principles of collective free improvisation are promising. In order to be effective, however, using the ethos of free improvisation in a teaching setting must include more than lifting restrictions on sound creation. Although I have incorporated this practice into my teaching curriculum for several semesters, rarely has it been 100 percent successful. Even among professional improvising musicians, let alone newcomers, there are conditions that need to be met for a completely improvised performance to be successful.

Among highly experienced improvisers, shortcomings are bound to arise in these settings as well. At a free improvisation concert at All Saints Church Belhar in Cape Town (March 28, 2019), a group called The New Project gave what many in the audience around me perceived as a remarkable performance. To be honest, I did not share this opinion. As someone versed in this performance practice, I sensed that something fell short; it was certainly enjoyable, but not remarkable. An informal interaction with the musicians (Dylan Tabisher, vibraphone; Coila-Leah Enderstein, piano; and Carlo Mombelli, bass) immediately afterward revealed to me and my peers that, indeed, Carlo and his colleagues were lamenting that the performance never quite came together in that gig. It turns out that Carlo is not a regular member of that group, and group members were still getting acclimated to each other's idiosyncrasies. Freedom is simply not enough on its own, whether in terms of musical structures or in its broadest sense.

The mark of a successful freely improvised concert is not necessarily found in surface-level sonic attributes. The musicians worked well with each other, displaying individual competence and successful coordination in that there appeared to be no mistakes. Still, there was a standard set by the musicians that was not met; a particular desired result of interacting was absent.

In another instance, an improvisatory group I was working with played a live gig and later recorded in the studio and found the studio experience profoundly lacking. This in itself was not surprising, but the degree to which we felt this was notable. The recording studio environment reduces the risk-reward feedback loop that the presence of an audience provides. Collective free improvisation is a discourse of musical praxis in which musical structures, individual perspectives, and broader contexts for social interaction must be taken into account in order to achieve success.

For all of its promise, collective free improvisation cannot be casually inserted into a curriculum or performance environment with the expectation of having ideal outcomes. I have encountered two instances when a participant experienced extreme anxiety as a result of the free improvisation context. In one class session I conducted an exercise drawing from Pauline Oliveros's sonic meditations, after which one student related that they remained motionless and silent for the entire duration of the event because of anxiety. In another instance, I participated in a workshop led by Jen Shyu, a renowned improviser who is well versed in improvisatory music education workshops. Despite Shyu's care to establish an inclusive, judgment-free atmosphere, one participant began crying and hurried away from the room.

In each of these instances, establishing an inclusive ethos through language was not sufficient. Making an appeal in rational terms is not enough to defuse the embodied experiential state of anxiety. Also, there were insufficient sonic factors in place to shelter perceived individual flaws and vulnerability. Collective improvised music making is a process of negotiation. It is a dialogue among individuals negotiating the sonic and the social. The various shortcomings I have observed and experienced in group improvisation have demonstrated that it is not enough to simply employ a philosophical base of inclusion. An awareness of performance conventions and the support of musical structures are also needed.

With these things in mind, I direct my attention to musicians and groups working within the realm of Afro-jazz. A genre such as Afro-jazz has established performance conventions, albeit with regional variations. Characteristics such as the emphasis on improvisation, the view of performer as composer, and the valuing of innovation create a musical framework that encourages individual expression. There is a repertoire that frequently incorporates folk and popular music traditions, providing creative models to guide the music. The balance between individual expression and established conventions is important in facilitating inclusion and group solidarity, but as with free improvisation, there are challenges to this ideal.

Afro-Jazz: The Dialogue Between Jazz and African Music

I define Afro-jazz as a fusion of jazz and African indigenous styles. Conventional performance practices are informed by popular music, especially styles emerging within the African diaspora. Among many musicians I have worked with in Malawi and South Africa, Afro-jazz provides a means of asserting African expressive practices and subjective positioning within a broader cosmopolitan ethos. This is accomplished in part by balancing technical proficiency and stylistic versatility. In turn, some musicians leverage these in interesting ways to assert important aspects of their personal and collective identities.

In January 2019 I performed at a jazz event in Lilongwe, Malawi, where I also spoke with fellow performers about their views on jazz in their lives. Guitarist Owen Mbilizi described jazz as the "motherboard" of musical genres, and saxophonist Dan Sibale explained how it "teaches you the world." Their assertions speak to their own experiences and reveal a set of values they associate with jazz as a genre.

> OWEN: Jazz. It's a genre that encompasses all types of music, you know? R&B, blues, traditional, hip-hop; it has got all those elements in one genre. Which is different than the other genres. You cannot do jazz in hip-hop, but you can do hip-hop in jazz. You see what I mean. Jazz seems to be like the motherboard here of most of all music.
> DAN: Let me just add to that. It teaches you the world, so you can touch all angles. And then, trained in jazz, it allows you to maneuver in all the music genres.
> OWEN: And let me add to that. When, you know, when you can play jazz, you can play anything; literally you can play anything, with anyone, anytime. (Mbilizi and Sibale 2019)

According to Owen, not only does jazz encompass several styles of music, but it also demands a technical virtuosity in the individual performer, enabling them to participate in other genres. He asserts that if one can play jazz, they can play anything. The extent to which this is true is debatable, and indeed this claim falls short in many cases. What is notable is how he embraces the sentiment; being a jazz musician is more than simply being a practitioner of a genre, it is to be a musician's musician. He is not just a musician; he is a jazz musician.

Similarly, Dan cites the versatility afforded a jazz musician in terms of access and maneuverability as a cosmopolitan "citizen of the world." This is echoed in the statement of another saxophonist, Salim Daud Mussah, at the same event: "I play music because it's one of the ways to communicate with people to tell them what's inside of you, and I play Afro-jazz. I believe and I know that jazz is from Africa, and that's one of the way[s] I'm able to express myself to the world and the whole nation" (Mussah 2019). Here, there is reference to Africa not only in terms of Afro-jazz but jazz more broadly. The statement implies that Jazz or Afro-Jazz is used as a vehicle to reconcile individual and collective Malawian and African identities, once again, within a broader cosmopolitan framework.

Another instance when musicians I spoke with cited aspects of technical dexterity and stylistic inclusion as desirable elements is seen here with drummer Lyton Chisuse.

Once when you learn to play [a] normal song, or with other musicians who don't play jazz, the difference [is] that . . . in jazz there is [*sic*] more skills. You learn things that are . . . it's like mad. There is more mathematics. Yeah, so it opens your mind, to think more. Yeah, sure, so jazz is . . . I can say that's it's something which is . . . you cannot understand until you learn the techniques and the things that is [*sic*] in jazz so you can be able to play any song. You can play a normal song. You can play . . . more advanced jazz. You can understand [that?] Yeah, so jazz is nice. I really like jazz. Sure. (Chisuse 2019)

The skill and dexterity described here are framed as tools to allow stylistic versatility and even social access.

On one occasion in Cape Town, similar technical and music theoretical prowess was leveraged as a means to defy convention. Commenting on a song we had just rehearsed for the first time, trumpeter Jo Kunnuji had this to say: "I think . . . I was just disobeying. [laughs] I was disobeying the rules, he he he. That one for me I was just thinking outside of the box. And that comes from my knowledge of jazz and you know what one can do over a minor chord." Here Kunnuji cites his knowledge of jazz as the reason he was "disobeying the rules" and "thinking outside of the box." In this instance, his skill set was not used to access a genre outside jazz but, rather, to transcend the boundaries, both asserting individual agency and articulating a jazz aesthetic. In a later discussion during that same rehearsal Kunnuji discussed the music of Miles Davis stating, "He just keeps like a kind of sound like a modal sound. You know, sometimes it's edgy, it's like, so for me it still has the jazz in it. Jazz is that edginess [laugher]" (Agyefi and Kunnuji 2019). The edginess of jazz suggests an ethos of nonconformity, of not being bound by convention.

The ethos of using alteration to create new versions in line with the aims of individual performers is an important aspect that is shared by these musicians. The "mathematics" that Chisuse discusses, the individual identity that Salim discusses, and the disruption of rules that Jo discusses demonstrate this creative liberty. I suggest that jazz, as they have internalized it, is embraced out of a necessity to transcend the performance conventions and values found in African popular or traditional music. This, in turn, may contribute to the creation of a cultural cohort in which musical conventions and regional associations play a central role in forging senses of belonging.

Afro Jazz: Place, Space, and Nostalgia

One rather obvious index within Afro-jazz is the African continent, but in practice the references are more particular and often more personal, depending on the individual. In some cases the personal reference is to a home area, a region where one's family originates. This may operate as a regional identity that can be asserted, musically, to mark difference abroad or establish a shared reference locally. For Dan Sibale, the geographic and cultural references are embedded in rhythmic and melodic idiosyncrasies of the music.

CRAIG [VIDEOGRAPHER]: Which instruments are fused into it to make it Afro-jazz?

DAN: It's not about the instruments. It's about [how] every music has got a scale whereby when you know the note, there are certain kinds of moves that you can take, when you go here, when you come here at the center [central region of Malawi], there is something. When you go to the southern region, that region also has got something. You know? So, our Afro kind of rhythm is coming up whereby we can take this kind of, the music that we have, ourselves, and fuse it with jazz so that the world can give it an ear. You see, sometimes it's hard when you take it raw as it is. Sometimes it doesn't make sense. It's only us who will understand it. When they hear those progressions infused with ours, that means Malawi Afro-jazz can go anywhere. It's easy to sell. (Mbilizi and Sibale 2019)

Here, Sibale discusses these references having relevance on the local and international levels. The desire to gain access to a broader musical discourse without sacrificing aspects of the local style is a frequent concern among musicians in this region. It suggests an ongoing forging of relevant African modernities. It is also notable in this instance that the references were not to Malawi as a whole but to regions within Malawi familiar to Sibale.

The emotional connection to a particular place and its musical associations can be complicated in interesting ways by listening habits and locations. For instance, first-generation immigrant families may play music of their homeland to their children, which may create a multifaceted notion of place and family. In another instance, for Nigerian trumpeter Jo Kunnuji, South African jazz created a sense of nostalgia and "home" because of the associations allowed by recordings in his household when he was growing up.

RICK DEJA: So what role has that music [Cape jazz], what got you into that music ... when were you exposed to it? What does it do for you?

JO: Ok, growing up my dad had vinyl recordings, South African, [groups like] Ipithombi so that sound sort of lingered into my youthful days and eventually when I came here [to Cape Town] hearing it again was nostalgic for me. Hearing that and also because that sound is also very hymn-like. I grew up singing hymns so that's another avenue for me. I think that second inversion of chord one is something that I hear a lot in choral [music] like hymns, so for me it's a bit nostalgic because I grew up with this music and then hearing again I just want to, in fact in some cases if I hear it over and over again and I think about some things I cry. [laughs]

PAPA KOW MENSAH AGYEFI [GHANAIAN MUSICIAN IN CAPE TOWN]: Yes, yes!

JO: Because it's like you can't explain that. It's beyond words. It's like a feeling that you can't really explain. Like it's *home*. (Agyefi and Kunnuji 2019)

For Jo, South African jazz and popular musics have a strong association with his home and family in Nigeria. At the time of the interview he had been based in Cape Town for more than five years and was well established in the local jazz scene. He performs in a variety of settings drawing from a diverse repertoire that includes American jazz standards, Cape jazz, musical theater, and his original work fusing jazz and indigenous Ogu traditions from Southwest Nigeria.

I became aware of his interest in Cape jazz because occasionally I heard him practice in the office next to mine. Shortly after I arrived at UCT I heard him play a chord progression on the piano that reminded me of the renowned South African pianist Abdullah Ibrahim. I joined him in a mini jam session, and afterward we shared our admiration for South African jazz, a genre I had been drawn to as a teenager when it was introduced to me by a South African boarding school roommate. This interaction with Jo was meaningful to me. It was comforting to experience sharing this with another foreigner, a musical style with origins outside our birthplaces that served as a common thread and now took on sedimented references that included the location where we currently live. Music local to South Africa indexed both our current and previous homes in sentimental ways. Musical traditions frequently elicit strong connections for myriad reasons, and this seems especially so within the politicized setting of South Africa.

Afro-Jazz, Improvisation, and the South African College of Music

In the context of Afro-jazz performance, the foregrounding of African musical features, referencing national, regional, or local regional traditions, is especially significant in contexts of cultural imperialism where Western practices were favored over indigenous ones. The devaluation of indigenous African music has occurred variously throughout many African countries. It was most prominent under colonialism and was influenced by many Christian missions throughout much of the twentieth century. In Malawi and South Africa there still is often a stigma attached to indigenous cultural practices in relation to those introduced from overseas. Since the political transitions in these countries during the 1990s musicians have increasingly pushed for highlighting African expressive practices in their music (Ansell 2004; Deja 2019; Fenn and Perullo 2000).

With this backdrop in mind, the Pan-African Jazz and Popular Music Ensemble[2] was formed at the South African College of Music, University of Cape Town, in February 2019. The goal for the ensemble is to give students performance experience with repertoire from established African and diasporic recording artists from the mid-twentieth century to the present. It is open to music majors from any section in the music department, but participants so far have been primarily from the African music section along with a couple from the jazz section.

The gradual foregrounding of African music at UCT continues to be a work in progress. Judging by audience reactions at concerts featuring increased African content from jazz and African music students, the response from students of all backgrounds is overwhelmingly positive. Student evaluations and in-class discussions in academic classes that I have taught echo this as students express appreciation for African music and interest in having more African content in courses whenever possible.

One of the strategies for fostering inclusion in the ensemble has been to consider geographic and gender representation in selecting repertoire. Another strategy has been to encourage students to take initiative in song selection, co-arranging, improvising solos, leading sectionals, and adding choreography. In addition, taking liberties with the arrangements in line with a broader jazz aesthetic seems to help.

Highlighting the translocal aspect of Afro-jazz may offer some sense of inclusivity without erasing various local and indigenous practices so long as we as educators and practitioners resist normalizing aspects of music rooted in the global North in the name of universalism. That said, anecdotal evidence suggests that performances at the college which feature African music may be helping transform the perception of the College of Music as a Eurocentric space into one that is more representative of the Black African student body. Yet disciplinary divides between classical, jazz, and African music sections still linger because meaningful large-scale systemic changes take time to implement.

Even within the relatively progressive jazz ethos, there are challenges that come with institutionalized music education. The codification of jazz is perhaps a necessary tool for teaching specific aspects of interpretation and improvisation, but it may occasionally act as an obstacle to individual creativity. I have observed a few incidents when students expressed concern or frustration with learning jazz in narrowly idiomatic ways. This seems to take the form of "not getting it" or being unable to express themselves fully as creative musicians.

After participating in a group improvisation session in one of my classes, a student expressed profound satisfaction with the way improvisation was presented without the confines of a jazz context. In a separate and unrelated context, I overheard a student advocating to their peers the need for more emphasis on improvisation beyond the confines of a particular genre. A more detailed exploration of this matter came up in an interview I conducted with a colleague at UCT, Bronwen Clacherty, whose professional performance and academic background includes both jazz and African musics. She reflected on her experience learning jazz at university:

> It was a very academic approach to music and learning all the rules of how you're supposed to play. And I understand that, but I wasn't able to get it. And it was so frustrating, like, I remember being very frustrated. In my fourth year of studying

jazz, . . . looking at the students who've been before me, and that just seemed to come so naturally to them, you know? (Clacherty 2019)

For Bronwen and several others I have encountered, searching for a creative outlet authentic to one's self is a pursuit of paramount importance. Ultimately for her, free improvisation created a sense of home and a freedom from the confines she had felt as an aspiring jazz performer.

> RICK: I'm wondering, is there a, musically speaking, is there a musical community that you feel at home in, or a genre? . . . What musical situations do you enjoy most, maybe? Or are you most comfortable in?
>
> BRONWEN: So the performance that I did last year was the first time that I felt like I'd kind of come home. And I was in a place where I was performing where I wasn't thinking about things. I was kind of just in the music. . . . I was working with Mark, who's a guitarist from India, I don't know if you know him, and Cara, who's a good friend of mine. And we've actually never worked together musically, which is weird, but we're very good friends. And they were the two just in their approach to music, it felt like we were working without rules and if I felt safe, playing music with Cara especially because she's coming from a very similar place to me; probably music college kind of broke her slightly by making it feel like there's this way to play music and then if you go out of it, it's like, that's not music, you know. And so especially, I mean that's why I stopped playing jazz because I just felt like I wasn't getting it exactly how I was expected to. (Clacherty 2019)

Following her studies and early career as a jazz musician, she pursued learning and performing African music, particularly Xhosa bow music and Zulu maskanda through collaboration and mentorships with African musicians.[3] As she recalled that journey some interesting issues arose. One of them involved the limits of genre regarding ethics of participation, even when collaborative and transparent. An excerpt of a longer discussion with Bronwen illustrates this point:

> [Performing African music] started to feel like it wasn't a superficial thing, . . . but it started to feel like with the music, I was trying to be something that I just wasn't . . . to the point where I kind of set all that aside and stop performing all that music until I can kind of work out . . . how to make it happen again. In a way I felt like there was something ethically . . . wrong with recording albums with arrangements of other people's music. Or, I mean, it wasn't all other people's music. I had composed other songs that were kind of inspired by some of the concepts of the music; it just got to a point where I felt uncomfortable with what I was trying to do. (Clacherty 2019)

Part of her apprehension stems from an academic background that emphasizes critical reflection. The locus of music making within a collaborative cohort and shared musical values tends to mitigate some tensions, but larger power dynamics continue to play a role. Discussing her work with maskanda musician Come Ladies, she reflected on the benefit of music making when central to social interaction: "Working with Come Ladies was a big shift in realizing what different worlds we were from, that we lived in, but, like musically, it felt like there weren't any barriers like . . . we shifted to what needed to happen."

As much as music serves to mitigate broader social differences, it is perhaps limited in the degree to which it can penetrate one's life to offer a more quotidian sense of belonging in a context such as South Africa. On the subject of trying to be a part of South Africa via music, Bronwen said:

> I think the biggest thing for me in my whole musical career has been working out how I belong as a South African, as being white and English. Music was my way of, well, not only music, but in a weird way, I almost tried to kind of work out how I fit into that world in a [general] way. That's why I took Zulu as a second language in school. That's why I studied African music at college. It was almost like I was trying to dress myself with things that were South African. If you understand what I mean, it's like, that's the only way that I can. Like I was trying to make myself fit into that world that I wasn't part of. And I don't think I ever will be, as much and as hard as I try. (Clacherty 2019)

This statement suggests that there are somewhat daunting limits regarding the efficacy of music and belonging on a national level. The inclusivity and creative freedom that may be experienced within a musical ensemble, however, should not be dismissed. Perhaps the smaller interventions afforded by these musical interactions can encourage useful negotiations and reflective internal discourse. In this case, it seems to have coincided with, if not fostered, a strong sense of self-awareness and empathy.

Concluding Summary

Key components of the musical settings discussed here help with inclusivity and self-expression within a larger group or social context. Regarding collective free improvisation, the underlying premise that there are no right or wrong notes, and no prescribed single genre, sets up a basic framework of creative inclusivity. The emphasis on cooperation, especially listening and decentering prescribed hierarchy, may help with establishing a stronger sense of cohesion, and perhaps over time, a sense of belonging. But these are not enough in themselves. As a musical practice that deviates from conventions, there may be habits and areas of vulnerability that cannot be overcome through linguistic directive (i.e., "there are no wrong notes"). Other musical features such as dense textures, cyclic forms, and call-and-response may need to be added in order to mitigate anxiety among self-conscious performers or assist the creative process for those new to improvisation.

Regarding Afro-jazz, foregrounding African practices, especially ones that resonate with participants, helps amplify a sense of community for some individuals, particularly if these practices tend to be underrepresented or undervalued in a larger context. Connecting with jazz as a cosmopolitan genre generates cultural capital for participants and seems to afford some leverage in asserting individual or collective identity or demonstrating cultural competence and mitigating a marked status as cultural other. There are several defining musical features that, taken together, may help facilitate a sense of belonging and group cohesion. These include emphasis on improvisation and composition, valuing the ability to manipulate musical elements such as rhythm, melody, timbre, harmony, and song form in a nuanced way, and a tradition of embracing folk, popular, and art music aesthetics or traditions.

Yet there are times when established practices and canon become sources for dogmatic guidelines, and this in turn excludes and undermines senses of belonging and cohesion. Jazz and African musics are embedded in histories of racial tensions and inequity that could also pose challenges if not engaged with effectively. Although music making can mitigate and subvert established power structures, there likely needs to be a degree of self-awareness among practitioners.

All this being said, by eliminating restrictive conventions it is possible to open the field for wider participation. It is important to encourage individual creative input while acknowledging social and historical associations. The dialectical process of challenging and embracing conventions is useful to progressive music making that seeks inclusion. Free improvisation, Afro-jazz, (and jazz more broadly) all offer opportunities for socialization using nonverbal references and contexts where individual creative input is emphasized through various forms of improvisation and composition. This context encourages and rewards representation and recognition in a space for creating self-awareness.

For musicians like Jo and Bronwen, their periodic reflection and musical interplay extend beyond the performance group into the immediate institutional space and at times the surrounding community. The same may be said about Dan, Owen, Lyton, and Salim working within the Lilongwe Afro-jazz scene. As music educators, scholars, and musicians, it is useful to regularly interrogate just how musical sounds operate in relation to what they allow sonically and socially, as well as what they prohibit (Turino 2008).[4]

The temporary suspension, however brief, of perceived hierarchies and markers of difference can be an important part of musical settings. Based on the above discussion I suggest that balancing the power of music to foster collective belonging with allowing freedom of individual expression could be central to creating a set of best practices—practices that "narrow down the complex whole," are "grounded in experience," and are "stabilized in discourse" (Fiol and Perman, introduction to this volume, "The Phenomenology of Community"). Thus, my vision of advancing ethnomusicology includes fostering musicking cohorts and, I hope, forging empathetic human connections and equitable communities by moving from the potential to the actual (Turino 2009, 13).

Notes

1. See also the discussion of feedback in the introduction to this volume under "Community and the Arts as a Feedback System."

2. This tends to be colloquially referred to as the Pan-African Ensemble and is offered regularly as one of the World Music Ensemble courses.

3. Bronwen Clacherty ultimately went on to complete her PhD research in present-day Zanzibar, focusing on the song genre dandaro practiced among women's singing groups there.

4. One of the many lessons I took away from working with Tom Turino in my coursework and as my dissertation supervisor was a relentless drive to fully interrogate the role of sound in relation to human interactions in particular contexts and larger social change.

Bibliography

Ansell, Gwen. 2004. *Soweto Blues: Jazz, Popular Music, and Politics in South Africa.* New York: Continuum.

Bailey, Derek. 1993. *Improvisation: Its Nature and Practice in Music.* New York: Da Capo.

Deja, Richard M. 2019. "Malawi: Modern and Contemporary Performance Practice." In *Sage International Encyclopedia of Music and Culture*, edited by Janet Sturman, 1369–70. Thousand Oaks, CA: Sage.

Fenn, John, and Alex Perullo. 2000. "Language Choice and Hip Hop in Tanzania and Malawi." *Popular Music and Society* 24(3): 73–93.

Fischlin, Daniel, Ajay Heble, and George Lipsitz. 2013. *The Fierce Urgency of Now: Improvisation, Rights, and the Ethics of Cocreation.* Durham, NC: Duke University Press.

Flood, Liza Sapir. 2017. "Instrument in Tow: Brining Musical Skills to the Field." *Ethnomusicology* 61(3): 486–505. https://www.jstor.org/stable/10.5406/ethnomusicology .61.3.0486.

Ladano, Kathryn. 2016. "Free Improvisation and Performance Anxiety in Musicians." In *Improvisation and Music Education: Beyond the Classroom*, edited by Ajay Heble and Mark Laver, 46–59. New York: Routledge.

Stewart, Jesse. 2016. "Improvisation Pedagogy in Theory and Practice." In *Improvisation and Music Education: Beyond the Classroom*, edited by Ajay Heble and Mark Laver, 32–45. New York: Routledge.

Thomson, Scott. 2008. "The Pedagogical Imperative of Musical Improvisation." *Critical Studies in Improvisation* 3(2): 1–12.

Turino, Thomas. 1993. *Moving away from Silence: Music of the Peruvian Altiplano and the Experience of Urban Migration.* Chicago: University of Chicago Press.

Turino, Thomas. 2000. *Nationalists, Cosmopolitans, and Popular Music in Zimbabwe.* Chicago: University of Chicago Press.

Turino, Thomas. 2008. *Music as Social Life: The Politics of Participation.* Chicago: University of Chicago Press.

Turino, Thomas. 2009. "Four Fields of Music Making and Sustainable Living." *World of Music* 51(1): 95–117.

Turino, Thomas. 2014. "Peircean Thought as Core Theory for a Phenomenological Ethnomusicology." *Ethnomusicology* 58(2): 185–221.

INTERVIEWS CONDUCTED BY THE AUTHOR

Agyefi, Papa Kow Mensah, and Jo Kunnuji. Cape Town, August 22, 2019.

Clacherty, Bronwen. Cape Town, August 22, 2019.

INTERVIEWS CONDUCTED BY CRAIG MAWANGA WITH THE AUTHOR

Chisuse, Lyton. Lilongwe, January 26, 2019.

Mbilizi, Owen, and Dan Sibale. Lilongwe, January 26, 2019.

Mussah, Salim Daud. Lilongwe, January 26, 2019.

11 Visions of Community and the Perils of Safeguarding a Himalayan Festival

STEFAN FIOL

One sunny afternoon in June 2019, the village of Salood-Dungra was abuzz with news that bureaucrats from the Indira Gandhi National Centre for the Arts (IGNCA), India's premier arts organization, would soon be arriving. Everyone was aware that the delegation was coming to check on how the funds resulting from the 2009 UNESCO Intangible Cultural Heritage designation of the local Ramman festival had been put to use. Perceived dominant (so-called upper) caste schoolchildren ironed their costumes and rehearsed dances while the newly constructed storeroom above the temple (for official purposes called a "museum") was unlocked, its computers were turned on, and the plastic over the furniture was dusted. Dominant-caste residents gathered to welcome and garland the bureaucrats as they stepped out of their vehicles, while youth filmed the proceedings on state-funded cameras. Following a sumptuous lunch, the delegation was treated to a performance of Ramman dances by children from dominant castes accompanied by two children from lowered caste hereditary drumming families who played the dhol and the damaun. The village headman then asked me, the resident ethnomusicologist, to play some local drumming compositions that I had learned, presumably to enhance the prestige of the occasion. Following this, members of the delegation gave speeches in support of additional funding proposals that could turn Salood into a major tourist destination, including a two-year research fellowship that could be offered to a member of the village of unspecified background (assumed to be dominant caste or overseen by dominant castes), and a community resource center that could sell commodities to tourists (e.g., wooden masks and dolls representing deified ancestors featured during the Ramman rituals).

If ritual performances were once studied primarily as a window into understanding dominant ideas of community and culture, scholars regularly emphasize how they are the staging ground for the contestation and negotiation of diverse group identities (Comaroff and Comaroff 2009; Harnish 2021; Hüsken and Michaels 2013). As Karin Polit reminds us, ritual experience creates selves, relationships, and communities by inscribing broader cultural concepts on the person and on the collective body. Rituals are contexts in which social positions are performatively negotiated, defined and redefined" (Polit 2012, 34), and where nested community formations emerge in relation to territory, social group, and cosmology. Rituals allow for multiple communities to coalesce around shared meaning making (Turino 2000). Moreover, the impact of festivals extends beyond the time of performance, "enacting values and embodying meanings" that shape lasting notions of belonging and community (Ohri 2016, 668).

Publications about UNESCO's Intangible Cultural Heritage (ICH) program and its impact on local communities have multiplied exponentially since 2010 in anthropology, folklore studies, and ethnomusicology (Schippers 2016; Peselmann, Bendix, and Eggert 2013; Howard 2012; Grant 2012; Geismar 2015; Harris 2020). Ethnographic approaches typically detail the perspectives and processes of either "on the ground" culture bearers (Foster 2015; Norton and Matsumoto 2018) or state-level or international-level bureaucrats (Brumann 2021; De Beukelaer, Pyykkönen, and Singh 2015; Meskell 2018). This chapter joins a relatively short list of studies that ethnographically examine the interstitial spaces of engagement between state-level and local-level actors of differing status (Harris 2020; Lowthorp 2015).

Heritagization—the creation of a shared historicity, legacy, and significance around a cultural practice or place—entails varying degrees of codification, state surveillance, monetary capitalization, and the operationalization of multiple and often competing discourses of community differentiated by caste, class, gender, residence, and regional ethnicity. According to the UNESCO Committee on ICH, "the spirit of the Convention is such that communities should be seen as having an open character, not necessarily linked to specific territories" (UNESCO Intangible Cultural Heritage n.d.). The UNESCO convention's open interpretation of the notion of community makes sense when one considers the divergent scales of the traditions supported by the convention, including traditions that are geographically diffuse (e.g., Vedic chant, yoga) and geographically narrow (e.g., Durga Puja in Kolkata). At the same time, the convention mandates that the process of inscription "cannot be done without the free, prior and informed consent of the community or group concerned. Their involvement is also required in the preparation and implementation of safeguarding programmes that benefit from international assistance" (ibid.). The process of safeguarding heritage thus requires slippage between community as an abstract group of culture bearers who identify or are identified by others with a specific set of practices, and community as a more concrete set of (undifferentiated) individuals who mediate the process of inscription alongside state functionaries.

In contrast to these top-down conceptions of community, ritual participants experience belonging within a community (or nested communities) through participation in highly charged, affective, and embodied experiences that reinforce social inclusion or exclusion in myriad ways. Experiences of ritual singing and dancing engender multiple and iterative processes of community making and unmaking that involve the transactional obligations between deities and devotees, the complex dynamics between individuals from unequal social groups, the allure of income-earning opportunities, the weight of custom, and the pleasure of moving and sounding together.

Performances of Ramman have successfully generated (or fed into) a number of narratives of community that I examine below, but each of these narratives is predictably rooted in the overlapping ideologies of Brahmanical patriarchy, neoliberal capitalism, cultural nationalism, and caste supremacy. For this reason, post-inscription performances of Ramman ultimately fail to contribute to inclusive community building in the sense theorized in the introduction to this volume as a process of attending to difference, feedback, and mutual but asymmetrical indebtedness between heterogeneous social groups.

This chapter highlights the incommensurable ideals of community espoused by differently positioned individuals in the wake of the ICH inscription of Ramman. Drawing inspiration from Akira Kurosawa's film *Rashomon* (1950), I employ a strategy of writing that juxtaposes the perspectives of four distinct subjects: a lowered status drummer, a dominant caste village leader, a state-employed folklorist who oversaw the nomination process, and a participant from a neighboring village. The juxtaposition of these subject positions reveals the contested nature of the heritagization process as a conglomeration of interests shaped by relations of power and relative insiderness or outsiderness. Whose values and priorities are foregrounded in the heritagization of festival performance? How is the festival understood to support particular visions of community that either reinforce or undermine structures of social oppression?

A Brief Overview of Ramman

I briefly describe what the Ramman festival entails before turning to the social positions and processes related to heritagization. Ramman is one of many varieties of masked dance-dramas locally referred to as *pattar* that are performed in the Dasoli and Nagpur blocks of Chamoli district, located in the Uttarakhand Himalayas of North India. Ramman is performed annually in late April (Baisakh) in three villages: the twin villages of Salood-Dungra (hereafter Salood), Dungri-Barosi (hereafter Dungri), and Selang (figure 11.1). These three Ramman festivals likely diverged from a single ritual performance in the distant past, and they remain identical in most respects. As I explore below, however, the

Fig. 11.1. Map of Uttarakhand showing the location of Salood in Chamoli District.

inscription of just one of these versions of Ramman (the one in Salood) has created resentment and inequitable consequences in the region.

During the fourteen-day festival, bards recite narratives about the gods while dancers wear elaborately carved wooden masks and follow the direction of and move to the rhythmic patterns (*baja*) of hereditary drummers performing on the dhol, a large barrel drum, and the damaun, a small kettledrum. The name *Ramman* derives from the Ramayana, and the final day of the day festival offers an abstract rendering of numerous episodes from the great epic including the birth of brothers Ram and Lakshman, Seeta Svayamvar, Seeta Hiran, Hanuman Milan, Lanka Dahan, and Raj Tilak. Although the historical record is spotty, Ramman is likely the vestige of a longstanding Ram cult brought by Vaishnavite and Ramanandi pilgrims visiting Joshimath and Badrinath.

During Ramman a heightened sense of community is fostered by the interaction of high gods, demigods, saints (or rishis), ancestors, and human participants. The space of *lila* ("divine play") is one in which the world is creatively suspended and fluidly reconfigured with each performance (Sax 2002). The majority of the danced episodes feature deities who are either in statis, where they represent images or tableaux vivants (*vigraha murthi*), or in motion, where they are dramatic personae (*lila murthi*) (Purohit 1993, 135). Among the latter are deified ancestors in male-female consorts (e.g., Lala-Lati and Mwar-Morin) who are a source of levity and humor, juxtaposing ideas of who local residents were historically (e.g., forest dwellers and hillbillies) with who they believe themselves to be now. Ramman distills historical and cosmological narratives, creating a "usable past" for local communities (Lowenthal 1985). The Maal dance reenacts a local early nineteenth-century guerilla conflict between local Garhwalis and the conquering Gurkha army. Two dancers in red (holding muskets and representing the Gurkha soldiers) face off against two dancers in white representing the Garhwalis. A number of divinities are propitiated in the festival including Suraj Ishwar (the Sun God), Ganesha, Narsingh (an avatar of Vishnu), and the Pandavas, heroes of the other great Indic epic, the Mahabharata. Also included are ritual enactments of comical social deviants, including Burhdeva (or Narada), a semi-divine trickster figure in a human body, who eats, marries, sleeps, and breaks taboos. Another episode features Baniya-Baniyan, traders from the southern plains who attempt to swindle the mountain people. On the final day of the festival, a character called Kurujogi personifies a pervasive pastureweed found in agricultural fields (*Cythula tomentosa*); wearing a costume bedecked with the sticky weed, he throws clumps of it at unsuspecting attendees, causing havoc and frivolity.

Presiding over the entire festival is the tutelary deity of Salood, the local god Bhumiyal, whose radiant silver mask is affixed to a long pole and who processes to all dominant caste homes in the village. Bhumiyal dances at the beginning and end of each day's ritual proceedings, and often between other "scenes" as well. Bhumiyal is the guardian of the land (*kshetrapal*); some manifestation of this divinity can be found in nearly every village across the central Himalayas, and indeed across much of South Asia, underlining the centrality of agriculture in ritual life (Prakash 2019). In this sense, Bhumiyal can be understood as the patriarch of a community of divinities, each of whom have their own place of worship (*dyo*) in the village. Ramman is thus a setting for a variety of intersecting narratives and ritual performances that offer powerful cosmological frameworks (Purohit 1993) and multiple overlapping expressions of community—past and present, earthly and divine, local and regional.

Garib Das, Hereditary Drummer

In 2016–17 I undertook a nine-month study of drumming in Salood. I chose to stay in this village because of the presence of twelve families of hereditary drummers that would facilitate work on a larger comparative project exploring drumming as historiographic method. My family and I arrived with a reference from Kushal Bhandari, the headmaster of a local college, who had arranged for a room for us in his nephew's house. Though I came to study with lowered status drummers, I knew that my access to many aspects of village life would be limited if I circumvented dominant caste intermediaries (cf. Polit 2012).

I began visiting drummers in their homes, explaining the goals of my project and requesting their participation. I experienced only warmth and agreement, but as the weeks wore on, I found that few were willing to engage with me apart from casual banter. The exception to this was a drummer named Garib, who appeared eager to work with me from the start. He was a widower with five young children and little in the way of steady income; tragically, Garib's name means "poor." Although many Dalit families live in conditions of poverty, Garib and his family were nearly destitute. They lived among other lowered caste families in a small hamlet at the bottom of the mountain on which Salood is perched. These sites had a water source separate from that for the rest of the village, a fact that was vitally important to the dominant caste residents of the village, who feared pollution from the intermixture of substances.

All participants in Ramman were amateur performers whose primary occupation was farming, with the exception of the drummers, who depended on their earnings from performance and had a *hereditary obligation* to perform during this festival.[1] Like the other drummers, Garib Das had inherited a group of patron families, including the Bhandari family, for whom he performed at family-level rituals including weddings, naming ceremonies (*namkaran*), haircutting ceremonies (*mundan*), and family healing rituals (*jagar*). Although I sought assurances that Garib's participation in my research was voluntary, I have no doubt that his indebtedness to his patrons extended to working with me, at least initially. This was a challenging context in which to try to build any semblance of an equitable relationship.

Garib compared his role as a hereditary drummer to that of the Brahmin priest: Both labor in the ritual economy, serving as intermediaries between people and gods, conveying the genealogies of their patrons, and relying on customary offerings for their services. The only difference, Garib once stated, was that the Brahmin performed his services inside the home, whereas the drummer performed outside. Yet in candid moments Garib admitted that there were vast differences between his social position and that of a priest. The relationship between a drummer and his patron rested on a platform of mutual if asymmetrical indebtedness. A drummer, not unlike a bonded laborer, was required to perform whenever his patrons requested; in turn, his livelihood (historically consisting of a fixed amount of their agricultural yield and a monetary token of appreciation), and indeed his *life*, were contingent on their beneficence (Qureshi 2002, 93).

In spite of the social inequity he experienced, Garib Das was proud of his role as a hereditary drummer. He explained that only drummers possessed the knowledge and skills needed to invite, move, and propitiate the gods during the

Fig. 11.2. Garib Das (right) performing with hereditary drummers during Ramman.
Photo by the author.

Ramman festival (figure 11.2). Garib compared his feelings of intense devotion
and gratitude to Bhumiyal, the presiding divinity (*devta*) of the village, as those
of a personal servant (Das) to a king. During possession rituals held during Ramman, Garib's drumming summoned Bhumiyal to possess the body of his human
medium, always a dominant caste person and typically a man. In a stereotypical
movement, the possessed man held the straps of the dhol and embraced Garib
around the neck while dancing animatedly. Such physical contact between a
dominant caste man and a drummer was unknown in other contexts, but the
agency of the god enabled this intimacy. Still, there were limits to the ways in
which Garib could know Bhumiyal. Following longstanding caste-based prohibi-
tions in the village, drummers and other members of lowered castes could not
enter Bhumiyal's temple or directly touch any of his sacred implements for fear
of pollution; nor could Bhumiyal visit lowered caste homes. These social taboos
evoked some sadness for Garib, but he noted that Bhumiyal communicated *in
spite of them*. Once while he was drumming for Bhumiyal, one of the pieces of
fabric (*saru*) attached to his bamboo pole fell onto Garib's dhol (Fig. 11.3). He saw
this as a direct blessing from the devta, a special recognition of his devotion, and
he was allowed to keep it. Through the telling of such stories, Garib foregrounded
the purity of his faith and the virtue of his direct relationship with Bhumiyal as
a means of overcoming oppressive caste restrictions.

Garib and the other hereditary drummers in Salood performed for several
large-scale festivals that occurred every one to three years (Ramman, Pandava
Nritya, and Nandashtami). These festivals, which lasted from three to fourteen

Fig. 11.3. Hereditary drummers playing while Bhumiyal dances. Photo by the author.

days, required enormous sacrifices of time, money, and other resources on the part of the entire village. Garib and his fellow drummers had an established rotation system according to which they performed in pairs during festivals; when any drummer found it difficult to perform because of age, illness, or fatigue, another drummer stepped in to support him. Historically, drummers received a token amount of compensation at the conclusion of a festival in the form of several kilos of rice and between $3 and $5 per person.

In 2009, the year Ramman was nominated to the ICH list, a festival committee was formed with Kushal Bhandari as chair (see below) and membership consisting exclusively of dominant caste men, with one exception. The formation of the committee was the result of a need to regulate and enforce "safeguarding" strategies, thereby catalyzing a process of standardizing and inscribing knowledge of the ritual. It is not surprising that Garib felt that the committee had wrested control from the drummers who had historically retained knowledge of the dances, rhythms, and ritual structure of Ramman. For as long as anyone knew, drummers had been responsible for orally transmitting this knowledge in pre-festival rehearsals and by means of drumming and verbal instruction during the festival.[2] A ninety-five-page booklet about Ramman published in Hindi and English by IGNCA omits any mention of the leadership role of drummers, stating only that "dhol-damaun players are diminished in the knowledge of their art form" (Kaushal 2017). Hereditary drummers had thus lost a position of respect as the progenitors of the tradition, and their importance had been reduced to that of marginalized bit players.

One of the main responsibilities of the newly formed Ramman committee was to administer resources that had accrued following the ICH inscription. From the 42 lakhs (approximately US$50,000) that had come from regional and national agencies, Garib and several other drummers received 2.5 lakhs over the course of two years to teach drumming to village youth.

The remainder of the funding was used to support dance, ballad-singing, and mask-making workshops and the purchase of computers, cameras, scanners, and other equipment that could be used to train people in festival documentation. Ironically, all of these resources were kept in a storeroom above the temple, a space that, following customary law, *lowered caste members of the village are prohibited from accessing*.[3] So the idea that these funds benefited everyone in the village—a claim made by representatives of the Ramman committee—was contradicted by the evidence. For instance, six new sets of drums (dhol-damaun) that were purchased with these funds were stored above the temple and could only be handed over to drummers at the discretion of the committee. One rainy evening during Ramman 2017, I couldn't help but consider the irony of this arrangement as I watched Garib playing rhythms of praise to Bhumiyal on a dhol with a split drumhead while only meters away, locked up in the temple, lay the six sets of new instruments.

Over the course of my time with Garib I came to understand his complex positioning inside and outside various kinds of communities. By drumming, he viscerally forged a connection with Bhumiyal and other deities, with dancers, and with his drumming partner on damaun. Yet the experience of fostering intimacy between others was attenuated by personal experiences of exclusion and casteism. The physical and ritual boundaries erected between him and Bhumiyal, and between him and his patrons, were undergirded by the constant threat of intimidation, stigma, and violence. Even the possibilities of community with other drummers were mitigated by experiences of trauma, poverty, and competition. In the final weeks of my stay, nearly nine months after arriving, two other drummers disclosed why our relationships had been strained since my alignment with Garib. Fed up with financial exploitation and threats of violence from dominant castes, the drummers of the village made a verbal pact in 2015 to refuse to perform any of their hereditary obligations until they began to be treated fairly and be compensated at a fair wage for their labor. Given the caste-based violence that occurs with regularity in the region, this was an extraordinary act of courage. Yet without the drummers' participation, Ramman could not take place. This threat motivated a local village leader to approach the District Magistrate with their demands, with the result that each drumming family was awarded enough funds to build an additional room onto their residence. While this was a significant concession, the drummers remained unsatisfied, arguing that they should receive a sustainable income and pension as they played an indispensable and physically demanding role in the festival.[4] Members of the Ramman committee resented this declaration of autonomy and sought ways to undermine it. Bhandari pressured Garib—his family's own drummer and the most economically vulnerable among them—to perform and break the drumming strike. This created great resentment among the other drummers, who considered Garib an opportunist and a "scab."

The inequities and tensions between and within social groups did not begin with the ICH designation, but the latter has further strained these relationships because some dominant caste individuals have been given control of the resources and performance elements of the festival. Yet all of the drummers, including Garib, were nevertheless proud of the inscription and the attention it garnered. When I asked Garib whether the ICH inscription could in any way compromise the divine power (*shakti*) of Bhumiyal, his response was unequivocal: The inscription was *evidence of* the superior shakti of Salood's Bhumiyal. "When there are so many masked dance dramas (pattar) and so many different divinities (devta) in this region, why is it that ours was chosen?" he remarked. "Universal heritage [*vishwa dharohar*] 'passed' Ramman, and this is proof of its power." At the same time, however, Garib was skeptical that the ICH designation would result in any positive changes for him or his family. Officials wanted to know how his participation sustained local heritage, he claimed, but he wanted to know "how participating in Ramman would sustain him and his family." Heritagization was an elusive and distant goal that offered little concrete benefit and had only exacerbated the harm experienced by hereditary drummers.

Kushal Bhandari, Village Entrepreneur

In November 2008 the delegation from IGNCA arrived without warning in Salood and asked if they could view a performance of Ramman. The timing of the request was odd because villagers were in the middle of a different large-scale ritual performance (Pandava Nritya), but Kushal Bhandari implored his fellow villagers to organize a separate demonstration. He was hopeful that if the delegation left the village impressed, it could lead to opportunities for himself and his fellow villagers. Outside attention might also generate more local interest in Ramman. He had noticed a pronounced and continuous decline in villagers' attendance and involvement in the ritual since his childhood that he attributed to urban out-migration and the incursion of roads and televisions in the villages. Would the attention of a national arts organization, he wondered, inject new resources and pride into ritual performances?

It was only natural for Bhandari to assume a leadership role. As the headmaster of a regional high school, he was someone whom the delegation would respect and someone who already commanded respect within Salood. Bhandari hailed from one of the most influential dominant caste families in Salood, a fact reinforced each year during Ramman in one of the climactic ritual sequences, when the god Narsingh (an incarnation of Vishnu) chose a male member of the Bhandari clan to wear the mask and dance as his human medium. In his articulation of sadness concerning the decrease in villagers' participation in Ramman, I sensed feelings of nostalgia for the Bhandari clan's historical prestige. He revealed that male members of his family used to enter the temple complex during Ramman dancing heroically to what he called "Bhandari baja," a rhythmic pattern that was played exclusively for them by their hereditary drummers. He later called on Garib Das to play this rhythm in his courtyard while he and other men from the Bhandari clan danced with arms outstretched. It was clear that this was not a personal memory but a collective memory that circulated within the clan, signifying their power and masculine bravado. The loss of this practice indexed a loss of caste privilege. When I later asked Garib Das about this rhythm, he said that he had always known it as "Discu baja," one of several rhythms used for collective dancing by anyone and not exclusive to the Bhandaris. I interpret Garib's act of renaming as a subtle refusal to endorse the caste superiority of the Bhandari clan.

Several weeks after the delegation left the village, Bhandari was overjoyed to receive an invitation to demonstrate Ramman at a conference in Delhi dedicated to Ramayana-based performance traditions across India. With only a month to prepare, Bhandari, who had no dramaturgical experience apart from ritual theater performances as a young man, took charge of the production, the first that would occur outside the village. He narrowed down a sequence of selected scenes and organized a team of twenty drummers, dancers, and singers. They all traveled to Delhi to rehearse for three days with the renowned Bansi Kaul. The latter worked with the performers to condense their ritual performance to ninety minutes, eliminating redundancies with the goal of keeping urban spectators entertained. Some of the drummers I interviewed spoke with awe about Kaul's ability to cut out rhythms that he deemed unnecessary and to arrange scenes in a strict order. Instead of having them follow their usual practice of playing in individual dhol-damaun pairs, Kaul appointed one drummer to be the leader and asked all of the others to follow his lead, which caused no small amount of conflict between the drummers. Kaul also drew a circle within the performance space and asked that all participants confine their movements within this space; this modification was explained as a way of mimicking ritual rather than adapting movement to the proscenium stage, with which they were unfamiliar. Kaul's modifications were not directly conceived of as part of the ICH mission of "safeguarding" Ramman; they were theatrical adaptations that he considered necessary for sustaining the interest of urban cosmopolitan audiences.

It is significant that many of these reforms were later brought back to the village and incorporated into ritual performances.[5] Analyzing video footage of Salood's Ramman from 2008, 2009 (the year of ICH inscription), 2010, 2012, and 2015, I noted a marked increase in standardization and formalization, coinciding with ever-larger audiences. Conversations with participants confirm that prior to 2008 the order of scenes (lila) was rather informal and decided on the spot; after 2008, however, the order followed a strictly notated sequence. The IGNCA team, in conversation with Bhandari, encouraged the revival of certain elements of ritual practice that had become dormant, such as the ballad-singing tradition (which required finding older exponents from Bhalla village to teach younger singers) and the role of Burhdeva, a trickster figure who plays a narrator role, the costumes and dance steps of the Rani-Radhikas (consorts of Krishna), and the roles of the Khylaris, who come to steal from the plains traders (Baniya-Baniyan).

Bhandari also enforced a number of other reforms including a new code of conduct, which included a strict ban on the consumption of alcohol before or during the performance, the wearing of a loincloth (*dhoti*) by any ritual functionaries, the construction of a clear boundary (*angan*) around the performance arena (a practice introduced by the Delhi director Kaul), a separate space for chief guests to view the performances, and a loudspeaker system to narrate the proceedings in formal Sanskritized Hindi. Some of these reforms were carried over from theatrical performances in Delhi. Others were adopted because of the marked increase in the attendance of outsiders in Salood's Ramman and because of what Bhandari assumed these outsiders *expected* to see in a performance of "ritual theater" (as inscribed by the ICH Commission): a clearly bounded arena for dancers and spectators, a strict code of conduct, an interpretation of the performance, and links to ancient Sanskrit ritual practice (e.g., the wearing of dhotis and modifications of language).[6]

Bhandari's position as the intermediary between villagers and national-level funding organizations brought risks and rewards. In the aftermath of the first performance of Ramman in Delhi in 2008, he faced a crisis back in the village. The presiding village deity, Bhumiyal, took offense at the removal of the masks and insignia (*nisan*) from the village. The masks used in Ramman were ritually consecrated objects that carried great ritual power, and they were only taken out of the temple once a year during the festival. Some of the villagers were fearful of the consequences of this perceived infraction, and they held Bhandari responsible. On his return to the village, he organized a possession ritual in which Bhumiyal, speaking through his human medium, conveyed that several goats needed to be sacrificed to assuage his feelings of offense. When the invitation came for Ramman to be presented again in Delhi in 2009, Bhandari only secured the consent of the village panchayat after arranging for a second set of unconsecrated masks to be made.[7]

At the time of writing, adaptations of Ramman have been presented at least a dozen times in festivals across the country; Ramman was even chosen to represent the state of Uttarakhand on a float during India's Republic Day Parade of 2016. Although Bhandari claimed not to have benefited financially, he leveraged his position to secure awards and promotions. He was able to invite chief guests to Ramman each year, including several chief ministers of Uttarakhand, resulting in considerable political influence and personal prestige. Despite this influence, he expressed frustration to me on several occasions about the amount of work involved in organizing Ramman-related events and the perceived lack of interest and cooperation from his fellow villagers. He lamented what he saw as a lack of support for developing Ramman, singling out the drummers as particularly ungrateful for new performance opportunities.

Molly Kaushal, National Folklorist

When I sat down with Molly Kaushal in her office at IGNCA in Delhi in July 2019, each of us had recently returned from a demonstration of Ramman in Salood, and I was curious to hear her perspectives. As the person most responsible for nominating Ramman to the ICH Commission, she was pleased with the enthusiasm of the performances but was not overly optimistic about the steps that villagers had taken to safeguard the festival. "Someone should first develop something that will bring in money," she exclaimed, "and then . . . see how that money is going to be used. You know, it's very important to get the tourists in. It's very important to sell." She noted that Salood's location just a few miles off the main highway to Badrinath makes it well positioned to attract tourists. It is also just a twenty-minute drive from Joshimath, a major tourist hub, and could easily serve as a day-trip destination.

She also disapproved of some of the ways in which the Ramman committee had used the funds, including the use of acrylic paints to make the masks instead of the traditional vegetable dyes. The Ramman committee had allocated approximately one quarter of their 42 lakh budget to the construction of a new temple to Bhumiyal. Because government funding cannot be used for the building of a temple, however, it was officially named a museum. Kaushal did not mind this creative wordplay, but she was put off by the use of ceramic tiles within the temple as opposed to stone and clay. "And that's the time when . . . I said, 'I'll stop all money because my mandate is to maintain what the traditional performing space is.'" But later she relented, saying, "I also understand that the communities that are on upwardly mobile [paths] would want to show their temple as a piece of architecture and they may not appreciate what their own dilapidated temple looked like. So it's ok, it's fine, [that] they have their own sense of aesthetics. After all, it's still community-based. Otherwise it would be interference, which I don't want to do."

In these statements Kaushal alternates between two distinct positions: that of a cultural bureaucrat with a keen eye for what tourists and cosmopolitans view as authentic ritual theater, and that of a neutral facilitator who selectively empowers local cosmopolitans (in this case Bhandari and other members of the Ramman committee) to assert control over the representation and management of the festival. Although she was not shy about recommending strategies and critiquing local efforts, she insisted that the role of IGNCA was to support and encourage from afar. "Unless Dr. Bhandari has the weight of the community behind him," she remarked, "it's not about funds, it's not about giving money. It's about, you know, creating that into an economic resource which is a cultural resource. That is something that the community alone can do."

Kaushal demonstrated a detached pragmatism when discussing Ramman, comparing it to various other village-based traditions with which she had worked. She noted that Ramman was just one example of a broad range of masked dance-drama traditions performed throughout the central Himalayas, some of which rival Ramman in terms of their richness and complexity. Moreover, India is a country with many thousands of traditions that are "representative" and worthy of safeguarding. "The people of Salood should be grateful [that Ramman was inscribed]," she said, "but what will they do with the opportunity?"

The process of nominating Ramman was both fortuitous and contingent. Shortly after inviting the Ramman troupe to the IGNCA-funded conference on Ramayana-based traditions of India (2008), Kaushal learned that UNESCO's Masterpieces of Oral Intangible Heritage program had been superseded by a new program, the Representative List of the Intangible Cultural Heritage of Humanity. This change in UNESCO's orientation prompted Kaushal to consider nominating a "little tradition" such as Ramman as opposed to one of the better-known "great traditions" that had been nominated earlier (e.g., Vedic chant). She noted that the ICH Commission was eager to recognize smaller, more localized traditions because of a belief that they could more easily be monitored for success. Kaushal then reached out to several regional folklorists, including

Data Ram Purohit, as well as Kushal Bhandari. She did not, however, feel it was necessary to discuss the benefits and drawbacks of an ICH designation with a broader cross-section of Salood residents, leaving that work for Bhandari.

As mentioned above, Kaushal's team from IGNCA visited Salood in 2009 to document Ramman in its ritual setting, and they produced a video documentary as part of the ICH nomination process.[8] At thirteen minutes, forty seconds in length, the documentary follows the prescribed format of the submission videos, with comprehensive footage of the different facets of the festival. Predictably, given the salvage agenda of the Indian state and the ICH Commission, the commentary emphasizes "vanishing" aspects of the festival, including the loss of knowledge about mask-making, drumming, dancing, and ritual singing. The commentary also underlines that Ramman is "organized by villagers, and each caste and occupational group has a distinct role": Members of the Lohar (ironsmith) caste collect firewood; members of the Bajgi drumming caste perform on the dhol-damaun each day of the festival; members of the Thakur or Rajput castes perform the roles of dancers and festival organizers; members of the Brahmin or priestly castes from nearby Barosi village perform rituals inside the temple and help prepare the village feasts; and members of the Bhalla caste are invited from Bhal village and Subhai village to sing ballad narratives. The commentary emphasizes the communitarian aspects of the festival, proclaiming that Ramman participants are "oblivious to the barriers of caste and creed" and forge a sense of "unity among the different village communities." Garib Das's experiences of labor and stigma during the festival tell a different story about caste privilege and difference.

Such idealized representations are to be expected in contexts where heritage-based organizations inscribe and assert rationalized control over cultural traditions that are fluid and contested. Marking any performance tradition as representative of ICH entails processes of codification, elimination, elaboration, and selective reification and raises questions about purism, ecological balance, and the efficacy (or lack thereof) of intervention (Grant 2012). To her credit, Kaushal responded with surprise and concern when I related how caste-based discrimination impacted the distribution of resources within the village. Yet casteism was for her an internal village-based matter, not something that could be addressed or mitigated by an outside agency. Rather than using her position of privilege to safeguard the rights and livelihoods of Salood's most vulnerable, she evaded this responsibility, assuming that the preservationist values of the heritage industry, and development of the festival on the basis of commercial diversification, would be inherently good for *all* residents. But this was demonstrably not the case in Salood, nor in nearby villages, as I would come to learn.

Pratima Devi, Resident of Dungri

In 2017 I was able to attend and review video footage of two other Ramman festivals, in the villages of Dungri and Selang, located one and five kilometers from Salood, respectively. In terms of the ritual structure and performance practice, these Ramman performances were practically identical to Salood's, replicating the vast majority of the masked characters, dance steps, and rhythms.[9] Yet the settings were radically different. In both Selang and Dungri, I was the only outsider present, and there were no signs proclaiming the event, no media contingent, no amplification, and no announcements in Hindi. These festivals were private, intimate rituals focused on building a sense of community between village residents and their gods.

When I asked Pratima Devi, a sixty-five-year old grandmother from Dungri, what Ramman meant to her, she reframed the question in terms of the lack of resources in her village in comparison to Salood. She lamented that there were no longer any living elders in the village who knew the sung narratives (this was true in Salood as well). Dungri residents were also victims of the theft of sacred masks in 2004, she noted, but they had fewer resources than Salood to make new masks, so they had to make do with fewer of them. She commented on how the Salood Ramman (post-inscription) had come to influence several aspects of their own performances, including the recent addition of the procession of Bhumiyal to each of the residents' homes, the community ban on the consumption of alcohol, and the requirement that all performers wear the dhoti. In years past, drummers from nearby Helang village were hired to perform for Dungri's Ramman because there were no hereditary drummers living in Dungri. Because these drummers lacked intimate knowledge of Ramman rhythms and dances, however, they had been hiring a drummer from Salood to assist them since 2017. These observations were not made critically but in a matter-of-fact way, as if to say that there was no avoiding the behemoth that Salood's Ramman had become (figure 11.4).

In Selang I heard similar refrains. The residents were incredibly proud of their own festival but lamented the fact that there were not enough resources to do it well and that knowledge among elders was waning. According to several testimonies, when the IGNCA delegation arrived in 2008 on a fact-finding mission they arrived first in Selang and asked about its Ramman. After some discussion, they continued on to Salood. Kaushal explained it thus:

SF: So I was told that your [IGNCA] team went to these other villages and inquired?
MK: Yeah, so it was, "We used to do it . . . not anymore" [*hota tha . . . ab nahi hai*]. And they did not volunteer to approach or come and say that we also have it. So obviously at that point as a very living tradition that was getting done every

Fig. 11.4. Signboard proclaiming "Ramman: Safeguarding World Cultural Heritage" on the road leading to Salood, Selang, and Dungri. Photo by the author.

year, [it] was only Salood. Other villages kind of did not have it as they claim now to have it. . . . But now that it's become a recognized tradition . . . there are many to lay claim to it.[10]

I spoke to residents from Selang and Dungri who, in contrast to this statement, insisted that Ramman had been performed in their villages every year continuously without interruption. They continued to wonder how their village's present and future would be different if the delegation had chosen to document one of their Ramman festivals instead of, or alongside, Salood's. Laxmi Rawat, one of the three members of the IGNCA delegation, said in 2019 that she continued to receive letters from (presumably dominant caste) Selang residents who were upset about their festival's not being safeguarded.

With hindsight, it is reasonable to ask why IGNCA members did not conduct a more thorough survey of Ramman traditions before settling on Salood's version. Although the ICH Commission inscribed Ramman with reference to the Garhwal Himalayas, thus technically allowing other locations to claim the designation, the fact is that only Salood's Ramman was documented and only Salood residents received post-inscription resources from the state. And while the majority of people with whom I spoke in Dungri and Selang wished that the financial benefits of inscription could have spread beyond Salood, this wish was counterbalanced by Pratima Devi, who remarked that Dungri's Bhumiyal had more divine energy (shakti) than Salood's Bhumiyal precisely because the former had not been taken out of the village. This sentiment was echoed by a number of older women, one of whom said that in Salood "they have sold their Bhumiyal" (*unke Bhumiyal ko bech diya*).

The Perils of Heritagization

With each passing year since 2009, the year of its nomination, Ramman has become more and more of a spectacle, regularly hosting more than one hundred outsiders and media personnel. In 2019 I was told that the festival went well except for the fact that the villagers were so distracted by the presence of a drone overhead filming the proceedings that many of them missed some of the pivotal moments of the ritual. Pratima Devi's fear—that a loss of divine energy would accompany Ramman's exposure to the outside world—points to a broader contradiction of the ICH process: Safeguarding almost always requires exposing ritual practices to external commercial and aesthetic values, which then pose a direct threat the local cultural values that the ICH Commission is seeking to protect in the first place (Comaroff and Comaroff 2009). Even as the commission has come to value "representativeness" over "masterpieces," and even as it has enshrined a commitment to community engagement in its safeguarding procedures (Smith 2013, 390), heritagization remains a top-down process. Even the designation of Ramman as "representative" has elevated it and distinguished it from similar traditions. "From UNESCO's metacultural global vantage point, a selected element may be just one of many on a list, but from the perspective of the culture, state, or community it represents, the element occupies a singularly vaunted position in contrast to all the other elements that were not selected" (Foster 2015, 4).

In order for Ramman to be vetted and recognized as a viable tradition of "ritual theater," IGNCA brought it to Delhi and repackaged it for cosmopolitan consumption. Each time this occurred, the performers returned to the village with a slightly different perspective on how Ramman could or should be presented in the village. Moreover, the delegation that came to Salood to document the tradition and prepare the nomination report and documentary focused on "vanishing" elements that needed safeguarding or revival, rather than the ways in which Ramman had already adapted to changing local conditions. The logic of IGNCA's safeguarding plan rested on an assumption that modernization had entailed a loss of heritage and that the only way to sustain the festival was via commercialization. Molly Kaushal recognized the ICH inscription as a global branding opportunity that could generate tourism, labor diversification, and long-term economic sustainability. The IGNCA directed considerable financial resources to a newly formed local Ramman committee with the expectation that residents follow their development plan (and an implicit threat of rescinding further resources if they did not). Yet the financial investments resulting from inscription, though ostensibly made for the benefit of all, have reinforced caste-based oppression and division within and between the villages.

In addition to the four subject positions I have described above, there is a fifth that begs consideration: my own. Just as the director Kurosawa shaped the frame of each of the four subjects in *Rashomon*, I have framed the narratives of my subjects, and my own politics should be made transparent. While I have tried to report the experiences of all four subjects in equal measure, I feel accountable to attend to the social inequities that are exacerbated (consciously or unconsciously) by agents in the heritagization process. This accountability is inextricably tied to my own complicity in class, caste, race, and gender inequities based on my privilege and postcolonial positionality in South Asia as a white, cisgender male researcher.[11]

Returning to the definition of *community* as relations of sameness and difference that carry a sense of mutual indebtedness (see the introduction to this volume), we might ask how the heritagization of Ramman has enabled particular visions of community to emerge, evolve, or decay. For Garib Das, this process has, at least in part, undermined the goal of the festival, which is to reinforce bonds of mutual (but asymmetrical) indebtedness between Bhumiyal and his devotees, between patrons and drummers, and between members of his own translocal drumming caste community. For Kushal Bhandari, Ramman heritagization has brought a largely unmet opportunity to restore familial prestige and to strengthen the unity of the village as a community of interdependent but hierarchically organized caste groups. For Molly Kaushal, heritagization is a process of inscribing traditions that solidify the nation-as-community, with Ramman serving as a representative "little tradition" that, unfortunately, has not yet become a model of sustainability for others. And for Pratima Devi, the heritagization of Ramman is a cautionary tale about how village communities can be undermined by outside commercial interests, resulting in spiritual impoverishment. Underneath their statements of regional pride, each subject reinterpreted the ICH designation in relation to their own positions within structures of privilege and oppression and their unmet ideals of community.

Heritagization did not generate these distinct visions of community, nor was it the cause of their incommensurability. Heritagization merely raised the stakes by generating a public platform on which existing discourses and practices of community (un)making competed and clashed in real time. The visions of community that circulate among dominant caste village leaders, state agencies, and UNESCO boardrooms might appear to be egalitarian and equitable at a discursive level, but they are built on a foundation of neoliberalism, nationalism, caste supremacy, and invisible labor. The failure of top-down strategies to engender community at the level of the festival performance, the caste group, or the village comes from not recognizing these underlying power discrepancies and not finding ways to ameliorate them. Without cognizance of the ways in which dominant ideologies of community are power-blind, and without centering oppressed voices in discussions of what community means, the good intentions of community-building only perpetuate structural inequities and undermine possibilities for reparation and healing at the heart of community formation.

Notes

1. Members of some dominant caste families also have the hereditary obligation to dance or perform ritual tasks during Ramman, but these responsibilities have minimal bearing on their livelihood or occupation outside the festival context. In contrast, many Bajgi drummers depend on drumming for their livelihoods, but they supplement this income with agricultural and skilled labor. In general, drumming for weddings and rituals *outside the village* can bring reasonable income, while drumming for rituals *inside the village*, as for Ramman, provides drummers with minimal compensation.

2. This responsibility was explicitly indexed in one ritual episode during Ramman when the dhol player instructed Mwar, a deified ancestor, on how to behave and escape dangerous beasts. Mwar deliberately misinterpreted these instructions, to great comical effect.

3. The Indian Constitution forbids any form of discrimination on the basis of caste, but villagers claim that the ritual sanctity of the temple prohibits the entry of drummers and other Shilpkars (artisans) or Scheduled Castes (formerly untouchables). Those who have recently endeavored to enter temples in other parts of Uttarakhand have been shamed, stoned, and even murdered by their co-villagers.

4. A pension program for lowered caste artisans of Uttarakhand was introduced by the Harish Rawat state government (2014–17) but was rescinded by the next administration before these drummers could apply.

5. I am struck by the similarities to Turino's analysis of the modernist reforms that the group Quantati Ururi adopted and brought back to Conima from Lima (1993, 130–66).

6. The anthropologist Victor Turner and the performance theorist Richard Schechner have theorized the mutual interactions between theater and ritual, suggesting that they intersect and diverge in important ways (Schechner and Appel 1990; Turner 1982). Following these scholars, I find it helpful to interpret performances of Ramman along a continuum of experience between ritual (context-sensitive, internally directed, sacred, and participatory) and theater (externally directed, secular, and presentational). While Ramman has always been *both* ritual and theater, theatrical elements have become more prominent in performances of Ramman leading up to and following its inscription, as the modifications of Bansi Kaul demonstrate.

7. Sadly, in 2004 a thief raided the temples of Salood, Dungri, Bara Gaon, and Lata, making off with most of the consecrated masks used for pattar (masked dance rituals). Salood was able to replace these masks rather quickly, but some of the other villages did not have the expertise or the resources to do so. Salood now owns three sets of masks: one consecrated set that remains in the temple to be used during Ramman only, a replica set for touring performances, and a replica set housed permanently at the IGNCA in Delhi.

8. To view the documentary and get a feel for the ritual context in 2008, search "Ramman UNESCO" on YouTube or visit https://www.youtube.com/watch?v=TNvPNwOvWOg. Note that the new temple had not been built, and many reforms had yet to be incorporated at the time this documentary was made.

9. The differences that I noticed appeared rather minor from my perspective, but they were still quite significant to insiders. For instance, the fact that in Selang, Bhumiyal dances with Ram, Lakshman, the Maals, and Narsingh were interpreted as a major transgression in Dungri and Salood, where Bhumiyal dances alone.

10. Interview with Molly Kaushal, June 13, 2019, at IGNCA, New Delhi.

11. For a fuller account of my positionality and its impact on this ethnographic setting, see Fiol 2023.

Bibliography

Avieli, Nir. 2015. "The Rise and Fall of Hoi An, a UNESCO World Heritage Site in Vietnam." *Sojourn (Singapore)* 30(1): 35.

Brumann, Christoph. 2021. *The Best We Share: Nation, Culture and World-Making in the UNESCO World Heritage Arena*. New York: Berghan.

Comaroff, John, and Jean Comaroff. 2009. *Ethnicity, Inc.* Chicago: University of Chicago Press.

De Beukelaer, Christiaan, Miikka Pyykkönen, and J. P. Singh. 2015. *Globalization, Culture, and Development: The UNESCO Convention on Cultural Diversity*. London: Palgrave Macmillan.

Fiol, Stefan. 2023. "White Caste Supremacy and Dis/Connection in Fieldwork Encounters." *The Routledge Companion to Ethics and Research in Ethnomusicology*. NY: Routledge, 105–16.

Foster, Michael D. 2015. "Imagined UNESCOs: Interpreting Intangible Cultural Heritage on a Japanese Island." *Journal of Folklore Research* 52:(2–3): 217.

Geismar, Haidy. 2015. "Anthropology and Heritage Regimes." *Annual Review of Anthropology* 44(1): 71–85.

Grant, Catherine. 2012. "Rethinking Safeguarding: Objections and Responses to Protecting and Promoting Endangered Musical Heritage." *Ethnomusicology Forum* 21(1): 31–51.

Harnish, David. 2021. "Tolerance of Ambiguity: Negotiating Religion and Sustaining the Lingsar Festival and Its Performing Arts in Lombok, Indonesia." *Religions* (Basel, Switzerland) 12 (626).

Harris, Rachel. 2020. "'A Weekly Mäshräp to Tackle Extremism': Music-Making in Uyghur Communities and Intangible Cultural Heritage in China." *Ethnomusicology* 64(1): 23.

Howard, Keith. 2012. *Music as Intangible Cultural Heritage: Policy, Ideology, and Practice in the Preservation of East Asian Traditions*. SOAS Musicology Series. London: Ashgate.

Hüsken, Ute, and Axel Michaels, eds. 2013. *South Asian Festivals on the Move*. Wiesbaden, Germany: Harrassowitz Verlag.

Kaushal, Molly, ed. 2017. *Ramman: World Intangible Cultural Heritage*. New Delhi: Indira Gandhi National Centre for the Arts.

Lowenthal, David. 1985. *The Past Is a Foreign Country*. Cambridge: Cambridge University Press.

Lowthorp, Leah. 2015. "Voices on the Ground: Kutiyattam, UNESCO, and the Heritage of Humanity." *Journal of Folklore Research* 52(2–3): 157.

Meskell, Lynn. 2018. *A Future in Ruins*. New York: Oxford University Press.

Norton, Barley, and Naomi Matsumoto. 2018. *Music as Heritage: Historical and Ethnographic Perspectives*. New York: Routledge.

Ohri, Lokesh. 2016. "Political Yields from Cultural Fields: Agency and Ownership in a Heritage Festival in India." *Ethnos* 81(4): 667–82.

Peselmann, Arnika, Regina F. Bendix, and Aditya Eggert. 2013. *Heritage Regimes and the State*. Göttingen, Germany: Göttingen University Press.

Polit, Karin. 2012. "Staging Ritual Heritage: How Rituals Become Theatre in Uttarakhand, India." In *Ritual Matters: Dynamic Dimensions in Practice*, 29–48. London: Routledge.

Prakash, Brahma. 2019. *Cultural Labour*. New Delhi: Oxford University Press.

Purohit, Datta Ram. 1993. "Medieval English Folk Drama and Garhwali Folk Theatre: A Comparative Study." Ph.D. diss., H.N.B. Garhwal University.

Qureshi, Regula. 2002. *Music and Marx: Ideas, Practice, Politics*. Critical and Cultural Musicology. New York: Routledge.

Sax, William S. 2002. *Dancing the Self: Personhood and Performance in the Pandav Lila of Garhwal*. New York: Oxford University Press.

Schechner, Richard, and Willa Appel. 1990. *By Means of Performance*. London: Cambridge University Press.

Schippers, Huib. 2016. "Applied Ethnomusicology and Intangible Cultural Heritage." *The Oxford Handbook of Applied Ethnomusicology*, 134–56. New York: Oxford University Press.

Smith, Laurajane. 2013. "Discussion." In *Heritage Regimes and the State*, 389–98. Göttingen, Germany: Göttingen University Press.

Turino, Thomas. 1993. *Moving away from Silence*. Chicago Studies in Ethnomusicology. Chicago: University of Chicago Press.

Turino, Thomas. 2000. *Nationalists, Cosmopolitans, and Popular Music in Zimbabwe*. Chicago: University of Chicago Press.

Turner, Victor. 1982. *From Ritual to Theatre: The Human Seriousness of Play*. Performance Studies Series. Cambridge, MA: Performing Arts Journal Publications.

UNESCO Intangible Cultural Heritage. N.d. "Involvement of Communities, Groups, and Individuals." https://ich.unesco.org/en/involvement-of-communities-00033.

Epilogue

STEPHEN BLUM

Readers of this book will have sensed how deeply the contributors value their friendship with Tom Turino. Each essay engages with issues and values that are prominent in his teaching and writing—and that ought to become more prominent in all areas of music scholarship. He consistently reminds those who get to know him in person or through his writings that we have options for a better life that we can recognize and follow up on. Experiencing "*different ways of knowing*" (Turino 1990, 408, his italics) as we work and play can help us identify and resist pressures to channel our lives in directions that injure individuals, communities, and all life on earth. Nothing need prevent us from "developing alternative, sustainable ways of living" (Turino 2009, 95), to experience teaching as what Joanna Bosse calls *co-learning* and "affective assembly and coalitional performance" as "a strategic form of political performativity," in David McDonald's apt formulation.

Those who share Tom's concern with making our ideas clear (Peirce 1878; Turino 2015) can emulate his readiness to interrogate problematic uses of terms, as when he noted the absence of "a clear conceptualization of musical or cultural systems" in efforts of ethnomusicologists to treat both as "organic interacting systems" in work of the 1970s and 1980s (Turino 2015, 386–87).[1] A major weakness in studies of such large interacting systems was the tendency in much sociological theory of the Cold War to associate *system* with consensus and stability; ethnomusicologists have done better at modeling more limited systems within specific practices (tuning systems, rhythmic systems, notational systems, and so on). Some doctoral students in my cohort of the 1960s were suspicious of representations of musical, social, or cultural consensus in writings of prominent ethnomusicologists: Gerard Béhague (PhD, Tulane, 1966), Tom's supervisor and my friend, was one such and I was another (as voiced in

Blum 1978, 19 on Hood 1971, 300–1). Assessing the "ideological history of Latin American ethnomusicology," Gerard emphasized the importance of "specialized and comprehensive ethnographic study of a given musical community, its history, and *dynamics* in contemporary perspective" (Béhague 1991, 63, my emphasis). Tom's dissertation research (Turino 1993) did exactly that, following Conimeños as they moved back and forth between their Andean village and Lima.

The meanings of *system* vary according to the aims and needs of specific theoretical projects, and the same can be said of *community*. Taken as a whole, this book treats the term's flexibility as beneficial and necessary. Like social interactions that transpire outside a system or that may form, maintain, or disrupt a consensus, processes of *Music Making Community* became a topic of ethnographic study, with emphasis on how the actors involved perceive and participate in those processes and their outcomes. It's the right topic for a book honoring Tom Turino. The title designates continuing projects that confront (or skirt) difficulties of various types, and our contributors describe specific ways people understand and accept, desire, resist, or argue about experiences of community in one or more of the word's many senses. Those experiences commonly involve awareness of "*lived social relations* at particular historical moments which are linked to ever broader contexts across space and time" (Turino 1990, 407, his emphasis). Participation in musicking[2] depends on a sense of responsibility toward other participants (of the past, present, or future, as relevant) and can strengthen positive feelings of human interconnections on multiple levels.

Stefan Fiol is concerned with how ritual experience forges "nested community formations . . . in relation to territory, social group, and cosmology." He also had to consider interactions between residents of the village of Salood and the state functionaries working to inscribe a ritual they share with others in the UNESCO Representative List of Intangible Cultural Heritage. The functionaries assumed that residents of Salood would approve of inscribing the ritual and showed little interest in discussing the inscription project with residents of what they did not see as nested community formations but as a singular and homogeneous subject. Failure to consult with members of communities on projects of potential relevance to their welfare is also an issue in Veit Erlmann's account of the making of the South African Intellectual Property Laws Amendment Act 28 of 2013. Erlmann shows how the term *indigenous community* was "a project of discursive bricolage," used in the service of different material interests. At no point during the three years leading up to passage of the act was input from members of South Africa's oldest indigenous community, the Khoisan, solicited or considered.

How participants in musicking recognize their affinities with others who are or might become involved in that musicking (and who may not be physically present) is an issue running through the book. Eduardo Herrera approaches it through a study of "in-group/out-group sonic dynamics" among neighborhood-based fans of soccer teams in Buenos Aires; fans can affirm their affinity with an in-group by singing its praises while also directing abuse at competing out-groups. Herrera focuses on a team identified with a neighborhood that has many Jewish residents, which fans of other teams take as a cue for singing chants charged with viciously antisemitic language. He names several European teams whose players and fans are also targets of antisemitic chanting. After reading two papers on the Anlo-Ewe *haló* (songs of abuse) (Anyidoho 1982; Avorgbedor 1994), a practice outlawed in 1960 by the government of Ghana, I mistakenly thought of communal musicking with the potential to precede or accompany communal violence as relatively infrequent; rather, like the much larger topic of music and violence (physical, symbolic, socioeconomic) it was relatively unstudied before this century (e.g., Ochoa 2006; Araújo with Grupo Musicultura 2006, 2010; McDonald 2009; and presentations at annual meetings by the Society for Ethnomusicology's Special Interest Group on Music and Violence).

Musicking is an extremely common *response* to violence. David McDonald's account of the Palestine Music Expo (PMX) in Ramallah focuses on Palestinians who "encounter and challenge the myriad forms of violence that frame their world" as they participate in the PMX. Some critics of this festival object to what they see as an overly narrow representation of Palestinian music and culture, meant to appeal to international audiences by excluding performers of folk, classical, and religious music. McDonald reports on their views as well as on the experience of those for whom PMX was "an enactment of an alternative Palestine richly desired by its participants." Here he recalls "the crucial interplay between the possible and the actual" (Turino 2008, 16) that often makes musicking (and so much else) a meaningful experience.[3] McDonald describes an episode at PMX when protesters chanted their objection to one singer's position in favor of voting in the Israeli election and "competing notions of community, nation, and citizenship were given opportunity for growth and transformation" through musicking.

Even with so many meanings serving such diverse interests (including those of the so called international community in whose name threats are continually issued against alleged "rogues"), an ethnomusicologist may find that *community* is not the right term for the sociality produced and sustained, at least in part, by musicking. Ioannis Tsekouras emphasizes the genealogy of the concept of community, which he associates with "experiences of organic solidarity" in his account of the Pontic Greek practice of parakathi or muhabeti "dialogical participatory singing": He argues that the experiences of organic *sociality* afforded by parakathi do not create community (Greek *kinotita*) as understood by participants. With reference to the distinction between *cultural formations* that share a relatively comprehensive set of habits and *cultural cohorts* that have deliberately prioritized a selection of habits (Turino 2008, 112–16), Tsekouras suggests that for Pontic Greeks community lies in between the two as "a model of affective sociality defined by the nostalgia for the inevitable loss of Pontos," the region along the coast of the Black Sea from which the Greek population was exiled during and after World War I. He identifies three different socialities relevant to the cohort engaged in parakathia, none of which makes them a community in their own estimation.[4]

While the PMX challenges forms of violence that are ubiquitous in the everyday lives of Palestinians, the Pontic Greeks' "nostalgia for a pre-modern rural past" evokes an imagined communal life prior to the trauma of expulsion from lands where their ancestors had lived for well over two millennia. Although what Donna Buchanan terms the "multilayered social formation" of Bulgaria's Armenian diaspora can also look back on a history of traumatic experiences of expulsion, for neither of the diaspora's two segments does any such nostalgia appear to be as central to experiences of community as Tsekouras found it to be among Pontic Greeks. Descendants of refugees from the pogroms of 1894 and 1915 against western Armenians and of the population exchanges of 1922 that also expelled the Greeks of Pontos from the new state of Turkey make up the oldest segment of the diaspora in Bulgaria, substantially enlarged since 1991 by eastern Armenian immigrants from the post-Soviet republic of Armenia, itself involved in a conflict with Azerbaijan over Nagorno-Karabakh. Despite these differences in origins and language, the diaspora's institutions promoted a "politics of belonging" oriented toward collaboration and inclusivity, toward the future rather than the past.

Tom Solomon's chapter takes competition as a topic that embraces "different kinds of social relationships that constitute musical communities." Types and degrees of informality or formality and of participatory or presentational musicking (as distinguished in Turino 2008, 23–65) are major variables in his comparison of his seven models, illustrated with examples from highland Bolivia. The first model, song dueling among friends "who enjoyed each other's company and enjoyed making music together," would accommodate the *parakathia* of Pontic Greeks. Another model is highly organized song dueling between small groups at a festival, each representing a specific locality and having a soloist who improvises over instrumental accompaniment. Three models involve simultaneous performance in which one ensemble may try to play louder and longer than another or, in the case of an (urban) brass band versus (rural) panpipes at a saint's feast-day celebration, will prevail effortlessly by the nature of the instruments. In his conclusion, Solomon argues that musical competition can "bring people together in many different kinds of communities" without necessarily "prefiguring or structuring other domains of social life."

Sylvia Bruinders points to the Christmas bands of Cape Town as examples of nonviolent competition among "musical collectivities" whose members feel responsibilities toward one another and also treat rival bands with respect. She notes that the bands exemplify musicking that is at once participatory and presentational. In one instance of interaction with outsiders, band members urged outside adjudicators to consider and respect "the bands' own criteria" in their evaluations. The practice is cultivated by Christian descendants of slaves imported from around the Indian Ocean, a larger "community" classified as "coloured" whose rights as citizens of the republic are affirmed by each band's display of respectability.

Music cannot "make community" (in whatever sense of the term) without what Tony Perman terms a sense of "mutual indebtedness." Reflecting on his engagement with the North American mbira community, Perman emphasizes the debts that members of communities incur in the course of musicking, which may extend well beyond their immediate communities. North American mbira players may acquire knowledge that carries "ever-deepening burdens of debt and obligation" and activates experiences of empathy and of "thinking with others." Perman's chapter squarely faces several difficulties that may prevent that from happening and shows how mbira players can learn to make good use of a "Zimbabwe-centric theory of community" in maintaining an indispensable attitude of humility.

Two other chapters also focus on issues of music as education for living (to cite the title of Catherine Ellis's 1985 book on Aboriginal music of South Australia) and of becoming human through music (Music Educators National Conference 1985). Ways in which musicking can "foster both individual expression and inclusivity" is central to Rick Deja's discussion of his experience with ensembles performing Afro-jazz and free improvisation at the South African College of Music at the University of Cape Town. He provides students' reports of their ensemble experiences and, like McDonald and Perman, is keenly aware of "the crucial interplay between the possible and the actual" (Turino 2008, 16), striking an appropriate tone of humility as he mentions practices that are "*potentially* valuable," "musical features that, taken together, *may help* facilitate a sense of belonging and group cohesion," and the like (my emphases). Deja makes a convincing case that the "egalitarian inclusive ethos" of free improvisation makes it "a potentially valuable musical practice to counteract damaging social hierarchies . . . found in many South African contexts"—and in countless others, his readers will be quick to add. His chapter should stimulate further consideration of the ethical presuppositions attached to pedagogies of improvisation and other modes of performance.

Joanna Bosse provides an instructive account of her experiences in developing and teaching a "performance-based" course on African music for first-year undergraduates in Michigan State University's Residential College of the Arts and Humanities. She found several ways to make performance central to the course, so that students would not consider the energy devoted to performance less significant than other course activities. One of her major aims was "helping students regain trust in their kinesthetic wisdom," which required sensitivity on her part to anxieties that some might feel at performing alongside their classmates in unfamiliar ways.

I regret that Peirce's spirit did not become a stronger presence in this country's ethnomusicology before Tom's teaching and writing. Benjamin Ives Gilman, author of landmark publications on Zuñi melodies (1891) and Hopi songs (1908), was one of Peirce's undergraduate students and contributed a paper to Peirce's *Studies in Logic by Members of the Johns Hopkins Community* (Gilman 1883). After further study with William James at Harvard, Gilman taught courses in the psychology of music at Harvard, Princeton, and Columbia before devoting most of his career to curatorial work at Boston's Museum of Fine Arts. When Charles Seeger (1977, 108) postulated "a limited compatibility between the semiotics of speech communication and of music communication," he did not mention Peirce's typology of icon, index, and symbol as possible relations between a sign and its object when he compared two ways to communicate a world view: "speech, by symbolizing it; music, by embodying it" (43). Both Tom Turino (2008, 5–16, 2014) and Gary Tomlinson (2015, 185–97) have developed that contrast more fully with explicit reference to Peirce, emphasizing the iconicity and indexicality of signs exchanged in musicking. "Indexical experience plus a perception of iconic similarity with other people and forms of life," writes Turino, "is the basis for feeling direct *empathic connection*" (Turino 2008, 16, his emphasis). "Musicking in the world today is the extended, spectacularly formalized, and complexly perceived systematization of ancient, indexical gesture-calls," Tomlinson notes; this "formalized systematization" produced "a human activity unique in the degree to which it highlights somatic experience while structuring it according to complex, abstract, and relatively recent outgrowths of our cognition" (Tomlinson 2015, 205, 289). Peirce's theory of signs provides a basis for attention to empathic connection as well as to formalized systematization.

Our title might lead some readers to suspect that these essays reproduce a model criticized by Jim Sykes: "I often feel the ubiquity of studies showing how 'music *x*' produces a feeling of 'community *y*' [which] fail in their objective: by showing how music plays a role in constructing (rather than simply expressing) identity, we still reinforce the idea that music history simply *is* about how music produces identity and place" (2018, 4, his emphasis). This book does not endorse the idea that musicking has functioned primarily to produce unified identities, nor do we equate community with identity and place. *Community* does not retain or acquire a stable meaning as the book proceeds. As only a small sampling of the varieties of lived social relations that humans have explored through musicking, the histories and communities evoked in these eleven chapters are complex and diverse. Although the three minority communities within nations (Greeks whose ancestors were expelled from the Pontus, Armenian immigrants in Bulgaria, the coloured in South Africa) and the Palestinians living under Israeli occupation do need to concern themselves with how to represent their situation and desires to outsiders, their musicking is by no means limited to that issue. The chapters by Bosse, Perman, and Deja describe communities that connect people through an engagement in co-learning. Residents of the "nested community formations" discussed by Fiol could experience their lived social relations with shifts of attention among cosmology, territory, or social group, as circumstances warrant. In *The Dawn of Everything: A New History of Humanity*, David Graeber and David Wengrow (2021, 8) pose a relevant question: "Is not the capacity to experiment with different forms of social organization itself a quintessential part of what makes us human?" The universality of musicking makes that capacity abundantly evident. David Graeber (1961–2020), an activist who participated in Occupy Wall Street, had much in common with Tom Turino, squarely rejecting the orthodoxies that squelch our sense of human possibilities.

Notes

1. In "How to Make Our Ideas Clear," Peirce remarked that appeals to comprehensive systems can get in the way of clear thinking: "It will sometimes strike a scientific man that the philosophers have been less intent on finding out what the facts are, than on inquiring what belief is most in harmony with their system" (1878, 299 and 1986, 273). Philosophers are not the only academics prone to that bad habit.

2. One benefit of the term *musicking* is that it can encourage attention to the full range of activities it may be a part of (worship, mourning, games, and so on), whereas discussion of *music making* often ignores accompanying activities and centers on music, sometimes without even attending to how and why it is made.

3. Peirce saw "a potentiality for future growth as essential to present meaning" (Short 2007, x).

4. The types of sociality involved in such genres of dialogical participatory singing as *parakathia* are a major concern of the ICTM Study Group on Multipart Music Making (see Ahmedaja and Haid 2008; Ahmedaja 2011, 2013, 2017; Macchiarella 2009, 2012, 2014).

Bibliography

Ahmedaja, Ardian, ed. 2011. *European Voices II: Cultural Listening and Local Discourse in Multipart Singing Traditions in Europe*. Schriften zur Volksmusik 23. Vienna: Böhlau. Accompanying CD and DVD.

Ahmedaja, Ardian, ed. 2013. *Local and Global Understandings of Creativities: Multipart Music Making and the Construction of Ideas, Contexts and Contents*. Newcastle upon Tyne: Cambridge Scholars Publishing.

Ahmedaja, Ardian, ed. 2017. *European Voices III: The Instrumentation and Instrumentalization of Sound; Local Multipart Music Practices in Europe, In Commemoration of Gerlinde Haid*. Schriften zur Volksmusik 25. Vienna: Böhlau.

Ahmedaja, Ardian, and Gerlinde Haid, eds. 2008. *European Voices I: Multipart Singing in the Balkans and the Mediterranean*. Schriften zur Volksmusik 22. Vienna: Böhlau.

Anyidoho, Kofi. 1982. "Kofi Awoonor and the Anlo-Ewe Tradition of Songs of Abuse (*Halo*)." In *Toward Defining the African Aesthetic*, edited by Lemuel Johnson et al., 17–29. Washington, DC: Three Continents.

Araújo, Samuel, with Grupo Musicultura. 2006. "Conflict and Violence as Theoretical Tools in Present-Day Ethnomusicology: Notes on a Dialogic Ethnography of Sound Practices in Rio de Janeiro." *Ethnomusicology* 50(2): 287–313.

Araújo, Samuel, with Grupo Musicultura. 2010. "Sound Praxis: Music, Politics, and Violence in Brazil." In *Music and Conflict*, edited by John Morgan O'Connell and Salwa El-Shawan Castelo-Branco, 217–31. Urbana: University of Illinois Press.

Avorgbedor, Daniel. 1994. "Freedom to Sing, License to Insult: The Influence of *Halo* Performance on Social Violence Among the Anlo-Ewe." *Oral Tradition* 9(1): 83–112.

Béhague, Gerard. 1991. "Reflections on the Ideological History of Latin American Ethnomusicology." In *Comparative Musicology and Anthropology of Music: Essays on the History of Ethnomusicology*, edited by Bruno Nettl and Philip V. Bohlman, 56–68. Chicago Studies in Ethnomusicology. Chicago: University of Chicago Press.

Blum, Stephen. 1978. "Changing Roles of Performers in Meshhed and Bojnurd, Iran." In *Eight Urban Musical Cultures*, edited by Bruno Nettl, 19–92. Urbana: University of Illinois Press.

Ellis, Catherine J. 1985. *Aboriginal Music, Education for Living: Cross-Cultural Experiences from South Australia*. St. Lucia, Queensland: University of Queensland Press.

Gilman, Benjamin Ives. 1883. "Operations in Relative Number with Applications to the Theory of Probabilities." In *Studies in Logic by Members of the Johns Hopkins Community*, edited by C. S. Peirce, 107–25. Boston: Little, Brown. Reprint, Amsterdam: John Benjamins, 1983.

Gilman, Benjamin Ives. 1891. "Zuñi Melodies: Hemenway Southwestern Archaeological Expedition 2." *Journal of American Ethnology and Archaeology* 1:63–91.

Gilman, Benjamin Ives. 1908. *Hopi Songs*. Hemenway Southwestern Expedition. *Journal of American Ethnology and Archaeology* 5. Reprint, New York: AMS Press, 1997.

Graeber, David, and David Wengrow. 2021. *The Dawn of Everything: A New History of Humanity*. New York: Farrar, Straus and Giroux.

Hood, Mantle. 1971. *The Ethnomusicologist*. New York: McGraw Hill.

Macchiarella, Ignazio. 2009. *Cantare a cuncordu: Uno studio a più voci.* Second ed., revised. Udine: Nota. Accompanying CD.

Macchiarella, Ignazio. 2012. "Theorizing on Multipart Music Making." In *Multipart Music: A Specific Mode of Musical Thinking, Expressive Behavior and Sound.* Papers from the first meeting of the ICTM Study Group on Multipart Music (September 15–20, 2010), Cagliari, Sardinia, 7–22. Udine: Nota. www.multipartmusic.org/multipartmusic/node/4.

Macchiarella, Ignazio. 2014. "Exploring Micro-Worlds of Music Meanings." *El oído pensante* 2(1). *Portal de Publicaciones Científicas y Técnicas.* http://ppct.caicyt.gov.ar/index.php/oidopensante.

McDonald, David A. 2009. "Poetics and the Performance of Violence in Israel/Palestine." *Ethnomusicology* 53(1): 58–85.

Music Educators National Conference. 1985. *Becoming Human Through Music: The Wesleyan Symposium on the Perspectives of Social Anthropology in the Teaching and Learning of Music, August 6–10, 1984, Wesleyan University, Middletown, Connecticut.* Reston, VA: Music Educators National Conference.

Ochoa, Ana María, ed. 2006. "Dossier: Música silencios y silenciamientos; Música violencia y experiencia cotidiana." *Transcultural Music Review* 10. http://www.sibetrans.com/trans/trans10.

Peirce, Charles S. 1878. "How to Make Our Ideas Clear." *Popular Science Monthly* 12 (January 17): 286–302 [available through Google Magazines, open access]. Reprinted in *Writings of Charles S. Peirce* 3:257–76. Bloomington: Indiana University Press, 1986.

Seeger, Charles. 1977. *Studies in Musicology, 1935–1975.* Berkeley: University of California Press.

Short, T. L. 2007. *Peirce's Theory of Signs.* Cambridge: Cambridge University Press.

Sykes, Jim. 2018. *The Musical Gift: Sonic Generosity in Post-War Sri Lanka.* New York: Oxford University Press.

Tomlinson, Gary. 2015. *A Million Years of Music: The Emergence of Human Modernity.* New York: Zone.

Turino, Thomas. 1990. "Structure, Context, and Strategy in Musical Ethnography." *Ethnomusicology* 34(3): 399–412.

Turino, Thomas. 1993. *Moving away from Silence: Music of the Peruvian Altiplano and the Experience of Urban Migration.* Chicago Studies in Ethnomusicology. Chicago: University of Chicago Press.

Turino, Thomas. 2008. *Music as Social Life: The Politics of Participation.* Chicago Studies in Ethnomusicology. Chicago: University of Chicago Press.

Turino, Thomas. 2009. "Four Fields of Music Making and Sustainable Living." *World of Music* 51(1): 95–117.

Turino, Thomas. 2014. "Peircean Thought as Core Theory for a Phenomenological Ethnomusicology." *Ethnomusicology* 58(2): 185–221.

Turino, Thomas. 2015. "On Theory and Models: How to Make Our Ideas Clear." In *This Thing Called Music: Essays in Honor of Bruno Nettl,* edited by Victoria Lindsay-Levine and Philip V. Bohlman, 378–90. Lanham, MD: Rowman and Littlefield.

Contributors

STEPHEN BLUM joined the CUNY Graduate Center faculty in 1987, when the concentration in ethnomusicology was initiated. He has published several articles, books, and encyclopedia articles on general topics (composition, improvisation, music analysis, modern music history, cultural exchange) and on specific musical practices of Iran, Kurdistan, Central Asia, Europe, and North America. He has been active in the Society for Ethnomusicology and currently serves on the editorial boards of the *British Journal for Ethnomusicology* and the *Journal of the American Musicological Society*.

JOANNA BOSSE currently serves as the interim head of the School of Music at Carnegie Mellon University. She is professor of ethnomusicology and dance studies in the Residential College in the Arts and Humanities at the Michigan State University College of Music, where she also holds the position of associate dean of academic affairs and strategic initiatives. Her published work focuses on couple dance traditions like salsa, tango, swing, and ballroom. Her book *Becoming Beautiful: Ballroom Dance in the American Heartland* (2015) presents an ethnographic case study of amateur ballroom dancers who experience personal transformation through artistic engagement. Her documentary film *Becoming Beautiful* (2017) has screened on three continents and received several awards. Her research on whiteness, race, and performance appears in the *Journal of American Folklore, Dance Research Journal, Ethnomusicology Forum*, and elsewhere. Her recent research explores the health benefits of engagement in creative arts among nonspecialists, with current research projects focusing on seniors, dementia patients, and PTSD survivors. Before joining MSU, Joanna taught at Bowdoin College and Millikin University.

SYLVIA BRUINDERS is associate professor and head of ethnomusicology and African music at the South African College of Music at the University of

Cape Town, where she teaches courses in ethnomusicology, African musics, and World musics. A former Fulbright scholar, her dissertation on the Christmas bands movement in the Western Cape received the Nicholas Temperley Award for Excellence in a Dissertation in Musicology at the University of Illinois, Urbana-Champaign. She has published several journal articles from this research, and her monograph, *Parading Respectability: The Cultural and Moral Aesthetics of the Christmas Bands Movement in the Western Cape, South Africa,* was supported by a postdoctoral fellowship of the African Humanities Program and published by the National Inquiry Service Centerin 2017. She is currently the director of the Mellon-funded Pan-African research project Mapping Africa's Musical Identities, which includes six universities on the African continent.

DONNA A. BUCHANAN is professor of music (ethnomusicology), anthropology, and Slavic languages and literatures at the University of Illinois, Urbana-Champaign. A specialist in musics of the Balkans, Russia, and Eurasia, she is the author of *Performing Democracy: Bulgarian Music and Musicians in Transition* (2006) and the editor of two anthologies: *Balkan Popular Culture and the Ottoman Ecumene: Music, Image, and Regional Political Discourse* (2007) and *Soundscapes from the Americas: Ethnomusicological Essays on the Power, Poetics, and Ontology of Performance* (2014). Her scholarly interests include acoustemology, performativity, postsocialism, and the implication of sound in cosmology, social power, and the politics of identity. Director of the University of Illinois Russian, East European, and Eurasian Center from 2004 to 2007 and its acting director during 2018–19, in 1998 Buchanan also established "Balkanalia," the University of Illinois Balkan Music Ensemble.

RICK DEJA is senior lecturer in ethnomusicology and curator of the Kirby Collection of Musical Instruments at the University of Cape Town. He has a background in music performance (saxophone and guitar), audio production, and composition. His research interests include jazz and popular musics in Malawi and southern Africa, comparative philosophies of improvisation, music and social belonging, and organology and revitalization. He directs the Pan-African Music Ensemble at UCT and is currently writing about the Afro-jazz movement in Malawi, as well as pan-idiomatic improvisation and co-creation in Cape Town.

VEIT ERLMANN is an anthropologist/ethnomusicologist and the endowed chair of music history at the University of Texas at Austin. He has won numerous prizes including the Alan P. Merriam award for the best English monograph in ethnomusicology. Erlmann frequently presents at leading institutions around the world. He has also published widely on music and popular culture in South Africa (*African Stars*, 1991; *Nightsong*, 1996; *Music, Modernity and the Global*

Imagination, 1999) and sound (*Reason and Resonance*, 2010). His most recent publication is *Lion's Share: Remaking South African Copyright* (2022). In 2004 he became editor of the journal *Sound Studies* (https://www.tandfonline.com/toc/rfso20/current). For more on Veit Erlmann's activities, visit his website at www.veiterlmann.net.

STEFAN FIOL (he/him) is professor of music at the University of Cincinnati, College-Conservatory of Music. Fiol's monograph *Recasting Folk in the Himalayas: Indian Music, Media, and Social Mobility* (2017) received the Association for Nepal and Himalayan Studies Jim Fisher Book Award (Honorable Mention). Emergent areas of transdisciplinary research include the role of music and mindfulness in stimulating memory, cognitive function, and experiences of awe and flow; indigeneity and musical repatriation in the Guatemalan highlands; and the spatial and social analysis of central Himalayan hereditary drumming practice as a mode of historiographic inquiry.

EDUARDO HERRERA (he/him) is associate professor of folklore and ethnomusicology at Indiana University. Herrera is the author of *Elite Art Worlds: Philanthropy, Latin Americanism, and Avant-Garde Music* (2020) and co-editor of *Experimentalisms in Practice: Music Perspectives from Latin America* (2018). He is currently working on two book projects: *Sounding Fandom: Chanting, Masculinity, and Violence in Argentine Soccer Stadiums* and *Soccer Sounds: Transnational Stories of the Beautiful Game*. Herrera previously taught at Rutgers University, served as visiting associate professor at Harvard University in 2021, and was a Humanities Center Faculty Fellow for 2019–2020 at the University of Rochester. He is currently a director-at-large at the American Musicological Society (2022–2023) and has served as interim council chair for the Society for Ethnomusicology (2020–21) and as board member-at-large for the Society for American Music (2017–2020).

DAVID A. MCDONALD is chair of the Department of Folklore and Ethnomusicology at Indiana University. Since 2000 he has worked closely with Palestinian refugee communities throughout Israel/Palestine, Jordan, and North America. This work focuses primarily on the performative dimensions of trauma, violence, and exile. He is the author and editor of two books, *My Voice Is My Weapon* (2013) and *Palestinian Music and Song* (2013). His current research involves documenting contemporary Palestinian-American experiences after 911, focusing on the legal, political, and cultural ramifications of the US "war on terror"

BRUNO NETTL, with a PhD from Indiana University, was a professor emeritus of music and anthropology at the University of Illinois, where he began teaching in 1964. He was the author of numerous books about ethnomusicology, including *The Study of Ethnomusicology, Blackfoot Musical Thought, Encounters* *in Ethnomusicology: A Memoir*, and most recently, *Following the Elephant: Ethnomusicologists Contemplate Their Discipline*. He also edited multiple volumes and contributed articles to numerous journals and edited works.

TONY PERMAN (he/him) is a specialist in the music of Zimbabwe and the semiotics of music and emotion. He serves as associate professor and chair of the Music Department at Grinnell College in Iowa. His book *Signs of the Spirit: Music and the Experience of Meaning in Ndau Ceremonial Life* was published in 2020. His current work explores performing difference as a moral project of empathy, hope, and postcolonial restitution. Before coming to Grinnell, he also taught at Pomona College and Bowdoin College. He has played and taught the mbira and mbira dzaVaNdau for many years, having been taught primarily by Chartwell Dutiro, Tute Chigamba, Musekiwa Chingodza, Davison Masiza, Zombiyi Muzite, and Zivanai Khumbula.

THOMAS SOLOMON is professor of musicology in the Grieg Academy Department of Music at the University of Bergen. He has done field research in Bolivia on musical imaginations of ecology, place, and identity, and in Istanbul on place and identity in Turkish hip-hop; he has also published on various theoretical topics in ethnomusicology and popular music studies including postcolonialism, diaspora, and popular music analysis. His publications include articles in the journals *Ethnomusicology, Popular Music, European Journal of Cultural Studies*, and *Yearbook for Traditional Music*, as well as numerous chapters in edited volumes.

IOANNIS TSEKOURAS is an academic fellow on music at the National and Kapodistrian University of Athens, Greece. His research lies in the intersection of musicology with collective memory, ethnicity, and refugee studies. More specifically, he examines musical processes of emotional remembering, transgenerational trauma negotiation, and ethnic subjectivity in relation to the identity politics of the Pontians or Pontic Greeks. Tsekouras has published in both English and Greek in several journals and edited volumes. He is currently working on his book project, under the (working) title *Dialogues of Empathy, Chains of Affect: Pontic Subjectivity and Postmemory in Parakathi Dialogical Singing*.

Index

Abù Nafar (Father of Nafar), 204
action, 11, 20, 22, 27, 40, 110, 169, 184, 191, 192, 201–4; direct, 192, 193, 198, 201–3
activism, 11, 25, 192–94, 202, 204
Actor-Network Theory, 10, 108
Aegean, 44, 79
aesthetic, 110–12, 177, 201, 233–35, 239, 245, 261, 265; disposition, 67; egalitarian, 27; practice, 179; presentational, 71; value, 111, 265
affect, 22, 41, 202, 219
affectivity, 41, 54; community, 40, 46; experience, 49, 250; interkinesthetic, 21, 22, 100
Africa, 108, 131, 138, 143, 147, 238; #africa-forafricans, 223, 224; National Congress Party, 105; Sub-Saharan, 133, 140, 233. *See also* Africans; South Africa
African Americans, 17, 144
African diaspora, 237
African music, 133, 135, 138, 140, 142, 233, 239, 241–46, 276
Africans, 144, 147, 175, 176, 212, 233, 237–42, 245
Agawu, Kofi, 147
Agbekor (West African), 135
AGBU (Armenian General Benevolent Union/ Parekordzagan), 65, 66, 76, 77
agency, 21, 22, 27, 40, 46, 48, 51–53, 57, 108, 112, 143, 199, 201, 203, 216, 219, 220, 235, 239, 254, 262, 266
agents, 8, 21, 22, 28, 169, 215, 219, 222, 266; creative, 66
aguante, 89, 90
Ajax, 86, 100

Alabarces, Pablo, 89
All Boys, 96
allegory, 45; allegorical, 46
al-Jazeera, 202, 204
alter-politics, 202
America, 214, 216; Americanized, 212; antebellum, 209; education, 130, 132
Americans, 2, 9, 144, 209, 211–14, 216, 217, 220, 224, 227
Anahid, 72, 81
anarchism, 37
Anatolia, 42, 67, 79, 80; eastern, 64, 66
ancestors, 214, 215, 224, 227, 251, 274, 277; deified, 248, 252; worship, 73
ancestral conviction, 227
ancestral lands/home, 24, 67, 109, 176
ancestral past, 78
ancestral spirits, 73, 211, 220
Anderlecht, 86, 100
Andes/Andean, 5, 10, 151, 166, 169, 170, 272
animism, 29
anthropocene, 10, 11
anthropology, 249; cultural, 129
anti-colonialism, 11, 12, 27, 108, 192–94, 203
anti-essentialist, 104
antinomy, 108
antisemitism, 9, 86–91, 94, 96, 98, 99, 100, 273
anxiety, 70, 136, 200, 213, 216, 222, 235, 237, 244, 276
apartheid, 9, 27, 104, 108, 175, 184
appearance, 193, 194, 198, 200, 203, 204
appropriation, 110, 111, 212, 213, 219, 224. *See also* misappropriation

Arab-Israelis, 204
Arab Spring, 89
Arapaho peyote, 4
Argentina, 88, 92, 94, 95, 97, 99
Argentine Football Association, 96
Argentinos Juniors, 96
Armenia, 26, 62, 64, 66, 67, 71, 72, 74, 77, 78, 80, 81, 274
Armenian *naroden dom* (AND), 61, 63, 64, 68, 75
Armenian diaspora, 9, 26, 61–81, 91, 274, 277; in Bulgaria, 64, 66, 67, 77–79
artistic engagement, 200
artistic forms, 76
artistic practice, 65, 123
artistic production, 65
Artsakh, 72, 73, 81
Asociación Mutual Israelita Argentina, 94, 95
assemblage, 104; affective, 192–94, 198, 202–4, 271
Austin, TX, 4
Australia, 53, 110
authenticity, 62, 144
authority, 12, 104, 107, 109, 120, 122, 179, 201, 214, 235
autonomy, 257
Avakian-Bedrossian, Sonia, 76
awareness, interkinesthetic, 22, 80
ayllu, 24, 166
Aymara, 2, 10, 180
Azerbaijan, 72, 79, 81, 274

Badrinath, 251, 260
Baghdasarian, Sarkis, 73
Bailey, Derek, 234, 235
baja, 251, 258
bajgi, 262, 267
baladi, 78
Balkans, 63, 66, 74
Baniya-Baniyan, 252, 259
Bayart, Jean-François, 105
Bayern Munich, 86, 100
Béhague, Gerard, 271
Belfast marching bands, 174
Belgium, 100
belonging 12, 19, 22, 26–28, 38, 42, 80, 90, 99, 116, 123, 192, 193, 215, 232–34, 249, 250; multiple, 63, 77; politics of, 65, 105, 274; sense of, 75, 235, 239, 244, 245, 275; sentiments of, 76
Bhandari, Kushal, 252, 253, 255, 257–62, 266
Bhumiyal, 252, 254, 256, 257, 259–61, 264, 266, 268

bi-musicality, 129, 212, 220, 228
Black Sea, 42
Blum, Stephen, 10, 28
body, 12, 19, 21–23, 65, 73, 90, 118, 184, 186, 193, 194, 197, 198, 202, 204, 242, 252, 254; collective, 249; embodied experience, 129, 183, 250
body politic, 104, 191
Bohemians, 91
Bohemios, 92, 101
Bohlman, Philip, 1
Bolivia, 9, 27, 151, 152, 155, 170, 174, 274
bombo, 156
Bosse, Joanna, 26, 271, 276
Bourdieu, Pierre, 29
Brahmin, 253, 262
British Forum for Ethnomusicology, 170
Brown, Danielle, 11, 220
Bruinders, Sylvia, 27, 171, 275
Buchanan, Donna, 26, 274
Buenos Aires, 85, 86, 90, 91, 99, 273
Bulgaria, 26, 61–71, 73, 75–79, 274, 277
Bundio, Javier, 89
bureaucracy, 38, 122, 123, 159, 197; bureaucratized procedure, 156, 158
Burhdeva, 252, 259
Bustillo, Bolivia, 159, 160, 164
Butler, Judith, 86, 89, 100, 153, 194

California, 19, 209, 223
camaraderie, 176, 177, 186
Canada, 53, 217, 219, 225
Cape Malay Choir, 175; "Cape" sound 183
Cape Muslims, 175
Cape Town, 27, 106, 176, 181, 183, 184, 232, 233, 236, 239–41, 275
capitalism, 192, 221, 222, 250
capitalist society, 16, 186
capitalist values, 27, 174, 186
Capwell, Charles, 1
Carnival, 156, 160, 161, 168, 184
caste, 248–50, 252–58, 262, 264–66; privilege, 258, 262; restriction, 254; superiority/supremacy, 250, 258, 266
Caucasus, 66, 68, 74
Cederberg region, 106
Chacarita Juniors, 86, 91, 95, 96
Champaign, IL, 2, 77, 282
charango, 2, 5, 156, 159
Chayanta, 159, 164, 165, 168
Chicago, 97, 204
Chicago School, 39
Chigamba, Henry, 228

Chigamba, Julia, 225, 226
Chigamba, Sukeru, 228
Chigamba, Tute, 218, 226
Chimurenga Renaissance, 224
Chingodza, Musekiwa, 212, 214, 218–28
ch'ixi, 10, 11
choreography, 64, 70, 74; choreographic met-
    onyms, 65; choreographic models, 70
Christian genocide, 42
Christianity, 72; ethics, 175, 180; mission, 241;
    theology, 73
Christians, 73, 78, 81, 174, 176, 275; African,
    176
Christmas bands, 27, 173–76, 178–84, 186, 187,
    275; Board, 176, 178; sound, 179, 182; Union,
    173, 176, 178, 179
citizenship, 27, 117, 175, 180, 191, 192, 196, 273;
    artistic, 123
City and Suburban Christmas Bands Union,
    173, 178, 179. *See also* Christmas bands
Clacherty, Bronwen, 246
class, 17, 89, 99, 175, 181, 183, 186, 213, 235, 249,
    266
Clegg, Johnny, 106
Club Atlético Atlanta, 86–99
Cochabamba, Bolivia, 153, 155
codes of legibility, 191
codification, 242, 249, 262
cohort, 23–25, 38, 41, 56, 192, 233, 243, 246;
    cultural, 8, 11, 23, 24, 215, 232, 239, 274
collaboration, 39, 243; and inclusivity, 74, 274
collaborative musical ventures, 69
collective emotion, 88, 89, 100
collective punishment, 197, 198
Collins, Patricia Hill, 14
colonialism, 11, 12, 27, 38, 175, 197, 200, 211–13,
    216, 220–22, 226, 227, 241. *See also* anti-
    colonialism; decolonialization; postcoloni-
    alism; settler-colonialism
colonialist politics, 10, 11
colonial oppression, 106, 198
colonial science, 111
colonial space, 168
colonial systems, 224, 226
Colorado, 214
commens, 29, 218, 219
commodities, 70, 221; artistic, 73; cultural, 66
communal experiences, 88
communing, 10, 16, 18, 24
Communitas, 15, 16, 21, 22, 40, 44, 46, 49,
    52–55, 180, 192, 193, 228
community, 228; "decolonized," 226; defini-
    tion of, 8, 15, 19, 38, 39, 43, 117, 215; forma-

tion, 13, 16, 249, 267, 272, 277; imagined, 15,
    23, 89; indigenous, 26, 104–7, 109, 115–17,
    120–22, 160, 162, 272; loss of, 43, 48; mak-
    ing, 8, 9, 12, 17, 75, 77, 170, 198, 199, 216, 250,
    266–67; moments of, 27, 152, 170, 185; mu-
    sic, 41, 183–85; musical, 41, 46, 56, 151, 169,
    170, 184, 186, 211, 243, 272, 274; noncom-
    munity, 53–56; "odd" kinship, 225; proto-,
    21–22; traditional, 40, 41, 43, 48, 54, 55, 109,
    116, 117, 121; unmaking, 17, 22, 24, 28, 250
comparsa, 156, 160
competition, 92, 151–54, 158, 159, 161–64, 166,
    168–70, 173, 174, 176–80, 186, 256, 274; idi-
    om of, 151–53, 170; modes of, 152; musical,
    27, 151, 159, 160, 162, 169, 170, 185, 275
concert, 55, 61–63, 67, 76, 143, 144, 192, 193,
    236, 242
conflict, 27, 67, 72, 74, 81, 186, 252, 259, 274
Conima, 24, 267
Conimeños, 24, 25, 272
consensus, 192, 213, 234, 271, 272
conservative populism, 37
Convention on Biological Diversity (1992),
    109
conviviality, 152, 155, 160
coplas, 154, 160; *de Carnaval,* 156; *de Todos
    Santos,* 154
cosmology, 20, 29, 44, 249, 272, 277
cosmological element, 73
cosmological framework, 252
cosmological mapping, 164
cosmological whole, 166
cosmopolitan, 2, 38, 40, 181, 195, 196, 200, 201,
    233, 237, 238, 245, 259, 261, 265; formations,
    8, 63
costume, 70, 71, 74, 156, 252, 259
countervisibility, 203, 204
COVID, 86, 221
creativity, 8, 15, 76, 123, 226, 242
Creed, Gerald, 41, 75
Creole, 174, 184
Csikszentmihalyi, Mihaly, 20, 127, 192
cultural expression, traditional, 109, 110, 112,
    114, 115, 121, 123
cultural formation/cohort, 8, 11, 23, 24, 78, 79,
    184, 215, 232, 274
cultural practice, 9, 18, 174, 177, 179, 180, 241,
    249
Cusicanqui, Sylvia Rivera, 10, 18, 226, 227

Dalits, 253
damaun, 248, 251, 256, 262
Das, Garib, 252–60, 266

Dearintirach, 72, 81

debt, 8, 9, 210–13, 215, 216, 220–22, 224–26, 275. *See also* indebtedness

decolonialization, 13, 26, 146, 200, 213, 217, 226, 228, 229, 232

decolonial scholarship, 10, 12, 28–29, 110, 111

Defensores de Belgrano, 96

deity, 23, 73, 101, 250–52, 256, 259; animist 73

de-individuation, 90

Deja, 27–28, 240, 275, 277

Delhi, 267

democracy, 108, 123, 190; democratization, 75

Democratic Alliance, 105, 106, 113

demographic flows, 63

demographic movement, 68

Descola, Philippe, 29

development, 41, 110, 111, 120; cultural, 162

Devi, Pratima, 263–65

devta, 254, 257

d'hol, 15, 62, 73, 77, 248, 251, 254, 256, 258, 262

dialectical synthesis, 235

diaspora, 8, 9, 26, 53, 62–68, 72–80, 199, 215, 237, 241, 274; cultural position, 76; diasporic consciousness, 66, 68, 76; ethnodiasporic figures, 66, 68; "forgotten," 67; homeland interactions, 67; multi-site nature of, 63; transnationalism, 68

dichotomy, 43, 110, 112, 113, 169

differentiation, 9, 10–13, 15, 17–18, 20, 23, 25, 28, 40–42, 46, 54, 56, 70, 75, 215

discursive practice, 233

dislocation, 9

displacement, 26, 39, 54, 66

divinity, 252, 254, 257

doli, 77

Drahos, Peter, 110

dramatic personae, 251

drummer, 250–60, 263, 266; hereditary, 248, 251–54, 256–58, 263

drums, 62, 73, 77, 85, 112, 156, 183, 184, 213, 251; drumming, 248, 252, 254, 256, 257, 262, 266

duduk, 62, 68, 77

Dumbutshena, Rujeko, 227

Dungri-Barosi, 250, 263, 264, 268

Durham, UK, 170

Durkheim, Émile, 28

Durkheimian theory: dichotomy, 38; evolutionism, 39; jouissance, 40; reifications of society, 37

Dutiro, Chartwell, 212, 213, 216–19, 221, 224, 226, 228

dyo, 252

dysphoria, 93, 94

dystopian, 8, 12, 13, 100

ecological zone, 164–66

Efraimidis, Polys, 50

Egypt, 191

election, 180, 190, 191, 273

elective community, 39, 40, 55, 56

electroacoustic transmission, 218

emblems, cultural, 71

emotion, collective, 88, 89, 100

empathy 21, 45–46, 52, 194, 198, 209, 213, 214, 216–17, 224, 227, 235, 244, 275; theory, 88

enclave, 196, 197

Eoan Group, 187

Epistemology, 10, 22, 29, 104, 111, 113, 120, 129, 132, 133

Epitrapezia, 44, 45

Erevan (Armenian Cultural-Educational Association), 61, 65, 66, 68, 69, 74. *See also* Yerevan

Erlmann, Veit, 26, 272

Estadio Don León Kolbowski, 85

estrada, 63, 68, 78

estradayin, 78

ethnic cleansing, 198

ethnicity, 26, 39, 42, 57, 78, 86, 89, 90, 99, 110, 216, 233, 249

ethnography, 12, 131, 151, 153; applied 11, 41, 185

ethnomusicology, 2–4, 7–14, 16–18, 22, 25, 29, 38, 40, 41, 68, 88, 100, 129–34, 141–45, 153, 168, 169, 185, 204, 215, 218, 220, 246, 248, 249, 271, 272, 273, 276

ethno-regionalism, 42, 43, 47, 56

Europe, 2, 66, 195, 215; European, 50, 62, 67, 78, 91, 134, 175, 224, 273; Western, 130

exilic nationalism, 68

expert system, 118, 120, 124

Facebook, 50, 75, 223

fandom, 26, 85, 87–90, 93, 94, 98, 99, 101

feedback, 8, 9, 11, 13–15, 17, 18, 20, 22–27, 29, 169, 219, 236, 250; cycle 18, 22, 23, 25, 27; dynamics, 9, 28; loop, 15, 23, 26, 29, 219, 236; system, 14, 15

Fees Must Fall Movement, 232

Feld, Steven, 3, 5,

Ferguson, James, 28, 113

festival, 9, 27, 28, 43, 70, 75, 155–59, 168, 174, 190–204, 248–67, 273, 274

fieldwork, 5, 12, 68, 80, 129, 151, 152, 159, 160, 170, 181, 233

fiesta, 162–68

Fine Music Radio, 187

Fiol, Stefan, 28, 57, 100, 169, 170, 227, 228, 272, 277

Firstness, 13, 18, 19–20, 22, 29, 55

Floresta (Buenos Aires), 97

flow, 15, 20–22, 44–46, 137, 192, 214; collective, 20–22, 214

freedom, 27, 28, 77, 209, 218–25, 234, 236, 243–45; artistic, 220–22; political, 203

folk, 5, 62–64, 68, 70, 78, 80, 198, 199, 237, 245, 273

folklore 42, 43, 47, 48, 50, 52–54, 62, 64, 68, 70, 79, 90, 104, 105, 109, 110, 158, 164, 249; stereotype, 164; urban ritual, 158

Foucault, Michel, 75

Fulbright Hays Dissertation Abroad Research Fellowship, 170

gamelan, 184, 220

Ganesha, 252

Garhwal, 264

Garhwalis, 252

Gaza, 190, 194, 196–99

gaze, 193, 200, 201

Gemeinschaft, 38

gender, 51–53, 89, 216, 233, 235, 242, 249, 266; specific dances, 71

gendered differentiation, 70

gendered roles, 161

gendered sensibilities, 71

gendered subject, 153

gendered uniformity of figures, 70

genealogy, 37, 41, 222, 223, 253, 273

genocide, 42, 54, 62, 66, 68, 74, 76, 79, 80

Germany, 17, 75, 80, 91

Gesellschaft, 38

gestures, 26, 64, 65, 70, 71, 90, 137, 204, 276

Ghana, 184, 223, 273

ghoema, 182, 183; musical complex, 187

Gilman, Benjamin Ives, 276

god/godess, 72, 81, 251–54, 258, 263; demi-, 251

gos, 73, 74

governmentality, 39, 54

Graeber, David, 28, 201, 202, 277

Greece, 42, 52, 54

Greek diaspora, 9, 25, 38, 42–44, 46, 47, 54, 55, 63, 75, 77, 91, 116, 274, 277

Grinnell College, 210, 216, 226, 228

Grondona, Julio, 96

group: in-, 26, 78, 87, 88, 99, 273; out-, 26, 87, 88, 98, 99, 101, 273

Guadalupe, 171

guardian, 109, 252

guitar, 2, 113, 154, 156, 174, 183, 217

Gurkha, 252

habit, 8, 9, 11, 12, 15, 16, 19, 23–25, 50, 80, 85, 88, 89, 123, 131, 134, 138, 139, 144, 169, 186, 192, 203, 211, 212, 215, 217, 219, 240, 244, 274

habitus, 120

hachkar, 73

haiduk, 62, 77

Haifa, 195

haló, 273

Hamas, 198

Harney, Stefano, 8, 209–10, 213, 215, 222, 228

Harris, Tim, 106

hasapiko, 63

Hayastan, 67, 71, 72, 74

Hegel, G.W.F., 225

Herderian ethnology, 38

hereditary obligation, 253, 257

heritage, 28, 54, 62, 67, 70, 71, 78, 79, 122, 182, 249, 261, 262, 265; artistic, 72; cultural, 42, 43, 54, 72, 73; intangible cultural, 28; musical, 182; residents, 67; UNESCO, 73, 248, 249; universal, 9, 257, 272

heritagization, 28, 249, 250, 257, 265, 266

Herrera, Eduardo, 26, 273

heterogeneity, 108

heteronormative system, 12

heterotopia, 50

Hezbollah, 95

hierarchy, 16, 53, 55, 56, 164, 170, 197, 213, 235, 244, 245, 266, 275

Himalayas, 250, 252, 261, 264

historiographic method, 252

home, 5, 24, 63, 66, 67, 80, 85, 86, 159, 161, 164, 176, 196, 197, 216, 221, 239, 240, 241, 243

homeland, 42, 63, 67, 68, 78–80, 211, 240

homelanders, 72

homeostasis, 15

homogeneity, 108

homology, 168

homosociality, 44, 48

Hood, Mantle, 130, 228

hoodia, 106

Hopi, 276

hostlanders, 67, 78

Hristov, Dobri, 62

humanitarian crisis, 196

hybridity, 10, 80

Ibrahim, Abdullah, 187

ICH (Intangible Cultural Heritage program), 249, 250, 255–57, 259–62, 264–66

iconicity, 29, 45, 51, 62, 81, 218, 276

ICTM Group on Multipart Music Making, 277

identity, 10, 11, 15, 20, 23, 40, 66, 71, 78, 86, 87, 90, 92, 98, 99, 116, 158, 166, 178–81, 200, 212, 214–16, 234, 235, 239, 249, 277; Armenian, 75; collective, 112, 161, 180, 238, 245; and community, 17, 19, 24, 161, 162; cultural, 75, 111; formation, 8, 19, 65, 111; Malawian and African, 238; narratives, 37; politics, 39, 111, 117; Pontic, 42, 43, 46, 56; social, 24, 89, 152

ideology, 37, 42, 75, 104, 107, 122, 250, 266; graphic/graphical, 11, 68, 121, 272

Illinois, 1–5

imagination, 18, 75, 92, 112, 216, 235

imagining, 8, 26, 28, 49, 76, 201

immigrants, 8, 43, 68, 69, 79, 80, 91, 240, 274, 277

immigration, 91, 97

imperialism, 11, 224; cultural, 241

improvisation, 28, 45, 218, 276; collective, 27, 234; free, 27, 232–37, 243–45, 275; group, 234, 236, 237, 242; idiomatic, 234; non-idiomatic, 234; pan-idiomatic, 234

inclusivity, 17, 26–28, 74, 201, 232, 234, 235, 242, 244, 274, 275; participatory, 24

indebtedness, 8–11, 13, 18, 23, 27, 28, 40, 41, 56, 169, 211, 215, 217, 224–27, 250, 253, 266, 275. *See also* debt

indexical experience, 29

indexicality, 29, 78

Indiana, 5

Indian Ocean, 175, 275

indigenous, 20, 38, 103, 123, 166, 194, 197–99, 215, 219, 225, 233, 237; community, 26, 104–7, 111, 112, 115–17, 120–22, 160, 162, 272; culture, 2, 106, 109, 111, 112, 121, 164, 167, 168; people, 26, 104, 105, 109–12, 162; practice, 241, 242; property rights, 108

Indira Gandhi National Centre for the Arts (IGNCA), 248, 256, 257, 259–65, 267, 268

Indonesia, 184

inequality, 10, 16, 17, 25, 52–54, 209, 211–13, 215, 221, 222, 224

inherent audience, 26, 90

inheritance system, 14, 29

institution, 13, 26, 28, 65, 115, 130, 133, 143, 213, 217, 232, 242, 245, 274

intellectual property (IP), 103–9, 111, 112, 114, 116, 118, 119, 121–23, 272; Laws Amendment Bill, 105

interdependence, 8–10, 23, 169, 215

intermediary, 253, 259

internalized disposition, 79

interoception, 22

intersectionality, 11, 15

intertextuality 122, 123, 124

intervention, 9, 11, 26, 28, 110, 192–94, 203, 204, 244, 262

intimacy, 15, 16, 46, 49, 118, 140, 152–55, 160, 169, 170, 193, 212, 216, 254, 256, 263

Iowa, 214

Iran, 95

Irupata, 160–62

Ismer, Sven, 87, 88

Israel, 91, 92, 97, 98, 190, 196–99, 201, 203, 204, 273, 277. *See also* Jews; Jewishness

Italian immigrants, 91

Jarzyna, Luke, 211

jaylliphusta, 7

jazz, 2, 27, 130, 181, 233, 234, 243; Afro-, 9, 232, 233, 237–42, 245, 275; Cape, 183, 240, 241

Jeftha, Alan, 106

Jewishness, 86–92, 94–99

Jews, 86–89, 91, 92, 94–100, 197, 198, 273

Joshimath, 251, 260

jouissance, 40, 54

julajula, 164–67

kanon, 62, 77

kasamintu takiy, 159

Kaul, Bansi, 267

Kaushal, Molly, 256, 260–62, 263, 265, 268

kemence, 44

Kentucky, 3, 5

Khoisans, 104, 120, 272

Khylari, 259

kinesthetic wisdom, 134, 276

kinotita, 42, 43, 274

kinship, 16, 42, 225

"kin-state," 67

Kirkorov, Kirkor, 63, 68

kladhia, 45

knowledge, 10, 11, 46, 68, 75, 117, 129, 130–34, 136, 138–41, 143, 144, 179, 217–22, 225, 239, 253, 255, 256, 262, 263, 275; embodied, 26, 217, 220; expert, 104, 118, 122; indigenous, 26, 103, 105–8, 110–14, 121, 215, 219; musical, 130, 131, 134, 224; relational, 23; shared, 23, 218, 219; system, 28; traditional, 28, 104, 105, 109–11, 114, 115, 120, 121

Kokkinidis, Lefteris, 49

Kolb Learning Style Inventory, 141

Kolbowski, Leon, 92

Kousalidou, Symela, 51, 52

kshetrapal, 252

kumparsa, 160, 161, 168

Kurujogi, 252

Kutev Ensemble, 62, 68, 76, 77

Kyker, Jennifer, 214, 215, 221, 222, 227, 228

language, 8, 15, 19, 20, 22, 23, 29, 42, 46, 67, 99, 113, 121, 122, 130, 141, 144, 153, 155, 169, 218, 233, 237, 259, 274

Latin America, 91, 130, 131, 272

legitimacy, 143, 194, 199, 223

legitimation, 121, 193, 200

leverage, affective, 26, 88, 94, 97, 99, 100

liberalism, 104, 108, 112, 123, 219. *See also* neo-liberalism

lila, 251, 259

Lilongwe, Malawi, 238, 245

Lima, Peru, 24, 25, 267, 272

liminality, 40, 45

Linda, Solomon, 106

localization, 37, 40, 41

London, 187

Los Angeles, 187

los bohemios, 91

lyra, 44, 45, 47–50, 52, 53

Maal Dance, 252, 268

Maccabi Tel Aviv, 92

Macedonia, 79; Greek, 43, 51, 53

Mahabharata, 252

makombwe, 214

Malawi, 237, 238, 240, 241

Malay choirs, 175, 184, 187

Malta, 171

Mamita Pitunisa, 171

Maraire, Dumisani, 212, 224

Maraire, Tendai, 224

Marais, S., 106

marching bands, 174; road marches, 174, 176, 180, 183, 186

marginalization, 108, 174, 185

marginalized groups, 17, 27, 106, 108, 184, 193, 219, 232, 256

marginalized practices, 224

marimba, 209, 212

marriage, 159

Marx, Karl, 29

mask, 229, 248, 251, 252, 256, 258, 260, 262, 263, 267

maskandi, 106, 243, 244

masked dance drama, 250, 257, 261

master of ceremonies, 153, 157, 158, 162

materialism, dialectical, 29

materiality, 90

Mbare Township, Zimbabwe, 228

Mbeki, Thabo, 110

Mbembe, Achille, 225, 226

mbira, 2, 9, 27, 135, 180, 209–28; American players and enthusiasts, 211, 275

mbube, 106

McDonald, David, 27, 100, 271, 273, 275

meaning making, 139, 249

mediums, 21, 209, 211, 220, 254, 258, 260

Mentesidou, Parthena, 51

metaphoricity, 40, 45

meta-socialization, 50

metronomic, 45

Meyer, Leonard B., 129

mhondoro, 214

Middle East, 66, 77, 78, 190

migration 42, 78; out-migration 68, 258. *See also* immigrants; immigration

military, 197; Israeli, 196, 198; occupation, 196, 197

Miller, Kiri, 89

mimesis, 218, 220

mimhanzi, 7

minority, 66, 67, 75, 77–79

misappropriation, 106, 110–12

Mizque, Boliva, 153, 160

model, 15, 107, 109, 123, 132, 133, 144, 145, 146, 168, 186, 192, 201, 215; cultural, 63; of community, 16, 55, 152, 170, 274

Model Provisions (1977), 109, 115

modernity, 18, 37–39, 41–43, 49, 54, 56, 107, 110, 112, 118, 240, 265, 267; pre-modern, 39, 42, 47–53, 55, 56, 274

modern trauma, 42

Moten, Fred, 8, 209–210, 213, 215, 222, 228

mountains, 51, 65, 72, 73, 81, 252, 253

Mount Ararat, 72, 73, 81

movement, 65, 68, 69, 71, 77, 99, 166, 184, 254, 259

Mtukudzi, Oliver, 228

muhabeti, 38, 41, 43, 44, 48–52, 274

multinaturalism, 29

music: agency, 51; communication, 276; as culture, 168; margins, 67; as social life, 7, 132, 141, 145; traditional, 15, 106, 121, 129, 130 32, 211, 237, 239, 241, 245

musicality, affective, 44; (music) labor, 51–53, 76

musical network, 40, 55

musical theater, 241

musicking 7, 8, 12, 14, 16, 18, 21, 23, 25–27, 38, 40, 41, 144, 170, 209, 212, 218, 226, 232, 246, 272–77

musicology, 10, 131
musiki, 7
musique, 7
Muslims, 175, 176
mutuality, 169
Mwar, 267

naci, 96
Nafar, Tamer, 190, 191, 203, 204
Nagorno-Karabakh, 65, 67, 72–74, 274
Nairi, 64, 66, 69, 70, 74–78
Narsingh, 252, 258
National Association of Schools of Music
    (NASM), 129, 132, 146
nationalism, 2, 16, 17, 74, 110, 266; cultural,
    111, 250
nationality, 215, 216, 233
Native American music, 4, 131
Nattiez, Jean-Jacques, 3
Nazi, 96, 97
Ndlovu-Gatsheni, Sabelo, 228
negotiation, 38, 41, 56, 115, 234, 23, 244, 248
neoliberalism, 37, 63, 142, 200, 209, 219, 221,
    222, 224, 250, 266
Netanyahu, Benjamin, 190, 191
Netherlands, 100
Nettl, Bruno, 1–6, 283–84
network, 11, 28, 40, 47, 46, 53, 55, 78, 221
niche construction, 14
Nigeria, 241
nisan, 260
North America, 9, 27,195, 213, 214, 221, 224,
    228, 233, 275
nostalgia, 26, 42, 51, 54, 55, 239, 240, 258, 274;
    nested, 43
Nuwe Graskoue Trappers, 187

Oakland, CA, 225
objectivity, 11; analytical 37
obligation, 8, 9, 27, 28, 41, 55, 209, 215, 216,
    224, 226, 232, 250, 253, 257, 267, 275
occupation, 190, 194, 196–98, 200–204
oddkin, 215, 222
Ogu, 241
"One-Eyed Ford, The," 4
ontological, 22, 29; relativization, 37
ontology, 29, 41
oppression, 27, 28, 55, 201, 209, 213, 224, 250,
    254, 265–67
orientalist, 200
Other, 12, 14, 23, 27, 99, 111, 212, 216, 220, 221,
    245
Otherness, 12, 100, 211, 214, 216
Ottoman, 42, 44, 63, 66, 67, 73, 74, 77, 79

outsider, 75, 89, 151, 163, 164, 179, 181, 225, 250,
    259, 263, 265, 275, 277
ownership, 104, 109, 116, 121, 122, 179, 222

Palestine, 195; Music Expo (PMX), 190,
    192–96, 198–204
Palestinians, 9, 27, 190–92, 194–204, 273, 274,
    277; citizens of Israel ('48s), 190, 199
Pan-African Ensemble, 246
panchayat, 260
Pandavas, 252; Nritya, 254, 257
Panossian, Razmik, 67, 79
parade, 173, 174, 176, 180, 184, 202
parakathi, 25, 38, 41, 43–57, 274
parallel polyphony, 44
participant observation, 129, 132
participation, 4, 9, 12, 16, 24–27, 40, 44–46, 51,
    53, 63, 70, 80, 90, 99, 131, 136, 137, 154, 174,
    180, 184–86, 191, 193, 203, 219, 226, 243, 245,
    250, 257, 258, 272, 275; ritual, 28
participatory action, 192, 204
participatory dynamics, 193
participatory music (making), 3, 8, 16, 192,
    232, 235
participatory practice, 17, 90, 179, 214
participatory singing, 16, 43, 274
patriarchy, 10, 12, 51–53, 252; Brahmanical, 250
patron, 52, 164, 253, 256, 266
pattar, 250, 257, 267
PBS Newshour, 204
pedagogical imperative, 234
pedagogy, 26, 132, 143, 225, 235; performance-
    based, 129, 131, 140, 142, 145, 276
Peirce, C.S., 3, 5, 8, 13, 18, 19, 29, 55, 218, 232,
    276, 277
Pepper, Jim, 4
performance: coalitional, 192–94, 203, 204,
    271; festival, 163, 250, 266; idiom, 153, 155,
    164, 169; participatory, 16, 27, 174, 186; of
    place, 184; presentational, 16, 27, 174, 180,
    186
performative act, 153
performative moment, 191
performative space, 235
performativity, 50, 192, 194; political 193, 271
Perman, Tony, 19, 27, 57, 88, 100, 169, 170, 210,
    227, 275, 277
Persians, 78
personhood, 197, 215, 249
Peru, 5, 151, 180; Aymara, 2, 10, 180; music
    180, 185
Petkova, Vanya, 62
phenomenology, 88, 169, 212; Peircean 8, 13,
    18–25, 232

pilgrim, 164, 166, 251
pilgrimage, 164, 168
place, 49, 99, 118, 184, 233, 240, 249, 277
Platense, 96
plurality, 88
poetics, 44, 52, 53
policy, cultural, 65
political demand, 193, 204
political ecology, 110
political influence, 190, 260
political system, 197
political transition, 65, 232, 241
pollution 253, 254
PMX, 204
Pontianness, 47, 54, 55
Pontic Greek, 9, 25, 38, 46, 51, 274
positionality, 12, 266
positioning, 232, 237, 256
possession, 214, 220, 254, 260
possible and the actual, the, 8, 18, 203, 273, 275
postcolonialism, 10, 111, 216, 266
postmemory, 41, 43, 47, 56
postsocialist, 63, 66, 67, 79, 80
potential, affective, 22, 24
Potosi, Bolovia, 171
power, 10, 16, 17, 20, 27, 56, 75, 107, 108, 121,
    168, 170, 201, 202, 220, 222, 223, 227, 233,
    250, 257, 258, 266; affective, 81, 191; dynam-
    ics, 8, 12, 89, 243; political, 103; ritual, 260;
    structural critique of, 28; structure, 40, 245
practice theory, 168
precarity, 87, 193
presentational, 1, 3, 5, 8, 16, 26, 27, 63, 70, 80,
    174, 180, 186, 193, 275
privilege, 12, 52, 190, 219, 221, 225, 226, 258,
    262, 266
production, cultural, 68, 76, 104, 123, 184
protest, 16, 89, 90, 101, 191, 192, 194, 202, 273
proto-modern 38, 41, 43, 50, 54
purification, 81
purity, 10

Qhantati (Quantati) Ururi, 24, 267
Quechua, 153–55, 159, 161, 169

race, 15, 17, 89, 99, 104, 174, 213–15, 224, 233,
    235, 266; division, 110, social inequality 211
racial lineage, 223
racial segregation/tension, 232, 245
racism, 9, 11, 17, 27, 190, 212, 213, 216, 220, 221,
    226, 227, 232
Ramallah, 190, 194–96, 198, 202, 204, 273
Ramanandi, 251
Ramayana, 251, 258, 261

Ram cult, 251
Ramman, 248, 250–68
Rani-Radhika, 259
Rasmussen, Anne, 129
Rawat, Harish, 267
reciprocity, 8, 40, 45, 54, 225; anticolonial, 12
recognition, 53, 74, 103, 106, 111, 117, 180, 190–
    92, 194, 200, 201, 210, 215, 245, 254
recollection, affective, 43
"reel dance," 187. *See also* Rieldans
reflexivity, 40, 41, 46
refugees, 25, 42, 43, 54, 66, 79, 274
Rein, Raanan, 92
renewal, 108, 176, 184
representation, 18–20, 39, 46–52, 70, 104, 143,
    144, 179, 199–201, 242, 245, 261, 262, 265,
    271, 273
resistance, 135, 138, 144, 202; cultural 202; po-
    litical, 201
resources, cultural, 261
respectability, 180, 275; embodiment of, 180,
    181; parading, 27, 180
Rhodesia, 213
Rhodes Must Fall, 232
Rieldans, 185
rites: of passage, 21, 160; of reciprocation, 176;
    renewal, 176
ritual, 54, 62, 80, 155, 158, 160, 162, 168, 186,
    252–63, 267; complex, 164, 166; experience,
    249, 272; life, 21, 252; object, 260; perfor-
    mance, 248, 250, 252, 257–59; practice, 259,
    265; "ritualized friction," 174; theater, 258,
    259, 261, 265, 267
River Plate, 98
Rogers, Alice, 90
Rogers, Anne, 210
Roma, 100
Romanticism, 38, 39, 43, 50, 53, 54, 225
Rome, 86
rooibos, 106, 107
Rukuni, Mandivamba, 215, 226
Russians, 63, 91; Soviet cultural policy, 65

safeguarding, 249, 255, 259–62, 264, 265
saints, 251
Saint's Day, 154, 163, 166, 275
Salood Dungra, 248, 250–54, 257–65, 267, 268
"Sam Bass," 5
sameness, 9, 12, 13, 20, 21, 23, 266
Sanskrit, 259
saxophone, 181, 217
Scheduled Castes, 267
schizophonia, 211, 218, 220, 221; experiential,
    27, 219

science and technology studies, 108
Scotland, 187
Secondness, 13, 18–19, 20–22, 23, 24, 29, 55, 212, 214, 220
secularism, 219
sedimentations, 46
Seeger, Charles, 130, 276
Selang, 250, 263, 264, 268
self, 17, 19, 20–23, 44, 46, 85, 88, 211, 212, 216, 220, 221, 227, 243
self-awareness 20, 244, 245
self-determination 26, 112, 191, 192, 194, 204
self-fashioning, 55, 199, 200, 202
semantic predictability of language, 218
semantic purification, 218, 219
semiosis, 14, 15
semiotic, 8, 17, 22, 29, 209, 219, 220, 222
semiotics 3, 7, 276; Peircean, 3, 232
Serrano, Fernando, 98
settler-colonialism, 194, 197, 198
shakti, 257, 264
Shelemay, Kay Kaufman, 15, 41, 183
Shilpkars, 267
Shona, 135, 210; mbira, 135, 221; saying, 217
sign, 12, 14, 18, 22, 23, 88, 90, 218, 219, 232, 276; Peirce's theory of, 3, 276
Sikuras, 167
slavery, 144, 175, 212, 213; descendant of, 275
Small, Christopher, 40, 152, 168
sociability, 174, 186
social, the: concept of, 28
social body, 43, 53
social death, 196–97
socialism, 61, 67, 68, 79, 110
sociality, 14–16, 22, 25, 26, 37–41, 46–49, 50, 52–56, 173, 198, 273; affective, 43, 53, 56, 274
socialization 12, 38, 40, 41, 44, 46, 48, 50, 52–54, 56, 79, 222, 245
social life, 7, 8, 13–15, 22, 23, 25, 26, 28, 38, 91, 129, 132, 138, 140, 141, 145, 169, 210, 226, 275
social obligation, 28
social organization, 10, 159, 179, 180, 277
social position, 249, 250, 253
social self, 15
social theories of culture, 10, 28
Sofia, Bulgaria, 64–68, 76
solicitation, 201
solidarity, 16, 18, 21, 22, 25, 27, 38, 39, 53–55, 79, 94, 99, 174, 180, 185, 186, 191, 193, 198, 237, 273
Solis, Ted, 129, 144
solo, 173, 176–79
Solomon, Thomas, 9, 27, 75, 80, 174, 185, 274, 275

song dueling, 151, 153–55, 157, 159, 168, 169, 174, 274
sonic dialogue, 234
sonic duel, 167
sonic dynamics, 87, 273
sonic ethics, 16
sonic interaction, 10
sonic practice, 13
Sotiriadis, Dimitris, 47, 48
sound ideal, 181
soundscape, 10, 25, 233
sound studies, 10, 11
South Africa, 9, 26, 106–8, 110–17 120, 173–76, 178, 185–87, 232–35, 237, 244, 277; Cape Colony, 175; Cape Peninsula, 175; Cape Town, 27, 106, 176, 181, 183, 184, 232, 233, 236, 239–41, 275; Eastern Cape, 116; Intellectual Property Laws Amendment Act, 103, 272; National Assembly, 103; Western Cape, 119, 173, 174, 181, 182, 184, 187
Southern-Holt, Helen, 187
space, 16, 18, 20, 27, 38, 40, 47, 49, 52, 89, 111, 153, 159, 165, 167, 170, 185, 186, 193, 194, 197, 203, 234, 235, 245, 249, 259, 261; Eurocentric, 242; institutional, 12; sonic, 166, 168
status, 21, 26, 38, 41, 56, 73, 129, 219, 2296, 245, 249, 250, 252; marginal, 175, 179
Stein, Edith, 88
stigma, 53, 57 241, 256, 262
St. Joseph's Christmas Band, 173, 178, 180, 186, 187
strategic auto-essentialism, 164
subjective disposition, 100
subjective positioning, 232, 237
subjectivity, 17, 19, 46, 65, 77, 100, 103; indigenous, 103, 112; inter-, 17, 19, 21, 23, 184
supremacy: caste, 250, 266; white 213, 232
Suraj, Ishwar, 252
Surp Asdvadzadzin Church, 61, 63
symbol, 29, 276; context, 12, 15, 23; token, 118
symbolic 39, 46, 51, 100, 273
symbolism 29; solar, 73
syncretic, 44
systematization, 276
Szanto, Thomas, 88

tableau vivant, 251
taboo, 252, 254
Taggart, Cindy, 146
takipayanaku, 153, 154, 155, 169
Tarasti, Eeero, 3
tatbīa', 190, 191
Tatik u Papik, 73
Tawengwa, Tanyaradzwa, 228

Taypikala, 162
Tchilingirian, Hratch, 67
teknonym, 204
temple, 248, 254, 256, 258, 260–62
Texas, 5
theory of legislative practice, 104
Thiong'o, Ngugi Wa, 228
Thirdness, 12, 13, 18–20, 22–24, 29, 212, 218, 220
Thomson, Scott, 234, 235
Thrace, 42, 66, 79
Tinker Foundation, 170
Tölölyan, Khachig, 65, 66, 68
Tomlinson, Gary, 13, 14, 18, 29, 276
top-down, 250, 265, 266
topophilia, 99
Tottenham Hotspurs, 86, 100
trademark, 103, 107
tradition, 28, 38, 42, 43, 47, 51–57, 62, 70, 80, 106, 109–17, 121, 122, 135, 163, 213, 223, 233, 235, 241, 245, 249, 256–66
traditional cultural expression, 109, 110, 112, 114, 115, 121, 123
traditional work, 103, 104, 114, 115, 121
trans-Atlantic slavery, 212
transformation, 15, 21, 65, 123, 191, 273; political, 192, 193, 203; social, 68, 107, 191
trauma, 27, 39, 42, 43, 54, 62, 79, 80, 211, 256, 274
trickster, 252, 259
triptych, 38–40, 43, 47–50, 52–54
Tsekouras, Ioannis, 25, 52, 273, 274
TUB notation, 146
Tunis Model Law, 105, 109
Turino, Thomas, 1, 3–5, 7–11, 13–20, 23–26, 29, 38, 41, 56, 63, 65, 67, 70, 76, 80, 90, 145, 146, 152, 168, 174, 179, 185–87, 192, 193, 203, 214, 215, 228, 232, 235, 246, 267, 271, 272, 276
Turkey, 26, 42, 66, 67, 72, 73, 75–78, 80, 274
Turner, Victor, 21

ud, 62, 76
Undercommons, The, 217
UNESCO, 109, 115, 249, 261, 265, 266, 268; intangible cultural heritage, 73, 248, 249, 272
unhu, 13, 215, 216, 222, 226, 228
United Kingdom, 170, 105, 111, 214
United States, 2, 24, 53, 130, 147, 204, 211–15, 221, 234
University of Illinois, 2
Urbana, IL, 2, 77, 282
urban culture, 167, 168
urbanity, 38, 39

urbanization 42, 43, 48, 54
Uttarakhand, 267
Utopian, 8, 12, 13, 15, 17, 28, 216, 222, 224

Vaishnavite, 251
Vancouver Island, 217
Vardapet, Komitas, 68, 80
Vardavar, 72
vigraha murthi, 251
Villa Crespo, Buenos Aires, 85–87, 91–93; "Villa Kreplach," 91
violence, 16, 17, 26, 42, 66, 86, 88, 192, 193, 202, 204, 211, 256, 257, 273, 274
Virgen de Guadalupe, 171
Viveiros de Castro, Eduardo, 29
von Scheve, Christian, 87, 88
vulnerability, 86–90, 94, 99, 100, 145, 193, 196, 203, 204, 237, 244

Wailing Wall, 98
wayli, 164, 165, 168
wayñu, 161
Wayt'I, 166–68
Wengrow, David, 28, 277
West Bank, 190, 195–97, 199
Western society, 55; art/music 12, 131, 177, 179, 181; European Classical Music, 132, 233; practices, 241
Wiggins and McTighe's backward design, 139
Wisitas, 160
Wong, Deborah, 19, 67
Wong, Isabel, 1
World Intellectual Property Organization (WIPO), 105, 109, 110, 115, 121
world music, 146
World Music Ensemble, 246
Wupperthal, South Africa, 187

Xhosa bow music, 243

Yerevan, 61, 62, 64, 70, 71, 72. *See also* Erevan

Zanzibar, 246
Zhao, Sunny, 211
Zimbabwe, 2, 3, 5, 109, 209–18, 220–25, 227, 228, 275
Zimfest, 217, 223
Zoroastrism, 78, 81
Zucal, José Garriga, 89
Zulu, 106, 113, 116, 244
Zuñi, 276
zurna, 73, 74
Zydeco, 2, 4, 5

The University of Illinois Press
is a founding member of the
Association of University Presses.

———————————————

University of Illinois Press
1325 South Oak Street
Champaign, IL 61820-6903
www.press.uillinois.edu